WOMEN IN THE WORLD

Studies in International and Comparative Politics

Peter H. Merkl, Series Editor

LYNNE B. IGLITZIN   RUTH ROSS, EDITORS

Women
in the
World

1975–1985
THE WOMEN'S DECADE
Second, Revised Edition

Studies in Comparative Politics
Peter H. Merkl, Series Editor

ABC-CLIO

Santa Barbara, California
Oxford, England

*This book is printed on acid-free paper to meet library
specifications.*

Cover and book design by Tanya Cullen

Illustrations by Marci Siegel

Library of Congress Cataloging In Publication Data

Main entry under title:

Women in the world, 1975 – 1985.

   (Studies in international and comparative politics; 16)
   Includes bibliographies and index.
   1. Feminism—Cross-cultural studies. 2. Women—Social
conditions—Cross-cultural studies. 3. Sex discrimination
against women—Cross-cultural studies. 4. Women—
Legal status, laws, etc.—Cross-cultural studies. I. Iglitzin,
Lynne B. II. Ross, Ruth A. III. Series.
HQ1154.W88383 1985   305.4'2   85-6158
ISBN 0– 87436– 409– 4
ISBN 0– 87436– 473– 6 (pbk.)

10 9 8 7 6 5 4 3 2 1

ABC-Clio, Inc.
2040 Alameda Padre Serra, Box 4397
Santa Barbara, California 93103

Clio Press, Ltd.
55 St. Thomas Street
Oxford OX1 1JG, England

Manufactured in the United States of America

CONTENTS

Part Two: Developing Countries, 177

Part Three: Communist Countries, 381

FOREWORD

THE DECADE FROM the mid-1970s to the mid-1980s has been profoundly significant for women throughout the world. 1975, "International Women's Year," marked the beginning of worldwide awareness of the social, political, economic, and cultural concerns of women. Gradually, the realization dawned that many of the major problems women face—inequities in the workplace, in the legal system, in their families, and in the social and political culture of their individual countries—outweighed the specifics of nation, country, or ethnic background. We have come a long way in heightened consciousness of the wide range of problems encountered by women in their daily lives in the ten years since the publication of the first edition of *Women in the World*; nonetheless, we are still far from achieving definitive solutions to most of these problems.

The past decade has been a rich and productive one in research and scholarship on these issues, and the essays that comprise this book reflect the latest social science scholarship, from a variety of interdisciplinary and cross-cultural perspectives. The women and men who have joined together in this effort span a wide range of countries and ethnic origins. Many of the authors, while residing now in the United States, are native to, or were raised in, the countries of which they write. Those who were part of the original volume have found it most instructive to report on the progress, or lack thereof, in those countries. The authors new to this volume allow us to fill gaps by focusing on some important countries omitted the first time.

The book's subtitle, "The Women's Decade," is indicative of the focus we invited all our authors to employ. The editors presupposed that the decade just past was one of enormous legal, political, and economic change in women's lives, and that these changes would be worldwide in scope. A careful reading, however, illustrates the danger of assuming such widespread change, particularly when the scrutiny extends below the surface of political rhetoric or constitutional preamble. In many of the countries under study here, the past ten years have indeed seen major change in laws regarding abortion, divorce, rape, equity in the workplace, child support, and so on. Simultaneously, the surge of feminist scholarship begun in the late 1960s continued to flourish, resulting in the emergence of a wide range of research findings and the accumulation of valuable data by and about women.

Yet in other countries not only legal and political changes, but also research efforts, have been relatively sparse, often in contrast to a period of high activity immediately preceding these years. In some areas where significant changes were made in law and political structures, the recent years may well represent no more than a consolidation of gains previously won. In others, the quiescence of the recent past may well reflect a neoconservativism or retrenchment on the part of women leaders and women's organizations, as well as of the authorities.

Whatever emphasis they place on the most recent decade, most of our authors feel the need to remind us of the historical context so vital in any evaluation of contemporary events. For some authors, this context can only be provided by reaching into themes, practices, and attitudes stemming from ancient history. For most, the historical setting of the twentieth century, particularly the post–World War II era, is sufficient.

This variation in style, emphasis, and focus lends richness to our efforts and serves to remind the reader of the healthy limitations on any all-encompassing theme, such as the role of women. Variables of religion, geography, ethnic diversity, and class are only a few of the factors that create diversity and uniqueness, tempering our search for universals and commonalities.

A second edition allows us to take a second look. How well have the comparisons and generalizations made about women's roles and lives in diverse countries stood up since they were first asserted in the mid-1970s? If there was one overarching theme that ran throughout the earlier volume it was that of a "reality gap" between official governmental posture and legislative enactments, on the one hand, and traditionalism and general resistance to change, on the other. Put another way, a strong contrast emerged almost everywhere between women's status in public and political arenas, where changes were symbolically important and rather widespread, and women's lives in home and family, where traditional beliefs and practices continued to hold sway. Ten years ago our foreword stressed the "tension between the public image of women and their private lives," which cut across cultural and national boundaries. Despite this, we concluded on a strong note of optimism, citing the growing strength of women and feminist consciousness worldwide.

The picture today is somewhat more complex. Not a country described here has gone untouched by the emergence of "women's issues" in the forefront of political agendas everywhere. Laws, political systems, and economic and cultural institutions have been altered everywhere, at least in some measure, by the changing status of women. However, in not a single country have women gone much beyond the reality gap—the contrast between doctrine and deed, pronouncement and enforcement, superficial rather than profound, change.

Our authors vary widely in their conclusions and speculations regarding future trends and directions for the years ahead. Furthermore, the sense of hope and optimism, so apparent in the earlier volume, is somewhat less apparent. Many authors are guarded, more cautious in their conclusions, recognizing perhaps with the wisdom of hindsight, how powerful are the forces of tradition that militate against rapid change in fundamental beliefs, attitudes, and practices.

In the final analysis, the reader may join us in withholding judgment and predictions for the future, and be content to assess gains and compare progress, not against some hypothetical feminist standard, but against the context of each specific country. Evaluating where women are today in any country, as well as cross-culturally, can be done most informatively against the criterion of where they were yesterday and the day before. This reserves for the future any definitive answer to the question of where they will be tomorrow.

—Lynne B. Iglitzin
—Ruth Ross

INTRODUCTION

The Patriarchal Heritage Revisited

AS WITH THE FIRST EDITION of *Women in the World*, this volume of essays on the role and status of women in many countries in the world rests upon a conceptual framework that makes comparisons and assessments about the status of women possible.

The fundamental assumption that underlies our look at women in the world today is, as it was in the first edition, the existence of the patriarchal heritage. Patriarchy, as was asserted then and as is reaffirmed now, has molded and dominated much of recorded history in most parts of the world. Patriarchy continues to be a powerful factor affecting attitudes and institutional practices everywhere, albeit in varying degrees.

The patriarchal heritage involves a set of beliefs and attitudes as well as a body of institutions and practices, each of which has complementary and interrelated cause-and-effect results upon the other. In order to construct a full-blown model of patriarchy, then, one must identify the ideological sources of belief structures, the roots of which go back into history and prehistorical times. One must further analyze the major institutions in any society that serve to socialize men and women into conformity with, and acceptance of, patterns of behavior that reflect as well as reinforce these beliefs. Such institutions include, but are not limited to, the laws, political system, economy, media, education, religion, and the family, not necessarily in this order of importance. Any set of generalizations about the strength of the patriarchal heritage in a specific country today, taken either individually or in comparision with others, must pay attention to this entire gamut of beliefs and institutions— unquestionably, a major task.

In the earlier edition, the development of the patriarchal model focused primarily on the roots and outlines of patriarchal thought, and less on the institutions and practices that reflect the thought. In this Introduction we reverse the emphasis and summarize briefly the ideological components of the patriarchal world-view. More stress is placed on those aspects of a society that implement and reflect beliefs and attitudes, in order to enhance our ability as students, researchers, and feminists to assess women's status in the world today. If we are able to outline a set of criteria that can be used to measure degrees of patriarchy, we are able to better judge its strength. We can also compare its lasting effects on the lives of women in a particular country with women elsewhere, as well as with the lives of their mothers and grandmothers before them.

Patriarchal ideology, the belief in male superiority and female inferiority, is rooted in biology, culture, economics, and religion. Most of recorded history has been based on this fundamental dichotomy, and patriarchal assumptions have been legitimized on a number of grounds. From Aristotle onwards, patriarchal rule has been justified in biological terms, i.e., the greater physical strength of the male animal. "Natural" differences, whether physiological or genetic, have been used to rationalize the overwhelming male monopoly of rulership.[1] Indeed, such rationalizations continue to this very day. In their analysis of Hausa Muslim women in Nigeria, authors Callaway and Schildkrout assert that "the accepted view of sexual inequality in Nigeria . . . has its origins in the hierarchy of nature itself."

Cultural and anthropological sources that attest to the widespread existence of patriarchal rule in the family unit in different eras and societies have also been used to justify the legitimacy of patriarchal power.[2] From the biblical days of the ancient patriarchs, the clear distinction was drawn: Women existed solely to reproduce and to perpetuate the male line, while the power and integrity of the family prerogatives were passed on exclusively from father to son.

The shift in the economy of many societies from communal to private property also helped to solidify and institutionalize patriarchy. The confluence of patriarchal family structures and private property resulted in the exclusion of women from the ownership and disposal of property. Indeed, women themselves were treated as property in many cultures, dehumanized and handed down as part of the male's patrimony, to sons, brothers, uncles, and husbands.[3]

Perhaps the most important source of patriarchal belief systems remains religion. An ecumenical perspective is sadly most appropriate here, as patriarchal attitudes and values have been central to all the major Eastern and Western religions. Women have been variously blamed for the fall of man, for the existence of sin, for playing the role of sexual temptress, and for impurity and uncleanness. In one form or another, the various religions justified the double standard of morality on which patriarchy rests; that is, sexual permissiveness and freedom for males, strict chastity and fidelity for females. Religion rationalized and legitimized patriarchal practices already well established in economic, social, and political systems.[4]

The legacy of male superiority/female inferiority that allowed the institutions, values, and beliefs resulting in the subordination of women to arise and flourish is, unfortunately, still bearing fruit even as we approach the last decades of the twentieth century. While a brave minority of men and women not infrequently cried out against the injustices of patriarchy,[5] their voices went largely unheeded. Such patterns lasted so long and were so universally practiced that they had to be the result of a powerful process of socialization of both males and females from birth onwards.

The set of attitudes that lies at the heart of this socialization process we have termed the patriarchal model. A brief review of the elements of the model is in order here.

1. *Women are apolitical.* Women thrive on the security of home and hearth and prefer to leave the sordidness and turmoil of politics and public life to men. One consequence is that laws have almost universally been made by men with men as beneficiaries.

2. *The sexual division of labor reflects inborn differences between males and females.* The serving and helping functions, in home or workplace, are best suited to the female; virtually everywhere, it is males who monopolize positions of financial and political power.

3. *Women's central identity is as wives and mothers.* Within the family, the man is the breadwinner; in the outside world, woman is viewed first and foremost as sister, daughter, wife, or mother—if there is no significant male relationship in her life, she is somehow deficient.

4. *Women are childlike.* Women are dependent upon men, not only for sustenance, income, physical support, and

protection, but also for ensuring their good character
and moral righteousness in their behavior outside, as
well as inside, the home.

We have suggested that this model could be used as a standard
to evaluate the public policy impacts on women in any society.
Beginning with the broad theories of the model, often interwoven
and interrelated, it should be possible to evaluate concrete institutional practices and policies in such important areas as law,
politics, the economy, family, media, and education. Indeed, the
countries we have included in this volume span the entire continuum from traditionalism and patriarchy to modernity and egalitarianism. If the model is a useful one, it should allow us to analyze
and evaluate women's status in each of these societal areas.

The political and legal realm is a good place to begin. It should be
relatively easy to draw up a list of qualitative and quantitative
public policy impacts to permit us to evaluate the degree to which
women are *apolitical,* as the patriarchal model would suggest. Certain questions and areas for policy analysis come immediately to
mind:

How many women vote?

Is the number of women voters increasing?

What are the barriers to women holding political office?
Are these barriers diminishing? In what areas?

Are women getting into politics, either through elective
or appointive mechanisms?

Do the major political parties include women in
leadership positions?

Are "women's issues" on the political agendas of the
parties and their candidates?

Are human rights issues important? Do they impact the
status of women?

Do women exert any special influence in electoral
politics? Is there a "gender gap?"

Are there significant numbers of women elites? Are they
making inroads into the centers of power and decision
making in formal government structures? In
legislative branches? In executive branches? In
informal power networks, such as committees, interest
groups, nongovernmental organizations?

Are there exclusionary practices built into central
government and legal institutions that effectively rule
out women's participation?

Are there any revolutionary movements for social change that include women and women's issues in any major way?

When assessing these and related questions regarding women's political involvement, it is important that such comparisons be kept country-specific, and that the variables of education, socioeconomic level, and race be kept carefully in mind. Women's participation, or its lack, must in all fairness be matched with male counterparts in all demographic categories.

In the final analysis, the notion of "apolitical women," as the bedrock of patriarchal politics, comes down to the pyramid of power. To the degree that a country's political system can be considered patriarchal, we will find the fewest number of women at the top of the power pyramid, the greatest number clustered at the base. How true is this in each of the countries under study?

Similarly, one must scrutinize the constitutions, statutes and judicial opinions to determine whether the weight of the legal system tilts away from or toward patriarchal values:

Is there an official commitment to equality under the law? Does the constitution or similar fundamental document contain such provisions?

Do judicial opinions and statutory law reflect egalitarian or traditional patriarchal values?

Have there been constitutional and/or statutory enactments prohibiting sex discrimination in the workplace and in other areas of society?

Does the machinery of the legal system provide for enforcement? Is there a perception that these laws are actually enforceable and, indeed, are being enforced?

Focusing our attention on questions like these tells us much about the seriousness of a country's commitment to ending patriarchy and achieving equality of opportunity for men and women.

Assessing the strength of the *sexual division of labor* in any society—the second element of the patriarchal model—requires a careful review of the practices and policies of the labor market and, indeed, the entire economy. Once again, there are important areas for policy analysis and quantitative and qualitative questions for which answers can be sought:

Are women paid less than men for comparable work?

Are women clustered in sex-stereotyped jobs, in the helping and nurturing professions, e.g., teaching, nursing, librarianship, clerical?

Is the range of jobs open to men far broader than that
available to women? Are there entrance examinations
or other prerequisites that effectively rule out women
candidates?

Is sexual harassment in the workplace a problem? Are
offenders subject to legal penalties? Are these
provisions enforced?

Is there a marked difference between workforce
opportunities and roles for women in rural, as
compared with urban, areas?

Are women still slow to enter new careers and professions
hitherto blocked to them entirely?

Are women underrepresented in union leadership and
workers' councils?

To the degree that the answer to most of these questions is affirmative, it clearly indicates that, no matter the country under study,
the patriarchal model of sexual division of labor is still the norm,
rather than the exception. As one of our authors puts it, in discussing
women's status in Yugoslavia, women are still struggling to combine "modern public rules with paternalistic private ones."
Nonetheless, our country-by-country research indicates areas
where gains, as well as losses, have been made and calls attention to
those places where exceptions and contrasts to the general patriarchal practices prevail.

The third and fourth areas of the patriarchal model—women as
wives and mothers, and as *childlike*—embody the whole range of
attitudes that are incorporated into the social and cultural
framework of any society. Throughout history, pervasive
stereotypes of women have painted them as motherly figures, im-
moral temptresses, goddesses, or helpless children in need of paternal guidance. All the chapters in this book include, to varying
degrees, a focus on the specific practices and policies that make up
the social culture of any society. Thus the reader can attempt to
evaluate the degree of patriarchalism that exists there:

How strict or liberal are the laws on divorce and
abortion? If legislation exists permitting these options,
do women have access to the means of taking
advantage of them? Do the customs and traditions of
their religion, family, and geographic locale encourage
or discourage women from taking the steps necessary
to gain release from traditional patriarchal bonds?

Do women from urban, middle-class settings have
noticeably different options available to them
compared to their sisters from poor, rural villages?
How do formal and informal community constraints
vary from place to place?

What role do the religious leaders play in inveighing
against, or taking a tolerant position toward, divorce
and abortion?

What are the statistics on spousal abuse, wife battering,
and sexual violence? Although they may be legally
outlawed, what are the actual incidents of such
patriarchal practices as suttee, dowries and dowry
deaths, tyrannical rule over and seclusion of the
married woman?

Woman-headed households have now become a factor of
importance throughout the world, many of them from
the poorest levels of society. Are there day-care
provisions that assist women who must work outside
their homes to support themselves and their families?

Do working women continue to hold down two jobs, one
outside and one inside their homes, as they have
traditionally done under the patriarchal model?

To what degree do the major media institutions,
particularly television, serve either to perpetuate
traditional patriarchal stereotypes or to create new,
less oppressive images of male and female roles?

This social and cultural arena is a broad one, and our questions
could go on and on. In each of the countries studied here, these
questions and others like them, receive varying degrees of attention.
In each, the authors' analysis allows us to assess the progress, or
lack thereof, away from patriarchy and toward egalitarianism.

On last note. As we undertake to use the patriarchal model as a
measuring stick for evaluating the role, power, and status of
women, one point should be emphasized. Unquestionably, this
model is a product of Western, modern, industrialized, middle-
class, feminist scholarship. The value-based nature of the model is
unabashedly clear: Those aspects of society and its institutional
practices that are most traditional and patriarchal are bad; those
that are most modern and egalitarian are good.

We recognize that not all of the scholars involved in this project
may agree precisely with this formulation, particularly those who

focus on the non-Western world, where concepts of traditionalism and modernism often have quite different interpretations and connotations. Nonetheless, we believe that all will agree that the model as described here has strength and vitality. While formulation and language may change, and definitions of traditionalism and modernity vary from one era and one country to another, the fundamental perspective underlying all the scholarship in this field does not vary: It is wrong when one group (women) is oppressed or subordinated to another.

Furthermore, it is extremely important to describe and discuss the role, status, and concerns of women. In and of itself, such description and discussion enhances consciousness and awareness of the problem. Of course, the critique of conditions and prescriptions of changes that need to occur to ameliorate life for women is considerably less generalizable and more subjectively rooted in specific culture, class, and ethnic tradition. Nonetheless, we assert that beneath the subjective differences stemming from specific vantage points of race, class, economic development, education, religion, urban or rural setting, the underlying theme asserted above—an end to oppression and inequality for women—is shared by all.

—Lynne B. Iglitzin

NOTES

1. The fundamental work here is Aristotle, *The Generation of Animals*, in *The Basic Works of Aristotle*, ed. Richard McKeon (New York: Random House, 1941), Book 1, Chapter 20. See also Georg Hegel, *Philosophy of Nature*, ed. and trans. by M. J. Petry (New York: Humanities Press, 1970). Simone De Beauvoir, *The Second Sex*, ed. and trans. by H. M. Parshley (New York: Alfred A. Knopf, 1952) also details this argument over time.

2. See, for example, Lewis H. Morgan, *The League of the Iroquois* (Rochester, NY: 1851) and *Ancient Society* (1871; reprint, New York: World, 1963); Sir Henry Maine, *Ancient Law* (London: Murray, 1861); and J. J. Bachofen, "Mother Right," in *Myth, Religion and Mother Right*, trans. Ralph Benheim (Princeton, NJ: Princeton University Press, 1967).

3. The classic account of this is found in Friedrich Engels, *The Origin of the Family, Private Property, and the State*, 4th ed., reprint (New York: International Publishers, 1942). Simone De Beauvoir also reviews the history of this practice in her seminal work, *The Second Sex*.

4. A good review of religious misogyny is found in Katherine H. Rogers, *The Troublesome Helpmate* (Seattle: University of Washington Press, 1966).

Similar religious attitudes and practices are detailed in Carol Andreas, *Sex and Caste in America* (Englewood Cliffs, NJ: Prentice-Hall, 1971).

5. Feminist scholarship that searches out long-neglected sources of such voices, as in old diaries and letters, continues to uncover such voices. One might cite John Stuart Mill, Mary Wollstonecraft, and Elizabeth Cady Stanton, to name but a few of the prominent voices from the past.

WOMEN IN THE WORLD

Part One

Industrial Democracies

THE INDUSTRIAL DEMOCRACIES with their technological so-phistication and their need for skilled women in economic roles outside the home would appear to be ideal settings to reflect a changing position for women during the past decade. The 1975 International Women's Year Conference in Mexico City dramati-cally heightened the worldwide visibility of women's issues, and this might lead the reader to anticipate direct impacts on their status in nations where women and men have actively promoted legal changes. The realities of the position of women are explored in the following seven chapters, which analyze several European countries, Israel, Japan, and the United States.

In "Policy Impacts and Women's Roles in France," Joelle Juillard explores the effects of the extensive legal and political changes of the past decade, especially since the election of Socialist President Mitterand in 1981. His victory was attributed to women voters, and the new minister for women's rights has been influential in passing measures to ensure actual implementation of equal rights. Addi-tionally, Juillard discusses the important roles of the diverse ele-ments of the French women's movement, which has successfully focused public attention on women's issues and the many recent reforms. She notes that the gap between law and reality is closing, and that public opinion is more supportive. Nevertheless, she con-cludes that the partial "institutionalism" of some militant feminist issues has not irradicated inequality or sexism, or changed the important cultural status symbol of a *femme au foyer*.

Like France, West Germany has enacted extensive legal changes that include major reforms in marriage laws and modifications in divorce laws. Legislation also created maternity leave, and in 1986 will provide a child-rearing allowance for mothers or fathers who discontinue work. Educational reforms have increased the numbers of women who complete their education, but in "The Women's Decade in West Germany," Peter Merkl argues that the need is to motivate women to choose the traditionally male-dominated careers, rather than to remove any deliberate barriers. Although the new Green party and the Alternative List party actively promote women's policies, they, as well as the organized women in the other parties, trades unions, and the Autonomous Women's Movement, continue to be an elite group with limited impacts on the ideas of the majority of German women and men. Furthermore, Merkl says that Germany is responding to the neoconservative political turning point of 1982, which promotes traditional family ties and a wife's identity linked to her husband's career.

Ingunn Norderval focuses her analysis of Scandinavia on the formulation of equality policy. The modern women's movement has built upon a long history of feminist concern and a dominant emphasis on basic equality. She documents the current thrust toward dealing with oppression and liberation from the historic patriarchal social order by changing male as well as female roles in "Elusive Equality: The Limits of Public Policy." Feminists are pushing for a radical restructuring of family and social roles, but this is based upon what she calls the Nordic tendency to support "radical or leftish solutions" to national problems. In Scandinavia, she notes, much of the impetus for change has come from the government, rather than from grassroots demands, and the present economic crisis and the more conservative political climate have helped to relegate equality issues to the back burner.

In "Italy and Ireland: Women, Church, and Politics in Two Catholic Countries," the church continues its significant role in family relationships, procreation, and education, but its influence is nominal in women's employment and political participation. The women's movements have developed in response to each country's particular culture. In Ireland, Catholicism and nationalism are synonymous in reaction to British Protestant domination, and changes for women have been incremental. In Italy, the struggle to obtain divorce and abortion rights galvanized women's political actions, and feminist demonstrations aided the adoption of the new Family Law Code. Although the Catholic church itself has little interest in women's participation in public life, M. C. Porter and Corey Venning comment that centuries of socialization continue to persuade many women that their proper role is in the home. The church continues to dominate education in both countries, maintaining single-sex primary and secondary schools. The authors conclude, however, that neither the Irish nor Italian churches can prevail indefinitely against reforms being demanded by the women's movements in these countries.

In Japan, traditional cultural values continue to be important, in spite of the radical constitutional changes created by the occupation forces after the World War II defeat. In her chapter, "From the Moon to the Sun: Women's Liberation in Japan," Kazuko Sugisaki briefly traces the historic position of Japanese women and the careers of a few early leaders for women's rights. More recent women's political action has assisted in gaining major reforms in equal pay, inheritance, divorce, and consumer issues. Nevertheless, many women withdraw from the labor force for marriage and childbirth, and with the increased standard of living, do not reenter the labor force, but are pursuing leisure-time training and activities in privately sponsored cultural centers. Typical courses are flower arrangement, the tea ceremony, cooking, religion, literature, etc. Formal university education for adult women is limited because it is oriented toward young full-time students. Despite legal equality, the Japanese social system continues to be based upon male supremacy; women are unwilling to divorce, and they tend to endure the vestiges of their low status, which is based upon centuries of Confucian and Buddhist teachings.

Ellen Boneparth explores the contradictions in contemporary Israeli society, which support egalitarian sex roles but also maintain a public policy orientation that reenforces women's traditional roles through the patriarchal Jewish religion. In addition to an analysis of family patterns, her article, "In the Land of the Patriarchs: Public Policy on Women in Israel," discusses women's place in the workforce, and the Israeli policy that assigns parenting responsibilities to women. Boneparth maintains that the distinctions between the religious and state spheres reenforce the sexual division of labor and the patriarchal character of the society, and that this is evident in housing policy and incentives and services for child bearing and rearing. She concludes that it would take both a cultural and a political transformation if Israeli women are to expand their work roles and combine work and family for their own benefit.

In "The Gender Gap in American Politics," Marjorie Lansing focuses on the effects of the gender gap in recent elections. Her analysis of poll data shows that the women's vote and attitudinal differences between men and women have been factors in state and congressional elections since 1980. This variation was also evident in the two Reagan presidential elections, but was offset by major demographic circumstances and by widespread approval of the president's performance in office, despite the selection of Geraldine Ferraro to run as the first woman vice-presidential candidate. She traces the sources of the gender gap in long-term changes in the role and status of women and in their politicalization, especially since the defeat of the Equal Rights Amendment. She also analyzes the impact of the liberal and conservative elements of the women's movement and of several current public policy issues. She concludes that women have become a force in American politics because of the gender gap and because of their changing roles and socioeconomic status.

Policy Impacts and Women's Roles in France

Joelle Rutherford Juillard
University of Southern California

T he situation of French women appears to be less paradoxical than it was a decade ago. At that time, this writer was able to hold[1] that French women

> ... have finally benefitted in some respects from that important French cultural theme, equality; but they continue to fulfill the domestic and subordinate female role in France's strong family tradition. Individual women have achieved positions of prominence and may exercise considerable power in French society, but together they have not gained control over those matters that affect their lives. There is a great discrepancy between the formal, legal opportunities for French women and their actual achievements. Moreover, French women, except for a tiny fringe, are not discontented with women's place in their society.

The legal reforms enacted since have been more impressive in terms of enforcement mechanisms, as well as in implications for far-reaching societal changes. At the same time French women appear to be gaining some real determination over issues affecting workplace and home. There is thus less discrepancy than there was in 1975 between actual achievements and legal gains. Pressure to improve the status of women during this last decade has acquired a broader base. The French government, especially since Mitterand took office in 1981, has met most of the issue-oriented reformist demands as they have come up.

Since formal legal gains have been so impressive and real

7

achievements appear to be growing, the question of long-term attitudinal changes toward women's roles in French culture becomes paramount. To what extent can the important legal gains be attributed to changes in cultural attitudes, and to what extent do they seem to be producing changes in attitudes? It is fundamental shifts in orientations toward sex roles that will secure the theoretical gains in laws. Admittedly, change in attitudes toward women is extremely difficult to assess.[2] This discussion will review the remarkable progress made during the "women's decade" in equal rights laws and will appraise the role of the French women's movement in this progress. The real achievements of French women over these ten years in the crucial areas of education, politics, and employment will then be examined.[3] Finally, the relationship of these developments to public consciousness will be explored, suggesting prospects for the future.

First, and most strikingly, the legal status of women in France has improved dramatically since 1975, when it was already well advanced. Since the attainment of industrial maturity by French society at the beginning of the century, and in particular since 1945, numerous laws had been passed in support of equality. The vote was obtained (in 1945 when women's participation in the Resistance was cited as a major justification for enfranchising them), and "full equality" was proclaimed with the constitution of 1946. Marriage contracts were improved when the Code civile was amended in 1965 and with legislation affecting parental responsibilities in 1970. France had an equal pay law with a "decree of implementation" by 1973, and in the area of birth control and abortion significant progress was made. Although Françoise Giroud's position as secretary of state to the prime minister for the condition of women, created in 1974, was without a budget and almost without staff (to represent 51 percent of the French), several important proposals passed during its existence, including the opening of all civil service entrance examinations to women and of all *agrégations* to both women and men, income tax deductions for child care expenses, improved pensions for widows, and extended Social Security benefits for divorcees.

However, the reforms enacted since 1975 have put France with Sweden in first place for equal rights for women. In June of 1975 divorce by mutual consent was adopted, and in July of the same year two laws were passed to guarantee equal access to government employment. By 1975 the Loi Veil (Interruption volontaire de grossesse or IVG) had passed, and abortion was legalized, although expenses were not yet covered by Social Security and abortions were restricted to those who could afford them.

The most impressive reformist activity has occurred since the election of Socialist President François Mitterand in May of 1981. His victory is attributed to women voters, who, for the first time, were no longer voting disproportionately for candidates of the Right.[4] Mitterand immediately fulfilled his promise to create a minister delegate to the prime minister for women's rights. He appointed Yvette Roudy, a veteran Socialist who worked her way up through party ranks while she was translating American feminist writers into French and writing her own feminist works reflecting on the political experience she was gaining within the party and the French women's movement.[5] "Over the last 15 years we were a small group of feminists within the Socialist Party fighting very hard even to have the word 'feminism' accepted. . . . I brought to him [Mitterand] the importance of women's issues and convinced him that women's issues are political issues," she has said.[6] The ministry is for women's *rights* rather than for their *condition*, an important distinction from Françoise Giroud's largely symbolic post under immediate past President Valery Giscard d'Estaing. In contrast, Roudy heads a full ministry with a budget of about 110 million francs (a tenfold increase over Giroud's), a building, and a staff of 240 in Paris and in offices throughout France. Roudy arrived in office with a clear picture of what she wanted to accomplish after 20 years working for women's rights and in the Socialist party. What she has accomplished in three years has been so broad in scope that it bears consideration in some detail.

With a deep understanding of political culture in France, Roudy shrewdly set about immediately entrenching her ministry in the bureaucracy and increasing its visibility everywhere by the development of an administrative structure of 150 staffed information centers, Centres d'Information sur les Droits des Femmes (CIDFS), throughout the country, where women can obtain information about their rights and the recent laws. Each region has a delegate to the Ministry (Déléguées Régionales), linking Paris and women in the regions and providing information in both directions. *Guides* about women's rights are published annually and distributed through these centers, where trained *animatrices* interpret them and give free advice about civil rights, workplace and Social Security rights, professional opportunities, and family issues. Their goal is to direct more women to the proper public bodies and to enable them to approach these institutions with more confidence. The most far-reaching function of these centers, though, is the clientele being cultivated for the new ministry in a country where "solid bureaucratic-clientelistic connections" provide the best staying-power.[7]

Among immediate actions taken by the ministry was a wide campaign for awareness about birth control and the reform of the Veil abortion law. The information campaign increased women's knowledge of the resources available for family planning through prime-time television spots, signs providing information telephone numbers in the metro, and a large brochure distribution; the number of consultations in family planning groups doubled within a year.[8] The reform of the Veil law in September of 1982 vastly increased the number of hospitals required to perform abortions, and in December reimbursement by Social Security became law, making abortions available to all. The ministry's efforts to increase accessibility to legal abortions were successful after more than a year of controversy.

The improvements in family law have significantly eroded the patriarchal concept of "head of household," which had limited married women's rights to children and to social welfare benefits. Since last year income tax returns must be signed by both spouses, thereby enabling the wife to know her husband's income. Since July of 1982 the wives of independent workers, such as shopkeepers or farmers, who had always worked with their husbands unsalaried and without rights to social benefits or pensions, may choose a status as salaried collaborator or associate and be eligible for social benefits. Other reforms include the right of divorced women to apply for their children to receive "orphans' benefits" if their ex-husbands are delinquent on alimony payments, special benefits and subsidized housing for single mothers, and special insurance and partial pensions for widows.

Great strides have been made in equal employment opportunity law with the Law on Sexual Equality in Employment, passed in July of 1983. It was designed to fill gaps and provide implementation mechanisms needed in the wake of two ineffectual earlier laws on equal pay and equality in hiring. A public awareness campaign was immediately launched to support it, much of which was aimed at youth under a "Careers Have No Sex" slogan. The new law extended the principle of nondiscrimination to apply to all except a list of certain jobs in which the sex of the employee can be considered a necessary condition for performance, and Roudy is continually getting that list reduced.[9] It will no longer be possible for employment contracts and conventions to contain specific discriminatory clauses *(motif légitime)* other than those related to pregnancy, maternity, and nursing. Also, in training, job evaluation, and promotion, discrimination is liable to stronger penalties. Labor unions will be able to act in the courts on behalf of a woman employee with her permission—this article is designed to help overcome women's reticence in resorting to the law. Any dismissal by an employer of a woman employee as a penalty for instituting legal proceedings on grounds of sex discrimination can be invalidated, and if individual discrimination is established by a judge, and is illustrative of a general situation, the employer can be required to implement measures to redress inequalities. The measures for redress attest to Roudy's creativity as well as her political pragmatism. Instead of stiffer fines and longer prison sentences (which are not ruled out but which are not likely to change the way a firm is run), the employer is required to propose a plan of measures designed to establish equality. This original sanction with an educative dimension will entail comparative progress reports on the reduction of disparities made each year by *comités d'entreprise* in the firms. Also, a firm may on its own initiative draw up a plan to reduce disparities and be provided with governmental financial and technical assistance. Less than a year has passed, and the machinery of the law is still being put into place, but Roudy is optimistic: "Soon no doubt I shall be in a position to announce numerous agreements of employers who are ready to put such plans into effect straight away."[10] Indeed, the law does provide unprecedented implementation "teeth." The "watchdog" function is to be performed by a supervisory body, the Higher Council for Sexual Equality in Employment, charged with defining and implementing policy and linked to the Ministries of Women's Rights, Labor, and Employment and Vocational Training. Organizations of both employers and employees are broadly represented on this council, and it has a permanent secretariat whose purpose is to promote these plans for equality in firms and to provide data for all interested parties.

It is too soon to evaluate the success of this very strong equal employment opportunity law, which also provides for stronger revised equal pay regulations, better training programs with quotas to break down occupational segregation, and exclusion of sexist imagery from textbooks and other materials. However, Roudy has demonstrated her concern with the crucial issue of socialization related to employment. Joint action with the Ministry of Education has been undertaken, and textbooks are being revised by regional commissions whose task it is to critique them and make appropriate

recommendations to publishers. Roudy is particularly interested in
encouraging young women to go into "high-tech" jobs, which motivated her trip to study training programs at Carnegie-Mellon, Cal-
tech, and Harvey Mudd in April of 1984.

Finally, to conclude this discussion of the new ministry's achievements, the "Anti-Sexist Law" was proposed in March of 1983
amid great controversy. Its main purpose is to prohibit degrading
images of women in advertising, and it is still being debated. The
employment equality law did pass with support from both the
Right and the Left: Roudy attributes this cooperation to her conviction that if people in France elected a progressive socialist government rather than a conservative one, it was an indicator that in
general they were prepared to accept changes.[11] Modeled after
France's "anti-racism" law, which was adopted ten years ago, the
"anti-sexism" proposal has roused cries of protest against censorship. Although it is only intended to apply to depictions that could
be incitements to violence against women, it is far from certain that
it will pass when it does come up for debate in 1985.

If the new ministry has been successful in passing measures more
likely to ensure actual implementation of equal rights, the activities
of the French women's movement over the last decade are held to
have been a crucial factor.[12] The various movement activities have
had good media exposure, which can have affected public knowledge of and cultural attitudes about women's issues in a country
where the middle classes have a relatively high interest in intellectual debate. It is often claimed that feminist militancy is now defunct in France, since the important issues around which the disparate tendencies had mobilized resulted in demands that were
largely met by government reforms.

In the early 1970s feminism was seen by both French men and
women, generally, as a left-wing "fringe" of frustrated women and
frustrated intellectuals, and it did not show signs of becoming a
broadly based mass movement like that forming in the United
States.[13] Many more groups, however, began to get involved, representing diverse segments of the population, and feminist agitation
is credited with making possible the passage of the Equal Pay Act of
1973, the 1974 laws on contraception and abortion, the election of a
Socialist government in 1981, and the success of Roudy's ministry in
enacting strong measures since. The press began to treat feminism
with some respect. Indeed, the women's movement during the 1970s
brought about "a transformation of consciousness."[14]

The "Mouvement de la Libération des Femmes" (MLF) was the

name given by the French press during the summer of 1970 to the different radical women's groups that had been visible, especially in Paris, since late 1968. The original impetus for their formation was the discovery that equality for women had no more importance for their "revolutionary" male comrades than for the bourgeois enemy. While theories of oppression and liberation have been numerous, very diverse, conflictual, and often intricately esoteric, the political action attempted has been in the best reformist tradition—a series of limited and precise fights, ending in specific victories. In terms of French intellectual life and influence, ". . . it has often been stated that radical feminism is the only revolutionary force that has maintained the exuberance of May 1968; it is the only movement in France today that combines the conviction of a cause with a serious theoretical quest and unlimited occasions to test the relation between theory and practice."[15]

The MLF has been comprised of a number of groups: Psychanalyse et politique, Choisir, La ligue du droit des femmes, SOS Femmes, and Petroleuses seem to have been the most clearly defined and influential. The proliferation of feminist journals, bulletins, and reviews, most intermittent and on shoestring budgets, did have a self-imposed intellectual center, which seems now to be on the wane.[16] Psychanalyse et politique, which has controlled the most successful feminist publishing house in Paris, Editions des femmes, attempted to politically dominate the entire movement. Early, it had set itself apart by its hierarchial organization, led by psychoanalyst "Antoinette,"[17] its focus on Lacanian psychoanalysis, and its extreme separatism, based on theoretical opposition to "feminism" as the rejection of difference in egalitarian emphasis. Briefly, the messianic separatism and antifeminism of Psych et Po inspired much philosophical debate and writings.[18] When the group acquired a legacy of considerable financial resources, it began to seek increased political power, and as Antoinette became better known, the media began to present her stands on issues as those of the diverse MLF as a whole. Although representatives of other feminist groups within the MLF explained that there was no single organization and leader—that they only came together for specific actions—the public continued to assume an organization of common positions and spokespersons. Because the designation MLF had originated with the press, it was easy for Antoinette to appropriate leadership symbolically by registering the new home of her organization with the Paris Prefecture as "the MLF": in October of 1979 Psych et Po became MLF, and the power play was for a time successful despite protest. This struggle must be viewed in the

context of the political centralization of France, the cultural domination of Paris, where the media are not regionally dispersed, and
the fascination with language that has characterized French intellectual life. The opposing group of feminists endeavored to publicize the "imposture" in a polemical dossier against the MLF with a
preface by Simone de Beauvoir. By March 1982, news stories had
begun to explain that "MLF" did not represent the entire women's
movement, and many more television viewers were better versed in
the issues of feminism. Without exaggerating its importance, this
"MLF" struggle may be viewed as an illustration of how public
awareness and understanding were increased.

The public successes of the movement during the decade were, of
course, crucial. The abortion rights march in the summer of 1971
(following the Manifesto of 343, which had been printed in *Le nouvel
observateur*) and the Bobigny trial had mobilized public opinion,
resulting in the 1974 Veil law; when this law came up for review in
1979, massive demonstrations again mobilized effective pressure
for abortion rights. Public awareness was increased by such actions
as a sit-in of SOS Femmes, which resulted in government financing
of a refuge for battered women, and by the debates about rape that
led to harsher penalties for rapists enacted in 1980. Just before the
1981 election Gisèle Halimi, the feminist lawyer who founded
Choisir, organized a forum for the presidential candidates to dis-
course on "Which President for Women?" During a three-hour
dialogue with Choisir, Mitterand made his promise for the creation
of the new Ministry for Women's Rights. Choisir's continuing reformist activity was instrumental in creating the climate for the
1982 laws on contraception and abortion.

Because of the proliferation of government-supported projects to
meet reformist demands, the feminist movement is now seen to be
in a state of quiescence. The Ministry of Women's Rights has subsidized several projects recently advocated by feminist groups, such
as the Simone de Beauvoir Centre (an audiovisual center directed
by Delphine Seyrig) and the Center for Feminist Research and
Information (CRIF). Roudy herself discourages separatism and is
optimistic about continuing reformist successes and the future of
the movement: "To claim that feminism is defunct, when in fact it is
becoming institutionalized, is, it has to be admitted, something of a
paradox. The truth is quite the reverse—feminism has never been
such a live force, for at last it is being put into practice. . . ."[19] Indeed,
that time when there are no more battles to be won is not yet upon
France (witness the Anti-Sexist Law controversy). Regarding the
theoretical debates of French feminism, "Because the prestige of the

French word in French culture is far greater than the ridicule that impedes the feminist initiative, the future of French feminisms and the writing that engenders them and is engendered by them lies open."[20]

In the face of the great strides made in formal laws and the awakening of public consciousness enhanced by the activities of the women's movement, what is really taking place in French life? Do French women have any more control over those matters that directly affect them in the crucial areas of education, politics, and employment?

In 1975 France placed among the most egalitarian of European nations in terms of equal access to education, but the impediment to true equality was the segregation of young women into the liberal arts and traditionally female training fields.[21] Women in France were by no means denied access to the professions because they were cut off from higher education, but there was a striking discrepancy between their educational opportunities and the extent of their achievement in the French occupational structure. It was not serving them well to be just as numerous as men in higher education if professional education for the *real* market was so unequal.

There have been some signs that this discrepancy is being reduced. Although female students still cluster in the liberal arts, increasing numbers of women are going into medicine, engineering, and scientific research.[22] The French military academies are just now (spring of 1984) being integrated. The recent government emphasis on "high-tech" training programs and equal access to all *stages* should soon produce notable improvements.[23] The large-scale rewriting of textbooks now being undertaken by the Ministry for Women's Rights with the Ministry for National Education should increasingly raise public consciousness against traditional segregation. As to the conciousness that could be raised by feminist research in France, "women's studies" is little more than ten years old. In 1980 a well-attended women's studies colloquium in Lyon made some recommendations to increase research,[24] but they do not seem to have become a priority for the new ministry. Only the Centre national de recherche scientifique (CNRS) offers limited help to feminist research in universities. However, the ministry did create the well-funded audiovisual Centre Simone de Beauvoir, and Madame Roudy took an implied stand in 1981 against the extreme separatism of Psych et Po,[25] helping to smooth the path for intellectual collaboration. The ministry's priority has been the concrete practical measures to reform educational segregation, and, although significant statistical trends have not yet materialized to indicate substantial progress, reasonable optimism abounds.[26]

The presence of women in French political life is not quite as "token" as it was ten years ago. It was the leftward vote of women, as has been noted above, that was decisive in bringing Mitterand to power. This electoral shift resulted in part from the activities of the women's movement, as women, active in autonomous groups and parties and trade unions, demanded equality and greater participation.[27] In July of 1981 the first woman prefect (now called commissaires du peuple, of which there are 100) was appointed. The number of women seated in the National Assembly has increased from 5 (in 1975) to 28 at present out of 491 deputies—representing a gain, but a continuing extremely low percentage. In 1975 there were two state secretaries and one minister, and in the present government 6 women hold the position of minister (1), minister delegate (2), or secretary of state to a minister (3), as compared to 36 men cabinet members. Ministerial appointments continue to emphasize the point that although some women do rise to ministerial rank, they are confined to several departments for which they are believed to have a special vocation—education, health, and social concerns—and this principle also continues to hold for the work of female members of the National Assembly and Senate, who prefer to sit on committees dealing with those areas.[28]

Although feminization of politics remains very much a matter of token cases, it does not seem as clear as it did a decade ago that politics in France is likely to remain "the game women do not play."[29] Women made an important breakthrough in the March 1983 municipal elections: the number of women elected increased 66 percent; women represent 14 percent of all elected municipal officers, up from 8.4 percent in 1977; the number of seats now held by women in townships of less than 3,500 people has doubled.[30] These results may be an indication that women will in greater numbers assume departmental and regional responsibilities. More French women now seem to be interested in politics and hopeful that increased participation will affect changes towards full equality.[31]

Much of the recent strong legislation for equal rights is in the area of employment or has most direct implications for this area. The issue of employment is central: It is a necessary condition for women's progress towards autonomy, equality, and liberation; Simone de Beauvoir stated in 1972 that work is a *first* condition of women's independence, and although it is not felt to be a general panacea, it is evident that this attitude is becoming widely shared in France.[32]

In 1975 women were found to be segregated in the least-skilled, lowest-paying, dead-cnd occupations, taken mainly to supplement low family incomes, so that the relatively high participation of women in the labor force (compared to the rest of Western Europe) was not in any way indicative of equality between the sexes.[33]

Women now comprise 40 percent of the labor force, as compared to 37 percent in 1974.[34] This gain is largely due to increasing numbers of married women entering the job market: In 1981 62 percent of the female labor force consisted of married women, and in 1982, 65 percent (50 percent of these had two or more children).[35] There is greater continuity among working mothers as well: It is now the third pregnancy rather than the second that prompts a woman to break off her career; more working mothers either do not interrupt at all, or else not for as long.[36] Disparities in salaries appear to be gradually diminishing: In 1975 the average gap was 33 percent, and in 1980, 31 percent; the higher status the position, the greater the earning disparity.[37]

Occupational segregation, however, continues with but small improvements. The percentage of working women in higher-status positions (liberal professions and *cadres supérieurs*, or top-level executives and civil servants) remains about the same at roughly 5 percent.[38] Of 300 listed occupations in France, women continue to be channeled into about 30.[39] Women are concentrated in a few branches of industry, where 65 percent of the jobs are held by women: textiles, ready-made clothes, some branches of electronics, and food processing. Of the administrative positions held by women 67 percent are in service occupations; women in the civil service are still segregated into the middle and lower ranks and in those service sectors traditionally regarded as feminine.[40] At all levels of public-school teaching below the university, teaching careers (civil service) are significantly more professionalized and prestigious than in the United States. Since the economic crisis of 1974, more men have been entering elementary and especially secondary teaching; a quota was established to get men *lycée* professors up to 35 percent. However, at the university level (positions that command higher salary and more prestige), no quotas have been established to increase the number of women. There are imperceptible gains, except at the lowest instructional rank, where the percentage of women has risen from 25 percent in 1975 to 40 percent in 1983.[41] Thus, professional opportunities and achievements for women in France remain very much weighted on the side of public employment (teaching and government administration), rather than toward accomplishment in entrepreneurial and private professions. In medicine, for example, the proportion of women physicians remains what it was in 1975: 15 percent.[42] It will soon be possible to discern whether the recent emphasis on opening up or "de-sexing" training programs and the government campaign for public awareness ("Careers Have No Sex," launched by Roudy's ministry) will change these numbers.

Life in France has become more convenient for the working woman over the past decade. There are larger numbers of supermarkets and coin laundries, many now open on Sundays. Freezers are not as scarce, and shopping for many women is not the daily chore it once was. The interruption of the noon dinner, ever a cherished tradition in families, continues to make the real working day for French women longer. It seems, however, that younger husbands increasingly share homemaking tasks, especially parenting activities, although even in "helping" with children and shopping, the domestic work week is far from equal.[43] As to a final aspect of the working woman's situation, child care, the problem noted ten years ago was lack of space in public facilities. Although availability of state-subsidized centers has compared favorably with other common market countries and with the U.S., demand continues to far outstrip supply, despite some improvement.[44]

A decade ago working women were reluctant to avail themselves of what legal machinery did exist in order to challenge discriminatory practices in hiring, promotion, and pay. Now that the July 1983 Law on Sexual Equality in Employment has plugged the gaps in implementation left by the earlier laws of 1972 and 1975, and now that the vast regional informational infrastructure (Centres d'Information sur les Droits des Femmes) is in place, are discriminatory practices being increasingly challenged? The distribution of the annually revised *Guide des droits des femmes* and the provision of counseling and meeting places through the Centres has greatly increased awareness of and information about rights and procedures. (In 1982, 300,000 women used one of the CIDFs.[45]) It is not at all clear that the number of discrimination cases brought to court is growing, and when asked about this point, Minister Roudy seemed despairing.[46] Nor has the powerful concept of "comparable worth" been developed in France. The only recent progress related to the issue of defining the value of work is in having professional experience gain acceptance as a permissible substitute for diplomas in certain fields. As for attempting to determine what traditionally male job the work of a traditionally female librarian, sales clerk, or health aide is comparable to, French women have not demanded it, and until they do, it is doubtful that the new ministry will take it on.[47]

The key to the relationship between the formal, legal opportunities and the real achievements of French women is French culture, those attitudes that seemed to be changing so slowly, if at all, a decade ago. The great gap between law and reality has been seen to be closing. Not only are the laws themselves increasingly forceful, but public opinion is more supportive of equality for women, and the role of the women's movement in the transformation of consciousness through focus on specific reformist issues as well as philosophical debate has been held to be significant. What now may be concluded about these changing cultural attitudes themselves?

The tradition is long and deeply embedded: ".... surely no other Western culture has developed more elaborate and intricate ideas about women and more closely interwoven them with the 'high culture' and the style of life of whole social classes" than has France.[48] The ideal of the *femme au foyer* has had especially great strength and persuasion for the French, and its force cannot be underestimated in the convergence of diverse philosophic tendencies: Catholic conservatism, Romantic individualism, scientific progressivism, and antibourgeois radicalism. (Of course the Marxist and Socialist perspectives, which did not subscribe to this view, subsumed "the women's question" in a class analysis of society's ills.) The powerful domestic ideal has provided a role for women long seen as crucial and dignified rather than routine and secondary. In France, higher social status and education have not, as in the United States, implied greater support for women's equality. Being able to stay home and make the important contribution in the *foyer* is still a status symbol.

However, there is now in France unprecedented public sympathy for feminist demands. Feminist concerns have been received with respect rather than ridicule, and indications of this changing attitude are especially clear in the media.[49] A state television prime-time discussion on rape with Marie-Odile Fargier (her book *Le Viol* caused the same interest as Brownmiller's *Against Our Will*, which was translated) in 1978 is one memorable illustration. What was once thought to be of limited interest to a small fringe of feminists gradually became part of the Paris cultural scene: good examples are Annie Le Clerc's *Parole de Femme*, a popular play in the late 1970s, and Helene Cixous's *Portrait de Dora*, which was played by the renowned Renaud-Barrault theater company in the elegant Theatre d'Orsay. The most popular fashion magazine (*Marie Claire*) now includes a regular insert consisting of women's history, news of feminist activities, and practical information, edited by the well-known and outspoken feminist writer Benoite Groult, who has just been named by Madame Roudy to head a new commission on the feminization of names of functions and professions. Women's issues, from contraception, to re-entry into gainful employment, to sex stereotypes in culture are, "if not standard conversational content for most French citizens, at least acknowledged in the media now to an unprecedented extent."[50] That intellectual oracle, *Le Monde*, has run increasingly frequent analyses on such subjects as the evolution of feminism in neighboring Mediterranean countries and the awakening of feminist awareness among the thousands of women teachers in the state school system. *Le Nouvel Observateur*, the weekly news magazine of the comfortable, well-educated, and moderate leftist middle classes, has given feminist causes increasingly extensive and sympathetic treatment. *L'Express* (equivalent to *Time* or *Newsweek)* has published excerpts of bestsellers, such as Fargiers's, with enlightened discussion and works such as Michele Sarde's *Regarde sur les françaises, X^e – XXe siècle*, published last year, enjoy considerable prestige.

The significance of this gradual acceptance of feminist values by the French political and intellectual establishment is appreciated when one remembers that the stimulating French intellectual tradition has included rigid national stereotypes of femininity. A striking reminder, near the beginning of the "women's decade" (1977), was Jean-Paul Sartre's statement in the much-heralded film documentary *Sartre par lui-même* that he preferred the company of women because they are good-looking but that, once in a while, a brilliant woman might be interesting to him despite her lack of physical attributes. Although vestiges of sexism have been tenacious among such conscientious intellectuals, when the season's bestsellers include works with a feminist bias, [51] a questioning of the traditional gender order is taking place in the public consciousness. Since abortion, rape, and equal pay are matters that are now taken seriously by most power groups and that receive unprecedented publicity in the popular press, feminism can be said to have come a very long way toward legitimization throughout French society over the last decade.

It seems reasonable to expect that the remaining gap between discussion and action will continue to close. The economic recession and increasing need for two incomes per family is one factor leading to growing tolerance for women's equality in cultural attitudes; the change in cultural outlook in turn facilitates improvement in conditions for working women. The exaggerated reactions produced by the proposed Anti-Sexist Law indicate that the struggle is far from won. Designed to discourage sexist representations in only their most violent and degrading forms, the proposed law has neverthe-less been denounced by the press, and public support for it, gener-ally, has not been forthcoming. When the new ministry moves beyond encouraging a rethinking of attitudes toward employment into the deeper waters of pushing for a rethinking of the ways in which images of women reproduce their subordination, the resis-tance is still strong.

This resistance seems to indicate that the new ministry, under-standably, is having an easier time with reforms that are congruent with the traditional socialist consensus about the needs of women, emphasizing conditions favorable to women's economic indepen-dence. When the issue is one on which feminists have stood alone, such as analysis of the reproduction of cultural oppression and its eradication, dissension flares up.[52] The proposed new law may prove too "feminist" for public opinion—or too far afield from the traditional Left consensus about the desirable status for women—to be passed. Its fate will be very indicative of just how far cultural attitudes have progressed.

The present Socialist government certainly has other priorities, such as inflation, unjust distribution of wealth, inadequate housing and public transportation, outmoded educational institutions, and rigidly bureaucratic administration. At least women's issues are no longer lost among these pressing concerns. Nor can one agree with those observers who hold that "feminism has gone out of style" for want of foci for real opposition in the cooperative climate of the present government, as contrasted to the clarity of polarized protest in face of a conservative government during the 1970s. There is still much inequality and sexism to be overcome, and it is far from evident that the majority of women or men in France have accepted the new image of the role of women forged over the last decade. The partial "institutionalization" (to some, co-optation) of feminist militancy is a new challenge for, as well as encouragement to, the continuing vitality of the women's movement in a positive atmo-sphere, where "... at this moment in France women are more hopeful and determined about their futures than they were a very few years ago."[53]

NOTES

1. Joelle R. Juillard, "Women in France," in *Women in the World* (Santa Barbara, CA: ABC-Clio, 1976), 115, 125–126.

2. Survey "measurement," always problematic, is possibly even more so in France. The material presented below, which will include some impressionistic content analysis of media, seems to be at least as reasonable a means of suggesting possibilities for permanent improvement of the status of women based on cultural acceptance.

3. In order to determine any improvements beyond the conclusions of ten years ago, presented in Juillard's "Women in France."

4. Jane Jensen, "The Work of the Ministère des Droits de la Femme," *Conference Group on French Politics and Society Newsletter* (Winter 1984), 3–9. Dorothy Kauffmann-McCall, "Politics of Difference: The Women's Movement in France from May 1968 to Mitterand," *Signs* (Winter 1983), 282–293. Conversation with Yvette Roudy, French minister for women's rights, at a dinner on April 18, 1984, during her visit to Scripps College, California.

5. Madame Roudy has translated into French Betty Friedan's *The Feminine Mystique*, Eleanor Roosevelt's *My Life*, and Elizabeth Janeway's *Man's World, Woman's Place*. Her own books include *La Réussite de la femme* and *La Femme en marge*.

6. Kathleen Hendrix, "Yvette Roudy: Feminist Force in France," *Los Angeles Times*, April 25, 1984, Part V.

7. Jensen, 7. This important point should be underscored in view of the backlash and implementation problems beleaguering reformist feminism everywhere.

8. Ibid, 4.

9. Yvette Roudy, "Discours," text of public lecture delivered at Scripps College, California, May 19, 1984, 6.

10. Ibid., 7.

11. Hendrix.

12. Elaine Marks and Isabelle de Courtivron, eds., *New French Feminisms* (New York: Schocken, 1981), "Introduction III"; Chantal Mareuil, "Women and Work in France," lecture delivered at the University of Southern California, April 13, 1983. See also Jensen, Kaufmann-McCall.

13. Juillard, 125; Catherine Silver, "Salon, Foyer, Bureau: Women and the Professions in France," *American Journal of Sociology* 78 (January 1983).

14. Kaufmann-McCall, 282.

15. Marks and de Courtivron, 33–34.

16. Leader Antoinette is reported to be traveling in the United States and seeking to live here after her attempt to found an exclusive labor union foundered last year.

17. The capital investment of one of her most convinced disciples set up the press.

18. The theoretical conflicts within the French feminist movement since 1968 are neatly summarized by Kaufmann-McCall. The differences with earlier feminisms are delineated by Marks and de Courtivron.

19. Roudy, 7–8.

20. Marks and de Courtivron, 38.

21. Juillard, 117–118.

22. However, the number of women students at the prestigious Ecole Polytechnique has increased from 4 to only 5 percent, according to a source at the Consulat de France of Los Angeles.

23. Sixty percent of candidates accepted in youth training programs must be women; joint action is being taken with the Ministry of National Education to provide training that will enable girls to break out of what Madame Roudy terms the "sexist ghetto." Press Department of the French Embassy, "France," June–July 1983, "France's Position on Women's Rights," 4

24. Such as an interdisciplinary commission to be created within the National Center for Scientific Research (CNRS), active solicitation for the creation of feminist studies posts by the Ministry of Education, formal liaison with the Ministry for Women's Rights, and further government-sponsored colloquia. (Education in France is nationally centralized and financed.)

25. Kaufmann-McCall, 291.

26. The optimism of Madame Roudy and her entourage at the Scripps College dinner is understandable, but the more well founded because it is shared by a diversity of reliable sources with whom this writer is in contact, both in France and in the United States.

27. Jensen, 3.

28. Madame Roudy confirmed this continuing trend at the Scripps College dinner.

29. Alain Duhamel, "Les Femmes et la politique," *Le Monde*, March 10, 1971.

30. "France's Position on Women's Rights," 5.

31. Madame Roudy noted at the Scripps College dinner surveys reported over the last few years in the French press that indicate greater interest in politics among French women as well as declining misogynous attitudes in French culture.

32. Mareuil.

33. Juillard, 118–121.

34. Maryse Huet, "La Progression de l'activité feminine est-elle irréversible?" *Economie et statistique* 145 (June 1982), 3–4.

35. *QUID*, 1984, "Femmes," 1413.

36. Huet, 4–5.

37. Mareuil. Hence, the gap is 37 percent for executives, 31 percent for *cadres moyens*, and 26 percent for laborers.

38. *QUID*, 1413, 1436.

39. Roudy, 5.

40. French Embassy, "Women in France," December 1982, 2.

41. Mareuil.

42. *QUID*, 43.

43. This writer's impressions are confirmed by a number of reliable sources; a recent survey is not available.

44. According to Madame Roudy at the Scripps College dinner.

45. Jensen, 7.

46. At the Scripps College dinner she underscored women's reluctance to bring cases to court, despite better laws and more information.

47. Hendrix's interview of Madame Roudy.

48. Silver, 843. For a more detailed discussion of this tradition see Silver, Juillard.

49. See note 2 above. Both participant observation and content analysis of media are possibly more valid "measures" of attitudes in France. Jennifer Stoddart's "Feminism in Paris," *Canadian Newsletter of Research on Women* (March 1978), is an excellent summary of the impact of French feminism in print on the cultural scene, and I am indebted to her discussion.

50. Ibid., 62.

51. See Stoddart for a complete description of such works in the late 1970s.

52. Jensen, 9. She analyses traditional egalitarian socialism in interaction with contemporary French feminism.

53. Mareuil, quoting Madame Roudy.

RECOMMENDED READINGS

Ambassade de France, Service de Presse et d'Information, "Women in France."
News of the latest regulations and statistics can be obtained from the Attaché de Presse; updated periodically.

Guadilla, Naty Garcia. *Libération des femmes: Le MLF*. Paris Presses universitaires de France, 1981.
A complete view of the women's movement in France and an analysis of the various tendencies since 1968, including an extensive list of feminist publications.

Jensen, Jane. "The Work of the Ministère des Droits de la Femme," *Conference Group on French Politics and Society Newsletter* (Winter 1984), 3–9.
A concise appraisal of the achievements of the new ministry in the context of French political culture.

Kaufmann-McCall, Dorothy. "Politics of Difference: The Women's Movement in France from May 1968 to Mitterand," *Signs* (Winter 1983), 282–293.
An excellent historical survey, distilling the theoretical conflicts within the contemporary feminist movement with their political ramifications.

Marks, Elaine, and Isabelle de Courtivron, eds. *New French Feminisms*. New York: Schocken Books, 1981.
An anthology of the leading feminist writers from Simone de Beauvoir to Monique Wittig, with a very useful introduction delineating the differences with earlier French feminisms and a detailed chart situating the history of feminism in the history of France.

Ministère des Droits de la Femme. *Guide des droits des femmes*. Paris: La Documentation Française.
A complete guide to the legal rights of French women, in a clear question-and-answer format, updated and published annually.

Silver, Catherine Bodard. "France: Contrasts in Familial and Societal Roles," in Janet Giele and Audrey Smock, eds., *Women: Roles and Status in Eight Countries*. New York: Wiley-Interscience, 1977. Pp. 259–299.
A *tour de force* on women in France, with extensive information and thoughtful discussion covering the development of French cultural definitions of women, family roles, employment and the French economy, the educational system, birth control, and political participation, all treated in historical depth.

Stoddart, Jennifer. "Feminism in Paris," *Canadian Newsletter of Research on Women* (March 1978), 62–67.

An informative discussion of the impact of French feminism in print on the general cultural scene and the implications for public opinion; such periodic examinations of media activities are extremely useful, and this one should soon be updated.

2

West German Women: A Long Way from *Kinder, Küche, Kirche*

Peter H. Merkl
University of California, Santa Barbara

The story of the changing roles of West German women since the 1960s is one of considerable progress in many respects. Nevertheless, it is also a story of retrenchment, of disappointment, and of frustration. By the late 1970s, the great German euphoria of planning and progress had given way to disillusionment and pessimism. Anxieties about the future in a world of limits seemed to paralyze the emancipatory thrust, and a new social conservatism suggested a return to traditional family roles. The entire country suddenly became aware that its birthrate was sinking farther and farther below the zero mark of population growth, and that this is the result of birth control pills and of the widespread preference of young women for a career outside rather than in the home. There is, indeed, a feeling of existential *Angst* among Germans of child-bearing age that makes them hesitate "to put children into this world," and even to tie the knot, despite their tendency to pair off far earlier in life than their parents did in their time.

In 1982/1983, also, a wave of neoconservatism brought the Christian Democrats back into power in what they like to call "the great *Wende*"(turning point). Officially sanctioned motherhood is back in style. Women workers and employees are fleeing back into family ties and even better-off, university-educated women are once more content to find their identity linked to a man's career, while radical feminists have withdrawn into an isolated subculture. Opinion surveys note with surprise the dramatic increase in intense and mutual trust in married couples and the general withdrawal from public

concerns into private social relationships. Yet social movements are
not so easily undone in their long-range impact: The newly raised
consciousness of women's rights achieved and options won lives on
in the new generations. And the rich flowering of women's writings
of the years since 1968 is read more avidly than ever: Christa Wolf's
Kindheitsmuster (childhood models), Helga Novak's *Die Eisheiligen*
and recent additions to her genre of mother-daughter relations,
Elisabeth Plessen's *Mitteilung an den Adel* and similar antipatri-
archal fiction, and countless socially engaged novels. The 20-year-
olds of today have more often absorbed the message in this form
than they are likely to have read translations of Betty Friedan,
or Simone de Beauvoir or their own feminists, such as Alice
Schwarzer, or the periodical *Emma*. These self-assured young
women may even reject feminism as too anti-male and show con-
tempt for the feminist vanguard of yesterday while making confident use of the options those "harsh and abrasive *Emanzen* (wom-
en's libbers)" conquered for them less than a decade ago.

The Era of Reforms

While the West German Basic Law of 1949 proclaimed the equality
of the sexes (art. 3, sect. 2), the "de-sexing" of German Law proceeded at a pace of decades. Obviously, the Federal Republic was
too preoccupied in those days with matters of economic recovery
and international security to get around to the status of women.
Finally in 1966, at the time of the first faltering of Christian Democratic (CDU/CSU) predominance, a federal government commission submitted a Report on the Situation of Women at Work, in the
Family, and in Society. This report constitutes something of a
benchmark against which to measure later developments, both in
its statistical stocktaking and its image of the social role of women.
The women are characterized by their heightened socioeconomic
expectations, mechanized households, fewer children, and
foreshortened periods of "active motherhood." The report also
strove to probe the functions and economic significance of women's
work in family and household and discussed the problems of
measuring its value, as might be required by an insurance claim.
Finally, it pointed out the inadequacy of the facilities and services
available to women in 1966, especially to working mothers. Even
though little action followed the presentation of the report before
the last CDU ministers left the cabinet in 1969, we can already
discern in it the breath of the dawning age of reform.

In 1969, a new government of Social Democrats (SPD) and Liberals (FDP) took over the helm of state and, after 20 years, sent the CDU/CSU to the opposition benches. The new social-liberal coalition was anxious to develop new initiatives in many areas of social policy—as well as in foreign policy toward Germany's eastern neighbors—and came out almost immediately with major enactments raising widows' pensions and giving equal rights to illegitimate offspring. Two years later, in the course of a major pension reform, they opened the Social Security rolls on a voluntary basis to housewives, a remarkable departure from existing conceptions of entitlement. In 1972, also, the federal government submitted a new Report on Measures for the Improvement of the Situation of Women and added a special section for Women's Policies to the Ministry for Youth, Family, and Health. There were also subtle but meaningful changes in 1974, such as permitting either employed parent up to five days of paid leave a year (per child) to take care of a sick child under eight years of age. Another such innovation changed the signature requirement in family passports from one page with "signature of pass holder and his wife" to two pages with a photograph and signature for each of them. In 1976, they legalized the adoption of the bride's maiden name as family name upon marriage if desired.

In 1977, after years of intense partisan debate, the social-liberal coalition presented the first installment of its blockbuster marriage and divorce reforms, which abandoned the old, prescribed division of marital obligations between husband and wife. In its place, the new law put equal partnership rights and consent: Husband and wife can now divide their obligations any way they like as long as their choice does not injure the rights of third parties, such as the children. Among other things, this change gave the woman's career or employment a new recognition and made the balance between unpaid housework, or child tending, and gainful labor strictly a matter of mutual agreement. The changes in divorce law replaced the requirement of assigning "guilt" to one partner with the recognition of no-fault "disruption" of the marital relationship.[1] From this principle of disruption followed different consequences of divorce. But the new law also recognized the need for maintenance of divorced persons unable to support themselves, at least for a time. The law mandated equal sharing of assets acquired during the marriage, or of the entitlement to retirement income, to reward ex-spouses for their years of unpaid work at home. In 1977, the ministry in charge also vowed to work toward the realization of legal equality in the family, at work, and in society by (1) informing women of their rights and options, (2) modifying traditional sexual role images, and (3) promoting women's participation in politics and social groups. The ministry also promised support for appropriate new initiatives of existing groups and substantial grants for the activities of the National Women's Council *(Frauenrat)*, a top coordinating committee of women's groups in the Federal Republic. Finally, and possibly for the first time, it showed interest in the problems of domestic violence against women and in supporting services, such as shelters, to help them.

The most spectacular issue of the reform years, however, concerned the revision of Criminal Code section 218, on abortion, which in its punitive essence dated back to Prussian laws of 1794 and 1851. The draconic punishments of "paragraph 218"—prison at hard labor—however, had already been ignored by German judges in all but the most shocking cases since before World War One, and there had been some modest reform efforts in the 1960s to limit the term of imprisonment to five years. With the sea change of 1969, however, German intellectual women of the Left began to assert themselves on this subject. Among other things, they picked up the battle cry of the French women's liberation group MLF and, in 1971/1972, stepped forward by the hundreds to announce in *Der Stern* magazine: "I had an abortion." Some men and doctors soon followed suit to indicate that they too had been involved in financing or performing abortions.[2] This open challenge to the law provoked an enormous debate and finally had some effect: The social-liberal coalition in Bonn, after years of internal wrangling—the SPD women had been for the complete abolition of section 218 from the beginning—produced a bill that promised to decriminalize abortion during the first three months and a network of counseling centers for women contemplating abortions. In 1974, the bill passed the lower house *(Bundestag)* but was amended considerably by the CDU/CSU-dominated upper house (federal council). One CDU state minister president, moreover, brought suit before the Federal Constitutional Court, which, in 1975, struck down the law on the grounds that it was in conflict with the constitutional guarantee of the "right to life," a clause the framers had inserted in the Basic Law in reaction to the murderous Nazi regime and not to shield "unborn life."

The old men of the court also indicated how a measure of decriminalization could be made compatible with the constitution, namely by exempting all cases from the general prohibition which met certain "indications": the long-legalized medical indication, the eugenic (birth defects), ethical (rape), and the "social" one, that is, cases involving severe social, economic, or psychological hardship. In this form, the abortion bill was finally passed by all the parties (!) in 1976. This solution was still a disappointment to the women's movement and drew almost universal female criticisms, also because "indication status" had to be granted in each case by predominantly male doctors and social workers whose lack of sympathy was often known ahead of time. There was also the problem of the flat refusal of public clinics and medical personnel in CDU/CSU-dominated states to perform abortions, and of these state governments to carry out the federal law at all.[3] But the Catholic church was never reconciled with it, anyway, and has continued its counter-propaganda, likening abortion to the Nazi holocaust and referring to its advocates as "murderesses." By the early 1980s, moreover, it seemed to have found a vulnerable spot of great impact: Cases involving the "social indication" had been by far the bulk of West German abortions (75 percent of 91,000 in 1982) and, in the 1976 compromise bill, were to be paid for by the national health insurance. Beginning with legal challenges in 1981, the Catholic anti-abortion campaign took aim at the funding for "social abortions," that is, for large families and for the poor, and the question is now before the Federal Constitutional Court. With the return to power of the Christian Democrats in Bonn, furthermore, a number of politicians have taken up the idea of curbing "the abuse of the social indication," allegedly for reasons of economy. In the state of Baden-Wuerttemberg in 1983, for example, an overwhelming majority at the state convention of the CDU passed a resolution to this effect. The SPD women's group, ASF, sooner or later expects an all-out political effort to roll back even the imperfect abortion legislation of 1976.[4]

Education and Employment

An appreciation of the changing status of German women in the Women's Decade requires also a look at the changes in education and employment. For nearly a hundred years, women in Germany have been gainfully employed in very large numbers, but their work was always concentrated in ghettos of low-paying and relatively unskilled work: as unpaid family helpers on farms and in small family enterprises, as farm help and domestic workers, in certain industries, and in the ever-growing secretarial pool. One major reason for this inequality, at least until recently, appeared to lie in the vocational and qualified education gap. As recently as 1965, young women only made up about 40 percent of the students of the secondary *Gymnasium*, 16 to 18 percent of evening schools, and as recently as 1970, they were less than a third of the university-bound youth. In the elementary schools, by way of contrast, they were represented in numbers corresponding more or less to their share of each age cohort. By the end of the decade of the 1970s their proportions had risen considerably: They were now 49 percent of *Gymnasium* students, nearly 50 percent of enrollees in evening schools, and over 40 percent of the university-bound.

To be sure, these statistical trends tend to obscure qualitative differences both before and after the Women's Decade. In the first postwar decades, for example, the sex-segregated public elementary and secondary girls schools of some states offered a substantially different education aimed at least in part at housewife-and-mother functions. The entire socialization process of young women, beginning with the home, inculcated images of a domestic future, including at most a transitional period in relatively unskilled work before matrimony. The researches of Helga Pross and Walter Jaide have shown that these patterns are slow to overcome and that, especially, a Catholic rural or a working-class background in a predominantly Catholic state made it unlikely for a woman to complete a *Gymnasium* education and to attend a university-level institution. Before the 1970s, the vast majority of young girls and their parents simply did not anticipate a qualified career and, in disproportionate numbers, passed up the appropriate channels of training. Even in vocational training, the bedrock of the German nonacademic employment system, women were more than two-thirds of the elementary school graduates that did not seek an apprenticeship. Those who did, moreover, generally stuck to a narrow choice of typical trades: saleswoman, beauty operator, secretary, ladies' tailor, and rural help. At the university, too, women's choices overwhelmingly ran toward the shorter courses of study—education, literature and languages, art, music, and medicine; and a high dropout rate was the bane of all female educational careers.[5]

The result of the educational and vocational education changes of the 1970s has been a substantial increase in the percentages of women with a completed general education, and a more modest increase in those with completed vocational training. Between 1970 and 1978, the proportion of employed women with vocational training has risen from 38 to 52 percent, while among the men it increased from 65 to 69 percent. Women are notably behind in the so-called dual system, which combines an apprenticeship or trainee position in a company with vocational school courses: There were only half a million women in such positions as compared to a million young men. The kind of vocational education curricula in which women are concentrated, moreover, such as commercial education, are not the ones leading to qualifed, skilled careers. They are also underrepresented in the continuing vocational programs that lead to the careers of skilled technicians or master certificates in a trade. Typical "women's vocations" such as paramedical education, on the other hand, are overpopulated by women. Looking back on a decade of, in some respects, disappointing growth, the Federal Ministry of Education and Science and several appropriate state programs concluded that the best chance toward breaking through the old pattern was with efforts to open up traditionally male occupations and their required training to female applicants. It is not a matter of removing deliberate barriers against women as much as a need to motivate young women to choose these careers.[6] The difference between qualified career employment and the patterns of the past is already reflected in slight changes in salary differentials: Women workers' wages were "only" 31.3 percent behind male wages in 1978 (1960: 40.3 percent). Female white-collar employees were 35.5 percent behind (1960: 44.1 percent). Only 2 percent of women had monthly incomes in excess of DM 2,500 (versus 14.1 percent of the men), but 53.4 percent (versus 12 percent of the men) had less than DM 1,000. This reflects the disproportionate number of women in less skilled functions, a shorter working week—little overtime, and often only part-time employment—less work in shifts, and less seniority, rather than direct wage discrimination, according to a recent government study.[7] Women also have long suffered more frequent and longer periods of unemployment. In 1979, their average unemployment rate was 5.2 percent as compared to 2.9 percent for the men.

In 1975/1976, the European Community (EC) issued guidelines regarding equality at work that, four years later, led to a German EC Anti-Discrimination Law with the following provisions: The principle of equal treatment between men and women was to apply to the start, maintenance, and conclusion of the labor contract, including also the remuneration. Jobs had to be advertised publicly and without sex-specific labels. In cases of complaints of sex discrimination, the burden of proof was on the employer's side. This enactment followed upon a new flurry of governmental activity, beginning with a 1979 law adding to the maternity leave of six weeks prior and eight weeks after the baby's birth a mandatory four months paid vacation for employed new mothers. Their jobs also cannot be discontinued during this period. There followed other laws guaranteeing maintenance for single or widowed parents and similar subjects while parliamentary commissions worked on a pension reform that promises equal treatment for both sexes.[8]

Not to be outdone by social-liberal "largesse" toward working mothers, the Christian Democratic opposition came up with a "child-rearing allowance" to give women a free choice between raising children and a career outside the home. Norbert Blüm, the present labor minister, first launched the idea at the 1981 convention of the CDU Social Policy Committees (Sozialausschüsse). When the CDU/CSU came to power in 1982/1983, however, there was a big economy campaign underway to curb runaway budget deficits, and the realization of such a program had to be postponed. There were also a number of budget cuts in social programs, including some of benefits to women. But in the meantime, the item was inserted into the budget of 1986 at a rate lower than expected: Beginning in January of that year, mothers or fathers willing to give up their work for good will receive a monthly child-raising allowance of DM 600 for ten months. Unlike earlier versions of the allowance, applicants are not limited to those who were gainfully employed, but emphatically include women faced with the choice between motherhood and employment for the first time. This measure, furthermore, is accompanied by income tax relief for parents and, for those below the minimum level of taxation, a monthly subsidy of DM 44 per child. Unemployed parents are to receive the subsidy until the child turns 21. Both the inducements for combining work and family and for choosing to stay home have suffered from the recent recession and budget deficits: Day care fees have gone up, retraining oppotunities under the Labor Promotion Act have been curtailed, and opportunities for part-time work have not picked up the slack created by the impact of welfare cuts on the more numerous female clients.[9]

A particularly controversial Christian Democratic plan to institute a "Mother and Child Foundation—Protection of Unborn Life" is still being debated in the Bundestag. According to its sponsors, it is an effort to provide up to DM 5,000 in financial assistance to needy pregnant women. Social Democratic and Green women deputies, on the other hand, see in it a calculated maneuver to undermine the "social indication" for abortions. They also point out that the proposed sum falls far short of the cost of raising a child, or even of resolving the impact of an unwanted pregnancy in marginal circumstances. The CDU/CSU had already launched a governmental commission of inquiry on women in society and debated the subject on several major occasions before the *Bundestag*, so we can sketch the Christian Democratic conception of the role of women in some detail.

For the CDU/CSU, in spite of its economic individualism in other matters, family policy and women's policy are one and the same thing. Women are to conform to their family function before they can be individuals, and the state—otherwise restrained from intervening in society—is given the mission to enforce this conformity in one way or the other. When major social and cultural changes, as in the 1960s and 1970s, create disruption or problems of adjustment like divorce or abortion, moreover, the state should intervene to restore the *heile Welt* (intact society) that is dreamt of in romantic and religious visions of the German family of the past. Thus, any ambition of women to seek individual fulfillment—otherwise specifically sanctioned as "realization of one's personality" by the Basic Law and court interpretations—is seen as "egotism" in conflict with the preordained family role, just as any social-liberal advocacy of the interests of children against their parents seems heresy. The economic contribution of women is fitted into this view of society, alternatively, either as service to the family or in essentially auxiliary functions to the family budget and the national economy. Christian Democrats might even prefer for women to have no permanent outside work, but, for a businessmen's party, the need for all this cheap labor is too compelling to do without it.[10] CDU and CSU party programs and handouts, therefore, frequently include mention of employed women but always with these conservative overtones.

In 1980, still under the government of Helmut Schmidt, the *Bundestag* requested a status report from the executive on how well the requirements of the EC initiative against sexual discrimination at work had been carried out. The government report, submitted under the new government of Helmut Kohl in 1983, contains a wealth of information on various relevant angles of the question. Among the findings, for example, was the striking difference in responses between the giant German Trade Union Federation (DGB) and the German Employers Federation (BDA). The DGB declared flatly that the EC antidiscrimination laws had "in practice had no positive impact whatsoever and had not contributed to women's equality at work," and it pointed to its earlier and unheeded criticisms of the law. The BDA, on the other hand, could not come up with any particular instances of noncompliance or missing points of emphasis in the implementation. It concluded "that there neither was nor is any need for such an antidiscrimination law in employment."[11]

The report then proceeded to present a flood of cases of discriminatory practices in work training, sex labeling of jobs in private industry and public agencies, rejection of a job applicant or transfer because of pregnancy, male job quotas, different mandatory retirement ages, wage differentials, dismissal for complaints against discrimination, and many other clear violations of existing federal law. The report also listed proposals for improvement such as giving female job applicants in certain "unreconstructed" branches of employment priority over men with equal qualifications or strengthening the representation of women in the works councils of larger enterprises. The CDU/CSU author of the report, the Federal Ministry for Youth, Family, and Health, promised to monitor future developments but rejected financial penalties or mandatory employment, remedies many of the experts had suggested. The ministry also rejected female quotas for works councils, but promised to review and revise the regulations that still bar women for antiquated health reasons from certain jobs. Otherwise, the government envisioned only voluntary initiatives to remedy the situation and not a new antidiscrimination statute.

This look at the educational and economic changes of the Women's Decade would not be complete without some attention to those who least benefited from the decade of reforms, older women and the poor. One way of drawing the line is with the help of the statistics of the *Institut für Berufsbildung* (Vocational Education), which clearly show that the improvements in job-related training between 1970 and 1978 benefited mostly employed women under the age of 45. This age division is particularly important in West Germany, where from age 45 on women constitute an ample majority of the population. Owing to the male casualty rate of two world wars and increased female life expectancy, there are far more older women than men, especially aged 65 and more, where there are 172 women for every 100 men. About one-fourth of all West German women is expected to be over 60 by 1985, so that their problems make up a large part of the women's problems in general. Of these 60-year-olds, moreover, half are widows—due to the custom of marrying older men and their own longer life expectancy—and nearly that many live alone.

The chief problems of these older women are economic and social in nature. The West German welfare state offers all of them a minimum level of support that frees them from dependence upon their children or other relatives. But it has not as yet developed new social role images, and habits of social contact and communication, that could take the place of the family-oriented socialization patterns of most of them. With rare exceptions, depending also on her financial resources, the typical German widow leads a rather lonely life once she is done with her employment, a husband, and the raising of children. Even their remarriage rate is far lower than with the men, and the taking up of a second career, or even part-time work, after retirement is rare.[12] A widow's pension is 60 percent of the disability pension of her deceased spouse (provided she was at least 45 or taking care of a child under 18, or a handicapped child, at the time of his demise), which in 1980 averaged about DM 825 a month for white-collar and DM 583 for blue-collar workers. The pensions of employed women tend to be substantially lower than those of comparable men because of lapses in the continuity of their employment and the other factors making for inequality. Average female white-collar pensions in 1980 were DM 688 a month (versus 1,459 for males) and female workers' pensions DM 377 (versus 1,052 for males). More than half the employed women retire prematurely on disability pensions, of which half are less than DM 300. A comparison of male and female pensions in 1980 shows that 62 percent of women pensioners received less than DM 500 a month (versus only 10 percent of male pensioners), while 65 percent of male pensioners got DM 1,000 or more (versus only 2 percent of women). Growing old for German women, consequently, perpetuates the economic inequality of by-gone decades and assures them a status of relative poverty. Worse yet, even the government's current pension reform plans in essence deny employed women the full fruits of their labors in favor of the widows' pensions of those who never worked outside the house. The pension reform under discussion, in other words, would penalize women for seeking employment.

Women and the Parties

Political participation has been relatively high among German women since the days of the Weimar Republic, but the level of participation has tended to be mostly at the level of voting and passive membership. In the early years of the Federal Republic, for example, the election turnout among women was only about 5 percent below that of the males, although women tended to vote far more heavily for CDU/CSU and men more for the SPD. From the 1961 elections on, various observers noticed an increase in the

younger (up to 30) women's turnout and predicted that women's
political behavior would soon be indistinguishable from that of the
men both in turnout and in party preference,[13] a prediction that has
more or less come true in the 1970s. Women have also become more
numerous among the membership of political parties. For example,
in the SPD, which boasts a long record of support for women's
causes, the percentage of women members climbed from 15.4 percent in 1946 to 17.3 percent in 1970 and 23.4 percent in 1982. The
CDU, from a lower level, reached 13.6 percent in 1970 and 21.4
percent in early 1983. The FDP women's share grew from 15 percent
in 1970 to 24.5 percent in 1982. Yet the share of women in the Federal
Executive Committees of the three established parties until recently
was far less than their share of the rank and file: In 1976, the SPD had
8.3 percent, the CDU 9.1 percent, and the FDP 12.1 percent women in
their top policy-making bodies. By 1982, this share increased in the
SPD to 17.5 percent while in the other parties there was no change or
even some slippage. Only the antiestablishment Green party had two
women members on its three-member Executive Council and, in
1984, ousted the incumbents and opted for an all-women council.

The women's share of the *Bundestag* membership has fluctuated
randomly between 5 and 10 percent since 1949. Currently there are
51 women deputies (9.8 percent) with the Green delegation alone
boasting 10 (37 percent of the Greens), but this ratio of 9.8 percent
had already been approximated once in 1919 under the Weimar
Republic. For a while the *Bundestag* president was a woman
(Annemarie Renger). There seem to have been plenty of women
candidates in the last two parliamentary elections, around 20 percent, but the electoral system screens out all but the toughest political professionals. In the state parliaments (*Landtage*), the women's
share is between 6 and 15 percent, and again the Greens have a
particularly high proportion of women deputies. In local government councils, women occupy only around 11 percent of the seats. In
metropolitan areas they often make up over 15 percent, and there are
a few cities, such as Munich, Freiburg, and Tübingen where their
share tops 25 percent of the city council. There has been a noticeable
increase in all these rates in the last ten years and, by the beginning
of the 1980s, the first, if still rare, women mayors began to appear in
some small towns. Otherwise, positions of executive leadership,
such as county supervisors (*Landräte*) or higher executive positions
have resisted women candidates. Behind the political advancement
of women since the early years of the Federal Republic have been
gradual increases in political interest that also reflect the rise of a
more democratic, postwar generation. In 1979, polls disclosed how

many more women "sometimes discuss politics" as compared to 1953: 16 percent (versus 4 percent in 1953) said they did it "frequently," 45 percent "occasionally" (1953: 21 percent) and only 39 percent (1953: 75 percent) "hardly ever."[14]

What has been the role of women politicians in the established parties? Each party seems to have its own approach. Beyond reestablishing a central women's bureau and forming women's groups in some localities, the postwar SPD for the first two decades after 1949 still seems to have been committed to the protection of women as housewives and at work. There were ritual assertions of equal rights but certainly no talk of emancipation. The party's Executive Council had a quota of five female representatives until 1971, when activist women insisted on the rescission of the quota because they wanted to earn the positions in their own right: Their representation then dropped to two. At the same time, the activists against considerable resistance established an Association of Social Democratic Women (ASF), which was founded in mid-1972. The century-old tradition of working-class and socialist solidarity militated against a separate pursuit of women's interests and continues to do so in the form of ideological debates while well-entrenched, lower-class, antifeminist prejudices resist the desire of women for emancipation from the fetters of homemaking and family. The ASF view of women's policy, while unhappy with the recalcitrance of the SPD, also differs from the antifamilist feminism of the Autonomous Women's Movement. The ASF believes that the replacement of the family by alternative life-styles is utopian to most Germans and, in times of crisis, advocating such a life-style will literally drive people back into the arms of the CDU/CSU. Instead, the ASF would promote better coordination between the family and career roles of both men and women, along with substantial steps to ease the present employment and career problems of women. The ASF view of the family is based on partnership and sharing of child-raising and household duties, along the lines familiar from Swedish practices and discussions.[15]

The ASF has about 40,000 members from among the 200,000—perhaps 16,000 activists—and most of them are young, well educated, and more middle-class than working-class. As a group, the ASF tried to steer a centrist course within the party but has received very little cooperation and support, and little representation on party and public bodies. Instead, the SPD repeatedly snubbed the ASF by drawing up its planks on women's policy without the ASF.[16] Since the SPD was the major government party during the era of reforms, it is easy to understand the disillusionment of women activists since about 1976, both with the party and with the course of reform.

Women activists are in a strong position in the other great bastion of the German working class, the trade unions. After decades of slow growth, their share of the membership of the DGB increased more rapidly from 15.3 percent in 1970 to 20.17 percent in 1981. Being mobilized into employment in times of boom and then sent home to home and children when recession strikes, along with the heady air of the era of reforms, politicized and activated many of these employed women to look out for their rights. Their share of the membership of the works councils of their respective enterprises rose even more, from 11.4 percent in 1968 to 19.3 percent in 1981, which places them into important positions at the grassroots level. In the DGB itself, they hold about one-tenth of the offices at the local, district, county, and industrial levels, and few (2 to 4 percent) of the presiding seats at any level. Their policies naturally concentrate on the equality and rights of working women and their interests in appropriate training and in the social benefits of unemployed, disabled, and retired women workers. Their demands, as early as at the DGM Women's Conference in 1977, included a women's quota in training programs for so-called men's occupations, more day-care centers, and the 35-hour week. They have also been strong advocates of equal sharing of child-rearing and household duties by couples, the abolition of section 218, disarmament, and the rejection of military service for women. There are, of course, differences in policy emphasis among the different industrial unions: The most radical proposals, both of a feminist and a left-wing description, usually come from the Metalworkers Union (IGM) or the Union of Education and Science (GEW), which includes women teachers and scientific personnel.[17]

The coalition partner of the SPD, the small FDP, has a much better record than the SPD in this respect. An old-time European liberal and middle-class party, it has always championed individual rights, including those of women. The FDP in fact was behind most of the initiatives making for women's progress in education, and on subjects such as abortion, and is determined to defend the latter against the efforts to restrict the "social indication."[18] Women politicians have long been prominent in the FDP at all levels. But many of these women deputies and party members were so unhappy over the final parting of the ways between SPD and FDP in 1982 and the new CDU/CSU-FDP coalition that they left the party. The FDP has also suffered a long series of reverses in West German state elections, and most recently, in the elections to the European Parliament that cast doubt on its future as a viable, national party. The current coalition in Bonn is clearly dominated by the Christian Democrats, whose conservative approach to women's questions we have described above. In this context, the FDP with its current crises is unlikely to show much initiative in women's issues while its coalition partner is preparing the assault on the public funding of both social indication abortions and Pro Familia counseling centers.

The most interesting political party, with regard to women's policies and activists, is the new Green party, which is currently represented in the *Bundestag*, most state diets, and a growing number of city councils. The part of the Greens' program dealing with women begins with the sentence, "For thousands of years, women have been particularly oppressed and exploited . . ." and goes on to protest sex discrimination, miseducation, ("in passive femininity"), and economic exploitation at work and at home. The Greens aim at a "humane society based on fully equal rights of the sexes and within the framework of an ecologically sound environment." More specifically, the program demands completely equal education and training, including mandatory home economics for both sexes, equal job opportunities and job security, and the recognition of household and child-raising activities as a full-fledged job with pension rights. Military service for women, furthermore, is rejected, and there is a long paragraph about violence against women. Four million West German women, the authors of the program estimate, are beaten and abused every year, "victims of a society in which power and oppression are exercised and suffered every day." The Greens demand state support for "autonomous" and self-governing women's shelters, antidiscrimination committees chaired by women, women judges for courts trying cases of abuse or rape, and the prosecution of abuse and rape by spouses.

There are further planks on child rearing, maternity benefits, and especially abortion, where important Green principles stand on both sides; that of the self-determination rights of the mother and father and that of protecting life, and the latter not just in the one-sided version of "unborn life," but of all life and especially of the living children. Here the Green plank demands free supply of and information on methods of birth control, public financing of *all* abortions, the absence of state or medical "advising" of women faced with this decision, and also no prosecution of women and doctors who have performed abortions. There are also planks

against legal and social or economic discrimination against lesbians and male homosexuals, as well as against a sexual education
in stereotypical prejudices against alternative sexual orientations.[19] While the Greens stand out with their commitment on
women's questions, it should be emphasized that they are primarily
an environmental and pacifist party. Most of the public opinion
polls taken of their views, and other descriptions of the Greens,
never even get around to their stand on women's policy, which, of
course, is equally true of the other parties. The public roles of
women in the Federal Republic suffer from a curtain of invisibility
and neglect in the media and in the public awareness. Books in
English about West German politics and society, with rare exceptions,[20] ignore the entire complex of questions, just as the subject is
nearly invisible in most American government texts.

The Berlin affiliate of the Greens, the Alternative List (AL) is a
metropolitan version of Green attitudes, with heavy emphasis on
the alternative counterculture and, in particular, feminist issues
and subculture. The most recent AL Election Program strikes a
militant tone, rejects the "normality" of marriage and family, and
contains two full pages of discussion, pro and con, of whether
housewives should receive a salary. Instead of the traditional family, the AL favors alternative groups in which parents or women
share cooking, parenting, and leisure activities. The program also
details its concern with employment problems, training, pensions,
and wages; it demands lengthening of the legal paid maternity leave
and public baby-sitter funds, and the complete freezing of abortions
(another five-page section) and availability of birth control. Particular attention is given to the subject of violence against women, rape
in marriage, and sexual harassment, and the judicial procedures
regarding all of these. Finally, the AL program concerns itself at
length with such problems as women's psychiatric therapy, the
conditions in women's prisons, the woman's image in the media,
and the oppression of lesbianism. There is also a demand for the
indemnification of surviving gays and lesbians who were imprisoned in Nazi concentration camps.[21] The alternative subculture
also speaks through its organized groups and newspapers, which
often take up such urban women's problems as the need for safe
transportation late at night when public transportation is inadequate or shut down.

This account of the political parties would not be complete with-
out mention of the recent attempt to launch a Women's party
(Frauenpartei). A recent public opinion poll of the Sigma Institute of
Berlin, commissioned by the German edition of Cosmopolitan

magazine, asked a sample of 2,549 women over 18 throughout the Federal Republic about their views toward such a development: 13 percent responded they would vote for it, another 22 percent said that maybe they would, and these potential supporters included a high proportion of women over 50. Probing these women's attitudes further, the institute became aware of the depth of their distrust of the Bonn politicians, including prominent women politicians, and this especially among working mothers. They simply doubted the sincerity and dedication of the established parties to their concerns and expressed particular impatience with the absence of true equality in marriage, family, and at work. Their policy priorities were (1) penalties for sex discrimination at work (2) pension credit for years of child rearing, (3) better opportunities for part-time work in one's chosen occupation, (4) three years of a "mothers' salary" after the birth of a child, (5) better health care for sick children of employed parents, and (6) adequate day care and schools that keep the children for the full working day. There have been attempts to launch a Women's party in West Germany in 1951 (two), 1970 (two), 1975 (again two), and 1979, none of them free from bitter internal feuds and factionalism. In 1980, there was serious discussion of an election boycott by women to protest the inadequacy of the alternatives presented.[22] In the 1984 elections for the European Parliament, a Women's party received 94,000 votes (0.4 percent), while the Greens, with over two million (8.2 percent) of the popular vote elected seven deputies, eclipsing the FDP's representation. Given the disappointment of activist women with the larger parties, it would hardly be surprising to see the emergence of a viable women's party or, alternatively, a more determined push of the Green party for the vast reservoir of the women's vote in the future.

The Autonomous Women's Movement

The hard core of the West German women's movement is the Autonomous Women's Movement, a congeries of groups, feminist journals, bookstores, and services that started in the heady days of 1968 when a handful of SDS women rebelled—to the shock of the majority of SDS women—against the implicit male chauvinism of the leadership of the student rebellion that wanted to liberate humanity. These "brides of the [student] revolution" then founded Women's Councils in big cities from which men were excluded and which pilloried the duplicity of the male student leaders with biting satire. The logical genesis of the movement was described tellingly

by Ulrike Meinhof in her left-wing magazine *Konkret*, the same
person who later became a leader of the Baader-Meinhof terrorist
group.[23] The campaign against section 218 of the early 1970s then
brought to a head the real issue of the women's movement: Would a
Marxist defeat of capitalism really free women from the old patriarchal oppression, or from the "male-dictated" definitions of the
feminine role? Only the most doctrinaire leftists could fail to see the
emergence of the women's interests quite independently from those
of their false friends to the left and the right, and the resistance to
the abolition of section 218 from everywhere, including parts of the
SPD in the government, opened many eyes. Consciousness-raising
groups advanced the discussion from abortions to birth control and
female sexuality and made the first decisive inroads into the vast sea
of self-ignorance and myths that had characterized German women
up until then.[24] Women's centers, cafes, taverns, programs, a profu-
sion of new groups and services followed in rapid succession.

By 1974, the movement involved perhaps a few thousand activists, a dozen centers, and 150 groups. Feminist magazines were
sprouting everywhere and were eagerly bought. Police raids and
harassment actually helped to mobilize and broaden support, and
to bring rebellion out of the closets. The themes, for example, of the
activists of the Berlin Women's Center in 1974 show that the movement had reached maturity in half a decade: women's sexuality,
violence against women, employed women, housewives' salaries,
self-help, karate, and street theater, although there were serious
problems of direction and organization. On the one hand, there
were well-trained left-wing organizers ready to bureaucratize and
centralize the movement. On the other hand, there were anarchists
and arch-feminists who distrusted bureaucracy and believed in
spontaneous action; and there was an ever-growing mass of newly
interested women who had never been politically organized before.
The sheer numbers tended to water down the commitment and
dedication of the original core of the movement, and its resolve to
keep out the men. At the same time, attention turned increasingly to
the economic issues, job discrimination, the so-called low-salary
(Leichtlohn) job classifications, and the paragraph of the Civil Code
(section 1356) that prohibits outside work for married women who
cannot "meet their duties in marriage and family" and simultaneously enjoins them to work "if required by the poverty of the
family." The issues of the value of unpaid housework and child
rearing and of equal household obligations of husband and wife
joined the list of economic complaints.

The second half of the 1970s was a time of frustration and disillusionment even though the movement grew stronger every day. The message began to hit home, probably contributing to the decline of the marriage rate and birth rate and the increase of the divorce rate. The recriminations between the sexes turned bitter, and the coming out of gay orientations was often interpreted as the real essence behind the feminist revolution. Vast national closets of physical abuse and exploitation of women were opened up for all to see, and it became more and more difficult for defenders of the status quo to pretend innocence or ignorance. New feminist publishing houses spread the word through annual yearbooks and women's calendars with circulations approaching 100,000. Blockbuster exposés such as Schwarzer's *Der Kleine Unterschied und seine grossen Folgen* (the little difference and its great consequences) sold a quarter of a million copies.[25] A housewives' survey commissioned by a magazine, *Brigitte,* to ascertain how "contented" German women are became the cause of the most bitter recriminations among women. The terrorist wave of the late 1970s and its repression also generated attitudes and legal means against other protesters and protest movements such as the women. The German press became extremely vituperative against prominent feminists and yet could not but report the growing power and sophistication of the movement. Women's university-level seminars and summer courses were developed. Women's teashops, taverns, and bookstores flourished. New projects such as shelters for abused women were launched, and taboo topics such as domestic violence even began to show up in popular tabloids. It is difficult to tell now whether the surfacing level of violence against women was actually higher in the late 1970s or whether this was rather a matter of the greatly increased level of reporting by a vastly heightened awareness of rapes outside and inside the home, and the wave of consciousness-raising disclosures has gone on to this day, when the topic of sexual harassment on the job and at school is broached in books and magazines.[26]

In 1977, the first issue of the radical feminist journal *Emma* appeared with a quickly sold first run of 300,000. It followed by a few months another feminist magazine, *Berliner Zeitschrift,* now known as *Courage. Courage,* unlike *Emma,* talks about "natural femininity" and motherhood, which have once more become fashionable in the movement. The circulation and readership of these two, even though they overlap, offers a gauge for estimating the current size and character of the Autonomous Women's Movement. In 1983, *Emma* had a circulation of 130,000 and *Courage* one of 70,000, and

we can assume that about twice as many women read them. Given
the overlap, we would estimate that about 250,000 to 300,000
women are reached, and 60,000 to 70,000 feminists make up the
movement. Of the *Emma* readers 87 percent are under 40, 80 percent of the *Courage* readers under 30, and in both cases, the majority
is in their twenties. Both bodies of readers are far more educated
than the general female population. Between 55 and 58 percent
have an *Abitur* or university degree (versus 8 percent of women
aged 15 – 40), and another 32 to 39 percent are still in school or
training (versus 7 percent of the comparable female population). Of
Emma readers 52 percent are employed, nearly half in office work.
Only 26 percent of *Courage* readers are employed. *Emma* readers
also answered questions about their beliefs: Only 5 percent of them
consider marriage the ideal, whereas 45 percent prefer communal
living, and 65 percent can think of "better forms of living together"
than marriage; in other words, 95 percent have little use for the
institution. Whether with regard to occupation, raising children, or
dividing the household work, 80 to 90 percent reject any sex-specific
roles. It should be mentioned that one out of two *Emma* readers has
a child, or wants one, and similar proportions live together with a
man; 96 percent reject the use of birth control pills, presumably
because of their side-effects, and not for traditional reasons.

One out of eleven of the *Emma* readers is active in the women's
movement, and one out of four calls herself a feminist. Two-thirds
are glad the Autonomous Women's Movement exists, and 40 percent
express their sympathy for it. The following proportions share its
goals:

Equal wages for equal work	86%
Truly equal rights with men	77
Elimination of all discrimination against gays	71
More women's shelters	70
More women in public office	63

What parties did these *Emma* readers favor in 1976, and who were
they planning to vote for in 1980? 71 percent had voted SPD, evi-
dently still representing the vote for the era of reforms, although one
out of three did so while "grinding their teeth." By 1980, nearly 100
percent of them thought that "none of the parties represented the
majority of the people" and, including the SPD partisans among
them, that "all parties are wholly or in part against women." Consequently, one out of three would have voted for the Greens, had
there been an election in late 1979, and three-fourths (two-thirds of
the SPD partisans) would have given serious consideration to a

women's party with a feminist program. Nearly every other *Emma* reader was toying with an election boycott, including one third of the SPD adherents.[27] No one knows as yet what the *Emma* readers really ended up doing as the great battle of 1980 unfolded between Helmut Schmidt (SPD) and Franz Josef Strauss (CDU/CSU). But the survey still ascertained the readers' views of the two political supermen: They both were given almost identical profiles, with features such as "authoritarian," "power hungry," "hostile to women," and "arrogant." When asked if they would favor a female chancellor, on the other hand, 21 percent of the *Emma* readers agreed readily, especially those over 30. Seventy-eight percent would like to see first whom or what this female candidate would represent. The caution is understandable although the respondents may not have realized the depth of realignment that a strong female candidate can, in fact, bring about.

Conclusion

There can be little doubt that the Women's Decade in West Germany saw a tremendous amount of change in the condition and attitudes of women, even though the climate of opinion has changed decisively from the halcyon days of reform to the conservative *Wende* (turning point) of 1982/1983. There is no way that the conservative power-holders can ever get the genie of the women's new roles back into the bottle of tradition again, no matter how they may chisel away at public financing for "social" abortions or other programs and services for women. There are, nevertheless, some concerns about the depth of the changes that have come to pass. First of all, even the multifaceted world of organized women in the parties, trade unions, and the Autonomous Women's Movement clearly represents a rather limited elite whose varied currents of thought cannot simply be taken to represent the state of mind of the masses of German women. Their limited efforts to pass along the word convincingly to these unenlightened masses, furthermore, have suffered from their internecine feuds and their stridency. What is needed are milder voices with a vast communications network such as the established but more conservative women's magazines or the bully pulpit of government leadership to reach the 30 million German women beyond the readership of *Emma* and *Courage*. Long-range changes of greater depth will also follow upon a successful revision of schoolbooks and children's literature, which are replete with stereotypical images reinforced by the home.

A third concern involves the impact of the ideas upon German
men. While men will undoubtedly receive a message of sorts when
their partners rebel and leave them, this is not necessarily the right
message, nor is it likely to be well received in this form. The exclu-
siveness of the Autonomous Women's Movement has its advantages,
but it also carries a high price: It fails to educate males sympathetic
to women's emancipation and to encourage them to carry the word
to the masses of men who by their own hostility and unenlightened
prejudices perpetuate traditional views and systems with regard to
women. What is needed, perhaps, are intermediary networks that
both avoid male interference with women's groups and yet give
them the benefit of education in the values they need to accept and
to pass on to others of their sex. The impact of communal living on
participating males may conceivably serve as a conduit that
changes the mind sets with which German males grow up, or it may
not. There are too many different group settings, and many tend to
be more of an escape by each commune member from oppressive
circumstances outside than a brave new world of lasting mutual
satisfaction. In any case, they have not been around long enough to
be studied carefully enough so that we could be certain of their
long-range socializing effects on male and female, or on the relations between the generations. As the ASF has observed, moreover,
alternative life-styles are quite "utopian" to the masses of Germans
and likely to remain so.

For lasting changes in the minds of the masses of German women,
especially the abused and oppressed, and by implication also their
males, the final barrier to overcome will always be the internalized
values of an obsolete patriarchal society. To quote Margrit Brück-
ner, a professor of social work writing in *Emma* about a case of an
abused wife,[28]

> The prevailing patriarchal understanding of femininity and of
> women's role is not only pressed upon women but it has become
> a part of our selves. If we only see women as the victims of a
> patriarchal society, we deny our own ability to overcome our
> oppression. The insight into our own participation in the pre-
> vailing relationship between the sexes is the precondition of our
> ability to change it.

When the mass of German women drops its attitudes of acquies-
cence in the ideas and practices of a by-gone society of *Kinder,
Küche, Kirche*, no male will be able to oppress them again.

NOTES

1. See the commentary of Ekkekard Schumann in Schumann, ed., *Unser Recht: Crosse Sanmlung deutscher Gesetze* (Munich: DTV, 1982), 284–285. The new principle is, in a nutshell, that "the economically more capable marriage partner has to pay maintenance to his/her needy ex-partner regardless of guilt or non-guilt (in the disruption of the marriage)." For a brief historical survey, see P. H. Merkl, "The Politics of Sex: West Germany," in Lynne Iglitzin and Ruth Ross, eds., *Women in the World* (Santa Barbara, CA: ABC-Clio, 1976), 129–148, esp. 140–142.

2. See Alice Schwarzer, *So fing es an! Die neue Frauenbewegung* (Munich: DTV, 1983), 20–30, 124.

3. See Karl-Jürgen Bieback, "Soll der Paragraph wieder nur die Armen treffen?" in Susanne von Paczensky and Renate Sadrozinski, eds., *Die Neuen Moralisten. § 218-Vom leichtfertigen Umgang mit einem Jahrhundertthema* (Reinbek: Rowohlt, 1984), 18–35.

4. In 1907, 30.6 percent of German women over 16 were gainfully employed, half of them in agriculture. In 1978, their percentage was 31.6 percent, after several decades of somewhat lower figures.

5. See Helge Pross, *Ueber die Bildungschancen von Mädchen in der Bundesrepublik* (Frankfurt: Suhrkamp, 1969), 11–31. Professor Pross was also responsible for the 1966 report on the situation of women and also wrote *Gleichberechtigung im Beruf* (Frankfurt: Athenaeum, 1973), on equal access to occupational careers.

6. See *Frauen '80*, Federal Ministry of Youth, Family Affairs, and Health, Bonn, 6–12.

7. Ibid., 16–19. The 1950s practice of "discounting" women's wages has been stopped.

8. The exchange rate between the DM and the dollar, which had drifted down as low as DM 1.75 to the dollar, was at DM 2.85 in the summer of 1984, which, however, may not be an accurate reflection of the internal purchasing power of the DM. See also the special issue on sex discrimination, *Das Parlament* 34 (August 27, 1983).

9. See Hanna Beate Schöpp-Shilling, "Affecting Equal Opportunities for Women in the Federal Republic: Recent Trends and Developments," *German Studies Newsletter* 2 (April 1984), 16–20. See also the survey of women's economic conditions in Carola Pust et al., *Frauen in der BRD* (Hamburg: VSA, 1983), Chapter One.

10. See the *Abschlussbericht der Enquête-Kommission Frau und Gesellschaft* (Bonn: 1980) and the quotations from CDU and CSU party programs in Heino Kaack and Reinhold Roth, eds., *Handbuch des deutschen Parteiensystems*, 2 vols. (Opladen: Leske, 1980), I, 63–65, 234–238. Also Anke Riedler-Martiny, "Die Partnerin ohne Konturen: Das Frauenbild der CDU/CSU," *Neue Gesellschaft* 23:4 (1976), 295–299.

11. See also Vera Slupik, "Verrechtlichung der Frauenfrage-Befriedungspolitik oder Emanzipationschance?" *Kritische Justiz* 15 (1982), 348–366. The EC commission considered the German record on

this matter less than satisfactory. Quotes in "Unterrichtung durch die Bundesregierung," Deutscher Bundestag, 10, Wahlperiode, Drucksache 10/14 (March 31, 1983), 7–15 (hereafter referred to as *Unterrichtung*).

12. See Pust et al., 96, 106, 109.

13. See Günter D. Radtke, *Stimmenthaltung bei politischen Wahlen in der BRD* (Meisenheim: Haim, 1972), 40–41; Gabriele Bremme, *Die politische Rolle der Frau in Deutschland* (Göttingen: Vanderhoeck, 1956), 65. Only the FDP and extremist parties like the NPD (neo-Nazis) and DKP (Communists) still show a considerable sex differential. The current turnout figures are 88.2 percent for men and 87.1 percent for women (1980).

14. Quoted by Pust et al., 179.

15. Among these are measures to set minimal levels of income for women and steps to assure women's opportunities for training and retraining. See esp. Pust et al., 203–216; Karin Hempel-Soos, "Die ASF zwischen SPD und Frauenbewegung," *Neue Gesellschaft* 27:2 (1980), 111. See also the resolutions of the 1977 SPD convention in Hamburg on family policy in *Neue Gesellschaft*, 27:2 (1980), 133–140, and the contributions about the traditional image of women by Christine Schmarsow and Anke Brunn, ibid., 115–122.

16. The ASF on key occasions received support from party chair Willy Brandt and Chancellor Helmut Schmidt, but generally had to make its way by complaints, confrontations, and hints of pulling out to form a new women's party. See Gerard Braunthal, *The West German Social Democrats, 1969–1982*, (Boulder, CO: Westview Press, 1983), 128–134.

17. See esp. Pust et al., 160–177.

18. See the *Programm zur Gleichberechtigung* of the FDP party congress of Mainz in 1978, p. 4, where the original version of the bill, that is, the legalization of all abortions until the end of the third month, was endorsed in spite of the negative court decision and reissue in the present form. The campaign against financing the "social indication" was specifically addressed along with FDP support for the original version in the 1983 election program. See *Freiheit braucht Mut, Unsere Wahlaussage*, 22. Also Liselotte Funcke, "Chancengleichheit und Partnerschaft in der Familienpolitik," in H. D. Genscher, ed., *Liberale in der Verantwortung* (Munich: Hanser, 1976), 99–113.

19. See Die Grünen, *Das Bundesprogramm*, 32–35, 39. See also Die Grünen, *Wahlplattform 1982* (Landesverband Bayern), 41–44.

20. One of the notable exceptions is David P. Conradt's *The German Polity*, 2nd ed. (New York: Longman, 1982), 37–38, 72–75.

21. The pro side argues, among other points, that only remuneration would create the leverage of strikes by the employee, while the other side sees in such remuneration a mockery—involving only "pocket money . . . like the CDU child rearing allowance"—and a confirmation of a capitalist relationship between husband and wife. *AL Wahlprogramm zu den Neuwahlen am 10. Mai 1981*, 23–24.

22. See "Wahlboykott?," special issue of *Emma* (1980), which includes voices from each party as well as an essay, by Dorothee Vorbeck, on why a women's party may be dysfunctional to the political goals of women, ibid., 67.

23. See "Frauen in SDS oder in eigener Sache," *Konkret*, December 1968. The various German left-wing terrorist groups all have a large percentage of women members whose armed struggle is expressly directed, among other targets, at male domination and oppression. See Hans-Josef Horchem, *Extremisten in einer selbstbewussten Demokratie* (Freiburg: Herder, 1975), 26–27.

24. See Schwarzer, 20–39. The polls of women's views on section 218 also show the growing swath cut by the movement. By 1973, 83 percent of German women were for the abolition of section 218 (71 percent in 1971), just as the legislative debate began.

25. Frankfurt: Fischer, 1977.

26. See, for example, Sibylle Plugstedt and Kathleen Bode, *Übergriffe, Sexuelle Belästigung in Büros and Betrieben* (Reinbek: Rowohlt, 1984). This book is a collection by the Greens and was launched in connection with an incident in their own party in Bonn.

27. Regarding the parties being against women, two-thirds flatly said yes and one third "in part." See "Wahlboykott" issue of *Emma* (1980), 10–18; on the women's party, 44 percent of the readers said yes and 31 percent "maybe," with 62 percent of the activists saying yes. On the boycott, 25 percent of the readers (versus 38 percent activists) flatly said yes and 20 percent "maybe."

28. See "Die Liebe der Frauen," *Emma* 6 (June 1984), p. 25.

RECOMMENDED READINGS

Federal Ministry of Youth, Family Affairs, and Health. *Frauen '80.* Bonn: 1980.

Pacsensky, Susanne von, and Renate Sadrozinski, eds. *Die Neuen Moralisten. § 218-Vom leichtfertigen Umgang mit einem Jahrhundertthema.* Reinbek: Rowohlt, 1984.

Das Parliament 34 (August 27, 1983). Special issue on sex discrimination.

Plagstedt, Sibylle, and Kathleen Bode. *Übergriffe Sexuelle Belästigung in Büros und Betrieben.* Reinbek: Rowohlt, 1984.

Pross, Helge. *Gleichberechtigung im Beruf.* Frankfurt: Athenaeum, 1973.

Pust, Carola, et al. *Frauen in der BRD.* Hamburg: VSA, 1983.

Schöpp-Schilling, Hanna Beate. "Affecting Equal Opportunities for Women in the Federal Republic: Recent Trends and Developments," *German Studies Newsletter* 2 (April 1984), 16–20.

Schwarzer, Alice. *Der kleine Unterschied und seine grossen Folgen.* Frankfurt: Fischer, 1977.

————. *So fing es an! Die neue Frauenbewegung.* Munich: DTV, 1983.

"Wahlboykott?" Special issue of *Emma* (1980).

3

Elusive Equality: The Limits of Public Policy

Ingunn Norderval
Møre and Romsdal College

Introduction

T*he decade of women's policy.* This is the label the Norwegian sociologists Runa Haukaa and Harriet Holter apply to the 1970s in Scandinavia. Here, as elsewhere in the West, this was a period when increased attention was focused on the imbalance in men's and women's position in society, as the modern feminist movement, imported from America, gained strength and infused both interest organizations and political parties with new perspectives and vitality. Under the impact of the tremendous activity and energy of the women's movement, women's issues were put on the political agenda. As result, public policy was employed in varying degrees, in a conscious attempt to make equality a meaningful concept and enhance the opportunities for democratic participation in societies regarded by many as the most equal and democratic in the world.

This chapter endeavours to examine and explain some of the central features of Scandinavian equality policy, and to assess their effects. It is a subject that has received relatively little attention: the growing literature on women and politics has tended to stress the input side of the political system, articulation of demands and interest group activity. Much less is known of the output side, the public policies that are the result of the political process and their effects.

One may distinguish between three main stages in the policy process:

1. Getting recognition that a problem exists, and placing it on the public agenda
2. The formulation and legitimation of a course of action to solve the problem
3. Implementation of the policy, and reaction to this implementation[1]

The following analysis will apply this perspective to the equality policy in the Scandinavian countries, with the emphasis on the last two stages in the above schema: government policies and the forces that impinge on and limit the effectiveness of implementation of these policies. The major focus will be on Norway, which is of particular interest from a public policy standpoint since, as the country long considered the most backward in the area in regard to women's rights, it has recently employed some of the most radical measures to ensure their equality.

The data base for the chapter consists of official publications, statistics, and the growing body of research in Scandinavia on women's status and political behavior. In addition, active work within the Norwegian Labor party has provided useful insights into the policy process and its consequences for the part women play in the political system.

The Position of Women in Scandinavia

The Scandinavian countries have long had a reputation as pioneers and pacesetters in the movement for women's rights. Already in the eighteenth century, Sweden's Hedvig Charlotta Nordenflycht launched the first serious sex-role debate. Her contemporary, the Danish-Norwegian philosopher and writer Ludvig Holberg, shared her idea that lack of education was the primary cause of women's backwardness, and posed their emancipation as an ideal that would benefit the entire society. Not until another century had passed, however, did their views gain prominence among intellectual and political elites. Beginning in the middle of the nineteenth century, formal barriers to equality were gradually removed. Equal inheritance rights for both sexes were established during the 1850s, and women's right to engage in trade and commerce ensured. Before the turn of the century, high schools and universities had opened their doors to women, who in turn began to enter the professions. By this time, women were legally independent in all the countries, except in the case of Swedish married women, who remained under the guardianship of their husbands until 1920.

Scandinavian women were also among the first to win entry to the polls. The suffrage movement gained strength during the last decades of the nineteenth century, and in 1901 Norwegian women received partial voting rights in municipal elections. In 1913, as the third country in the world, Norway extended the vote to women on the same terms as to men in all elections. In Finland, women had received the vote in national elections already in 1906, but had to wait until 1917 before they enjoyed the same rights as men in municipal elections. Denmark and Sweden followed suit with universal suffrage legislation in 1915 and 1921, respectively.[2]

The suffrage did not, however, change women's role in the policy process much immediately. While their voting participation, low at first, rose steadily until it approximated that of men, women's representational activity continued to be low. With the exception of Finland, only a few women were sent to the legislative assemblies during the interwar years. The world's first female cabinet minister, Denmark's Nina Bang, was appointed in 1924, but by and large the "take-off stage" in women's legislative and governmental representation was not reached until after World War II. Since then, their presence has increased steadily in both legislative and executive fora, and is today, with the exception of Iceland, the highest in the West. (See Figure 3.1.) The region has also had its first woman prime minister, Norway's Gro Harlem Brundtland, and in Iceland, Vigdis Finnbogadottir is president.

This development illustrates that political integration of a newly enfranchised group is a process that requires time. During the first phase of the process, the voting rates of the group increase from the normally low participation at first, to a level similar to that of the "old-timers." (See Figure 3.2.) The second phase is reached when the new groups not only have a large turnout at the polls, but also begin to send a larger number of representatives from their own midst to the legislative and other decision-making bodies.

Normally, little conflict attaches to the first of these phases, but the second may entail problems. During the first phase, political elites have an active interest in increasing their strength by attracting the new electorate to their folds, and an "open door" policy prevails. Far less generosity may characterize the second phase, when the newcomers vie with the established electorate for direct power and influence through their own representatives. While the first phase may be seen as one of *distributive policy*, the giving of something to somebody without at the same time depriving someone else, the second phase is one of *redistributive policy*, the taking from one group and giving to another.

FIGURE 3.1

Women's Representation in the Scandinavian Parliaments

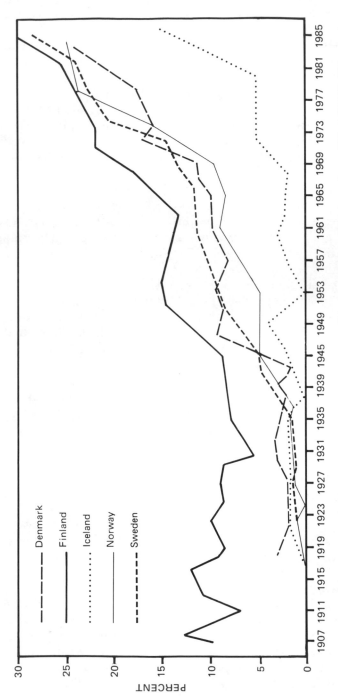

Source: Torild Skard, "Women in the Political Life of the Nordic Countries," *International Social Science Journal* 35: 4 (1983), 645.

FIGURE 3.2

Differences in Men's and Women's Voting Rates in Parliamentary Elections

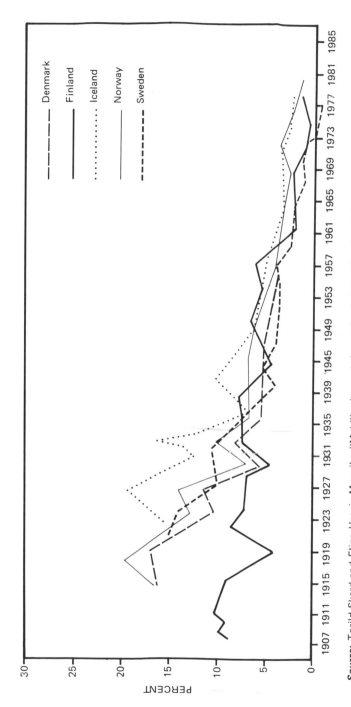

Source: Torild Skard and Elina Haavio-Mannila, "Mobilisering av kvinner til valg," in Elina Haavio-Mannila et al., eds., *Det uferdige demo-kratiet* (Oslo: Nordisk Ministerråd, 1983), 63.

Granting the suffrage to women obviously did not deprive men of theirs. But when women began to demand that they be represented by other women and that their interests receive higher priority in the allocation of resources, this could not be achieved without denying men some of "their" seats and "their" budget allocations. It follows that the second phase of the integration process will entail more conflict than the first, and be more difficult to achieve.

So, Scandinavian women tend to stress all that remains before integration can be said to exist, even though, by global standards, a great deal has been achieved. "Suffrage has not given women political power on a par with men. On the contrary, one may say that women's distance from and lack of power in the political system remain a fundamental weakness in our democracies," declares a recent study.[3] In spite of the formal rights enjoyed and the formal equality, women are still oppressed. Traditional role patterns and a sex-differentiated economy persist, and combine to preserve a political system where women are on the periphery and where, according to Harriet Holter, their institutional participation is inversely related to the importance of the institutions. Women have achieved, maintains Holter, "penetration of superfluous or shrinking institutions":[4] They are admitted to, or gain greater influence in various social institutions as the functions of these are reduced and they become less important to society. As the family's functions are reduced, the egalitarian ideal wins acceptance, with both women and children getting more say in family matters as the overbearing *pater familias* becomes rarer. As society becomes increasingly secular and nobody goes to church, women are admitted to the ministry. As representative political institutions lose their positions as centers of power, women are admitted in greater numbers. But the women thus admitted to high public office frequently find that they have little influence on agenda setting, particularly if they are interested in representing women's interests and push so-called women's issues.

In short, alongside the egalitarian ideology to which everyone pays lip service, there is another ideology that assumes women's needs and articulated interests to be less important than those of men. There exists systemic sexual oppression: Individual women may be able to acquire economic, political, and social resources and gain influence in the system. But *women as a group* are unable to do so, and are consequently not in a position to benefit from the formal equality offered by the system.[5]

Policy Formulation and Legitimation

The modern women's movement, which in the 1970s infused new life and vitality into the work for women's rights in Scandinavia, could build on a long tradition of feminism in the region. This continuity with the past made the "new feminism" seem both less sudden and less radical than might otherwise have been the case, and helped provide legitimacy for new policy demands. The growing body of scholarly research on the "sex-role problem" from the 1950s on, also lent legitimacy to the movement. This research had produced solid evidence of the inconsistency between the egalitarian ideals of the welfare state and the socialization processes actually at work.

One may distinguish between three different perspectives in Scandinavia concerning women's roles—three perspectives that correspond to different stages in the women's movement and public policy toward women: the traditional, the equal rights, and the liberation perspectives. Let us consider each of them briefly.

The traditional perspective emphasizes men's and women's essential differences but equal worth, and the complementary roles that flow from this. It demands greater social recognition of the value of the work performed by women in their traditional roles, but does not question the traditional role division itself nor the social structure within which this role division is functioning. The earliest Scandinavian women's movement represented, by and large, this perspective. Women's demands for the vote and for education were couched in instrumental terms: They would be able to carry out their traditional roles in a better way if given political rights. As one member of the Norwegian Storting enthused during the suffrage debate in 1893: ". . . women, who are thus admitted into public life, will become more capable people, . . . better suited for taking care of their daily, housewifely duties; for spiritual interests and spiritual advancement quite naturally lead to improvement even in such routine, daily doings as cooking and housekeeping and all entailed in this."[6]

The second perspective stresses men's and women's basic equality, and the need for social policies that will enable women to take their place alongside men in the occupational and political world. But it does not fundamentally question women's roles as those primarily responsible for homemaking and child rearing. It is thus essentially a dual role perspective, and the public policy it stresses is one that will facilitate the individual woman's chance or opportunity to take on a public role in addition to her private one.

Today, under the impact of the feminist movement, a third perspective has come to the fore: an oppression and liberation perspective, with the focus on the patriarchal social order as a source of oppression, and demand for a thoroughgoing restructuring of this male-dominated society as a prerequisite to woman's full participation. "The goal is not to obtain a part of men's power position, but to remove all oppression," declare the new feminists. Men as well as women need to be liberated.

The second perspective, with its emphasis on equal rights, is still the dominant one in Scandinavia. But the new feminism, with its demand for radical restructuring of family and social roles, is becoming more prominent among women and social scientists, and has won some recognition at the policy-making level for the demand that the private sphere of reproduction and the public sphere of production must be integrated if equality is not going to be merely equality in regard to competitive opportunities, but equality in regard to results.

To understand the receptivity to such views in Scandinavia, one must appreciate the degree to which the people in this area have emphasized the ideals of equality and solidarity as central democratic values, and built them into the very concept of the welfare state. The Finnish sociologist Erik Allardt shows in his survey of attitudes in the four major Scandinavian countries that concern about equality is deeprooted, and that people favor even more leveling in order to attain it: To realize equality, they have been willing to take radical steps. As the historian Hans Fredrik Dahl observes, the Nordic way "seems generally to lead to the left, to radical or leftish solutions to almost all national problems."[7]

Scandinavian women have been able to benefit from this bent for "radical and leftish solutions," legitimating their demands through insistence that basic system values are violated by women's underdog position. And while many remain impatient with the political will to achieve rapid change, the fact remains that the 1970s have brought institutionalization of equality policy in Scandinavia and a many-pronged attack on traditional sex-role patterns and their supporting structures. The radical position that the changing of women's position requires changing male roles as well has become the basis of government policy, as reflected in Norway's reply to the United Nations on the status of women in that country:

> In Norway, one has increasingly recognized that equality between the sexes depends on changing the man's position, particularly so that he may get an increased responsibility for his

children and opportunity to participate more actively in the life of the family.

It is the responsibility of society to motivate and stimulate such attitudes in men, while simultaneously creating conditions that make it practically possible for men to participate to a greater degree in the care of the children.[8]

The Equal Status Councils

Between 1972 and 1978 all the Scandinavian countries established Equal Status Councils as major props of the equality policy. Although it is assumed that work for equality will be undertaken within all public agencies and at all levels, it seemed advantageous to have special institutions entrusted with responsibility for initiating and coordinating all the various aspects of equality policy.

Included among the tasks of the Equal Status Councils are research, submission of reports to public bodies, drafting of legislation, and in general responsibility for promoting equality in the labor market, in education and training, politics, and even within the family. The instructions to the Finnish Delegation for Equality Questions are illustrative. The delegation's tasks are

1. to work as a coordinating body for the various fields of research aiming at achieving equality between men and women in the community;

2. to prepare reforms for increasing equality in collaboration with authorities, government and municipal institutions, labour market organisations and other associations;

3. to observe and promote the realisation of equality in community planning and to take initiatives and submit proposals for the development of activities in fields of research, education and information concerning equality;

4. to take initiatives and submit proposals for the development of legislation and administration which could have effect on equality;

5. to keep up with developments abroad in questions connected with equality between men and women in society, and

6. to administer research and planning assignments connected with this field on special instructions from the Minister's Secretariat.[9]

These are quite clearly very general instructions, so it is very much up to the councils themselves what to make out of the office.

With the exception of Denmark, all the countries have also adopted provisions for municipal equal status committees. Norway is the only country where these seem to function: In that country, over half the municipalities have established such committees, against only 18 percent in Sweden, and 13 and 4 percent in Iceland and Finland, respectively.[10] At the regional level, cooperation between the various national Equal Status Councils is carried on through the Contact Group for Equality Questions, established by the Nordic Council of Ministers in 1974. The group, which has one representative from each country, has devoted considerable time to drawing up proposals for Nordic cooperation and action programs on equality issues.[11]

The value of the Equal Status Councils lies primarily in their work as initiators, coordinators, and watchdogs for women's rights. On the symbolic level, they serve as a reminder that equality is taken seriously. Through their research reports, they have demonstrated the continuing discrepancy between the positions of men and women in both private and public employment, and the persisting differences between the educational patterns of boys and girls, which reinforce the sex-differentiated economy with its demonstrated negative consequences for women. Through their legislative proposals, they delineate solutions to these problems.

In sum, one may say that the national Equal Status Councils have performed a useful service by maintaining a steady searchlight on equality issues, and making information available to organizations, employers, schools, and people in public office. The municipal committees, on the other hand, have not functioned very well. As already indicated, it is only in Norway that one finds many of these—in 1982, 257 of the 454 municipalities had established such committees.[12] However, even here, research has shown that most of them are very ineffective, and about 20 percent did not have a single meeting in the course of a two-year period.[13] The reason for this contrast between the national and the municipal committees must be sought in the greater degree of voluntarism characterizing the latter: The municipalities *may* appoint them if they choose, and their tasks are not clearly spelled out by the central authorities. In the competition for funds, the local committees have low status and receive little priority.

The Equal Status Laws

One of the major tasks of the Equal Status Councils has been the drafting of proposals for equal status laws. With the exception of

Finland, all the countries have now passed such laws, which are quite similar. They are generally based on the principle of *gender neutrality*, and forbid discrimination of both men and women. Thus, the Norwegian Law on Equal Status, passed by the Storting in 1979, states in its main provision quite simply that "Discriminatory treatment of women and men is not permitted." While gender-neutral, however, it also acknowledges that discrimination is primarily a problem that women have to contend with, and consequently permits the use of special treatment to improve women's conditions:

> Differential treatment which is consistent with the law's purpose in that it furthers the equal status of the sexes is not in conflict with the first clause. The same applies to women's special rights which flow from the existing, unequal situation of women and men.[14]

Quotas for women that, for instance, might result in the bypassing of more qualified men, will not be in conflict with the law, nor can the law be used to demand military service for women.

Although the equal status laws generally are *prohibitory laws*, forbidding discrimination, both the Norwegian and Swedish laws provide for concrete, positive steps to be taken to ensure equality. The Swedish law, which only applies to the labor market, has two main parts: one forbidding discrimination, and one compelling employers to take active steps to promote equality. The Norwegian law stipulates that "Public authorities shall create conditions that are favorable for attaining equality between the sexes in all areas of society."[15] In addition, the Norwegian law contains a provision, lacking in all the others, that compels representation of both sexes on all public boards and committees. If such a body has four members or more, each sex must be represented with at least two members. However, while the law thus ensures minimum representation, it also makes clear that the desired end is equal representation: "When a public organ appoints or elects councils, boards, committees, etc., it shall aim at as equal a representation of both sexes as possible," states paragraph 21.[16]

This feature of the Norwegian Equal Status Law has proved very valuable. Modern political systems are characterized by a removal of power from the legislative to the administrative branches, where corporate interests have attained great influence through their representation on a host of councils and committees. This development has been seen by many as an expansion of democracy, giving the affected parties an opportunity to participate in the framing of the rules they are governed by. But for women, this rule by committee has in fact been a problematic development. At a time when women have begun to gain acceptance to the legislative and executive bodies, power slips away from these organs to the corporate channel, where women are much less likely to be recruited, since they are so poorly represented in the business community, the labor unions and their leadership, and the whole corporate structure from which public boards and committees are drawn.[17] Through the equal status law's provision, women are now assured representation on public boards at all levels of the political system, from the local through the provincial and to the state level.

Already in 1973, Norwegian government regulations were adopted that required organizations entitled to nominate candidates for *departmental or cabinet-appointed* committees and boards to submit as many female as male candidates, and to nominate twice the number of members they were entitled to. In this way, the departments got a substantial list of available candidates to make their final selections from. Even though no legal requirement existed for women's appointment, as Figure 3.3 shows, their representation on public boards rose from only 11 percent in 1972 to 17 percent five years later. Under the impact of the equal status law, this figure has risen further, and women's representation on public boards was 27 percent by 1982. On the newer boards, it was over one-third.

The Equal Status Ombud

In Denmark and Iceland, cases arising under the equal status laws may be tried in the courts. Norway and Sweden, on the other hand, have established special offices, *equality ombuds*, charged with their enforcement, and the Finnish proposal for an equal status law also contains a provision for such an ombud. According to the Norwegian law, the equal status ombud shall "on its own initiative or on the basis of applications from others help to ensure that the regulations of the Law are observed."[18] If the ombud's recommendations for voluntary settlement of a complaint are not adhered to, the case may be brought before a board of appeals. Theoretically, the cases may go from the board of appeals to the courts, but this has never happened.

Since the Norwegian equal status ombud began her work, the number of complaints and cases initiated by the ombud herself have

der neutrality (one cannot obtain equality through equal treatment of groups whose positions are vastly dissimilar); the principle that the goal is to be reached through voluntary compliance and attitude change; and the principle that equality shall be relegated to a secondary position if it is in conflict with other values.[24] Principles such as organizational freedom, religious freedom, freedom of speech, and even the principle of worker-employer negotiations determining the solutions of labor market conflicts are all accorded more significance than women's equality, which policy-makers have been unwilling to back with force. This lack of willingness to use compulsion to achieve the end of public equality policy reflects the lower degree of priority assigned to the goal, declare the critics.[25] In short, the political will to obtain genuine equality is not strong enough.

The Limits of Public Policy

Assessment of the effects of Scandinavian public policy toward women vary. "The contraceptive pill and the loop have changed women's lives to a much greater degree than public equality policy," declares one critic.[26] Still, without doubt, changes have occurred. As many girls as boys now get higher education. Women's labor force participation has increased markedly, most notably in Norway, where over 60 percent of married women now have some kind of work outside the home, in contrast to only 9.5 percent in 1960. Women's presence in elective and appointive public fora has more than doubled in the last decade and a half.

But the persistence of old patterns is also noticeable. Girls' career choices are still narrower than those of boys, and the occupationally active women tend to be concentrated in typically "female" jobs. In all the countries, women earn less than men—in fact, they are the new proletariat. Women who *have* made it to the top report of having done so in spite of discrimination and opposition from male colleagues and subordinates, whose attitudes may be illustrated by the statement of one male administrator: "The biggest thing wrong with career women is that they are born with the wrong sex."[27] And there appears to be a tapering off in the rate of increase in women's political representation: In the 1983 municipal elections in Norway, the proportion of women increased by only one percentage point. At that rate, it will be a hundred years before half the city councillors are women. As the authors of *The Unfinished Democracy* observe, "we have neither achieved an integrated labor market, integrated political institutions, nor equal sharing of work in the homes. The goal of public equality policy is still in the far distance."[28]

Does Democracy Defeat Women?

Turning now to the forces that impinge on and limit public equality policy, we shall look at political participation and representation of women in Scandinavia. Why is it not higher?

Explanations of political participation have tended to focus on two major sets of variables: the supply and demand factors. While the former stress the qualities of the individuals or groups concerned, their skills, resources, and motivations, the latter emphasize the political structures themselves, the rules of the game, the formal and informal mechanisms that ensure access for some and exclude others.

Obviously, as a group, compared with men, Scandinavian women still possess less of the resources we know to be associated with political participation and recruitment to high political office. Their education and income are lower, their occupations less prestigious, their organizational memberships fewer and less relevant to the needs of the political world. In short, they move in environments less rich in political stimuli than those of men. For the women who *do* possess the political resources associated with the characteristics listed aove, the double burden of home and career often prevents active political involvement. Indeed, marriage is a resource for men but a political handicap to women. As a study by Beatrice Halsaa Albrektsen has shown, the gap between men's and women's political involvement actually widened with an increase in such conventional resources as education, income, and occupational activity, *except for the unmarried women*, whose political involvement was almost as high as that of the married men![29]

So, if we emphasize the *supply factors*, we may say that the more limited supply of women than of men accounts for their poorer representation. Their political party membership figures are lower, too, than those of men; recent figures from Norway show only 12 percent of women as against 20 percent of men to be party members.[30] Only the Christian parties in Denmark, Finland, and Norway have a majority of women among their members. In most of the parties women now appear to constitute between 30 and 40 percent of the membership.[31]

Much of the research on women and politics has focused on the supply factors. However, recent writings by Scandinavian feminist social scientists have stressed the *demand factors* as constraints on female political participation. The political structures themselves are a hindrance to women. Men are the gatekeepers to the political system. They have defined the entry rules, and they send out the invitation and screen the recruits. As well, the *redistributive* aspect of politics is underscored: Male gatekeepers perceive women as threats to their positions in a system with limited rewards.[32] And throughout, "the iron law of power" prevails: The more power, the more men.[33]

On the surface, this view may seem at odds with the reality of Scandinavian politics. Several parties have now adopted quota rules to ensure women's representation in all party fora and on the ballots. This development has proceeded farthest in Norway, where the Socialist Left party, the Labor party, and the Liberal party have all adopted rules demanding at least 40 percent representation for each gender in all party organs and on the ballots. The "contagion from the left" also appears to ensure that even parties that do not have such formal regulations feel compelled to adhere to them in practice. Thus, as Table 3.1 shows, women's representation in the Central Executive Councils of most of the parties is quite high, in some cases higher than women's proportion of the party membership. The exceptions are the two parties on the extreme ends of the political spectrum, the Progress party on the right, and the Communist party on the left. Maybe most remarkable is the fact that the Christian People's party and the Center party, both quite conservative parties whose major appeal has been to the rural population, have increased women's representation on the Executive Council to 45 percent. The "iron law of power" thus appears to be in the process of modification, as several parties have higher proportions of females in their governing bodies than in the membership. Only the Christian parties have 50 percent women or more among their members.[34]

Leading politicians within several Norwegian parties have commented on the tendency of women to fare better at the higher levels. Thus, Astrid Gjertsen, the minister of family and consumer affairs and a Conservative, observes:

> It is my impression that the parties at the local level are less conscious of equality issues than the central institutions. This indicates that the parties' own equality ideology, which dominates in the party programs, is not always taken seriously in the same way by the organizational apparatus and the local party branches.[35]

TABLE 3.1

Women's representation in Norwegian political parties

Party[a]	MEMBERS OF PARLIAMENT			NATIONAL CONGRESS			NATIONAL COUNCIL			EXECUTIVE BOARD			WORKING COMMITTEE			HIGHEST POSITION OF A WOMAN
	Total	Women	%	Total	Women	%	Total	Women	%	Total	Women	%	Total	Women	%	
Left Socialist	6,740	2,696	40	225	107	48	27	11	41	15	7	47	7	3	43	Vice-president
Labour	160,000	?	40	300	113	38	22	10	45	15	6	40	3	1	33	President
Liberal	11,482	4,861	42	209	85	41	35	16	46	9	5	56	—			Vice-president
Christian	?		55 (?)	256	83	32	37	10	27	11	5	45	5	2	40	Vice-president
Agrarian				187	61	33	42	15	36	11	5	45	4	1	25	Vice-president
Conservative	60,000	20,000	33	413	125	30	—			62	12	19	5	2	40	Vice-president
Progress	167,544	?	40-45							7	1	14				Executive board member

Source: Torild Skard, "Women in the political life of the Nordic countries," *International Social Science Journal* 35:4 (1983), 647.

[a]Parties not represented in Parliament are not included: The Workers' Marxist-Leninist Party, the Communist Party and the Liberal Peoples Party.

And the Center party's Svein Sundsø expresses similar sentiments:

> It seems that women prosper, relatively speaking, in those areas governed and controlled by the central party apparatus. But in relation to the lower levels of the organizational hierarchy, or the voters, there women do more poorly.[36]

Local politicians, for their part, tend to emphasize the problems associated with meeting quota demands. At the lower levels, the number of activists are few, and the party meetings poorly attended. The faithful are overjoyed for each new member, and quite ready to bestow favors in the form of party offices, they insist. But being a precinct leader, a cashier, secretary or study circle leader— these are thankless tasks that few seem to want, and the nominating committees typically receive more noes than ayes when trying to field a full slate of officers for the approval of the annual meeting. Even when it comes to nominations for seats in the municipal councils, the demand may exceed the supply, making the party nominating committee's task an onerous one.

According to this view, then, the party system and politics at the lowest level are remarkably open, characterized not so much by gladiatorial contests between eager officeholders, as by reluctants who out of a sense of civic duty assume the burdens imposed on them. Far from a conspiring oligarchy of party bosses being at the core of the problem of women's representation, it is democracy itself that defeats women, as voters reject the female candidates who have agreed to be nominated by the parties.

Norwegian elections results lend some substance to this view. The Norwegian Municipal Elections Act gives voters a very direct influence on who is elected to the municipal councils through a device known as *kumulering*— cumulation, which permits voters to eliminate the names of candidates on the party ballot, while giving an extra vote to other candidates by writing in their names. To a limited extent, the names of candidates from other parties may also be added to the party slate. Candidates thus added will get a double vote when the ballots are counted.

For women, cumulation by the voters has proved to be a double-edged sword: While it permits organized efforts to elect more women, election analyses also show that a disproportionate number of the candidates eliminated over the years have been women. Campaigns by women's organizations to increase female representation by taking advantage of the cumulation possibilities resulted in some notable improvements. There were also some much publicized "conspiracies," identical changes of the ballots by a handful of voters, which resulted in majorities for women in a few city councils, among them Oslo and Trondheim, in 1971. However, on a nationwide basis, it is quite clear that men are in fact cumulated more often than women, for men have in all recent elections constituted a larger proportion of the elected municipal councillors than of the list candidates. In the municipal elections of 1983, there were concerted efforts in some municipalities to eliminate women from the ballots, possibly the result of a "backlash" to feminist attempts to increase women's representation. Research indicates that most of those who eliminate female candidates are men, and that the sturdy old fisherman and party politician from one of the western provinces expressed the sentiments of quite a few of his sex when he said, "There are many who think that women have gotten enough."[37]

For the convinced democrat, this poses a dilemma on which one party official commented. In the 1983 municipal elections, women's political hopes were dashed and a setback experienced, he said,

> Not because the party said "stop, no further." What we experienced in the last elections was that the voters said "stop a while, now you advance faster than we can follow." The breaks were applied. All with a democratic ideal must give the people the right to say this. The people have the right to make a mistake, even if this goes against our ideal and goals of the party organization. People have a right to hold that the earth is flat, if they so wish.[38]

To point out that democracy may be a constraint on women's political fortunes does not absolve the party organization of responsibility for recruitment and promotion of women, and thus for redistribution of political power. The role of the party as gatekeeper to the political hierarchy is probably more important in Scandinavia than in most political systems. "Self-recruitment" does not exist in the sense than an individual may "throw her hat in the ring" and "run for office." The political culture emphasizes modesty: Jobs are not sought, but offered to the candidates. Appearing to want a political career may be the surest way not to get it.

In such a system, the need for sponsoring godparents or mentors is crucial. A political hopeful must have someone who mentions her name and pushes her ahead as a potential candidate for party and public office. The party leadership and secretariats are in a unique position to play this role and to exercise influence and control over who is defined as an available candidate. They lift people out of obscurity, groom heirs for the next election, and place their names in nomination for public boards, committees, and councils, thus making them into well-known figures for whose candidacy a "spontaneous" demand may later rise. Obviously, there is much of an element of unwitting oligarchy in this process. When asked to propose names for this or that committee or board, people first tend to think of those they know, and the very structure of the system thus strengthens those groups that already are represented. All the political godfathers represent an enormous built-in asset for continued male dominance of the political system.

Political leaders at the local level commonly assert that they have problems finding women who are willing to accept public positions, and that women's reluctance to serve now is the real reason behind their poor representation. Existing survey research from Norway does not support this position. It shows that a *majority of both men and women* do not wish to hold positions of this kind: only 21 percent of the electorate were willing to accept any kind of political job. But of the women willing to serve, only 22 percent had in fact been asked, while 37 percent of the willing men had been asked![39] Quota rules in those parties that have them now force the leadership to "look a little harder" for willing female candidates. Still, the rules are practiced halfheartedly, and sometimes deliberately set aside. Their infraction is then excused with the argument that "we must be practical, and after all, this has nothing to do with sex, it is simply finding the best person for the job." There have also been instances when the 40 percent quota is used as a *maximum* for women's representation, rather than as a *minimum.* Thus, in one municipal party, the nomination of a third woman to the five-member party group in the municipal executive council was argued against on the ground that "this would be in violation of the 40 percent rule."

The last example suggests that there is also *deliberate oligarchy* at work, a very conscious exclusion process, intended to hinder the political advances of one person and promote those of another. The locus of this deliberate oligarchy is often the party secretariats, which possess enormous power in that they define agendas and make the first proposals for the executive organs of the parties to react to. So, the moles who succeed in getting the ear of centrally placed party people are in an advantageous position to reap future political rewards. Although the system at first glance appears gender-neutral, it in fact works against the women, because, as relative newcomers to the political game, they are less skilled in the art of politicking behind the curtains, and discover too late that they have been outwitted. What women need, therefore, are more godmothers who can sponsor them and alert them to the ways of the moles, so they can "beat the system." An illustration of such godmothering is offered by the female politican who told of quietly grooming as her own successor to an elective office a younger woman against whom the party secretary and the ambitious young functionaries around him have applied more or less subtle exclusion mechanisms. She is not called on to perform party tasks that will give her public exposure and increase her visibility.

As women gradually penetrate the party leadership and are able to play the role of godmothers, the political process will be easier for other women. Still, however, the rule is that positions of leadership are an almost exclusively male preserve. Even at the local level, very few women serve as party leaders, and at the national level they are even rarer. Sweden and Finland have had some deputy party leaders, but Norway is the only country where women have served as national party leaders. It is especially the parties on the left side of the political spectrum that have been willing to elect female leaders. The Norwegian Labor party is headed by a woman, earlier Prime Minister Gro Harlem Brundtland, and the Socialist Left party, the Liberal party, and the Liberal People's party have all had women leaders. Most of the other bourgeois parties in Norway now make it a practice to have women deputy leaders.

The redistributive aspect of politics and the difficulties this represents for women is underscored by the formal and informal rules governing the elections. All the Scandinavian countries feature proportional representation and a party slate system, which normally favor the election chances of women when compared with elections in single-member districts. However, the fractured party systems, with several parties competing for just a handful of seats in each election district, ensures that most parties only win one or two seats. This is most clearly the case in Iceland, and combined with the small number of representatives in the *Allting*, just sixty members, the result has been that many of the district parties are in effect in the same position as parties in the single-member system: They can only hope for one seat, and that tends to go to a man. In comparison with the other Scandinavian countries, Iceland has had exceptionally low female representation, under 5 percent during most of the postwar period. Only in 1983 did women's representation reach 15 percent.[40]

Examination of Norwegian election results during the postwar period has also shown a clear relationship between the number of seats controlled by a party in a province, and women's election changes: The larger the number of seats, the greater the chances that women are elected. Conversely, those provinces where a party can elect only one or two representatives have seldom been served by a woman. As only the Labor party is large enough to count on three or more representatives in most provinces, and the Conservative party to win two or more in most provinces, this explains why most of the women elected to the Storting have been sent there by these two parties. In those provinces where they only capture one seat, they have been no more likely than the rest to nominate women at the top of their tickets. However, this trend is now slowly changing. Evidence that ideology does play some role is found in two of the smallest parties represented in the Storting, the reactionary Progress party, and the Socialist Left party. Both elected four representatives in 1981. In the former, all are men, while the latter has 50 percent female representation.[41]

The complex makeup of many of the Norwegian provinces also complicates women's election chances. Custom dictates that geographical, cultural, and economic groupings all must be represented on the ticket, and this may lead to the exclusion of extremely able women from the ticket because "their" group or geographical area is already represented.

In the absence of more central control of the parties' nominations, it is likely that women's representation will continue to lag behind that of men. Central coordination of the nominating process, for the smaller parties that obtain only one seat in most provinces, would place women at the top of the tickets in half of these, and would increase women's representation. However, provincial autonomy is jealously guarded, so for all practical purposes there is a built-in ceiling on female representation: The most women can hope for is half of the seats in those provinces where a party wins more than one seat. In order to attain this, parties would have to alternate their male and female candidates on the list, a practice that so far only the Socialist Left party, the Liberal party, and, to a somewhat lesser degree, the Labor party have practiced.

Similar problems occur in the matter of appointment to the many boards and committees that, according to the Equal Status Law, always shall include members of both sexes, and aim at equal representation. Nominations to such bodies are submitted by many different groups, which may all propose only the names of men, expecting someone else to nominate the women. The very democratic structure itself, laboriously erected to ensure citizen participation, may thus be a hindrance to effective implementation of the equal status legislation, whose purpose is *also* democratic participation.

The imperative to produce female candidates has undoubtedly made it less likely that women are passed over. As the Labor party's Thorbjørn Jagland has observed: "We have over 3000 local chapters in the country. Many of them have *almost only* male members. If they are going to fulfill the requirements, which they *must*, they simply have to recruit more women."[42] It is equally clear that much remains to be done. In the summer of 1984, Equal Status Ombud Eva Kolstad sent out letters to most of the 454 Norwegian municipalities, alerting them to the fact that they were in violation of the law as far as the composition of their public boards was concerned. Only *one* municipality, a small rural community in Northern Norway, had fulfilled the law's intent of close to equal representation of the genders.[43] In most of the others, not only were women underrepresented, but they were concentrated in the typical "women's committees," those whose tasks are extensions of the female caretaker role, the committees of health, education and social affairs.

Conclusion

The popular notion of democracy as the creator of equality receives no more than qualified support from this survey of women's position in the Scandinavian countries. Extension of equal rights to women has not been the result of a "bubbling up" of grassroots demands that are then finally placed on the government agenda. Rather, we see an instance of Karl W. Deutsch's "cascade model": Demands arise among the elites, and cascade downward, until they finally receive support at the mass level.[44]

Much of the impetus for change has come from the public sector. Governments, as Torild Skard says, "have been the main initiators of change in the division of labor based on gender, while the important organizations in the economic sector have for the most part dragged their feet."[45]

The major obstacle to rapid change and limit to public policy must be sought in the prevalence of deep-rooted traditional orientations to their respective roles among both genders. Public policy is often frustrated, wittingly or unwittingly, at lower levels, just as central party directives are overlooked by subordinate organs.

The present economic crisis, combined with the more conservative political climate of recent years, also has helped to relegate equality issues to the back burner. In some labor unions, there is now quite open talk of "one wage earner per family." Such arguments are not heard only from men. It was a woman, prominent in the Norwegian Labor party's women's organization in one of the western provinces, who argued at a recent conference that "we must increase respect for the housewife's occupation. This will keep more women at home, and free jobs for the men and young people."

Still, even though it is important to emphasize that the power relationships in Scandinavia have not been fundamentally altered, one must also note the positive devlopments that have occurred. The parties have nominated and elected an increasing number of women at all system levels, and women have succeeded in placing new items on the political agenda. Maybe most significantly, children's attitudes to women's political participation indicate that attempts to alter traditional sex-role orientations through public policy are succeeding. Thus, a comparative study of Canadian and Norwegian children's views on women and politics indicates more egalitarian attitudes among Norwegian children than among the Canadians. This is particularly true of the boys.[46]

So, while Scandinavian women have not yet attained an equal share in political power, a foundation for the future has been laid. As political scientist Beatrice Halsaa expresses it, "Women are no longer hostages in politics, we now constitute a minority."[47]

An earlier version of this article was read as a paper at the meeting of the Association for the Advancement of Scandinavian Studies in Canada, Canadian Learned Societies' Conference, Guelph, Ontario, June 6, 1984.

NOTES

1. For a discussion of the public policy process, see, for example, Charles O. Jones, *An Introduction to the Study of Public Policy* (Belmont, CA: Duxbury Press, 1970).

2. Elina Haavio-Mannila et al., eds., *Det uferdige demokratiet* (Oslo: Nordisk Ministerråd, 1983), chap. 2. See also Ingunn Norderval Means, "Political Recruitment of Women in Norway," *Western Political Quarterly* 25 (September 1972), 491–521.

3. Haavio-Mannila, 1. This and other translations from the Norwegian are by this author.

4. Harriet Holter, Om kvinneundertrykkelse, mannsundertrykkelse, og herstekniker," in Kristian Andenæs et al., eds., *Maktens ansikter* (Oslo: Gyldendal, 1981), 227.

5. Ibid.

6. *Stortingstidende*, 1893, p. 1645.

7. Hans F. Dahl, "Those Equal Folk," *Daedalus* 113: 1 (Winter 1984), 93.

8. Likestillingsrådet, *Kvinnens stilling og integrasjon i utviklingen* (Oslo: Likestillingsrådet, 1975), 1.

9. Nordic Council of Ministers' Secretariat, *Measures for Equality between Women and Men in the Labour Market in the Nordic Countries* (Stockholm: Nordic Council, 1979), 27–28.

10. Haavio-Mannila, 212.

11. Nordic Council of Ministers' Secretariat, 25–26.

12. Haavio-Mannila, 212.

13. Ibid., 214.

14. Law on Equal Status, paragraph 3. The law is printed in *Likestillingspolitikk* (Oslo: Department of Consumer Affairs and Government Administration, 1982), 64.

15. Ibid., paragraph 1.

16. Ibid., paragraph 21.

17. For a discussion of women's role in the corporate channel, in the business and labor leadership, see the following works: Helga Hernes, *Staten—kvinner ingen adgang?* (Oslo, Universitetsforlaget, 1982), 85; Edda Espeland, *Er du blitt sjef, jenta m* (Oslo, Gyldendal, 1984); and Marit Hoel, *Den kvinnelige arbeiderklassen* (Oslo: Universitetsforlaget, 1983).

18. Law on Equal Status, paragraph 11.

19. *Likestillingspolitikk*, 11. This publication by the Department of Consumer Affairs and Government Administration offers a good introduction to Norwegian equality policy.

20. Ibid., 64.

21. Torild Skard and Elina Haavio-Mannila, "Equality between the Sexes," *Daedalus* 113:1 (Winter 1984), 162.

22. See *Likestillingspolitikk*, 34–38, for an account of the various steps taken under the Action Plan.

23. Ibid., 24–25.

24. Haavio-Mannila, 231.

25. Ibid., 229.

26. Ibid., 233.

27. Edda Espeland, cited by Tone B. Jamholt in *Arbeiderbladet*, March 27, 1984, p. 6.

28. Haavio-Mannila, 230.

29. Beatrice Halsaa Albrektsen, *Kvinner og politisk deltakelse* (Oslo: Pax, 1977), 174.

30. Kari Rolstad og Brit Førde, *Kvinner og politikk* (Oslo: Likestillingsrådet, 1983), 8.

31. Haavio-Mannila, Table 2.2, pp. 67–68.

32. See, for instance, interview with Torild Skard, "Framgangen kommer ikke flytende på ei fjøl," in Rolstad og Førde, 18–20.

33. Skard and Haavio-Mannila, 155.

34. See Table 2.2, pp. 67–68 in Haavio-Mannila.

35. Likestillingsrådet, *Rapport fra kontaktkonferansen med organisasjonene*, 28–29 februar 1984 (Oslo: Likestillingsrådet, April 1984), 14.

36. Ibid., 122.

37. For a discussion of the Norwegian Municipal Election Law and some of its effects, see Ingunn Norderval Means, "Women in Local Politics," *Canadian Journal of Political Science* 5 (September 1972), 365–388; and Torild Skard, "Personvalget til kommunestyrene—partistyring eller velgerdemokrati?" *Tidsskrift for samfunnsforskning* 23 (1982), 359–382.

38. Likestillingsrådet, *Rapport fra kontaktkonferansen*, 125.

39. See Stein Ugelvik Larsen and Audun Offerdal, *De få vi valgte* (Oslo: Universitetsforlaget, 1979), 94–97.

40. See Torild Skard, "Women in the political life of the Nordic countries," *International Social Science Journal* 35: 4 (1983), 644.

41. For a discussion of the relationship between proportional representation and women's election chances, see Wilma Rule, "Why Women Don't Run: The Critical Contextual Factors in Women's Legislative Recruitment," *Western Political Quarterly* 34 (March 1981), 60–77. See also Means, "Political Recruitment of Women in Norway"; Torild Skard, *Utvalgt til Stortinget* (Oslo: Gyldendal, 1980).

42. Likestillingsutvalget, *Konferanserapport*, 116.

43. Equal Status Ombud Eva Kolstad in an interview with *Romsdals Budstikke*, July 6, 1984, p. 8.

44. Karl W. Deutsch, *The Analysis of International Relations* (Englewood Cliffs, NJ: Prentice-Hall, 1968), 101–110.

45. Skard and Haavio-Mannila, 162.

46. Ingunn Norderval, "As Children See It: Canadian and Norwegian Children's perceptions of Politics," *Skrifter* 1982:3 (Molde, Norway: Møre and Romsdal Regional College, 1982), 11.

47. "Kvinnene ikke lenger gisler i politikken," *Aktuelt Perspektiv*, May 4, 1984, p. 8.

RECOMMENDED READINGS

Allardt, Erik, et al. *Nordic Democracy*. Copenhagen: Det Danske Selskab, 1981.
A comprehensive introduction to the political and economic institutions, and social and cultural affairs of the Scandinavian countries, written by the area's leading social scientists.

Haavio-Mannila, Elina. "The Position of Women," in Allardt et al. Chapter 24, pp. 555–588.
Haavio-Mannila is generally considered to be Finland's foremost expert on women's role in society, with a vast number of publications to her credit. In this article she examines women's movements and political activities in the context of their economic and educational position.

_____ , et al. *The Unfinished Democracy—Women in Nordic Politics*. Oxford: Pergamon Press, 1985.
This is the first booklength comparative study of women's political participation in the five countries. It is the result of a cooperative project started by women political scientists participating in the workshop "Women in Politics" at the European Consortium for Political Research in Berlin in 1977. The various chapters examine the function of the women's organizations, women's electoral participation and their role in parliamentary and local politics, as well as their representation in the corporate channel. One chapter is devoted to public equality policy and its effects.

Hernes, Helga Maria, and Kirsten Voje. "Women in the Corporate Channel: A Process of Natural Exclusion," *Scandinavian Political Studies* 2 (1980).
The authors document the extent of women's underrepresentation in public boards and committees, and also present a profile of the women who do get appointed.

Holter, Harriet. *Sex Roles and Social Structure*. Oslo: Universitetsforlaget, 1970.
The first major work by a Scandinavian social scientist to examine women's social, economic, and political position in the area.

Nordic Council of Minsters Secretariat. *Measures for Equality between Women and Men in the Labour Market in the Nordic Countries*. Stockholm: Nordic Council, 1979.
Very informative report on the situation of women in the labor market, and the regulations that affect equality in working life.

Norderval, Ingunn. "As Children See It: Canadian and Norwegian Children's Perceptions of Politics," *Skrifter* 1982:3. Molde: Møre and Romsdal College, 1982.

The article addresses itself to the question of whether regime efforts to influence children's sex-role attitudes have any effects.

Skard, Torild. "Women in the Political Life of the Nordic Countries," *International Social Science Journal* 35:4 (1983), 639–657.

Concise and informative presentation of the political position of women in the area, with the main emphasis on Norway.

————, and Elina Haavio-Mannila. "Equality between the Sexes—Myth or Reality in Norden?" *Daedalus* 113:1 (Winter 1984), 141–167.

The article examines the development of the feminist movement through its various stages, and women's present positions in the economic and political systems of the Nordic countries. This special issue of *Daedalus*, entitled *The Nordic Enigma*, contains several excellent articles on various aspects of Nordic culture, which provide a useful background for understanding women's situation.

4

Italy and Ireland: Women, Church, and Politics in Two Catholic Countries

Mary Cornelia Porter
Barat College
Corey Venning
Loyola University of Chicago

The women's movement, like the socialist movement, is international, and has developed in a variety of cultures and social, economic, and political systems. In this article we examine the impact of the women's movement in two parliamentary democracies whose political cultures, while different in many respects, have been significantly shaped by Catholic doctrine and the Catholic church as an institution.

In both nations the status of women and their roles in social, economic, and political life have been directly and indirectly determined by the church, especially as pertains to matters of crucial concern to it—procreation, the regulation of family relationships, and education. In areas such as female employment and political participation, the church's interests are now nominal.

Those sociopolitical and religious similarities would suggest strong resemblances in the configurations, goals, and effects of the womens' movements, especially as regards objectives opposed by the church. That this has not been the case illuminates the necessity for understanding and assessing the movement in each country within its particular, even idiosyncratic, context. In the examples at hand, what might now be a routine success for Italian women may be a resounding triumph for their sisters in Ireland. We must make our judgments in terms not only of results, but also of efforts and feasibilities.

Catholic doctrine holds that all souls are equally precious to God. Women have attained the highest degree of sainthood, and greater holiness is ascribed to the Virgin Mary than to any other mere human being. Spiritual worth and responsibility for sin are in no way determined by the sex of the actor.

But in the worldly effects of behavior, anatomy is destiny. Women's primary earthly functions are maternity, nurture, and sacrifice. In marriage, which if valid is indissoluble, the husband prevails unless the wife's obedience would cause her to sin: Woman is to man as the church is to God, and should serve him accordingly. In practical and canon-law terms violation of the rule of marital fidelity and other forms of sexual misbehavior are more serious when committed by women. Artificial contraception and abortion are forbidden. These prohibitions are recognized to have greater practical effect on women than on men.

Positions in the church hierarchy are reserved to clerics. Women are categorically excluded from the priesthood and from minor orders, and therefore from church governance. The Virgin herself could not receive the sacrament of Holy Orders, or serve as an acolyte—an office usually performed by 10- to 14-year-old boys. The recent revision of the Canon Law Code accepts somewhat greater lay participation in church affairs in general, and does permit women to be diocesan business managers and (nonpresiding) judges in diocesan tribunals.[1]

The church does not see itself as a repressive force with regard to women's status, and in many respects its teachings and policies advance the goals of human (including female) dignity, social justice, and peace. In recent decades it has accepted trends toward increased formal education for women and their participation in the political process. Though he does not welcome women's extradomestic employment and has expressed hope that the necessity for it may be eliminated, the present pope has denounced sex discrimination in the workplace. Statements on these matters by church officials are invariably accompanied by references to woman's true role as mother and center of the family.[2]

While church teachings are universalistic, their reach and impact are not. Variations in adherence to papal pronouncements on family planning are illustrative. Thus, despite the fact that Italy and Ireland are overwhelmingly Catholic (Italy, 99 percent; Ireland, 95 percent), and despite the special status the church has enjoyed in both countries, church influence, church-state relations, and popular attitudes toward Catholicism and the clergy are quite different in each. The womens' movements in Italy and Ireland have developed in reaction to particular, as well as the more general Catholic, cultures.

Historically the church and the family have been at the center of Italian life. Under the 1929 Concordat between the Vatican and the Italian state, Catholicism was Italy's state religion, and the church had considerable authority over family law and public education. Notwithstanding this pervasiveness of the church in Italian affairs, Italy has for centuries also had a strong anticlerical tradition.[3] In early 1984 a Concordat revision eliminated an Italian state religion and placed full secular authority in the Italian government and legal system.

The Irish church appeared, until the 1960s, to command the total allegiance of its communicants. However, rising levels of education, the "Europeanization" of once parochial Ireland, the development of social as well as political rapport with the once detested "Brits," the pervasiveness of television, and the youngest and fastest-growing population in Europe have combined to erode the social (if not the spiritual) authority of the church.[4] Nonetheless, old habits and allegiances die hard, particularly in rural and conservative Ireland. Due to over 300 years of British *Protestant* domination, exploitation, repression and religious persecution, Irish Catholicism and Irish nationalism became synonymous. The church attained and has enjoyed a dominion that is neither easily challenged nor willingly relinquished.

The Irish Constitution no longer "recognizes" the Catholic religion, the "Catholic article" having been repealed in preparation for possible reunification with Northern Ireland. This repeal may be window dressing, for the Irish Constitution embodies and lends secular legitimacy to Catholic dogma. It forbids divorce and the remarriage of persons divorced in other jurisdictions. It defines the family in terms of marriage (thus denying illegitimate children the full protection of the law). While it holds all citizens equal before the law, immediate modification permits legislation "having due regard to differences of capacity, physical and moral, and of social function." It assigns to women a special place, not unlike that given Mary by the church.:

> In particular the State recognizes that by her life within the home the woman gives the State a support without which the common good cannot be achieved. . . . The state shall, therefore, endeavor to ensure that mothers shall not be obliged by economic necessity to engage in labor to the neglect of duties in the home.

The Irish Constitution, in sum, reflects the Church's view that "women's role in life is fulfilled as mother and homemaker."[5]

The Italian and Irish womens' movements share a number of characteristics. Each had its short-lived predecessor.[6] Each is composed of those who would work within and those who insist on fundamental change in the social, legal, economic, and political systems. Of late, splinter groups, exclusively concerned with matters such as violence against women, control of reproduction, unmarried mothers, welfare equity and other economic concerns, and lesbian rights, have proliferated. The Irish government provides modest funding for shelters for battered women, rape victims, and unmarried mothers. In both countries, but especially in Ireland, obligations imposed by the European Economic Community (EEC) and other international and inter-European organizations have resulted in great changes in the economic status, and concomitantly in the legal and political status, of women. In both countries women's groups have challenged the teachings and authority of the church. In Italy, the church has retreated in some respects. In Ireland, it has made some grudging concessions. In both countries it has fought back.

Beginning in 1970 Italian women were galvanized into intense and ultimately successful action by the issues of divorce and, later, abortion. These struggles provided them with invaluable political experience. Further, party-connected women's groups, which had theretofore faithfully followed party leaderships, asserted real independence in the face of their parties' lukewarm support for or outright opposition to divorce and abortion reform.

Feminist demonstrations and other activities were also effective in pressing for adoption of the new Family Law Code, establishment of family counselling centers throughout the country, and for other private and governmental undertakings significant to women's interests. On the whole, the record of the Italian women's movement during the past 15 years is impressive and, in view of the insignificant public roles assumed by Italian women for many generations past, surprising.

Beginning in 1982 some observers have commented on an apparent weakening or "burnout" in Italian feminism. Economic recession, severe in Italy, no doubt retards women's progress there as elsewhere. And Italian feminism, never tightly organized, always displaying much splintering and separation of groups along ideological and life-style lines, may indeed appear to be in danger of becoming moribund. But appearances, and judgments based on habits and customs of other societies, can be misleading; witness the ease with which feminists obtained 350,000 signatures (50,000 were required) on a recent petition to revise the current laws on rape and sexual violence. Italian feminists rely on a loose and decentralized network, with coordination, representation, and action as need for them is perceived.[7]

The Irish women's movement was launched by Dublin journalists and academics in the late 1960s. While it received media attention, the government's establishment in 1970 of a Commission on the Status of Women brought the movement into the mainstream of Irish politics. The commission's first report provided an agenda for the movement, a Magna Carta around which women (and men) of varying views could rally. This and three subsequent reports documented a wide array of discriminatory laws, practices, and attitudes, and proposed remedies and reforms—most of which have been legislatively and/or administratively implemented. There are those, however, who charge that the government has coopted the movement and isolated feminists who demand the legalization of divorce and abortion and the availability of contraceptives to all who want them. While more moderate feminists may also favor such measures, they do not do so publicly, preferring consensus building to confrontation.

The splintering of the women's movement into about 50 disparate groups has been offset by government action. Official agencies such as the recently established cabinet-level Office of Women's Affairs and Family Law Reform and the Employment Equality Agency and quasi-official groups such as the Council for the Status of Women, the Women's Representative Committee and the National Women's forum have articulated issues; lobbied the political parties, the bureaucracy, and the Parliament; and have sought to broaden the base of the movement by reaching out to rural women, homemakers, and women who work on family farms. In this sense the Irish women's movement may be *sui generis*.

The Irish women's movement and progress toward the realization of its goals have been immeasurably aided by Ireland's membership in EEC, the International Labor Organization (ILO), and other European institutions. In a direct sense, the EEC was the burr under the saddle as far as economic matters go, and freed the

movement to turn its attention to social issues. Senator Mary
Robinson, long associated with the movement, claims that it would
be difficult

> to assess how quickly there would be progress on a purely
> internal level to achieve equality of opportunity in Ireland if
> there were no pressure from the European level. Certainly the
> legal effect of the time limits stipulated in the Directives for
> their implementation is a welcome guarantee of equal progress
> in these areas.[8]

One of the areas in which the church ostensibly has little interest
is the participation of women in public life. Yet the church's example in its own governance and centuries of socialization have
worked to persuade women that their proper activities are confined
to the private sphere. Which is not to say, as witnessed by experience in non-Catholic countries, that Catholicism is the only, or
necessarily the most important, force inhibiting female participation in politics and government! But, as has been pointed out,
compared with women in Protestant European countries, women in
Catholic countries "remain the most timid in enjoying what rights
they have received—including the right to vote and discuss
politics."[9]

This timidity notwithstanding, the significant changes in the
overall situation of women in Italy during the past 15 years testify to
their effectiveness in pursuing goals they see as important. It should
also be remembered that for Italians their political system and
"politics" narrowly defined have played a less important role in
ongoing social and personal life than in most other Western countries. In any case, women comprise 51 percent of the Italian electorate. That they have consistently voted in larger proportion to their
numbers than have Italian men can no longer be ascribed, as it once
was, to the success of clergy and Christian Democrats in sending
docile communicants to the polls.[10] Women's representation in the
national parliament and in regional local governments—very significant in Italy, whose regions display a high degree of distinctive-
ness and whose local and regional governments hold a greal deal of
de facto authority—is comparable to that in other Western European countries, and higher than in the United States. Women are
also taking positions within Italy's national political elite: Since
1978 women have been president of the Chamber of Deputies, ambassador, and undersecretary of state for foreign affairs.

Given Italy's weak coalition governments, the bureaucracy is
arguably the real power within the national governmental struc-

ture. There women continue to be concentrated in the lower grades, with evidence of systematic, though illegal, discrimination.[11]

The first report issued by the Commission on the Status of Women remarked on the "subdued and muted" participation of women in Irish public life. While there are sociological explanations for the phenomenon, political practices and institutions are equally salient. Political dynasties and local political machines dominated Irish politics. Political access is thereby typically restricted. Ironically, however, such arrangements have assured continuous female representation in the lower house: When male relatives of deceased deputies are either unavailable or unsuitable, their widows, sisters, daughters, and even granddaughters have been recruited as candidates. Once elected, some of these women are permitted to assume back bench leadership positions—when their parties are in the opposition.

Further, deputies do not formulate public policy; their function is to respond to government initiatives. If they wish to remain in office, deputies are expected to demonstrate loyalty to their parties, local organizations, and their constituencies. They are *not* expected to take independent stands on issues.

In the Senate, whose members are indirectly elected from lists of candidates presented by the prime minister, various organizations, and the universities, and which is historically a forum for political mavericks, women do speak as women. Nonetheless, since the lower house of Parliament (like the British House of Commons) is more powerful than the Senate (somewhat similar to the House of Lords), it is there that strong representations of women's views as such would be most effectively raised.

While the women's movement appears thus far to have had little direct impact on female participation in national electoral politics or on female deputies' consciousness about women's issues, the movement is nonetheless responsible for considerable change. In the first place, as attested to by the recommendations of the Committee on the Status of Women and the formation of the Women's Political Association, women have made female political participation an issue. Thus, what has been described as the political inertia of a majority of Irishwomen has been psychologically counteracted. Second, women are no longer so uniformly swayed by the political preferences and opinions of male relatives, and younger women (and men) believe that women should assume public roles. Third, women are discovering that litigation may succeed where politics fails. Irish appellate courts, for example, have invalidated the ban against the importation of contraceptives; held that women, like

men, are obliged to perform jury service; sustained a challenge
against legislation that placed a heavier tax burden on married than
unmarried working couples; and held that a married woman without dependents had wrongfully been denied unemployment compensation. Fourth, politically ambitious women who lack the
requisite family ties are testing other routes to Parliament, such as a
term or two in the Senate, experience in local government with the
concommitant opportunity to build a political base, and participation in youth and women's groups. In the fifth place, the political
parties are genuinely committed to increasing female participation
in electoral politics, and each has adopted a policy on women.
Finally, Parliament has established a Committee on Womens'
Rights, which suggests that women running for and elected to
public office may in future comfortably identify with women's
issues.

Despite the Government's articulated interest in encouraging
women to enter public life, few are in policy-making and high-status
posts. To the disappointment of the Committee on the Status of
Women and the Economic Equality Agency, the recission of the
"marriage bar," which had prohibited women from entering the
public sector (teaching excepted) has thus far had little across-the-
board effect on female presence in the civil service. This may, however, change with time. Further, women are rarely to be found in
positions that provide access to promotion, or on the boards of
state-sponsored and advisory bodies such as the Law Reform Commission and the National Economic and Social Council. It was not
until 1978 that a woman (whose political career began, not surprisingly, with her succession to her father's seat in Parliament) was
appointed minister.

Female visibility in government is restricted to matters that concern women or require the traditional womanly social services
skills—which is not to say that such jobs are negligible. Women
predominate on umbrella and advisory groups such as the Women's
Representative Committee and the Employment Equality, whose
members represent the minister of labor, the trade unions,
employer's groups, and women's organizations. They are well represented on the National Service Board and the National Council
for the Aged. In 1982 a woman member of Parliament was appointed
as minister of state for the newly created Office of Women's Affairs
and Family Law Reform. The implementation of her ambitious
program calls for the involvement of all government departments
and full support of Parliament.

In sum, women are slowly entering Irish public life—under their own steam as elected representatives, as bureaucrats, as cabinet officers, as lobbyists, and as public interest litigants. "The rate of progress," admits a political scientist and member of Parliament, "does not hold out any hope of a sudden and dramatic transformation, for the battle for full equality" has just begun. But, he adds, "it has begun, and that's something that could not have been said even ten years ago." Irish women are now on the political agenda.[12]

Since their enfranchisement in 1945, Italian women have been under no formal limitations on their rights and duties as citizens, and there have been few legal barriers to employment in civilian occupations. Barriers to equality in these areas have been sociopolitical, not legal.

This was not the case with matters of sexual and family relations. Until 1970, and in conformity with church-state relations under the 1929 Concordat, Italian law governing such matters conformed to the canon-law model. There was no legal divorce. In most circumstances abortion was a major criminal offense on the part of all concerned. Dissemination of contraceptive information and distribution of contraceptive materials were restricted. Wives were subordinated to husbands, and children to fathers, in all aspects of family relations and in inheritance. In some respects Italian law went beyond the rules of the church in confirming patriarchal authority. Laws on marital infidelity reflected a thoroughgoing double standard. Illegitimates had no rights of inheritance and for practical purposes no legal claims on their parents. Reflecting the mores of the preindustrial and culturally traditional south, liability for prosecution for rape, seduction, or corruption of a minor female was extinguished by marriage of perpetrator and victim, and men convicted of crimes of honor against erring female relatives and their partners were punished lightly, if at all.

In 1970, divorce—on limited grounds hedged with restrictions and formidable procedures—became possible. In 1973 advertising of contraceptive information and devices was legalized. In 1975 a new Family Law Code came into effect. It places spouses on equal legal footing; reduces the extent of both authority and obligation as between parents and children; substantially equalizes the status of all children, legitimate or otherwise, vis-à-vis their parents; and permits marital separation by mutual consent or where continued cohabitation is intolerable or severely prejudicial to the well-being of family members. The new code establishes a Family Counselling Service.

In 1978 abortion was legalized, with provisions for its performance at public expense and in effect on the sole decision of the woman who seeks it.

Each of these changes is fundamental to the condition of Italian women, and each elicited considerable opposition from the church and other status-quo-oriented elements in Italian society. The divorce and abortion issues especially occasioned prolonged and intense public debate and demonstrations. Both new laws were submitted, after their passage, to nationwide public referenda, which sustained them by impressive majorities. In all these cases, steady and imaginative campaigning on the part of women's groups of many ideological persuasions was perhaps decisive to success of the reform measures.

The anomalies resulting from the institution of these new laws under the postwar Consititution, into which the 1929 Concordat with the Vatican had been incorporated, were resolved by the conclusion in 1984 of a new agreement, mentioned above, between the Vatican and the Italian state.

That laws are on the books does not of course assure full adherence to them, or full knowledge of or utilization of their provisions by their presumed beneficiaries. The record varies with class and region. The Italian divorce rate (about 10,000 per annum) is minute compared with that for most Western industrialized countries. The birthrate, which has approximated that for the rest of Western Europe for two decades, has not changed significantly as a result of legalization of contraceptive information and sales. The abortion rate is about the same as estimates of abortions performed before legalization. The new Family Law Code appears to conform closely to actual Italian urban and northern practice of both working and middle classes. Especially with regard to abortion, in some parts of the country practice diverges rather widely from the formal provisions of the law. For example, many physicians (though a decreasing number over time) make use of the law's "conscience" clause permitting them to refuse to perform abortions in public facilities.

It should also be noted that there has thus far been little change in the letter of the law with regard to crimes of honor. Marriage still wipes out liability for prosectution for rape, itself not a criminal offense but an "offense against morality" whose prosecution is the responsibility not of the state but of the victim. But crimes of honor against wives, sisters, daughters, and their paramours, are no longer treated lightly in any part of the country. And in contrast with the recent past, rape victims not only are increasingly willing to bring suit against their violators, but also have strong community support—even in the south. Even in the south, such victims increasingly refuse to marry the men who have "dishonored" them. A current effort, strongly supported by Italian womens' groups, to reform the laws on rape, seduction, and crimes of honor bids fair to succeed.[13]

Irish family law, which has traditionally followed rules established by the church, is undergoing rapid change. Major reforms, some of which predate the women's movement, define and protect the legal and property rights of married and legally separated women. Others provide state assistance to unmarried mothers who keep their children and to divorced as well as deserted wives. Proposals under debate or consideration include facilitating the procedures and broadening the grounds for obtaining annulments and legal separations, revising the law of domicile so that Irish wives would no longer be regarded as dependents and would be as free as their husbands to establish residence abroad and sue for divorce, and guaranteeing the succession rights of illegitimate children. Irish courts, in a narrow category of cases, have recognized foreign divorces. Some of these developments lend legitimacy to practices and attitudes that run counter to church teaching or upon which the Irish church frowns. Her bishops, however, are most directly threatened over the divorce issue.

Marital breakdown in Ireland is dramatically on the rise, and the courts are "flooded" with applications for separation. "Few areas of Irish life are untouched by the problems faced by men and women who cannot terminate a marriage that has clearly failed." Unmarried couples who are unable to divorce their spouses, and the offspring of their unions, lack the protections of the laws of property, inheritance, guardianship, and adoption. Should such couples separate, he would be at her mercy as concerns his relationship with and rights to their children, and she at his concerning claims to their property. She would not be eligible for a deserted wives allowance. Should he die, she could not make application for a widow's pension. It is estimated that 70,000 men and women (Ireland's population stands at 3.6 million) are in this legal limbo, and the financial and emotional toll is said to be heavy. One such unmarried father has resorted to the European Commission on Human Rights—an embarrassment to a country that has "made something of a fetish of its respect for European institutions, particularly on the human rights issue."

The Women's Representative Committee has recommended the elimination of the constitutional definition of the family in terms of marriage in order that "freer," "more mature," "wide-ranging and compassionate debate" on the divorce question might take place. (The committee was careful to avoid taking a stand on the matter of divorce itself). In 1981 just over one-half and in 1984 over two-thirds of the public favored varying degrees of liberalization of the constitutional ban against divorce. The Divorce Action Group, which leads a lobbying effort, attributes changing attitudes to "a whole generation of young Irish women coming along who won't tolerate things that we didn't think about until we were much older." An all-party Committee of the Parliament will probably recommend legalization of divorce. Should the government decide to proceed with a constitutional referendum, the political battle will be "bitter" and socially divisive.[14]

The ban against the prescription, advertisement, and sale of contraceptives fell within the Irish Constitution's definition of obscenity. Beginning in the 1960s the prescription of birth control pills as "cycle regulators" and a black market in contraceptives were officially tolerated. (Opposition to the ban became something of a sport when a group of feminists took a well-publicized trip to Northern Ireland on what was dubbed the Pill Train, and on their return tossed what they believed to be birth control, but were actually aspirin, tablets to the interested spectators who greeted their arrival.) Following the Irish High Court's invalidation of the prohibition, a reluctant government relaxed the ban to the extent that married couples could obtain contraceptives—but by prescription only ("an Irish solution to an Irish problem"). The bishops' reaction was to advise physicians and pharmacists that they need not comply with requests. There is now considerable pressure, some coming from within the government, to make contraceptives available to unmarried persons and to permit over-the-counter sales.[15] Such changes would, of course, be requisite for reunification with the Protestant North.

Abortion is not permitted and abortions are not performed in Ireland. Irish women go to England to terminate their pregnancies and are not prosecuted for doing so. Only one organization admits openly to running an abortion referral system and to providing medical and psychological assistance. Authorities do not interfere with its operations. Women seeking abortions leave weekly on regularly scheduled chartered flights to Birmingham. While accurate figures are hard to come by, it has been estimated that "the number of Irish women who have abortions is about the same per 1,000 of the population as in Great Britain." The decision to induce termination is apparently made with as much dispatch by Irish women as it is by their counterparts in the United Kingdom. The majority have made the decision after consultation with the man responsible for the pregnancy.

This defiance of church teachings alarms church leaders. Equally alarming is the EEC Document on Women's Rights, which endorses abortion among other means of safe contraception. The bishops' warning that Ireland might as a consequence have to withdraw from the European Community fell, of course, on deaf ears. Further, the church is painfully aware that reunification demands the liberalization of abortion. When Pope John Paul in a 1979 visit to Ireland "prayed that Ireland would not fail the test" regarding abortion, the Irish hierarchy responded with demands for a constitutional ban against it.

The hue and cry for a referendum became a political football in the 1982 elections. The "flagging" Prime Minister Charles Haughey, in order to "prove himself a better churchman than his advancing rival, Garrett FitzGerald," supported a referendum. So did FitzGerald, whose Fine Gael-Labour coalition won. In Parliament all women deputies voted for the amendment. Women in public office remained silent; as did women's groups receiving state funding. Two deputies, one of them chairman of the Labour party, campaigned against the referendum—and lost their seats.

The public campaign was marked by great divisiveness and inflammatory rhetoric. The pulpits became rallying points, and arrangements were made for cloistered nuns who had never left their convents to come to the polls. Opposition to the amendment came from a broad coalition, including Women's Right to Choose and Protestants who viewed the enterprise as blatantly sectarian. The weekend before the September 1983 vote FitzGerald, regretting his earlier endorsement, withdrew his support. Only half the eligible electorate turned out to pass the amendment by a two-to-one margin—hardly a ringing endorsement. Several Dublin districts returned a negative vote; indeed the returns were marked by a rural-urban division. Whatever the reasons for the poor showing, many potential voters were said to be confused by the amendment's murky wording, which FitzGerald and a number of lawyers said could be interpreted as *legalizing* abortion.

For all practical purposes the amendment will have little, if any, effect. Growing numbers of Irish women will continue to obtain abortions in England. Apprehension about the future of the New Ireland Forum proved unfounded as representatives of the Republic and Northern Ireland continued their negotiations. Prime Minister FitzGeraled felt confident enough about his and his coalition's political support to place himself (however belatedly) in direct opposition to the subsequently victorious bishops. The Irish, it was recently pointed out to the authors, "are extremely good at symbolic gestures which will not change anything on the ground."[16] Nonetheless, the abortion amendment should be viewed as the Irish church's response, not only to the increasing secularization of Irish society, but to the women's movement as well. The fact that the bishops could push for and get a constitutional prohibition against abortion is indication enough that they can—and will—fight back.

Changes in women's employment and education in Italy and Ireland have been affected less by church attitudes—which themselves have undergone what amounts to transformation on these subjects over the past 40 years—than to economic opportunities and exigencies, and to other secular influences.

Women are now one-third of the Italian labor force, and over half of all Italian working women are married. Most are in the services sector, but compared to other Western industrialized countries a high proportion are in manufacturing and agriculture. A great many Italian women, like their male counterparts, work in small family-based enterprises in which women do much of the work and have considerable managerial responsibility, but remain in formally subordinate positions. Most women agricultural workers are southern peasants. Before the current worldwide economic constriction, many of them were left on the farms by their men, who emigrated to the industrial north or to northern Europe. While the circumstances of these women have been extremely difficult, their having been thrust from positions as mere breeders, field hands, and domestic laborers into roles as *de facto* family heads has worked to broaden their experience and give them increased confidence in their abilities. Significantly, some who previously supplemented family earnings with in-home piecework in glass, lace, leatherwork, and other crafts have, often under feminist aegis, organized cooperatives in which they themselves assume marketing and managerial functions.

In conformity with EEC and ILO rules, equal pay laws are on the books in Italy. As in other countries, practice does not fully reflect the law; though narrowing, wage differentials exist. Women's pay is typically about 75 percent of men's for comparable work. A 1977 law prohibits hiring discrimination or dismissal on grounds of sex, marital status, or pregnancy. Female employees may take a total of 12 months' paid maternity leave, with option for another 6 months, at full pay and no prejudice as to continued employment or promotion. Public facilities available at nominal cost to young children of working mothers have been mandated since 1971, and many are in operation. Though reliable data are not available as to the degree to which all these benefits and protections are actually available to, or known to, women workers throughout the country, on-the-spot observers are fairly sanguine, but emphasize regional and urban-rural variations.[17]

The Irish government is likewise committed as a member of EEC and ILO, and in response to women's demands, to radical change in the role of women in the economy. In this sense the women's movement has impacted dramatically. Among the goals of legislation recommended by the Committee on the Status of Women and enacted by Parliament (not without some foot-dragging) are the establishment of equal pay rates, the elimination of all forms of discrimination in employment, provisions for equality of opportunity, job protection for pregnant employees, and paid maternity leaves. Progress is monitored by the Employment Equality Agency, which is also authorized to make further recommendations; to investigate complaints; and with the Labour Court, which has the final say, to adjudicate disputes. Irish trade unions, once male bastions, now admit women to their governing councils and are concerned with issues of women's pay and working conditions.

The effects of these reforms are not yet fully known. The EEC has commissioned a study to collect data and provide analysis. In the meantime, it is apparent that women are still concentrated in low-status, low-paying jobs with little opportunity for advancement. Indeed, compared with the EEC as a whole, Ireland has fewer women in higher-status jobs. Sex segregation in employment persists. While the employment rates for women have risen modestly, women represent only 28 percent of the workforce, a rate which lags well behind that of Western Europe, and which, according to an EEC report, is not expected to change for some time. This may, in part, be explained by an economy plagued by the highest unemployment rate in Europe, by unprecedented deficits and an inflation rate that has been as high as 20 percent. Efforts to reduce deficits have resulted in funding cuts for women's shelters, and the Employment Equality Agency warns that it lacks the resources necessary to properly fulfill its mandate.

What may be more significant than the gap between the government's intentions on the one hand and realities on the other are demographic and attitudinal changes. Women have been marrying younger (although the age of marriage is again rising), having fewer children, and, unlike their mothers who finished rearing their (larger) families in their mid-fifties, will be possible candidates for the labor pool. The trend may have commenced: While the rates for employed married women are well below the European average, the past decade has witnessed a 13 percent increase. Admittedly, few women have entered prestigious professions or have risen in the private or public sectors, but this does not speak to expectations. The role models, however scarce, are there, and changes are occurring in an educational system that fosters sex-role stereotyping, discourages female accomplishment in science and mathematics, and generally dampens female ambitions. What are most significant are the psychological and sociological impacts that employment itself has on Irish women. A recent study, which controlled for background characteristics, concluded that employed as contrasted with unemployed Irish women held few of the traditional attitudes about sex roles, had confidence in themselves and the abilities of other women, were more likely to use contraceptives, were "significantly less religious," and "far more likely to support social change and policies which would lead to greater equality for women." Employment, in sum, provides a form of socialization diametrically opposed to the experience of generations of Irish women, and employed women constitute a potential social and political interest group.[18]

The central educational concern of the church has always been that the young receive approved spiritual and moral guidance. Few vestiges remain of papal opposition of the kind expressed as late as 40 years ago to equal educational opportunity for men and women. The present pope iterates that sex education is the responsibility of parents, and perhaps of pastors. The church still furnishes much of the personnel and management of both private and state-supported school systems in Italy and Ireland. In both, single-sex primary and secondary schools are typical.

There is little evidence of sex-based channeling in Italian primary and secondary education. Regional and other variations in quality of the required eight years' schooling seem to affect both sexes alike. In the last decade Italian feminists have initiated successful efforts to provide continuing education in women's studies and other important areas. Significantly, these efforts have been directed largely at working women.[19]

Over 95 percent of Ireland's schools are under church management, are single-sex, and, it is charged, condition girls "so that they may be easily slotted into the roles perceived as appropriate for them by society." Until recently, none of this occasioned much public interest. Now, however, there appears to be considerable support for a system of secular mixed schools. More tellingly, once the government considered its EEC obligations, it acknowledged that in order to equalize economic opportunity, basic changes would have to be made in curricula, in teacher attitudes, in textbooks, in vocational training, and in advising. Any serious possibility of reunification with Northern Ireland would be predicated upon the establishment of a wholly secular public educational system.

The effects of the educational system on opportunities for professional development and economic opportunities for women will linger for years to come. While at the university level the gap between entering males and females has narrowed appreciably, the gap between their chosen fields of study has not. Men predominate overwhelmingly in commerce and engineering, for example, and women in education and art. In law and medicine progress has been made to the extent that males outnumber females only about two to one. What must be emphasized here is that post-secondary education, not to mention postgraduate training, is not a possibility for the vast majority of Irish young. For this reason primary and secondary education are of crucial importance. As recently as 1981 22 percent of male and 3 percent of female school leavers obtained apprenticeships. And it was only recently that unemployed female school leavers became eligible for the dole long available to their male counterparts.[20]

For centuries Catholic teaching has profoundly affected the status of women and the roles they have played in public and private life in both Italy and Ireland. For the last 50 years, this influence has been augmented by the quasi-official position of the church in both countries. Today women's status and roles have changed radically. But the pace of change has not been the same in the two countries, and, as concerns family law and laws pertaining to procreation, the outcomes have been quite different. The changes that have occurred in both countries may be attributed to the women's movements, to the obligations that accompany membership in the European Communities, and more generally to the cultural revolutions of the 1960s along with the media's transmission of new ideas, trends, and fads across national boundaries.

The Italian movement has enjoyed dazzling successes in a relatively short period of time. The hard-fought and dramatic battles for the legalization of divorce and abortion provided momentum for the achievement of other successes such as the establishment of the new Family Law Code, and, very likely, reform of laws governing rape and crimes of honor. The Irish movement, by contrast, has measured its successes incrementally.

Much of the difference in the pace of change and character of outcomes is explicable in terms of the Catholic heritage peculiar to each country. Many Italians separate their religion from the institutional church. The former commands their devotion; the latter often elicits some cynicism. Additionally, the worldly Italian church, accomplished in the game of politics, has long since concluded that its institutional well-being is sometimes linked, among other things, to its willingness to accommodate to laws, arrangements, and attitudes of which it may not approve. It is finding ways to make at least temporary peace with divorce, contraception, abortion, and feisty Italian women who are good Catholics *and* feminists.

This is not the case for Ireland. Whatever the misgivings about the church's temporal (although informal) authority, it is, as an institution, taken as seriously as the faith it expounds. The Irish, historically, have no reason to doubt the motives of their bishops and their priests. Few politicians are willing to grapple with the church directly or publicly, although successive governments have been quite willing to look the other way as Irish women have found ways to obtain birth control pills, and openly take off for England to terminate pregnancies.

Having said all this, the fact is that the Irish church, like the Italian church, cannot prevail indefinitely. A significant segment of Irish public opinion favors the legalization of divorce, the general availability of contraceptives, and a system of public education in which the church has no responsibilities. (Since abortions are so readily obtained elsewhere, that issue may simply not be salient until reunification becomes a real possibility.) Add to this the consciousness that reunification (whatever the probability) must entail guaranteeing the civil rights of *Protestants*, there can be little doubt that the church must at least contemplate making the sorts of concessions that may now be perceived as striking at the core of its being.

In the meantime, it has been the women's movement that articulated and dramatized the issues, that lobbied for reforms, that mobilized the government, and that made it clear that henceforth Irish women would no longer accept the roles assigned to them by Ireland's traditional Catholic culture.

The authors thank the following persons for invaluable help in gathering information and in other aspects of preparation of this paper: John Blackwell, University College, Dublin; Basil Chubb, University of Dublin; Clara Clark, Organizing Secretary of the Council for the Status of Women; Renée Dominis, RAI, Rome; Nuala Fennel, Minister of State for Women's Affairs; Brigid Laffan, National Institute for Higher Education, Limerick; Maurice Manning, University College, Dublin, and Member of Parliament.

NOTES

1. Lincoln T. Bouscaren, *Canon Law*, 4th rev. ed. (Milwaukee: Bruce Publishers, 1966). The 1983 Canon Law Code revision (text not yet available) "deletes references to women as having the same canonical status as children and imbeciles—a status bestowed as a measure of protection but seen now as an assertion of inferiority," and also modifies the unilateral right of a husband to choose the marital residence. *Chicago Sun-Times*, October 27, 1983.

2. See, e.g., Pius XI, *Casti Connubi* (Encyclical), 1930; Pius XII, Allocutions of 10 September 1941 and 25 February 1942; John XXIII, *Gaudium et Spes* (Encylical), 1962; John Paul II, *On Human Work* (Encyclical), 1981; *Chicago Tribune*, September 13, 1983, sec. 1, 5; *New York Times*, December 2, 1982, 1; James H. Provost, "The Revised Code: A Promising Vintage," *America* (February 5, 1983), 85–88.

3. Anticlericalism is the view that church authority, unquestionably right and justified in spiritual matters, is misplaced in temporal law and politics.

4. Basil Chubb, *The Government and Politics of Ireland* (Stanford, CA: Stanford University Press, 1982), especially Chapter 2; Jonathan Marcus, "Ireland in Transition," *The World Today* (March 1983), 113–122.

5. Articles 40 and 41; Patricia Redlich, "Women and the Family," in Margaret MacCurtain and Donnacha O'Corrain, eds., *Women in Irish Society: The Historical Dimension* (Westport, CT: Greenwood Press, 1979), 82–91, 86.

6. Mary Cornelia Porter and Corey Venning, "Catholicism and Women's Role in Italy and Ireland," in Lynn Iglitzin and Ruth Ross, eds., *Women in the World: A Comparative Study* (Santa Barbara, CA: ABC-Clio, 1976), 93–97.

7. Yvonne Ergas, "Feminism and the Italian Party System: Women's Politics in a Decade of Turmoil," *Comparative Politics* (April 1982), 253–279; Dinah Dodds, "Extra-Parliamentary Feminism and Social Change in Italy," *International Journal of Women's Studies* (March 1982), 148–160; Renee Dominis, taped communication to author (Rome: December 27, 1983).

8. Dublin Founding Group, "The Civil Wrongs of Irish-women," IDOC (August 28, 1971); Chubb; Nell McCafferty, "Ireland's Paradox: 'The Womb and the Border,'" *Ms* (March 1983), 94–97; Committee on the Status of Women, *Interim Report on Equal Pay*, presented to the Minister for Finance (Dublin: The Stationery Office, 1971); Committee on the

Status of Women, *Report to the Minister for Finance* (Dublin: The Stationery Office, 1973); The Women's Representative Committee, *Progress Report on the Implementation of the Recommendations in the Report of the Committee on the Status of Women*, and *Second Progress Report* (Dublin: The Stationery Office, 1976 and 1978); Employment Equality Agency, *Annual Report and Accounts* (Dublin: Employment Equality Agency, 1977–1983); Council for the Status of Women and the National Women's Forum, *Irish Women Speak Out* (Dublin: Co-op Books Ltd., 1981); Bernadette Barry, *Women at Home* (Dublin: Council for the Status of Women, 1983); *Irish Women's Diary and Guidebook* (Dublin: Irish Feminist Information Publications, 1983); Mary Robinson, "Women and the New Irish State," in MacCurtain and O'Corrain, 58–70, 66–67.

9. Margaret L. Inglehart, "Political Interest in Western European Women: An Historical and Empirical Comparative Analysis," *Comparative Political Studies* (October 1981), 320.

10. Porter and Venning, 93.

11. Gisbert H. Flanz, *Comparative Women's Rights and Political Participation: Europe* (Dobbs Ferry, NY: Transnational Publishers, 1983), 217–219; O. Sepe, "Considerazione sulla posizione della donna nell'amministrazione statale in Italia," *Rivista Trimestrale di Diritto Publico* (1975), 2077–2111.

12. Mary E. Daly, "Women, Work and Trade Unionism," in MacCurtain and O'Corrain, 71–81; Paul Kellner and Mary Holland, "Can the U.K. Learn from the Irish?" *New Statesman* (February 19, 1983), 5–6; Brigid Laffan, "Alice in Wonderland: Women in Irish Politics," unpublished paper presented to the Women's Political Association, Dublin, November 1983; Nell McCafferty, "Ireland's Paradox" and excerpt from *Spare Rib* in *off our backs* (July 1982), 7; Maurice Manning, "Women in Irish Politics 1922–77," in MacCurtain and O'Corrain, 92–101; Robinson, "Women in the New Irish State." See generally Chubb, *The Government and Politics of Ireland;* Frank Litton, ed., *Unequal Achievement: The Irish Experience 1957–1982* (Dublin: Institute of Public Administration, 1982); Howard R. Penniman, ed., Ireland at the Polls: The Dail Elections of 1977 (Washington, DC: American Enterprise Institute for Public Policy Research, 1978); David E. Schmitt, *The Irony of Irish Democracy* (Lexington, MA: Lexington Books, 1973):

13. Valerio Pocar and Paola Ronfani, "Family Law in Italy: Legislative Innovation and Social Change," *Law and Society Review* (Summer 1978), 645–664; Dominis; Ergas; Dodds; articles in *New York Times, Economist, New Statesman*, 1976–1980.

14. See generally William Binchy, "New Vistas in Irish Family Law," *Journal of Family Law* 15 (1976–1977); Alan Joseph Shatter, *Family Law in the Republic of Ireland* (Postmarnock, County Dublin: 1977). Redlich, 85; Jon Nordheimer, "Searing New Social Conflicts Tear Irish Church and Family," *New York Times*, March 22, 1984, 8; *New Statesman* (March 12, 1983), 3; Porter and Venning, 98; Women's Representative Committee (1978), 60–79; The Law Reform Commission, *Report on Divorce A Mensa Et Thoro and Related Matters* and *Report on Domicile and Habitual Residence as Connecting Factors in the Conflict of Laws*

(Dublin: The Law Reform Commission, 1983).

15. Porter and Venning, 85–87; McCafferty, "Ireland's Paradox," 97; in invalidating the contraceptive statute, the Irish High Court was "influenced by constitutional developments on the subject in the United States," Binchy, 666, quoted in Chubb, 281; Nordheimer; *New Statesman*, July 11, 1980, 34. As the book goes to press the Irish Parliament has given preliminary approval, by a 83–80 vote, for the sale of contraceptives to anyone 18 years or older. "Political commentators here describe the vote as the first defeat ever sustained by the Catholic Church in a head-on confrontation with an Irish Government on social legislation." The "Pill Bill," is expected to be enacted despite threats against and harassment of its supporters. *New York Times*, February 21, 1985, p. 4, col. 6; *Chicago Tribune*, p. 3, col. 2.

16. For journalistic and political commentary on the referendum see Mary Holland, "Ireland's Bishops Decide," *New Statesman*, April 3, 1981, 6–7 and "Needlepoint Debate," *New Statesman*, February 25, 1983, 11; *New Statesman*, July 1980, 34; *New Statesman*, May 21, 1982, 12–13; "Misbegotten Referendum," *Economist*, September 3, 1983, 15; Nordheimer, "Irish To Vote Tomorrow on Abortion Measure," *New York Times*, September 6, 1983, 12. For an analysis of the vote, see "Abortion Vote Draws Only Half of Irish Electorate," *Chicago Tribune*, September 7, 1983, 10; BBC "International Call," September 24, 1983; *Irishwomen's Diary*, 146–147. For characteristics of Irish women obtaining abortions see R. S. Rose, "Abortion and Irish Women," *Irish Journal of Sociology* (1977), 71–119. The amendment reads as follows: "The state acknowledges the right to life of the unborn and, with due regard to the equal right of the mother, guarantees in its laws to respect and, as far as practicable, by its laws to defend and vindicate that right." (The referendum provides for the exceptions of ectopic pregnancy and cancer of the uterus, Marcus, 121). The authors appreciate the wise comments of an Irish academic, letter to Mary Cornelia Porter, February 21, 1984.

17. United Nations, *Statistical Yearbook*, 1981; International Labor Organization, *Yearbook of Labor Statistics*, 1982; Dominis.

18. See generally Commission on the Status of Women, *Reports;* Women's Representative Committee, *Progress Reports;* Employment Equality Agency, *Reports;* Eunice McCarthy, "Women and Work in Ireland," in MacCurtain and O'Corrain, 103–117; Daly; Robinson; John Blackwell, "Digest of Statistics on Women in the Labour Force," draft paper for EEA (September 1982) and "Statistics on Women in the Labour Force and Related Topics," draft paper for EEA (February 23, 1983). For the Irish economy, see Marcus; Holland, "The Prime Minister Who Cannot Tell a Lie," *New Statesman*, February 5, 1983, 4. For present trends and future implications, see Joseph Lee, "Society and Culture," Litton, 1–18, 12; Margaret Fine-Davis, "Social-Psychological Predictors of Employment Status of Married Women in Ireland," *Journal of Marriage and the Family* (February 1979), 145–158, 149. John Blackwell commented helpfully on this and other sections.

19. *Annuario Statistico Italiano, 1983* (Rome: Istituto Centrale di Statistiche).

20. Chubb, 30–31; *Irish Women Speak Out*, 48; For an overall view of the

problem see *Schooling and Sex-Roles* (Dublin: Employment Equality Agency, 1982); Economic Equality Agency, *Report* (1981), 35; Blackwell, "Education and Training," chapter on a study prepared for the EEA, 1982; *Schooling and Sex-Roles*, 36; McCafferty, *off our backs*, 7.

RECOMMENDED READINGS

Republic of Ireland

Chubb, Basil. *The Government and Politics of Ireland.* Stanford, CA: Stanford University Press, 1982.
Excellent coverage of Irish political institutions and processes, with insights concerning the importance of history, church influence and the forces of social change. Considerable attention to and analysis of the women's movement and its political and social ramifications.

MacCurtain, Margaret, and Donna O'Corrain. *Women in Irish Society.* Westport, CT: The Greenwood Press, 1979.
Collection of essays which first treat the position of women from the beginnings of recorded Irish history, through the periods of foreign conquests and domination, the Famine, the Revolution and the establishment of the Republic. The second part of the book is devoted to essays covering the contemporary scene— women's roles in economic and political life, and women in the family.

Government Publications: A number of publications document the status of Irish women, the problems they face in achieving equality and equity and the progress they have made. The publications contain a wide variety of recommendations and report on their implementation. Especially significant are:
Commission on the Status of Women, *Interim Report on Equal Pay: Report to the Minister for Finance.* Dublin: The Stationery Office, 1971 and 1973.

Women's Representative Committee, *Progress Report on the Implementation of the Recommendations in the Report of the Commission on the Status of Women.* Dublin: The Stationery Office, 1976 and 1978.

Women at Home: A Report on Nationwide Get-Togethers of Women (Dublin: Council for the Status of Women, undated); Mary Ena Walsh and the Council for the Status of Women, *Women in Rural Ireland: A Report of Get-Togethers Held in 1982* (Dublin: Council for the Status of Women, 1983); The National Women's Forum, *Irish Women Speak Out: A Plan of Action* (Dublin: Council for the Status of Women and Co-op Books, 1981).

Italy

Allum, P. *Italy: Republic without Government?* New York: Norton, 1973.
Good introduction to the structure of Italian national and regional government, with insight into the interaction of historical, political, and social factors.

Barzini, Luigi. *The Italians.* Boston: Atheneum, 1977.
Wide-ranging essay beautifully and accurately expressing the "flavor" of Italy.

Cornelison, Ann. *Women of the Shadows.* Boston: Little, Brown, 1976.
Conveys lives of southern Italian peasant women, and provides clues as to the sources of their strength.

Dodds, Dinah. "Extra-Parliamentary Feminism and Social Change in Italy," *International Journal of Women's Studies* (March 1982), 148–160.
Describes feminist groups in the Rome area; conveys a sense of how Italian feminists see themselves, and their typical forms of organization and interaction.

Ergas, Yvonne. "Feminism and the Italian Party System: Women's Politics in a Decade of Turmoil," *Comparative Politics* (April 1982), 253–279.
Fairly detailed and judicious account of Italian feminism in the context of the general sociopolitical situation.

5

From the Moon to the Sun: Women's Liberation in Japan

Kazuko Sugisaki
Meijo University

The Passive Revolution

August of 1945 marked sudden and tremendous changes in the history of Japanese women, as World War II ended with Japan's unconditional surrender. The 14 years of war, beginning with the Manchurian incident of 1931, devastated the land and the people of Japan. Close to three million soldiers in the battlefields and almost 800,000 civilians at home perished because of the wars. City streets were filled with hungry veterans, orphans, and many men and women without jobs. The people in Japan were not only without money, food, and a place to live, but many also were without hope for the future.

Women worked hard and efficiently during the war years and assumed responsibility for the domestic economy. They ran the factories, transportation system, shops, offices; they farmed and tended the animals. When the war ended in complete defeat, all their efforts and sufferings seemed to be nullified. They had lost family members; they had sacrified so much for the war, and now many of them had to face the postwar confusion alone. Although those were hard and depressing times, there were unforeseen results that came from women's war experiences. Their forced participation in all the fields of social activities gave them a strong sense of self-assurance. They proved they had the abilities to run society as well as men did. Unfortunately, they were excluded from government, the most powerful decision-making body of the nation.

Only ten days after Emperor Hirohito's own voice was heard for the first time in history as he announced Japan's surrender, Ichikawa Fusae, a long-time leader of the women's suffrage movement in Japan, organized the Women's Committee on Postwar Countermeasures with several other women. The committee petitioned the government, the General Headquarters of the Occupation Forces (GHQ), and each political party with the following resolutions:

1. Grant suffrage to women over the age of 20, and the right to run for office to those over 25
2. Change the government system on the prefectural and municipal levels to benefit women and children
3. Grant civil rights to women
4. Revise the Peace Preservation Laws[1]
5. Reorganize the civil service system to permit participation of women

Those who received the biggest benefit from the occupation policy after the war were Japanese women. Under the strong influence of the GHQ the new Showa Constitution was enacted on May 3, 1947, and it proclaims that "the Japanese people forever renounce war as a sovereign right of the nation, and the threat or use of force as means of settling international disputes."[2] Five articles assure fundamental rights for women. Article 14 states that all people are equal under the law, and there shall be no discrimination in political, economic, or social relations because of race, creed, sex, social status, or family origin. Article 15 guarantees universal adult suffrage. Article 24 requires that marriage shall be based only on the mutual consent of both sexes, and that it shall be maintained through mutual cooperation. Article 26 provides for equal education based upon ability. And Article 44 permits women to run for office.

In light of women's prewar dismal status in the areas of equality, discrimination, suffrage, and marriage, it might be helpful to examine their history briefly to better understand the significance of their new situation.

A Brief History of Japanese Women

In early Japanese history, women held powerful positions. During the sixth and seventh centuries *one-half* of the Japanese imperial rulers were women. They were strong leaders with a keen interest in cultural activities, but at the same time, they were the keepers of the calendar—a very important role when success and failure of agriculture depended entirely on the sun and other natural elements of seasons—in the shamanistic tradition.

A few of the great empresses are worth mentioning here. One is Empress Jingo (200– 269), who was revered as the great ruler second only to the legendary Great Sun Goddess. She led the army with her husband to Kyushu to quell an uprising. After her husband's death she led her soldiers on to Korea in the hope of conquering it. Empress Gemmyo (707– 715) established the first permanent capital of Japan in Nara. Empress Shotoku (764– 770) compiled *Manyoshu*, a collection of Japanese poetry that is still read and enjoyed by many Japanese. (The book has been translated into English as well.) These and many other empresses played important roles, and set standards for culture, religion, and the social mood of the time.

From the late sixth to the early ninth centuries, the rulers sent envoys to China, and they copied all aspects of Chinese civilization, including the form of government. With the foreign civilization came both a foreign religion and philosophy, Buddhism and Confucianism. In Buddhism and Confucianism, which rapidly permeated the upper society of early Japan, women's position was very low. According to the teaching of the Tendai and Shingon sects of Buddhism, for instance, women are placed in this world to interfere with men's attaining enlightenment, and for women there is absolutely no hope for salvation either in this world or in the next. Later, the Pure Land Sect modified the doctrine proclaiming that women can attain enlightenment; however, unless one became a devoted nun, the conditions were almost impossible to fulfill.[3]

The government issued the Taiho Law Code in 701 to bind subjects with very rigid moral laws based upon Confucian and Buddhist philosophy. Women could no longer be the head of a household as long as there were men in the family. Women also were forced to observe the teaching of three obediences: obey your father as a daughter, once married obey your husband, and obey your son when aged. The code also changed the time-honored maternal structure of the family.

Many centuries later, during the Tokugawa period (1600– 1867) when Tokugawa *Bakufu*[4] closed the country to the outside world except for the Dutch, who could come to a few sea ports in Kyushu, women's position had gone from bad to worse. As the Tokugawa asserted their centralized dictatorship, they installed a rigid class hierarchy. Primogeniture controlled inheritance; younger sons could be successors in waiting, but daughters had no right over the property. The families with no sons either had to adopt a son or have the husband of their daughter carry on their family name. A woman in the warrior class could own very little—some kimonos, tools, and furniture given by her father at marriage. If she also had money, it belonged to her husband to dispose of in any way he wished. If her husband's property was confiscated by his lord, her money was also taken away. Poligamy was common. If a wife could not bear a son, her husband took a mistress. A wife could not initiate a divorce, but her husband and his parents could at any time by simply giving her a divorce letter. If a wife committed adultery, she was liable for punishment by death. A divorced woman usually did not remarry unless so ordered, because she was bound by the virtue of chastity. All these incredibly unfavorable conditions of women were legalized by "house laws" issued by each feudal lord to control his retainers and their families in his fief.

Kaibara Ekken (1630–1714), neo-Confucian scholar who published more than 100 books on Confucianist morals, wrote a book for women called *Onna Daigaku* (Great Learning for Women, 1672), to teach them how to live. Kaibara claims that a woman must find no faults with her husband, and look to him as her lord whom she must serve with deep reverence. She should be trained for the domestic duties of weaving, washing, sewing, cooking, or in arts such as incense burning, flower arrangement, and the tea ceremony.

Compared with the position women in the warrior class held during the long feudal period, those of the merchant class possessed a little more freedom. Since the success of the family business depended more on personal abilities than on the order of birth or sex of children, property division was left to its owner's judgment. Therefore, a woman, if capable, could inherit property from her father. The wife of a big merchant, while not helping in the store openly, took great responsibility for personnel and domestic management. As the riches began accumulating in the hands of successful merchants, some of their wives had control over a great deal of money. However, their emotional freedom was still very much restricted, and as portrayed in Chikamatsu dramas,[5] a man and woman in love often had to resort to a double suicide when their relationship was not socially acceptable.

After two and a half centuries of despotic control of the Tokugawa Shogunate, the Meiji Restoration in 1868 disbanded more than 260 fiefs and declared that all the people in Japan were to live under one law, the Meiji Imperial Constitution. People were now free to choose their occupations. The first six years of primary education became compulsory for all children, including girls (1872). With Ambassador Iwakura and his mission, five young girls from ages 8 to 15 were sent to the United States to study (1871). Christian missionaries were now welcomed. Liscensed prostitutes were to be freed (1872).

These were impressive reformations on the surface. However, in reality, changes from the old system were slow and ineffective, especially for women. For instance, even though education became compulsory, the tuition parents had to pay for each of their children was so high that most of the farmers could not afford to send their youngsters to school. In 1897, 80.6 percent of boys but only 50.8 percent of the girls went to school.[6]

In November 1875 the government opened the first Teachers Training College for Women; however, less than 80 young women entered, and only 15 received credentials. But the number of similar institutions soon increased, and by 1882 more than 2,500 women were teaching at primary schools. In 1881 a Nurse Training School and in 1899 a Medical College for Women were opened. Educational opportunities for women certainly increased. And yet the principles of women's education were still based upon historic Confucian role of a lower status. The Imperial Rescript of Education was issued in 1890, and read at important ceremonies in almost every school until the end of World War II. Under its guidelines, women were still educated to be subordinate to men, namely, to become good wives and wise mothers, and the full development of personality for women as free independent individuals was essentially ignored. Fukuzawa Yukichi, who founded Keio University in Tokyo, said that "Japan was hell for women, and as long as they were treated so miserably, the country would remain uncivilized."[7] Christian schools for girls were opened by missionaries in many of the cities, and most of them are still prominent today. These schools, which were relatively free from the imperial authority, provided access to freer and higher-level education. Direct contact with foreign teachers, many of whom were eager and idealistic Christians, gave the students the opportunities to experience Christian ethics, democratic ideas, and Western social manners. Some of the courses modeled after the high-level colleges in the United States were conducted in English, preparing the girls to pursue further education overseas.

At the turn of the century, the Meiji government issued a new Civil Code; however, this code provided few changes for women. Laws governing family relations were still based on patriarchal authority. Perpetuation of the family line was considered most important, and feudal dictatorial family attitudes were apparent in every aspect. Primogeniture was the rule, and women had no right to inherit the family property. Women were legally considered incompetent, along with minors and the physically and mentally handicapped. Adultery committed by a wife was a crime. A divorce could be obtained with the mutual consent of a couple. But because a wife had no right either over her husband's property (even after she had contributed to it) or over her children, a divorce on equal terms was literally impossible. Reformation of this Civil Code was one of the main goals of the women's movements since its enactment, but it was not until 1948, after World War II, that the democratic code under the new Showa Constitution replaced it. Success in wars with China (1894-1895) and with Russia (1904-1905) justified the course Japan was following. Militarism and conservative nationalism were predominant trends, along with the development of modern capitalism. Women were kept subordinate, even though in the first factories women provided the cheap labor that enabled the development of capitalism. The Confucian womanly virtues of obedience and docility continued to be emphasized.

In revolt against these trends, Hiratsuka Raicho (1886-1971) started a magazine with several of her friends in 1911. It was the first magazine run totally by women. In the first issue of the magazine, *Seito* (Blue Stockings), Hiratsuka wrote: "In the beginning a woman was the sun. She was a true human being. But now she is only the moon. Her life depends on others. She can shine only when reflecting light from others. Hers is the face of the moon, pale and sick."[8] The women gathered for the magazine were well-educated intellectuals from the middle or upper classes. Because the magazine was literary rather than political, their main plea was for freedom of love and freedom of spirit for women. They challenged the customary virtues women were taught to obey. In the January issue of 1913, Hiratsuka wrote: "The new women wish not only to destroy morals and laws established by men's egoism but also to create a new kingdom upon spiritual enlightenment bestowed by the sun."[9] Several issues of *Seito* were banned by the government, and in 1916 it was terminated. However, its influence on the eager intellectual women of the time was enormous, and even today Hiratsuka's courage and ideas are an inspiration to women.

As early as 1879 a few women began a movement for women's rights. Kususe Kita, nicknamed "Grandma Women's Rights," lectured on the island of Shikoku. Kishida Toshiko in Osaka lectured and published in a newspaper the first article on equal rights written by a woman.

The brilliant career of Ichikawa Fusae, who had been a powerful political leader of Japanese women's movements all her life and died in office as a member of the Diet (Parliament) in 1981 at the age of 88, best illustrates the history of the movement during the first half of the twentieth century. She was born in Aichi Prefecture in 1893. Encouraged by her father, she pursued higher education and became a teacher. But when faced with salary discrimination (she received only one-sixth the salary of men teachers), she became disgusted and left teaching. She went to Tokyo and formed the New Womens' Association (1919) with Hiratsuka and Oku Mumeo, both of whom were already known activists. The association, along with other organizations, aimed at the abolishment of Article 5 of the Peace Preservation Law (see note 1). It took them three years to achieve this goal. In 1922 the two Japanese characters for *women* and *minors* were erased from Article 5, and women at last were permitted to participate in political activites.

Ichikawa, after breaking up with the other two leaders, went to the United States. She studied with a third-grade class in Seattle to learn English, and later took extension courses at Columbia University. Ichikawa met U.S. suffragists Alice Paul and Carrie Chapman Catt. She also met Jane Addams at Hull House. Her experience in the United States gave a strong impact to her career, and helped to form the issues she pursued during her lifetime: women's suffrage, social reform, and the preservation of peace.

Coming back to Japan in 1924, Ichikawa organized the Women's Suffrage League. By this time men over 25 had achieved suffrage, and it was thought that women would soon be granted this right. Women's organizations amalgamated and expanded. They lobbied at the Diet, and in 1928, 13 women's organizations collected 32,000 signatures to endorse the petition.[10] The bill for women's suffrage passed the Lower House in 1930, but was rejected by the Upper House. Ichikawa and others were prepared to reintroduce it, but a sudden shift in government policy occurred, and the movement was severely suppressed.

This period was called the Dark Valley of Showa. Beginning with the Manchurian incident in 1931, the militaristic government of Japan plunged the nation into consecutive wars, the last of which was World War II. Government-sponsored women's societies such as the Patriotic Women's Society and the Women's National Defence Association were organized, recruiting thousands of women in the name of patriotism. Ichikawa's association, even though she was proud of its members' higher intellectual level and free spirit, was also thrust into the war situation. During the wars she worked

for the Patriotic Press Association, and in 1940 she toured China
speaking on the theme of Greater East Asia Coprosperity, the slogan
the government propagated. It was for these activities performed
during the war that she was purged by the occupational authorities
in 1947, when she was preparing herself to run for the House of
Councillors. More than 169,000 signatures were collected to petition
her return to public life, but this was not granted to her until 1950.
Except for one defeat in 1971 Ichikawa was elected to the House of
Councillors from 1953 to 1981, when she died in office. With her
death, Japanese women lost their most sympathetic and forceful
leader. Now, nearly 40 years after the end of the war, many new
women leaders are coming onto the scene. For them the long history
of suffering of Japanese women is fortunately only a myth of the
past.

Women's Political Action in Postwar Japan

After the Showa Constitution in 1947 women gradually took greater
advantage of their new suffrage, so that by 1969 more women than
men voted in national elections. In 1980, 75 percent (a surprisingly
high percentage for the voters of any election) of women voted,
compared to 53 percent for men.[11] In the first election after the war
when women were at last allowed to participate, women members
of the Diet rose from 0 to 39, and finally leveled off at 25 in 1982. This
represents only a small percentage of the total Diet (3.3 percent) but
is significant historically. Of greater importance are the regional
self-governing organizations; here women represent one-third of
the total employees (1978).

In the 100 years since the Meiji Restoration, Japanese women
have come a long way. Ironically the policies of the occupation
coincided with the goals of Japanese women and produced many
dramatic changes: Women's suffrage is achieved, women are admitted to national universities, and licensed prostitution is abolished.
The principle of equal pay for equal labor is ensured. Housewives
organize, and a Eugenic Protection Law benefits mothers. Women
are no longer treated as imcompetent; they can inherit and own
property, and the law of primogeniture is finally abolished. Parental
consent is no longer needed for marriage. Divorce is obtained by
mutual consent and property is divided between husband and wife.

In 1955 the first Mother's Congress was held in Tokyo, anticipating
the World Congress in Switzerland. Two thousand mothers attended, including a mother with a baby tied to her back from a small

southern island whose expenses were paid with "one-yen-a-woman" contributions. The conference was divided into three sections: protection of children's happiness, preservation of world peace, and protection of women's life and rights. Thirteen resolutions were adopted, including: improvement of health and social insurance for women; increasing the education budget; screening harmful movies, comic books, and toys for children; prevention of traffic accidents; objection to forced retirement of women; and appeal for nuclear disarmament. Yambe Kazuko, director of the action committee for the 30th Mother's Congress of 1984, who had participated in it every year from the very first, said that ". . . the congress still provides opportunities for mothers to discuss their everyday problems even though women's status is now much improved and the nature of their problems is different. And the international cooperation of mothers becomes more necessary now that world peace is threatened by the increasing nuclear arms race."[12]

The first Consumer Conference was held in 1963. Consumerism, almost entirely supported by women, had become a strong and effective movement in Japan. Women's organizations paraded with their famous rice-paddle placards to keep consumer prices down. They were instrumental in the passage of the Basic Consumer Protection Law (1968).

These are only a few examples of women's political participation in the postwar period. Because of women's efforts the following laws to improve women's status were passed in the last two decades: Mother and Child Health Law (1966), Working Women's Welfare Law (1972), and Child-Care Leave Law (1975). Another landmark of women's progress was the appointment of Nakayama Masa as the first minister of health and welfare (1960), Ogata Sadako, the first woman minister in the Diplomatic Corps (1976), and Takahashi Nobuko, the first woman ambassador (1980).

Growing through Education

The "International Women's Year" in 1975 had a pronounced effect on Japanese women. Following the government's announcement of a National Plan of Action for the International Decade of Women, regional self-governing bodies announced their own plans of action. They invited many women to contribute to the process. In Kyoto, 20 of the 28 members of the planning committees were women. In Mie Prefecture, 13 of 25 members were women. Previously, women's participation in such planning was very rare. In the process of

initiating action plans for the women's decade, Japanese women
not only clarified goals for solving women's problems, but also
started the first step toward the goals.

According to the paper issued by the National Women's Education Center, one common goal these plans share is to acquire the
ability and strength to plan and choose their own way of life.[13] To
reach this goal Japanese women would have to make a great breakthrough and seek opportunities to train and improve themselves
both in work and education. The idea of permanent education has
lately been attracting such attention in Japan that it may be interesting to discuss how programs of life-long education for women
(especially for married women, since 95 percent of our women are
married by their late thirties) have been developed in recent years.

The number of women receiving higher education is growing
every year. Although compulsory education ends at the ninth grade
in Japan, 95 percent go beyond that grade.[14] After receiving education and training in institutions of higher learning, they are rea-
sonably well prepared to meet the demands of various jobs. Indeed
68 percent of women college graduates take jobs, but within a few
years most of them discontinue their work for marriage or
childbirth.[15] However, those women who withdraw from initial
work opportunities will very likely try to participate in some kind of
social activities in 10 or 15 years. After the period of childbirth and
intensive child care, women face another period, Period III, a time of
relative freedom.[16] With the average lifespan expanding, they now
enjoy 20 to 30 years of mature and healthy life in this period.
Because the number of children in each family has decreased (the
average is now two) and the use of electric appliances has lessened
the time spent for domestic labor, housewives during Period III now
have ample free time. Financially they have sufficient reserves so
that their monetary contribution is not necessary for the family. The
use of this free time has become an important concern; so much so
that it created a social phenomenon—the Culture Center.

The Culture Center is a learning institute mostly run by private
businesses such as big newspapers, department stores, television
networks, etc., that provides study opportunities for anyone who
wishes to learn. According to a survey taken by the Association for
Promoting Recreational Culture in 1978, more than 100 major centers were registered. A 1980 report issued by the Ministry of Education on systems of life-long learning says that in 1979 one out of two
persons had some kind of learning opportunity, whether in sports, a
hobby, art, or social and human sciences.

When the Asahi Culture Center run by Asahi, the newspaper with the largest circulation in Japan, opened in 1974, it offered only 38 courses, but by 1980 these increased to 130. Some of the courses offered are: flower arrangement, tea ceremony, classical dance, Noh mask making, dressmaking, knitting, cooking, psychology, Japanese literature, French language and literature, creative writing, Russian, Korean, Chinese, yoga, aerobics, etc. The registration fee is about 22 U.S. dollars. By paying the fee anyone can become a member of the center for three years, and can take as many courses as one wishes. Tuition for one course averages a little less than 100 U.S. dollars for three months. Lesson hours are flexible, and the same courses are scheduled repeatedly on weekdays, including Saturdays, from 9:00 A.M. to 8:00 P.M. Teachers at the big centers near railroad terminals and civic centers are rather well known through journalism or TV programs.

Almost all the culture centers are extremely successful because they meet the needs of women, especially during Period III. About 80 percent of the students of culture centers are women, of whom one half belongs to the age group from 30 to 50, and about 42 percent of these women are college graduates.[17] In the last ten years, the demand of the students shifted from mere popular hobbies to more serious courses such as religion, literature, philosophy, and psychology. This reflects a trend that women, previously confined to a role of wife and mother, now seek to enrich their cultural background through education. However, courses concerned with direct women's problems have not been successful at the centers. They were offered from time to time, but had to be closed because of lack of enrollment.

Women seem to turn, for such studies, to public institutions. Action Plans for the International Women's Year made by the government and many other regional self-governing bodies include study programs for women. The Public Hall (available in every community), the House for Working Women, Women's Education Center, and other such public institutions organized programs to study and discuss women's problems related to family situations, job discrimination, children's welfare, and other relevant subjects. These courses are offered free of charge or with minimum fees because of government subsidy. Lecturers for these programs may not be publicly well known, but are community leaders whose concerns are closely related to the community, or specialists in particular women's problems. In 1981, a total of 1,402,774 women participated in all kinds of study programs sponsored by the government.[18]

Nakano Ward of Tokyo provides a good example of a public study program. In 1980 Nakano Ward Office established a preparation committee for a women's seminar. The committee, mostly women, determined the purpose of the seminar. It was to deepen women's understanding of the problems involved in family situations, politics, occupation, and other social activities. It was hoped, in making an effort to solve these problems, the women of Nakano Ward would acquire an understanding of each other, and thus strengthen their cooperation. The main theme of the seminar was to be Women's Independence and Solidarity. Running for ten months from September 1980, with Ichikawa Fusae as the opening speaker, the whole seminar was very successful. Women studied such themes as: the historical significance of the International Women's Year, men's and women's roles, psychotherapy, children's welfare, recreation, welfare of the old, social problems rising from the increased percentage of the elderly; and women's liberation in Sweden.

When the seminar was announced 250 applied, five times as many as the alloted capacity of 50, and participants had to be selected by lot. The Nakano seminar was a great success in several different ways: (1) It was a real joint project of the ward administration and the residents; (2) women took an active part in the project from the very beginning; (3) subjects studied were those of immediate concern to women; (4) it attracted close attention as a model case not only of Nakano residents but also of those concerned with women's problems in many other cities of Japan; (5) it received such encouraging feedback from the seminar participants that the further development of similar projects became possible.[19]

While informal study opportunities for women have steadily increased, university-related formal educational opportunities are still very much limited for Japanese women. Compared with American universities, where numerous credit-oriented extension courses are offered to the public, Japanese universities have been mostly for young people under 25. Theoretically anyone with a high school diploma could enter a university. However, in reality, entrance examinations for national and private universities of higher standards are so difficult that it is practically impossible to pass unless one is well prepared. Also, without a proper scholarship system it is financially not feasible for working women or housewives to go back to school when the university curriculum is totally oriented to full-time students.

Rikkyo University, a large Christian university in Tokyo, was the first to open a channel for adult education. Starting in 1979, they adjusted the entrance examination so that adults who were long out of high school could pass. An English examination, a short critical essay, and a personal interview were all that were required. This first attempt to open the gate of an ivory tower to the public was widely publicized and welcomed as an epoch-making advance in the closed university system in Japan.

Whereas being admitted as a full-time student is very difficult, almost all national universities and many private universities have an auditor system. Anyone with the permission of the professor in charge can audit the course by paying tuition (70 to 100 U.S. dollars a course). But the units studied cannot be converted into credit toward a degree or diploma. There are also many national and private universities that offer lectures open to the public. Tōyō University, a Buddhist institution, presented open lectures even before World War II. These open lectures of universities offer a great variety of subjects from natural science to social and human science. Registration is almost as easy as for the Culture Center, but no credits are granted, which can discourage the auditors a great deal. In general, university programs for adult education are not yet fully developed in Japan. There is still a tendency in Japanese society to regard an adult woman student with curious scrutiny, and this can be a hindrance to women's life-long education.

In this section we have shown study opportunities offered to women during Period III. The almost explosive energy that these women have shown toward learning in the last decade is something new in Japanese history. Freed from financial and domestic responsibilities to a certain extent for the first time, they can aim at higher education. They began to learn to enjoy or to develop womanly skills, but then as their social and spiritual environment widened, and as they became more aware of the problems women are facing everywhere, their focus of interest has greatly shifted. The problems originated essentially from the deep-rooted social attitude of discrimination against women, and they are now making great efforts to face and solve these problems. Through learning, they are acquiring not only knowledge of the nature of the problems, but also finding friends and companions to work with toward the same goals. Many of the study groups formed at seminars have developed into effective grassroots activist organizations. These have evolved into women's movements for peace, nuclear disarmament, anti-inflation, and children's welfare, against pollution and job discrimination, and many others. Through their activities Japanese women are undoubtedly growing out of the confined past into the future of knowledge and its constructive application.

From Islands to the World

A 1981–1982 survey by the office of the prime minister gives us a portrait of the average Japanese woman: She values her family life very highly and is willing to make sacrifices for them; once married she is unwilling to divorce no matter how unsatisfactory the marriage may be; she feels Japanese women including herself are treated unequally both in the family and in society; but she is proud of her status as the decision-maker in family financial matters. It is ironic that such a quiet, conservative figure makes up 35 percent of the Japanese workforce, and that without the contribution of Japanese women, the country's economy would certainly come to a standstill.

The government promised to ratify by 1985 the United Nations convention on abolishing all forms of discrimination against women. But it was only in May 1984 that the Ministry of Labor completed an outline of a new equal employment opportunity law. The first draft prepared by the appointed committee provided for "compulsory enforcement," but when the government made the final draft public, many women activists were shocked to find the enforcement clause watered down to read "must strive to give women equal treatment."

It is a paradox that, in Japan, working women still suffer open and hidden discrimination while their contribution makes Japan's existence as a world economic power possible. There is no simple explanation for this. It may be that the whole social system has been so rigidly based on male supremacy that it is virtually impossible to bring rapid changes, or that Japanese men have been traditionally so accustomed to treating women as their inferiors that they are not even aware of the advantages of their superior position or the discrimination it produces. Or perhaps Japanese women themselves, having endured a low status imposed on them for generations by a society based on Confucian and Buddhist moral virtues, do not fully realize the extent of their discriminatory treatment. And regrettably there is still a prevalent tendency among middle-class women to look down upon the activists of women's liberation movements as not "ladylike." There is also a lack of interest in administrative and legislative issues that are beyond their immediate concern.

All of these ingrained problems must be dealt with to bring about a true liberation of Japanese women. But in her quiet unassuming way, the Japanese woman with her tradition of generations of decision making in the family will make steady progress toward this goal. She is no longer isolated in her struggle. The International

Women's Year made a tremendous impression upon the women of Japan. The unique Showa Constitution, which paved the way for women's liberation, also renounced war. Japan, the only country that has experienced atomic war, may now take the lead in the struggle to preserve world peace, and Japanese women, always beginning from their immediate, personal interests, in their private persistent manner, may lead the way.

NOTES

1. The Peace Preservation Law enacted in 1900 prohibited any group organization or movement that was thought to disturb the peace of Japan. It included a specific clause forbidding women and minors to attend political meetings or to initiate such meetings.

2. The English translation used here is taken from Kasahiro Watanabe, *Nippon Koku Kenpo ni Tsuite* [Study of Japanese Constitution] (Tokyo: Yohan Shuppan, 1980), 7.

3. To be saved, women had to read ten thousand holy scriptures and repeat several hundred thousand chants as well as other duties.

4. *Bakufu* or tent government. Shogunate governments were always called by this name as opposed to the symbolic central imperial government in Kyoto, *Chotei*.

5. Chikamatsu Monzaemon (1653–1724) wrote plays for *Jyoruri* or puppet shows in which heroes and heroines, unable to have their love fulfilled because of their social obligations, often committed a double suicide.

6. Inoue Kiyoshi, *Nippon Jyosei-shi* [History of Japanese Women] (Tokyo: Sanichi Shobo, 1982), 194.

7. Quoted in Inoue, 225.

8. Hiratsuka Raicho, *Hiratsuka Raicho Zenshu* [Collected Works of Hiratsuka Raicho], Vol. I (Tokyo: Ohtsuki Shoten, 1983), 18.

9. Ibid., 258.

10. Miyagi Eisho and Ohi Minobu, *Shinko Nippon Jyosei-shi* [History of Japanese Women, Revised Edition] (Tokyo: Yoshikawa Shobunkan, 1983), 237.

11. Prime Minister's Office, ed., *Fujin no Genjyo to Shisaku* [Present Situation of and Programs for Japanese Women] (Tokyo: Gyosei, 1983), 32.

12. An Interview in *Mainichi Shinbun*, June 7, 1984.

13. *Fujin Kyoiku Jyoho* [Report on Women's Education] 2 (Tokyo: The National Women's Education Center, 1980).

14. Prime Minister's Office, 53.

15. A recent survey taken during the university festival of the Nagoya National University shows that 50 percent of their women students do not intend to work after marriage. This means they would work only

three to five years after graduation. The figure for private women's colleges is 70 percent. *Mainichi Shinbun*, June 15, 1984.

16. A survey of the Ministry of Health and Welfare of 1971 gives a new cycle of a women's life, dividing it into four periods: Period I (ages from 0 to 18–23), growing and receiving education; Period II (from 24 to 45–53), raising the next generation; Period III (from 54 to 65–70), personal freedom; Period IV (70 to death), physical decline.

17. Kanda Michiko, ed., *Gakushy suru Jyose no Jidai* [The Age of Learning Women] (Tokyo: NHK Books, 1983), 89.

18. Prime Minister's Office, 18.

19. Kanda, 38–42.

6

In the Land of the Patriarchs: Public Policy on Women in Israel

Ellen Boneparth
U.S. Department of State

I n the last decade, many works have explored the myths and realities of the status of women in Israel. Some have portrayed pioneer women in the Yishuv seeking to translate an egalitarian sex-role ideology into meaningful participation in the economic, defense, and political decision-making structures of the new land.[1] Other studies of the post-independence period have shown women soldiers, restricted more and more as security is strengthened to peripheral roles in the Israeli Defense Forces;[2] aspiring female political leaders whose struggles within male-dominated political party organizations and government bureaucracies are obscured by one woman's successful climb to the top;[3] female workers, who, despite an impressive quantitative presence in the labor union movement, experience qualitatively (and quantitatively) different rewards from men for their work inside and outside the home;[4] and female members of agricultural collectives whose formal claim to equality is undermined by informal sets of attitudes and practices that restrict them to sex-stereotyped roles.[5]

What functions do myths about sexual equality serve? In Israel, as in any society, these myths put the responsibility for lesser achievements on women themselves, implying that if the society is characterized by equal opportunity, women personally must be to blame for failing to seize opportunities for self-actualization. Women internalize this blame, rationalizing their subordinate status with a variety of defense mechanisms ranging from expressions of satisfaction with their "natural" roles, to passivity, to outright hostility toward women or groups challenging the *status quo*.

At the institutional level, these myths remove the need to examine the status of women and effect systemic change. Myths of equality, individual rights and responsibilities, and free choice constitute a liberal ideology that conceals the patriarchal structure of the state, defined by Eisenstein as a "political structure [that] seeks to control and subjugate women so that their possibilities for making choices about their sexuality, child-rearing, mothering, loving and laboring are curtailed."[6]

How are women's choices curtailed in patriarchal society? Biology, namely women's capacity to bear children, is transformed into the institution of motherhood. Motherhood, the primary definition of women's role, is sustained by the state through a variety of public policies of both intervention and nonintervention in women's lives. As Eisenstein argues, "the state mystifies its patriarchal base by not only constructing but also manipulating the ideology describing public and private life."[7] Women are thus caught in the many contradictions of liberal ideology and patriarchal reality with little power to confront attitudes, policies, and practices relegating them to subordinate roles.

The contradictions of Israeli society are not unique to the status of women. They are the fruits of a hybrid societal development, mixing a variety of strains—ancient and young, religious and secular, capitalist and socialist, European and Oriental, developed and developing, peace-loving and aggressive, unified and polarized. Nor is the status of women in Israel unique in its contradictions. Women in Israel suffer similar forms of social, economic, and political oppression as women elsewhere, although certainly with a distinctive cultural flavor.[8]

What, then, makes Israeli women such a fascinating case study? From the perspective of women in other industrialized countries, Israel's long-standing egalitarian sex-role ideology, its potential institutional capacity to mobilize women—whether through the army, labor unions, or voluntary organizations—and its historical willingness to devote resources to the improvement of social welfare all appear to favor improvements in the status of women. Yet, the overwhelming thrust of Israeli public policy is toward reinforcing women's traditional roles. Why and how apparently progressive public policy retards the progress of women in Israel is the subject of this study.

Women and the Family

In Israel, the family is unquestionably the preeminent social institution. Traditional Jewish belief and law promote the family as the institution that not only provides the individual with a social identity but also provides the societal means for sustaining Jewish values and culture. Because the family is so highly valued, the role of mother garners high esteem. In the private sphere of the family, mothers are responsible for the care and rearing of children, the maintenance of the home, and the celebration of the weekly Sabbath ritual. Religious identity is derived through the mother. Jewish law regulates sexuality and sexual relations to assure women every possible opportunity for child bearing. Thus, over 5,000 years of traditional belief and practice support the ideals of family and motherhood.

Lest the role of women in Judaism sound too exalted, it must be pointed out that women's roles beyond the family are devalued or ignored and their participation in religious practice is highly restricted. Religious leadership (which, in effect, means community leadership), prayer, study, and scholarship are reserved for men. As many have observed, traditional Judaism is a highly patriarchal religion that neither recognizes women's spirituality nor their contribution to the community beyond the confines of the home.[9]

The centrality of family in Jewish tradition has been reinforced by the changing ethnic composition of the Israeli population resulting from the massive immigrations in the pre-state, and particularly, post-state periods of Oriental Jews from Asia and Africa. The Sephardim, who today constitute a majority of the Jewish population in Israel, brought with them a secular, as well as religious, value system that rendered the multigenerational family not only the primary social, but also economic, unit. In the precarious transition from homeland to Israel, the family remained critical, providing economic and psychic security in the struggle to adapt to a new, strange, and often hostile environment. While the Sephardic family has evolved in recent years to a smaller nuclear family, the culture continues to emphasize the roles of women in the home and the centrality of family life.

Perhaps the most remarkable manifestation of the vitality of the Israeli family is found on the kibbutz. The founders of these agricultural collectives in the early twentieth century, while not, for the most part, rejecting the institution of family, had notions of transforming it by collectivizing child rearing and domestic work. One of the goals of collectivization was to break down the traditional sexual division of labor. While the kibbutz pioneers never succeeded in eliminating distinctions between men's and women's work, particularly as concerns male participation in traditional female domains, economic survival made it necessary for women to work in the fields and construction, as well as develop their own productive specializations raising livestock and gardening. Once the kibbutzim emerged as established settlements, however, the traditional sexual division of labor fully reasserted itself, with men concentrated in the production sector and women concentrated in the service sector.

Countless studies of the kibbutz have traced the evolution of sex roles, using a wide variety of conceptual frameworks. Some studies approach the issue as the retreat from equality when, in fact, original source materials make clear that sex role equality was an ideological goal never actually realized.[10] What is most important, however, is the contemporary situation of women and family on the kibbutz. The birthrate on the kibbutz is somewhat higher than in Israeli society generally, with families averaging over three children. Work is increasingly sex-segregated. The trend, interestingly, is away from collective institutions and toward the nuclear family with children sleeping at home and households frequently eating at home and acquiring consumer items—which multiply domestic chores and increase family-centeredness.

No discussion of the centrality of the Israeli family would be complete without an understanding of the relationship of the family to the security of the nation and its people. War has been a constant theme from the settling of Palestine to the founding of the state to the periodic eruptions of conflict since independence. Underlying the contemporary security threat is the traumatic experience and memory of the Holocaust, in which a third of the world's Jewish population was exterminated.

Threats to Israel's security lie just under the surface of daily life; citizens are reminded of them by the disruptions caused by universal military service and long periods of reserve duty, by the price paid for maintaining a huge defense establishment, and by the presence of soldiers everywhere. The fragility of internal security is brought home by periodic terrorist attacks on the civilian population, by civil disorder erupting in the occupied territories, and by the constant security checks in supermarkets, movie theaters, and public places. In such an environment, the family becomes an island of security.

The family as a means of survival as well as a measure of security is evident in Israel's pronatalist goals and policies. Pronatalism is a popularly accepted response to the incalculable losses of the Holocaust, to the small size of the Jewish population in relation to its numerous Arab neighbors, and to the regular loss of life in Arab-Israeli conflicts. From the 1940s, when David Ben-Gurion called upon families to perform their "demographic duty" by having four to five children, to the 1950s when cash prizes were awarded to mothers of ten children, to the 1960s when family allowances were introduced starting with the third child, there has been a national consensus behind Israel's goal of increasing its population.

The literature on the Israeli family notes complementary themes of stability and change. Stability can be seen through the mid-1970s in the high rate of marriage and low rate of divorce. More recent studies point, however, to modest increases in the last few years in the age of first marriage, in the proportion of women not marrying, and in divorce rates, and suggest that these trends will continue into the 1980s.[11]

In contrast to marriage and divorce, dramatic change has occurred in fertility rates in Israel.[12] The decline in Jewish birthrates is accounted for by increasing levels of education among women, leading to an expanding female workforce and wider knowledge and use of family-planning techniques. The differences in family size between Ashkenazim and Sephardim are disappearing, reflecting a significant drop in fertility rates among the Sephardim and slight increases in fertility rates among the Ashkenazim and Israeli-born.

The family in Israel, therefore, is changing only marginally with respect to marriage and divorce, but significantly with respect to fertility and family size. While these latter trends do not generally portend a lessening attachment to the family as an institution, they do signify changes in family patterns that have particular consequences for women in their social and economic roles.

Women and Work

Women's work roles everywhere exist in relation to their family roles. If women are defined as having primary responsibility for child rearing, the family, and the home, they will by definition have secondary roles in employment outside the home. These secondary roles are, nevertheless, gaining in importance.

In Israel, as in all other industrialized societies, the major employment trend of recent years has been the expansion of the female labor force. In 1980, 40 percent of all Israeli women were working, an increase of 17 percent since 1955 as compared to a decrease in the male labor force in the same period of 11 percent.[13] The increase in women workers was greatest in the 1970s, a period of economic growth that saw a surge in the labor force participation rate of married women with children. By 1980, the participation rates of married and unmarried women had converged with, in all likelihood, married women pulling ahead in the 1980s.[14]

How have Israeli women been absorbed into the workforce? Bernstein traces patterns of female employment in the post-state period, showing that women have found employment primarily in those periods when there was a shortage of labor and primarily in those occupations that were undergoing a major expansion.[15] In the 1960s, a period of economic growth, women were recruited through government urging to work in occupations the state was seeking to develop—the clothing, textile, and food-processing industries, social services in education, health, and welfare, finance (at the clerical level), and trade (in those areas needing sales workers). In the 1970s, most women continued to find employment in service industries, the sector of the economy expanding most rapidly.

For the most part, service jobs have provided women with less-than-equal employment opportunities. First, the proportion of full-time women workers dropped rapidly in the 1970s, while the proportion of part-time workers increased almost as much.[16] Secondly, while the overall wage gap between men and women narrowed in this period, the earnings of women with higher levels of education, relative to men, declined.[17] Moreover, fringe benefits such as car, travel, and telephone allowances are not calculated in basic wage rates; since these fringe benefits are attached to managerial and professional jobs where women are in short supply, the gap between men's and women's earnings is, in reality, considerably wider. Finally, the female unemployment rate, while lower than in most countries, was almost half again higher than the male rate.[18]

In Israel, as elsewhere, women constitute a secondary labor force, a situation that is maintained, to a large extent, by occupational segregation. Women workers are concentrated in a small number of occupations: clerical jobs; low-status, low-paying professional jobs such as nursing, social work, and teaching; labor-intensive industrial jobs in textiles, food production, electronics, and computer manufacturing. Women are significantly underrepresented in managerial jobs, technical jobs, and industrial jobs requiring the use of heavy machinery. A large proportion of the more highly educated female labor force (13 percent) is found in government employment, which in the 1970s provided professional women—lawyers, engineers, pharmacists, doctors—considerable employment opportunities. The availability of these jobs, however, reflects the movement of men from government service to higher-paying jobs in the private sector; despite lower pay, the continuing attraction of these jobs for women involves regular and shorter work hours.[19]

The fact that Israeli women constitute a secondary labor force, working fewer hours on the job and earning less per hour than Israeli men, does not mean that they work less than men, as work in the home clearly substitutes for market work. Combining home and market work, married men and women work roughly equal numbers of hours per day, while unmarried women work more than married men.[20]

Entry into the labor force for Israeli women is, therefore, a mixed blessing. Occupational rewards, whether in terms of income, mobility, or choice of work, are restricted through pay discrimination and occupational segregation; at the same time, market work must be combined with work in the home. The centrality of the family makes it impossible for working women to avoid the strains of the dual burden of work and family.[21]

While changes are occurring both in employment and the family, these changes are not in themselves sufficient to challenge women's primacy in the home or marginality outside. The question then remains what role public policy plays in preserving or altering these patterns.

Women and Family Policy

In Israel, women's roles in the family are not only culturally prescribed but are also prescribed by a wide variety of explicit and implicit public policies. Women receive considerable policy support for their roles as wives and mothers as long as they function within a traditional framework that assigns men the predominant family role or that, in the absence of a husband, substitutes the support of the state. Recent shifts in public policy resulting from the changing social, economic, and political climate in Israel have exacerbated problems of women's status.

Marriage and Divorce

A first major consideration in understanding women's family roles concerns those realms where the state has agreed *not* to intervene—marriage and divorce. In 1953, the Rabbinical Courts Jurisdiction Law placed marriage and divorce in the hands of the religious authorities—the Orthodox Rabbinate, which has the sole right in Israel to perform marriages and grant divorces. The strictures of Orthodox Judaism on marriage have been discussed at length elsewhere,[22] but the issue of male control of women's personal status deserves emphasis. Matters of women's personal status are decided by an all-male clergy in courts where women are not even permitted to testify and where women attorneys are held in low regard.[23] Divorces are not granted without a husband's signature on the divorce decree.

It seems highly unlikely that the Israeli government will remove the religious monopoly over personal status in view of the power of the religious political parties and the acceptance of the majority of the population of the *status quo*. In fact, at the present time, the religious parties are proposing legislation that would give the religious courts absolute jurisdiction over matters (alimony, property division, and child custody) where currently religious courts and civil courts have joint jurisdiction.[24] In response to this situation, one minor political party, the Citizens Rights party, led by a woman member of Knesset, Shulamit Aloni, has made civil marriage a principal plank in its platform and garners enough political support to maintain minor representation.[25] Women's organizations that provide women legal advice spend most of their energies on matters of personal status,[26] and a small organization of religious women, Mitzvah, attempts to mediate in divorce cases involving recalcitrant husbands.[27] Dramatic cases of injury to women receive attention in the press, and a few religious scholars are working on reform through marriage contracting and liberal interpretations of religious law.[28] Despite these efforts and despite existing abuses, the system of marriage and divorce is maintained, on terms and conditions beneficial to men, a system that is acceded to, if not actually supported, by most Israeli women.

What does the state gain, beyond the avoidance of conflict with organized religion, through its policy of nonintervention in matters of personal status? Taking the state out of the domain of marriage and divorce conveys the clear message that there is a distinction between public concern for family welfare and private matters of family relations. Nonintervention enables the state to maintain a low divorce rate and to assign responsibilities for family relations to private voluntary organizations, religious and secular, which fill the gap in family services. In practical terms, the monopoly of the religious authorities relieves the state from dealing with all but the most serious problems of peace in the home *(shlombayit)* and, by extension, with the whole issue of family violence. At an ideological level, the religious/state, private/public distinction reinforces the traditional sexual division of labor inside and outside the home, bolstering the patriarchal character of the society.

Housing

A brief look at housing policy, a field where government has intervened in a significant way, reveals that it, too, promotes marriage. Housing policy is strongly geared toward home ownership rather than rental housing. As housing is expensive (a small apartment usually costs six to seven years' annual earnings), the government has an extensive system of mortgages and loans that, in most cases must be supplemented with financial assistance from families. Housing is constructed to accommodate parents and an average family size of three children rather than providing for singles or extended families.

Clearly, the goal of housing policy is to create a stable nuclear family. Unmarried adults living alone or together are ineligible for housing assistance from the government and, given social norms, are unlikely to receive assistance from families. The single-parent family has recently been added as a priority category for government assistance, but the Commission on the Status of Women noted in its report that requests for assistance from unmarried mothers are often negatively received.[29] Thus, the desire for better housing and home ownership provide a strong incentive to get married and are certainly factors when couples consider whether to remain married.

Child Bearing, Child Rearing, and Family Planning

Child bearing is also promoted through a wide array of incentives, services, and benefits to women. Mothers receive grants from the National Insurance Institute for hospital births equaling approximately 70 percent of the average monthly wage, as well as a layette grant equaling approximately 17 percent of the average monthly wage.[30] In addition, a large system of mother-and-child health

clinics provides free health care to pregnant and postnatal women
and their children up to the age of five.[31] Thus, the costs of child
bearing are borne to a large extent by the state, while the child's
health is implicity assumed to be the joint responsibility of the
mother and the medical establishment.

The admirable emphasis on children's health in Israel, what one
observor has called "quality control of children,"[32] because it is
viewed as the natural and sole domain of mothers, often produces
anxiety in women that they must rear quality products and guilt
and social condemnation from others when children experience
mental or physical health problems. Thus, the child-bearing role
carries over fully into child rearing, with child rearing becoming a
woman's, rather than a parental, responsibility.

Government support for child bearing can be seen equally clearly
in family-planning policy. The practice of family planning is curtailed not only by the attitudes of the religious establishment but by
the political, medical, and social welfare establishments as well.
The result is that women receive very little assistance with family
planning. Sex education is not included, in most cases, in the school
curriculum. The medical bureaucracy is notorious for failing to
provide women with information and access to alternative methods
of contraception.[33] Sterilization, an increasingly common method
of contraception in other societies, is highly restricted by hospital
policies.

Legal abortion in Israel has existed only since 1977. Prior to that
time, private abortions were implicitly tolerated, as seen in court
cases and police practices, in which prosecution of illegal abortion
was only sought when injury to a woman's health was at issue.
However, since private abortion services were expensive and only
located in urban areas, poor and geographically isolated women
had little access to abortion.[34]

Since 1977, government-supported abortions are available if
women seeking abortions meet certain criteria and are approved by
a hospital committee of doctors and social workers. The criteria
were tightened in 1979 through the revocation of the social clause,
which previously permitted abortions on the grounds of social and
economic hardship.[35] How widespread, then, is the continuing
practice of private, illegal abortion? Researchers and governmental
committees have looked into this question and have come up with
estimates ranging from 12,000 to 80,000 per year.[36]

Illegal abortion is thus a continuing response to the failure of
public policy to support family planning or legal abortion. Ironically, neither positive incentives for maternity nor disincentives

resulting from government restrictions have had the desired effect on the birthrate. The decline in fertility over the last 20 years shows the limits of pronatalism when promoted through reproductive policies. The policies, however, reveal a great deal about the government's willingness to intervene in some aspects of reproduction, and ignore others, in order to maintain the traditional nuclear family.

Family Violence

Family violence presents yet another example of governmental noninterference in order to reinforce traditional family roles. As in all countries, spousal abuse is a common practice, hidden from public view and inadequately dealt with by public authorities. The culture of violence is widespread, based on males' insecurities of status and manifesting itself in the behavior of husbands who isolate women in their homes, keeping them economically dependent even if the women are working, and resorting to physical beatings as ultimate sanctions.

Police are usually reluctant to intervene in cases of family violence either because they view family relations as the domain of the religious courts or because they view wife beating as a minor offense, which they themselves occasionally resort to.[37] The services needed by a family beset by violence are often unavailable because social workers are ignorant of the issues and untrained in intervention techniques.

The services that do exist for abused women in Israel (four shelters and a Family Violence Center) are run solely by women's organizations, which also provide the bulk of the funding. While government neglect of the problem is found to a lesser or greater degree in most societies, it is particularly striking in a society where the family is such a central institution. Apparently, the preservation of male authority in the family, even in violent situations, overrides the well-being of family members.

Child Allowances

Until the late 1970s, the underlying goals of social welfare policy were "to assure greater economic and social security for the population, to narrow economic and social gaps and to create in Israel a more egalitarian and just society."[38] Income maintenance was achieved by a system of child allowances, categorical grants, and income-tested social assistance programs. The trend in the 1970s was to extend child allowances from large families to all families with children and to replace tax deductions for children with tax credits in order to increase the relative benefits to low-income families. The wider eligibility and higher level of benefits through the system of child allowances initially lessened the need for other forms of social assistance, reducing the incidence of poverty among families between 1969 and 1977, with particular improvements for large families and families headed by aged and single parents. Since 1977, however, there has been an erosion in benefits from child allowances, in part because child allowances are adjusted to wage rates on a quarterly basis (while other benefits are adjusted to a monthly cost-of-living index), which, in a highly inflationary economy, results in a decline in benefit levels. In the last few years, the decrease in benefit levels and the increase in the proportion of families below the poverty line make it clear that the poor are living at a more deprived level today than in the 1970s.[39]

These universal policies of child allowances, moreover, fail to address the particular needs of poor women. Unless they fall into a designated category for special assistance (war widows, the disabled, etc.), poor women are generally not perceived as having any special problems by the social welfare establishment. Yet, an examination of the conditions of women in poverty by the Commission on the Status of Women in 1978 revealed them to be suffering from a very low sense of self-esteem, oppressive marital relations, social isolation, lack of information on and access to services (vocational, health, and family planning), and a lack of opportunities for personal development.[40]

Socioeconomically deprived women suffer psychological burdens that have an impact on family functioning and that are not necessarily alleviated by improving statistics on the incidence of family poverty. Recommendations from the Commission on the Status of Women for government-supported training programs, social activities, and family services for poor women (which are presently supplied to a limited extent by women's voluntary organizations) seem to have fallen on unresponsive ears. Female dependency is an accepted social norm for most policy-makers and social welfare professionals alike, and since low self-esteem is rarely expressed by women in antisocial behavior, it remains conveniently invisible.

Single Mothers: Widowed, Divorced, and Unmarried Women

In a society such as Israel, which places such a strong emphasis on the maintenance of the nuclear family, it is not surprising to find a dearth of public policy dealing with the needs of single-parent families. These families are overwhelmingly headed by women and presently constitute a rather small proportion (4 to 5 percent) of the population. Nevertheless, they present an important social problem, both because of evidence that they are slowly increasing in number and because their socioeconomic situation is deteriorating.[41] The National Insurance Institute reported, for example, that in 1979, after transfers, 48 percent of single-parent families were above the poverty line while, by 1982, the proportion living above poverty had dropped to 27 percent.[42]

In Israel it is necessary to distinguish between different types of female-headed households in order to show the various ways in which public policy affects or neglects their situation. The most advantaged group of single mothers are war widows, who have been a serious concern of policy-makers, at least to the extent that the government provides benefits equivalent to the deceased's wage in order to assure the surviving family a measure of financial security.[43] Although provided for financially, the social-psychological situation of war widows is quite complex. The special status assigned them by the government, combined with general societal sympathy and respect, leads them to be clothed, as one psychologist put it, in a "gown of honor."[44] Consequently, the reintegration of war widows into society is difficult because the women cling to their special social status.

Divorced female heads of households are in a worse condition than war widows economically, if not psychologically. While the National Insurance Institute introduced a progressive policy in the 1970s of paying delinquent husbands' court-ordered alimony and child-support payments of delinquent husbands directly to wives, there is a ceiling on these payments that makes it impossible for the divorced woman and her family to maintain anything near their previous economic standard. Moreover, while single-parent families are listed as priority categories for housing assistance and day care, neither of these policies goes very far in alleviating the economic pressures on the divorced woman. A proposal to provide a small additional income tax credit for one-parent families passed a first Knesset reading in 1984 but, even if passed, would provide too little to change the family's basic economic situation.[45]

The divorced woman in Israel faces social and psychological

problems that are intensified by the family-centeredness of the society. Psychologists report that, while the stigma of divorce may be lessening, divorced women receive little support for raising children alone or for finding employment. The emphasis, both socially and institutionally in communities or in single-parent groups, is on finding new partners, rather than on building viable lives as single parents. Interestingly, even the Commission on the Status of Women failed to make any recommendations for counseling and employment services for divorced women as are found in "displaced homemaker" programs in other countries.

Unmarried women with children are extremely rare in Israel and receive little attention from researchers or policy-makers. Yet, these women do exist and provide interesting exceptions to the social norm. It appears that many of the unmarried mothers are educated professional women in their late thirties who have chosen single motherhood over childlessness. While their choice is congruent with the general societal desire for children, their singleness could be interpreted as antifamily. A study of a very small sample of unmarried mothers indicated, however, that given the right circumstances, they generally would have preferred to have children in the context of a marriage or relationship.[46] While single motherhood by choice was practically unknown a few years ago, and remains highly uncommon, single mothers report that they are gaining social acceptance, although they are far from receiving governmental assistance for their chosen lifestyle.[47]

While explicit goals vary from policy to policy, the implicit goals of Israeli family policy are to support the patriarchal nuclear family and to assign parenting responsibility to women. Policy goals are achieved both through state intervention and nonintervention. Intervention through benefit programs in the fields of housing, maternity and child health, and child allowances directly support marriage and child bearing; nonintervention in marriage and divorce law, family planning, and family violence serves to maintain men as heads of households and women in subordinate roles. Women who seek control over their reproductive lives or who maintain families without the male heads of households receive minimal benefits from the state and are often compelled to turn to voluntary agencies or private (sometimes illegal) services for assistance.

The effects of these policies on family life are mixed. On the one hand, Israel has been successful in promoting and maintaining the traditional nuclear family as seen in the relatively stable demographic patterns discussed earlier. On the other hand, social tensions and problems are created by a monolithic approach to the family as evidenced by the deteriorating economic situation of low-income, usually single-earner families, by patterns of family violence, and by the social, psychological, and economic distress of single-parent families. Most importantly, women, whether in the context of traditional or nontraditional families, carry the main burden of family life on their shoulders, with the result that participation in either economic or political roles outside the family becomes exceedingly difficult.

Women and Employment Policy

While the state of Israel has always endorsed the role of women as workers and partners in nation building, and while policy exists in many areas to effect equality in the workforce and to assist women in their work roles, the impact of either ideology or policy on women's employment opportunities has been minimal. A review of three different policy approaches emphasizing antidiscrimination measures, education and training, and assistance for working mothers shows that the gains of Israeli working women have occurred, in large part, in spite of, rather than because of, public policy.

Antidiscrimination Policy

Antidiscrimination policy in Israel has its roots in the Declaration of Independence of 1948 and the 1951 Equal Rights Law, both of which seek to guarantee women's legal equality but which, as statutory declarations of principle, lack the force of constitutional law and guarantee nondiscrimination only in the public sphere.[48] The Women's Work Law was passed in 1954 to assure women workers equal status with men; the law, however, gave women workers special protection as women.

Israel has not seen fit to do away with protective legislation, although the government does make exceptions where desirable, as in night-work prohibitions for a few categories of women workers (nurses, hotel employees, computer programmers, etc.). Even the Commission on the Status of Women hesitated to recommend any major changes in protective legislation in view of "the traditions of a large part of the population" (that is, woman's traditional place in the home, especially at night) and the desire to continue protection against reproductive hazards.[49]

Efforts to eliminate "negative" discrimination against women

workers were expanded with the passage of the Equal Pay Act in
1964. While setting down the principle of equal pay for equal work
and making pay discrimination illegal, the legislation has had little
effect, as mechanisms for enforcement (complaint procedures, litigation methods, and sanctions for violators) have no real teeth.
Women who seek redress of pay discrimination must bring suit on
their own initiative and at their own expense without the assistance
of any independent public or voluntary agency to investigate, collect data, or argue the case. Since unequal pay scales are often
quietly acceded to by labor unions in collective agreements, the
unions have shown little interest in raising the issue of women's
wages. The difficulty of using the Equal Pay Law on women's behalf
is evident in the fact that, in the 20 years since the passage of the
legislation, only one equal-pay case has ever been brought to the
labor courts.[50]

A second area of employment discrimination—hiring and conditions of work—is also covered by statutes and contract law but
rarely litigated or enforced. A major case in 1973 established the
right of women to challenge discrimination in collective
agreements, as well as the right of judicial review not only in
public-sector but also in private-sector employment.[51] Ten years
elapsed, however, before a second case, currently being argued
(involving differential mandatory retirement ages for male and
female doctors) has been brought to court. Efforts to ban discrimination in hiring and training resulted in the passage in 1981 of an
Equal Employment Opportunity Law, which also provides gender-
specific job advertisements, but, to date, this law has also been more
or less ignored.

The failure to utilize antidiscrimination measures to improve
women's employment status is a result both of the inadequacies of
the law and the reluctance or inability of employees and employee
organizations to pursue the issue. The legal deficiencies include
placing the burden of litigation on individuals instead of building
class-action suits or using governmental enforcement agencies,
proving discrimination in the absence of data revealing patterns of
discrimination, and the lack of remedies—short of impractical
criminal sanctions and civil damages—that would result in obtaining employment for aggrieved parties.[52] It is clear that, in addition
to procedural problems, the enforcement of antidiscrimination
legislation is inadequate because it is in the hands of inspectors
from the Ministry of Labor who have only investigatory power and
who have little commitment to or knowledge about sex-
discrimination issues.

Education and Training

From the time of the Second Aliya when young, urbanized European Jews came to Palestine to devote their lives to farming, education and training for work roles have been a major concern in Israel. The primary objective in Israel, however, has been to train men, whether immigrant or nonimmigrant, as they are perceived as the family breadwinners. In contrast, the movement of women into paid employment as secondary wage-earners has been achieved with little regard for appropriate education or training.

Sex stereotyping in Israeli education and training is, as in other societies, pervasive. As the Commission on the Status of Women reported, the image of women portrayed in children's books is highly traditional.[53] The teaching profession has been progressively feminized, with women concentrated in the ranks of elementary school teachers, roughly equal proportions of men and women found among high school teachers, and men holding over 90 percent of school principal and supervisorial positions.[54] Finally, the status of women and issues of sexual equality are generally ignored in both the school curriculum and teacher training.

Despite the need of Israel to increase its population of industrial and technical workers, only 14 percent of the vocational college population is female (with no change in proportions over the last decade) and most of the female students are concentrated in computer programming, chemistry, or architecture, fields where working conditions, including the availability of part-time jobs, are perceived as desirable.[55]

The traditionalism of the educational system is matched by the traditionalism of the military, another arena where there is a significant potential opportunity to educate and train women. The Israeli Defence Forces, however, point to numerous disincentives to technical training for women. It is argued that female recruits lack the appropriate educational backgrounds, serve one year less than males, are not called for reserve duty after the age of 24, and are not likely to seek or find employment in technical fields once they complete their service. Yet, the army's need for technical workers in light of recent demands for a larger force of combat soldiers and in light of the increasingly technical character of the defense establishment makes women soldiers a logical source of personnel to meet the demand. In recent years, the military has opened an increasing number of occupations (approximately two-thirds of the total) to women and is utilizing women somewhat more in technical fields, although primarily as instructors of male recruits. Still, the overwhelming majority of women soldiers work as clericals, teachers, and social/recreational workers. Thus, while the military has the potential to be an instrument of social change by educating and training women, this potential in both peacetime and wartime situations is far from being realized.

Policy for Working Mothers

The most developed area of employment policy for Israeli women involves assistance for working mothers, who may take advantage of a wide variety of benefits provided to assist them with the burdens of child bearing and child rearing. With respect to child bearing, salaried workers are granted three-month maternity leaves at 75 percent of their salaries paid by the National Insurance Institute. New mothers may extend their leaves to one year (although after three months there are no allowances) without jeopardizing their jobs.

Maternity leave policy emphasizes the woman's place at home with little concern for the integration of family and work roles. Consequently, two modifications of maternity leave policy have been suggested. First, several observers have argued for greater flexibility, since making maternity leaves mandatory, while benefiting the overwhelming majority of women, may disadvantage a small number, particularly professionals with responsible jobs, who desire to return to work soon after childbirth. Second, it has been proposed that maternity leaves be made into parental leaves, enabling fathers or mothers to take time from their jobs for infant care. The Commission on the Status of Women, however, rejected this notion "out of consideration for the traditions and lifestyles of a large segment of the population," implying that child rearing as a joint family role is, as yet, too radical a notion to embrace in public policy.[56]

On the one hand, these policies may be viewed as progressive; on the other hand, they create certain problems for women. In the short run, they reinforce negative attitudes toward hiring women on the part of employers, who view women as unstable because they must take time off for maternal responsibilities. In the long run, these policies reinforce the societal view that parenting is not only a female role but also a *primary* female role, with work secondary.

An examination of child care policy makes this pattern even clearer. Child care in Israel has long been a recognized need, promoted since the 1920s by various women's organizations. The basic impetus behind the establishment of child care centers has been to assist women to go to work, rather than either to advance early childhood education (although the welfare agencies do support a large number of deprived children in centers) or to provide a means for all women, working or not, to engage in activities outside the home. Child care centers are run, for the most part, by women's voluntary organizations and are financed by a combination of government funds (particularly for the construction of centers), private organizational support, and fees paid by families on a sliding scale. The availability of child care was greatly expanded in the 1970s with an accelerated government building program; today the pace has slowed considerably, and less than half the need for child care is met by centers. The shortage of places has necessitated a priority system of placements with large families, single-parent families, and families in deprived urban areas and development towns heading the list.

The Israeli child care system is presently beset by many problems, both economic and political. The Likud government, in power since 1977, has not only decelerated the building of centers but has also cut back on child care subsidies. Women are paying approximately 50 percent more in fees in 1984 than in 1983, constituting roughly one-third of their income for each child. For women with more than one child in a center, it is harder and harder to justify working when child care costs consume most of the paycheck. Even the basis for determining fees—the woman's income—which was intentionally established to persuade women to work by keeping child care costs low, is threatened, as the government has proposed to use total family income as the basis for setting fees. The anti–working-woman political bias can be seen in the attitude of the finance minister, who, when asked about the impact of rising fees on working women, replied that they would be better off staying home and raising children.[57]

Child care problems for women are compounded by the scheduling of the work and school days. The school system works on a half-day with most children coming home for lunch. A number of child care centers operate on the same schedule, with only morning hours and long summer holidays. Clearly, the result for many working women is that they are only able to hold part-time jobs.

Solutions to this dilemma are obvious: extending the school day, beginning compulsory education at a younger age, providing afternoon programs for elementary school children and day camps for holiday periods. Obstacles to resolving this dilemma are also obvious: the considerable cost of extending child care and educational services and the lack of interest on the part of policy-makers in women's full employment opportunities.

An alternative approach would be to adjust the hours of the workday. Israelis generally work a 45-hour, five-and-one-half-day week. Since not only schools but also public, commercial, and business services are generally closed in the afternoons, after 7:00 P.M., and on the Sabbath, it is very difficult to combine work and homemaking. The Commission on the Status of Women recommended that services be opened some afternoons and/or late evenings to provide workers with greater opportunities to take care of domestic responsibilities. Likewise, the commission proposed that a five-day week with parallel child care schedules be introduced into industry.[58]

Generally speaking, Israel has done little in the area of flexible work patterns, a practice that in other countries has been found advantageous by employers and employees alike. In part, this can be explained by the fact that much of Israeli industry is small-scale and does not lend itself easily to flexible hours and shifts. Part of the explanation, however, also lies in the fact that employers derive greater benefits from utilizing part-time workers on short shifts than from adjusting work schedules to accommodate full-time women workers, either single or married, with heavy home and family responsibilities.

In conclusion, employment policy in Israel, like family policy, sustains traditional social patterns. Despite an array of antidiscrimination measures and a policy package to assist working mothers, the traditional sexual division of labor prevails, with men assigned roles as family breadwinner and women confined, for the most part, to economic roles that supplement family income. Clearly, many Israeli women accept and express satisfaction with secondary work roles in order to devote themselves first and foremost to culturally valued family roles. For those women, however, who, out of economic need or out of a desire for career advancement, seek more extensive involvement in the labor force, the barriers posed by family responsibilities and by public policy that fails to help them advance in the workforce or integrate work and family roles are severe. Thus, the ideological commitment in Israel to working women is less a commitment to a full economic partnership between men and women, and more a rationale for obtaining women's labor in the marketplace without significantly rewarding them for or relieving them of their unpaid domestic contributions.

Conclusion

It could be argued that, given the family-centeredness of Israeli culture, public policy that confines women to the nuclear family not only is congruent with the culture but actually strengthens the foundations of society. In this view, public policy, whether implicit or explicit, interventionist or noninterventionist, reflects, rather than forms, predominant social values. If the society values first and foremost stability based on family, motherhood, and child bearing, then limiting women's options by emphasizing their roles as wives and mothers is desirable.

Such a view fails to take into account several crucial variables. First, public policy notwithstanding, Israeli women's lives are changing. Family roles, while still primary, are gradually assuming less significance, as seen in the demographic changes occurring in marriage, divorce, family size, and female labor force participation. Public policy may retard but not abrogate those trends. Work roles, while still secondary, are gaining in significance as more women gain the education necessary to enter the world of paid labor. Public policy that, at best, only peripherally takes account of these trends, exacerbates women's dual burden, taking a toll not merely on women but on the family and work environment as well. Furthermore, short-term social stability may be achieved at the expense of long-term social stagnation and even disintegration. Public policy, by reflecting predominant social values but failing to allow for variation or adaptation, may create social tensions that undermine the stability that is so highly valued.

An alternative view of Israeli public policy would point to the individual, institutional, and societal costs of accentuating family roles and downgrading others. Let us examine these costs in the Israeli context. First, women as individuals suffer from a lack of life options. While marriage and motherhood may be the desired family style for women everywhere, in most industrialized societies these institutions are evolving along with women's desires for additional or alternative social, economic, and political roles.

Israeli women who opt for marriage and children but also seek extra-family roles experience the dilemmas of the dual burden of traditional family roles and new work roles to an enormous degree. The majority of Israeli women find themselves in this situation and present to the outside observer an impressive degree of energy and competence in managing their many responsibilities. The costs of this balancing act are evident, however, in women's sacrifice of

personal leisure, experience of role conflict, and inability to sur-
mount this burden to fulfill economic or political leadership roles.
The unmarried woman, with or without children, or the woman
who chooses not to have children, is considered an aberration. She
suffers a degree of social stigma as well as experiencing social
pressure to conform to the norm. Nonconformity often brings self-
doubt, defensiveness, and social isolation.

The traditionalist might argue that women's devotion to their
family roles, while costly to them personally, is nevertheless
healthy for the family. Certainly it is true that the emotional support and domestic services Israeli women extend to their families
offset much of the stress of the society as a whole. At the same time,
meeting the social expectations of the homemaker means perpetuating the stereotype of "supermom" and failing to provide
alternative role models for the next generation. In interviews with
Israeli women regarding their hopes for their children, the respondents often stressed the theme of greater autonomy for their
daughters and greater sensitivity and responsibility for family life
for their sons. Yet Israeli women, by their own examples, continue to
socialize their children to highly sex-stereotyped family roles.

Costs are even greater for nontraditional families in Israel. As has
been seen, the typical single-parent family finds itself in a strained
economic situation. As the number of these families is still small, it
may not be appropriate as yet to label this phenomenon "the
feminization of poverty." Since, however, the number of single-
parent families is slowly increasing and their economic status is
deteriorating, it may not be long before the problem takes on a more
widespread social significance. Already, Israeli social scientists and
social service professionals are beginning to turn their attention to
the social-psychological problems of single-parent families, including the effects of single-parenting on children and the need for
special welfare services for these families. The thrust of this professional attention, however, is more that single-parent families represent a deviation that must be remedied somehow than a
circumstance that, with responsive public policy and social awareness, represents as viable a life-style as the traditional nuclear family.

Beyond the costs to women and their families, the emphasis of
Israeli policy on family roles is costly for the society as a whole.
How? First, there is the loss of productivity resulting from restricting mothers, in particular, to part-time jobs and women, in general,
to sex-segregated occupations, primarily in the service sector.
While, in the short run, industry might benefit from having a large
part-time labor force to achieve flexibility and to avoid paying

fringe benefits, in the long run, part-time workers cost the economy by failing to advance in skill. Israel, seeking to accelerate its economic development, suffers from a shortage of industrial and technical workers; by failing to train and employ women in these jobs, the society greatly narrows its pool of available labor.

This situation becomes critical in times of military threat (as was the case in 1973) when the male civilian labor force is mobilized and women are unprepared to substitute for men in production. Even in the last few years when Israel has had more men in combat and has extended the length of reserve duty as a result of its involvement in Lebanon, the drain on the economy has been felt. The necessity of the state to maintain a large defense establishment makes it highly unlikely that labor shortages in important sectors will disappear even in times of relative peace. Thus, the failure to develop women workers in light of the country's security problems exacerbates its economic burden.

Beyond employment issues, a society that subscribes to egalitarian goals defeats itself by restricting women to marginal economic roles. Women are placed in a condition of economic dependency either on their husbands or, in the absence of husbands, on the state. While economic dependency reinforces social and psychological subordination ingrained in the culture of the more traditional elements of the population, thus avoiding tensions resulting from female role change, it is costly for the society by increasing economic inequality. In Israel, as elsewhere, the two-income family fares far better than the family with only a male breadwinner. Likewise, the family with a single parent working fares better than the nonworking single-parent family. A new class system is created based on family earning power. Public policy, by failing to maximize economic opportunity for women, aids and abets the social gap, with the lines in the future drawn less along ethnic divisions, as has been the case in Israel, and more along patterns of family composition.

What is needed is public policy that provides women with real opportunities for economic participation and that assists women and men in integrating their work and family roles. What is the likelihood that Israeli policy will adapt to changing family patterns and the changing needs of women? A study of public policy on working mothers in the United States, China, and Sweden concluded that the two critical variables underlying social policy benefiting working mothers are an economic need for female labor force participation and a political ideology of government responsibility for family welfare.[59] If these two variables alone were sufficient,

Israel, which meets these conditions, would present a rather different case than described here.

What has impeded the evolution of policy in Israel has been the traditionalism of the culture on the family and the inability of women who pay the price for this traditionalism to affect the policy-making process. Economic need and a social welfare orientation are, therefore, necessary but not sufficient conditions for change. In the case of Israel, both a cultural and a political transformation are necessary for the evolution of policy that would allow women to expand their work roles and combine work and family roles for their own benefit, that of their families, and society as a whole. In the Israeli context, demographic changes are slowly occurring that could lay the groundwork for a cultural transformation. Until women are able to use the policy-making process, however, to translate new social needs into effective policy, traditionalism is bound to prevail.

NOTES

1. Sarah Azaryahu, *The Union of Hebrew Women for Equal Rights in Society: A Selected History of the Women's Movement in Israel (1900–1947)*, translated by Marcia Freedman (Haifa: Women's Aid Fund, 1977); Dafna N. Izraeli, "The Zionist Women's Movement in Palestine, 1911–1927: A Sociological Analysis," *Signs* 7:1 (Autumn 1981), 87–114; Ada Maimon, *Women Build a Land* (New York: Herzl Press, 1962); Rachel Katznelson Shazar, ed., *The Plough Woman: Memoirs of the Pioneer Women of Palestine* (New York, Herzl Press, 1975).

2. Irving H. Breslau, "Women in the Israeli Defence Forces," *The Retired Officer*, September 1982, 16–19; Leslie Hazleton, *Israeli Women: The Reality behind the Myths* (New York: Simon and Schuster, 1977), 137–161.

3. Natalie Rein, *Daughters of Rachel* (Harmondsworth, PA: Penguin Books, 1979); Geraldine Stern, *Israeli Women Speak Out* (New York: J. B. Lippincott, 1979).

4. Deborah Bernstein, "The Plough Woman Who Cried into the Pots: The Position of Women in the Labor Force in the Pre-State Israeli Society," *Jewish Social Studies* 45:1 (Winter 1983), 43–56; Dafna N. Izraeli, "Israeli Women in the Work Force," *Jersusalem Quarterly* 27 (Spring 1983), 59–80; Dafna N. Izraeli, "Sex Structure of Occupations: The Israeli Experience," *Sociology of Work and Occupations* 6:4 (November 1979), 404–429; Dafna N. Izraeli and Kalman Gaier, "Sex and Interoccupational Wage Differences in Israel," *Industrial Relations* 18:2 (Spring 1979), 227–232.

5. Michal Palgi, Joseph Blasi, Menachem Rosner, and Marilyn Safir, *Sexual Equality: The Israeli Kibbutz Tests the Theories* (Norwood, PA: Nor-

wood Press, 1982); Naomi Nevo and David Solomonica, "Ideological Change of Rural Women's Role and Status: A Case Study of Family Based Cooperative Villages in Israel," *Working Papers on Women in International Development* 16 (East Lansing, Michigan State University, January 1983).

6. Zillah R. Eisenstein, *The Radical Future of Liberal Feminism* (New York: Longman, 1981), 16.

7. Eisenstein, 26.

8. Any complete examination of Israeli society necessitates a discussion of both the Jewish majority and the Arab minority. Such an approach is beyond the confines of this study both because of the dearth of secondary source material on Arab women and the difficulty of gaining access to Arab society and culture for primary research. The exclusion of Arab women from this study is painful as it parallels the polarization of Arab and Jew in Israeli society itself. Moreover, it implies that the differences between Jewish and Arab women are so extensive as to make comparisons meaningless. To the contrary, informal impressions strongly suggest that an analysis of the status of women and the impact of public policy on women's roles across the two cultures would yield an even deeper understanding of the contours and functioning of patriarchal society. Thus, the decision to focus on Jewish women in this study must be understood as a practical necessity that leaves both a theoretical and empirical gap that must be closed sooner rather than later.

9. Hazleton, 38–62.

10. Palgi et al.; Shazar.

11. Leo Davids, "What's Happening in the Israeli Family? Recent Demographic Trends," *Israel Social Science Research* 1:1 (1983), 34–40.

12. Moshe Hartman, "Number of Children and Work Experience of Married Women in Israel" (Jerusalem: Demography Center, Prime Minister's Office, June 1978).

13. Yoram Ben-Porath and Reuben Gronau, *Jewish Mother Goes to Work— Trends in the Labor Force Participation of Women in Israel, 1955–1980* (Jerusalem: Maurice Falk Institute for Economic Research, 1984), 1.

14. Ben-Porath and Gronau, 10.

15. Deborah Bernstein, "Economic Growth and Female Labour: The Case of Israel," *Sociological Review* 31:2 (May 1983), 263–292.

16. Ben-Porath and Gronau, 12.

17. Ben-Porath and Gronau, 21.

18. Ben-Porath and Gronau, 23.

19. Izraeli, 65.

20. Reuben Gronau, "The Allocation of Time of Israeli Women," *Journal of Political Economy* 84:4, Part 2 (August 1976), 201–220.

21. The extensiveness of the dual burden has even led one Israeli sociologist to conclude that the two-role model for women is oversimplified. Dafna Izraeli has proposed a third role that she calls boundary-spanning,

involving the "liaison" work women do, linking the family at school and at medical institutions, being responsible for home technical services (repairs) and financial services (banking), purchasing, and taking responsibility for social events, symbolic occasions, and recreation. These activities are not usually counted in time studies of domestic work because they do not occur on a daily basis. They occur, however, with enough frequency to consume a great deal of time. Women are assigned this role because their work status is generally lower than that of men and taking time from work is therefore less costly. Yet, this role catches women in a vicious cycle: because women are responsible for these functions, they must work fewer hours or take time off from work to perform them but, as part-time workers, advancement is almost impossible, reinforcing the idea that women's paid labor is less valuable than men's.

22. Hazleton, 38–62.

23. Interview with women attorneys in Israel, Spring 1984.

24. *Jerusalem Post,* March 8, 1984, 5.

25. Stern, 15–35.

26. Interviews with legal aid bureaus, Naamat and WIZO, Tel Aviv, Spring 1984.

27. Nitza Shapiro-Lebai, "Women's Participation in Social and Political Life," *The Status of Women* 3 (November 1982).

28. Leah A. Globe, *The Dead End: Divorce Proceedings in Israel* (Jerusalem: B.A.L. Mass Communication, 1981), 64–66.

29. Commission on the Status of Women, *Recommendations of the Commission on the Status of Women* (Jerusalem: Government Printing Office, 1978).

30. Joseph Neipris, *Social Welfare and Social Services in Israel: Policies, Programs and Current Issues* (Jerusalem: Hebrew University, 1981), 58–59.

31. Neipris, 65–67.

32. Interview with Professor Yohannon Peres, Department of Sociology, Tel Aviv University, Spring 1984.

33. Beersheva Women's Health Collective, "A Report on the Delivery Room and Obstetrics Ward of the Soroka Medical Centre" (Beersheva: 1976).

34. Eileen Basker, *Belief Systems, Cultural Milieu and Reproductive Behavior: Women Seeking Abortions in a Hospital in Israel,* unpublished doctoral dissertation, Department of Sociology and Social Anthropology, Hebrew University, June 1980.

35. It has been shown, however, that liberal hospital committees are using the criterion of possible danger to the mother's health more frequently since 1979, when the social clause was removed (*Jerusalem Post,* March 1, 1984, 3).

36. Interviews with women's health groups and professionals suggest that official estimates are low.

37. Interview with director, Family Violence Program, Naamat, Tel Aviv, February 1984.

38. Abraham Doron, "Social Policy for the Eighties," *Jerusalem Quarterly* 19 (Spring 1981), 77–78.

39. National Insurance Institute, *Annual Survey 1982*, in Hebrew with English summary (Jerusalem: National Insurance Institute, 1983), 35.

40. Commission on the Status of Women.

41. National Insurance Institute, 59, Hebrew text.

42. National Insurance Institute, 59, Hebrew text.

43. Widows of men who died as a result of work accidents are covered by a less generous pension program amounting to 70 percent of the husband's wages. Widows whose husbands died of nonwork accidents or illness receive no special benefits and generally face serious economic hardship.

44. Interview with acting director, Steiner Institute, Ben Gurion University, Beersheeva, Israel, February 1984.

45. *Jerusalem Post*, June 5, 1984, 2.

46. Iris Atzmon, "Case Study of Six Unmarried Mothers Who Chose To Raise Their Children," unpublished paper (in Hebrew), Department of Education, Hebrew University, September 1983.

47. Unmarried mothers formed an organization in 1982, Mothers without Marriage, which currently has 350 members. The organization's goals are to counter the isolation of unmarried mothers by bringing them into a social network, provide support for individual problem solving, and to lobby for government assistance in the form of tax credits and health and child care subsidies.

48. Frances Raday, "Equality of Women under Israeli Law," *Jerusalem Quarterly* 27 (Spring 1983), 81–108.

49. Commission on the Status of Women, 12.

50. Frances Raday, 97.

51. Frances Raday, 99.

52. Frances Raday, 102–108.

53. Commission on the Status of Women, 42–43.

54. Commission on the Status of Women, 43.

55. Interview with director, Vocational Training Unit, Department of Labor and Social Affairs, Tel Aviv, April 1984.

56. Commission on the Status of Women, 55.

57. Interview with director, Naamat Child Care Services, Tel Aviv, February 1984.

58. Commission on the Status of Women, 87.

59. Carolyn Teich Adams and Kathryn Teich Winston, *Mothers at Work: Public Policies in the United States, Sweden and China* (New York: Longman, 1980).

RECOMMENDED READINGS

Hazleton, Leslie. *Israeli Women: The Reality behind the Myths.* New York: Simon and Schuster, 1977.
An excellent, although somewhat dated, journalistic overview of women's status in Israel. A good introduction to the subject.

Izraeli, Dafna N. "Israeli Women in the Workforce," *Jerusalem Quarterly* 27 (Spring 1983), 59–80.
A survey of contemporary Israeli women's roles and positions in the labor force. Highly useful analysis of female employment trends and explanatory variables.

Lieblich, Amia. *Kibbutz Makom.* New York: Pantheon, 1982.
An oral history of three generations of kibbutz members; particularly revealing interviews with women kibbutz members about their lives and attitudes.

Palgi, Michal, Joseph Blasi, Menachem Rosner, and Marilyn Safir. *Sexual Equality: The Israeli Kibbutz Tests the Theories.* Norwood, PA: Norwood Editions, 1982.
A presentation of many different perspectives on the problem of sexual equality on the kibbutz; a fine summary of previous research and exploration of the future.

Rein, Natalie. *Daughters of Rachel.* Harmondsworth, PA: Penguin Books, 1979.
The only study in English of the fledgling Israeli women's movement. The interpretation and projection to the future is overly optimistic, but the book includes valuable documentary material.

Shazar, Rachel Katznelson, ed. *The Plough Woman: Memoirs of the Pioneer Women of Palestine.* New York: Herzl Press, 1975.
A beautiful collection of memoirs of pioneer women during the pre-state period and their struggles against sex discrimination.

7

The Gender Gap in American Politics

Marjorie Lansing
Eastern Michigan University

The Gender Gap

Women became a recognized force for the first time in American politics with the emergence of a gender gap in the 1980 election.[1] This gap widened in the 1982 election, when women were credited with providing the margin of victory for the election of governors in three key states, Michigan, New York, and Texas. The differences between men and women in 1984 in political attitude widened further, but the actual vote by women was disappointing to feminists, who had expected that the selection of Geraldine Ferraro as the first woman to serve as a candidate for vice-president would be a major factor in defeating Ronald Reagan, a president on record as opposing key feminist issues. With Ferraro leading the charge, 1984 was supposed to be a banner year for women in American politics. However Reagan's landslide victory over Walter Mondale meant that Ferraro's bid failed, and women candidates across the country were defeated in greater numbers than expected. Reagan's sweep of 49 of the 50 states obscured the facts, however, that the gender gap held in 1984, with a 10 percent difference in the vote by women as compared to men—the same lower vote for Reagan by women as in 1980. Although there are slight differences in the exit polls from which these data are drawn, women in almost all categories except those living in the region of the South and women over 60 years of age voted in lesser numbers for the Republican candidate, Reagan, than men did. Further, the gender gap was credited with making the difference in several crucial state races.

Women helped to oust Senator Roger Jepson of Iowa, a prime
supporter of New Right legislation. Women gave his opponent Tom
Harkin 56 percent of their vote, 4 points more than men did, as
compared to 39 percent for Jepson. Women gave 56 percent of their
vote compared to 46 percent by men to provide a margin that
elected the more liberal Democrat Paul Simon over Senator Charles
Percy in Illinois. The liberal Democrat Carl Levin in Michigan
received 55 percent of the women's vote as compared to 46 percent
of the vote by men. A full review state by state would reveal that
women were a factor in a number of other races, and other positions.
The victory of a woman, Madeleine Kunin, as governor of Vermont
depended on a heavy women's vote.

Thus the pattern of the women's vote in 1980 and 1982 was repeated in 1984, but the Reagan landslide is not to be minimized.
There were profound demographic shifts across the country that
helped to account for this landslide. He won every region, every age
group, and almost every demographic voting bloc. Mondale showed
strength in older, industrial cities, and won blacks, Jews, and older
people earning less than $10,000 a year. Despite the Reagan av-
alanche, however, the gender gap, the difference in the vote by men
and women, held on the national scene and in many state races. The
magnitude of the Reagan vote and the failure of women to deliver an
enormous vote in line with pre-election expectations obscured the
value of the gender gap in 1984. A first disappointment for feminists
was that despite widespread efforts to register and vote more
women, there was only a slight increase in voter turnout. Nevertheless, although a majority of women voted for Reagan, who received
59 percent of the vote, women were found in greater numbers than
men in the 41 percent of the vote received by Walter Mondale. The
following data are of interest since they present the subgroups of
voters marking the differences in votes cast for Reagan. Table 7.1
provides a comparison of the vote by men and women in the 1980
and 1984 presidential contests by age, education, race, region, and
marital status. The comparison validates the observation that a
pattern in both elections is found that shows that women gave a
lower vote to Reagan than men did with the exception of women
over 60 years of age, and men and women of high school education,
who cast a similar vote (60 and 61 percent). Women who contributed
to the gender gap were more likely to have less than high school
education or to have college experience, to be unmarried, and to live
in the East. Half as many black women (6 percent) voted for Reagan
as did black men (12 percent) Women who were voting in higher

percentages for Reagan were more likely found in the South; they were high school graduates; and they were married. Support for Mondale was 10 percent higher among women who are union members than their male colleagues, casting 68 percent for Mondale compared to 58 percent by men.

Thus, since women voted in the same proportions as men in 1980, and actually in greater numbers, why did Reagan win? Both women and men gave Reagan an extraordinary majority. Peace and prosperity had a great deal to do with it, as well as his image as a strong and decisive leader. When *The Los Angeles Times* asked voters to choose the single most important reason for their vote, "strong qualities of leadership" was the leading explanation. Mondale's best issues were nuclear arms control, environmental protection, civil rights, and particularly fairness—the same ones that had been influential for women in 1980. But in 1984 prosperity overrode the fairness issue—just as Reagan's record of peace tended to override concern about his administration's lack of progress on arms control. However, although the polling data reveal widespread approval of the president's performance in office, there was little agreement by voters on politics for the future. As a mandate for the future, the message of the 1984 election was far from clear, and this was especially true for women.

The consequences of the Ferraro factor in the 1984 election await long-term assessment. But in the short run, as the first woman ever nominated in America by a major party as well as the first Italian American, she made history. Her nomination at the National Convention of the Democratic party in San Francisco put the only significant dip in the polls that showed that more than half of the voters had decided to vote for Reagan in the early months of 1984, before the campaigns actually began. In brief, Ferraro had an immense psychological effect on many women, who were excited about her candidacy. Her campaigning appeared to have star-quality ability to raise funds for the party, and to attract crowds that frequently outdrew Mondale. However, severe tests came early in the campaign with controversy over her own and her husband John Zaccaro's finances. Feminists complained that the attacks on her finances far exceeded those generally made on male candidates. Further, she had difficulties with the leaders of her own Roman Catholic church, who publicly criticized her position supporting free choice on abortion.

It is not clear in the short run whether her candidacy helped or hurt the Mondale ticket. In the South it is apparent that she turned

TABLE 7.1

The Vote by Men and Women in 1980 and 1984 (in percentages)

	1980			1984		
	Reagan	**Carter**	**Anderson**	**Reagan**	**Mondale**	**Percent of 1984 Vote**
Total	**51**	**41**	**7**	**59**	**41**	
Age						
Men, 18–29 years old	47	39	11	61	37	11
Women, 18–29 years old	39	49	10	55	45	13
Men, 30–44 years old	59	31	4	62	37	17
Women, 30–44 years old	50	41	8	54	46	18
Men, 45–59 years old	60	34	5	63	36	11
Women, 45–59 years old	50	44	5	58	41	12
Men, 60 and older	56	40	3	62	37	9
Women, 60 and older	52	43	4	64	35	10
Education						
Men with less than high school education	51	47	2	54	46	4
Women with less than high school education	41	56	2	46	52	4
Male high school graduates	53	42	3	61	38	12
Female high school graduates	50	44	5	60	39	18
Men with some college	59	31	8	63	36	14
Women with some college	52	39	8	58	41	16
Men, college graduates	58	28	11	65	34	16
Women, college graduates	42	44	12	53	47	13

Race						
White men	59	32	7	68	31	41
White women	52	39	8	64	36	45
Black men	14	82	3	12	85	4
Black women	9	88	3	6	93	5
Region						
Men in the East	52	38	8	57	42	12
Women in the East	42	47	10	47	52	12
Men in the Midwest	55	37	6	63	35	13
Women in the Midwest	47	44	7	59	41	15
Men in the South	58	38	3	64	36	14
Women in the South	47	50	3	63	36	15
Men in the West	56	30	11	62	37	8
Women in the West	51	38	9	57	42	10
Marital Status						
Married men	N.A.	N.A.	N.A.	65	34	32
Married women	N.A.	N.A.	N.A.	60	39	35
Unmarried men	N.A.	N.A.	N.A.	53	45	12
Unmarried women	N.A.	N.A.	N.A.	50	49	16

Source: *The New York Times/CBS News Poll.* (1984 data based on interviews with 8,698 voters leaving polling places around the nation. Those who did not answer or said they had no comment are not shown. Neither are groups for whom the samples available were too small.) November 8, 1984, 11.

off women as well as men. Overall, a general confusion reinforces a long-standing observation that presidential nominees win or lose on their own merits: Voters do not vote for the vice-president per se.

Thus, the 1984 election was essentially a referendum on Reagan, and the judgment was immensely positive. Nevertheless the exit polls revealed significant and growing divisions in the electorate, and this clearly states the paradox for the decade under review in this book, 1975–1985. The conservative Ronald Reagan advocated turning the clock back for women. Further, groups such as the antifeminist evangelicals and a minority of women organized to defeat the ERA and to support pro-life measures became more strident in 1984. These groups had risen in part as a backlash to the women's movement of the 1970s. They attacked the women found on the progressive side as being opposed to traditional values, as disrupting family structure, and as deviant. Thus, the decade is puzzling. It saw both a political unity among a majority of women, yet an articulate, well-organized antifeminist group emerged with support from the Reagan White House. Of interest to this analysis is to explain the origin and development of the gender gap as it appeared in 1980.

The Demographics of Women

What are the causes of the gender gap? Survey data show that it is rooted in long-term demographic changes. The first of these has been the lowering of the birthrate. In the 1960s the development of the pill was influential in the rise of the women's movement. In the last decade, on average, women have been having fewer than two children. In this connection the Census Bureau reported that the size of the average household in 1982 was 2.72 persons, the smallest yet recorded, continuing the marked decline that has been underway since 1965.

This means that the conventional nuclear family in which the husband goes to work and the wife stays home is no longer the norm. The nuclear family accounts for only 16 percent of the households. The significance of this change cannot be overestimated. Forty-five million women are working in paid employment, some 50 percent of all women between the ages of 18 and 64. Over the past 25 years, for every two men entering the paid work force, three women entered. By 1990 women will constitute more than half of the American labor force.

Family structure has also altered, and the number of one-parent households has more than doubled since 1970. Compared with their

counterparts in 1970, women maintaining famili
younger, more likely not to have been married o
more likely to be black or Hispanic.

Women are gaining in numbers over men. Men st
percent advantage over women and end up with mo
to-one disadvantage. Young men lose their numeric ̲̲̲̲periority
over women by age 27. At every age above that, there are progressively more women than men in the United States because,
from one age to the next, fewer men survive. Women will continue to
outnumber men, and as the population gets older a larger majority
will be women. In close elections, therefore, women can make the
difference.

Another significant demographic change is the increase in the
proportion of educated women in the population, a topic we will
treat at more length later. Briefly, by 1960, of all persons aged 25 and
older who had been in college for four or more years, 39 percent
were women. In 1975 the proportion had grown to 41 percent, and it
reached 45 percent by 1980. Education widens the world view of
individuals and increases the sense of competence to live one's life
as one wishes. These consequences heighten the probability that the
individual will recognize the pervasive influence the political system exerts on day-to-day life and express her preferences by voting.
A key finding in voting behavior research over a quarter of a century
is that level of education is a prime predictor of voting. College-
educated women vote at higher rates than do lesser-educated
women. The fact that more women have been gaining college experience will continue to have an important impact on American
politics.[2]

The Women's Movement

Another factor with a profound influence on the political attitudes
of women is the women's movement, which affected their socialization. The women's movement entered its third wave in the decade
between 1975 and 1985. The movement had its origins in the long
struggle to secure the right to vote. Along with the extraordinary
Temperance Crusade, the drive for suffrage was a single-issue campaign, and once the goal was achieved, the first wave of the women's
movement dispersed. There was no sustaining ideology. Still,
women continued to rally around political causes, organized non-
partisan groups, and were mildly active as volunteers in community affairs and political parties.

The women's movement of the 1960s was the second wave. It rose as a protest movement in a rapidly changing society. An overwhelming fact of the time was the transformation of the role and status of women. Women recognized this change and took advantage of the new opportunities opening up to them. They now constitute a force in America comparable to the organized labor movement in the first half of the twentieth century. What began as a special interest protest emerged into a loose organization of individual groups that range across the full spectrum from liberal to conservative ideologies.

In 1975–1985, women lost the big battle for the Equal Rights Amendment. Yet, they became consciously aware as never before that the future of women's rights is a quintessentially political issue. The maturing of the women who learned the lessons of serious campaigning in the ERA fight ensures that the past will not overtake the future. The multitude of women who forged new political skills on behalf of the ERA have subsequently focused on a wide range of economic and social issues important to women. The impact of this movement should not be underestimated.

These changes in the social and economic roles of women have influenced their political attitudes. This has been a gradual process. From the 1950s on, while women did not constitute anything like a visible voting bloc, there have been distinguishable differences in attitude between the sexes. At times, women were slightly more inclined than men to favor racial justice, federal expenditures for so-called humanitarian programs, and nonviolence, thus favoring gun control, nuclear safety, and opposition to capital punishment.

In 1952 women's support for Dwight Eisenhower led the pollster Louis Harris to speculate on a potential women's vote. In 1972 women were slightly more favorable than men to George McGovern for his peace stand, and 7 percent fewer women than men voted for Richard Nixon. Women were half as likely as men to support the candidacy of George Wallace.

Throughout the period, the most committed difference between men and women has been over issues pertaining to peace or war.

By the 1980 election, these long-term changes were confirmed as women did for the first time vote as a bloc. Why did this occur in 1980?

Most analysts agree that three central issues converged in the 1980 election, with the major candidates presenting clear choices for alternate policies. This choice is unusual in presidential contests, when candidates tend to take the middle ground in order not to alienate constituencies found at either end of the ideological continuum. The 1980 election found women more negative than men on the Reagan candidacy in relation to the peace/war issue, economic discontent, and the women's agenda (pro-choice, pro-ERA, pro-equal status for women).

Candidate Choice

An intriguing question is whether the gender gap is simply a "gipper gap," that is, related entirely to the personality and leadership style of Ronald Reagan, or whether it is a more enduring phenomenon. This question is central to the agenda for ongoing study of gender differences in political behavior.

While this major analysis is drawn from the National Election Studies of the Center for Political Studies at the University of Michigan, data from various other public opinion surveys also make clear that there is a persistence of the pattern of the gender gap throughout the Reagan presidency. Although surveys vary, men in 1980 gave 55 percent of their vote to Reagan and only 35 percent to Jimmy Carter. Women divided evenly between these two candidates, 47 percent for Reagan and 45 percent for Carter. Significantly, these differences cut across all age categories, all income and educational levels, and all regions. An interesting difference was exhibited by married men and women, who showed less of a gap than single men and women. This difference continued in the 1982 congressional elections. This so-called marriage gulf is also a continuing pattern in the 1984 surveys. Some social scientists argue that Reagan's real problem is a "single woman" gap. Data from the 1980 election indicate

> *Political Party Choice.* Contrary to previous years, women expressed a 6 percent higher preference than men for the Democratic party and a 4 percent lower preference for the Republican party. This preference carried through the 1982 and 1984 federal elections. Party choice obviously did not correlate in high percentages in 1984. Party choice is not the same as candidate choice.
>
> *Economic Issues.* Women indicated more economic discontent than men, and saw their financial condition as worse compared to a year ago. Women were more liberal than men on social welfare issues. Women seem to have a higher compassion index.
>
> *International Politics.* Reagan's support for significantly increased defense spending and his Cold War view

were perceived as his most distinctive policy positions. Most analysts agree that women's perception of Reagan as a possible "war-monger" was central to their coolness to his campaign.

Women's Issues. Support for women's issues found remarkable agreement between men and women, with 55 percent agreeing that society discriminates against women, and 60 percent supporting the Equal Rights Amendment.

Environmental Issues. Women continued to be less favorable than men to a federal policy to build more nuclear plants. Women were also less likely than men to favor relaxing governmental regulations concerning the environment.

Women Elites in Politics

The development of the gender gap has the potential to propel more female candidates into appointive and elective office. The threat of a women's bloc vote gives a bargaining power that women in America have never had before. As a result, it appears that for the first time in American politics there is an advantage for a candidate to be a woman. Much of the impetus for women to pursue professional careers and to test their political skills in partisan campaigns has come from the women's movement. There is no clear evidence from the 1980 and 1984 elections that the gender gap was employed to the advantage of women candidates, but the gain seems to be that the prejudice of yesteryears against electing women candidates is disappearing. This notion was expressed by Nancy Sinnott, executive director of the Republican Congressional Campaign Committee: "We saw in 1980 the crumbling of the attitude [prejudice] in a lot of places in the country, and I can't think of anywhere it's a big problem now." Ruth Mandel, director of the Center for the American Woman and Politics agrees: "Women who get nominated have about the same chance of winning as a man. For a long time, a woman could land a nomination only if the situation called for a sacrificial lamb, someone to run against an unbeatable male. That time has passed."[3]

Only time will tell.

Unquestionably, the defeat of the Equal Rights Amendment by male-dominated legislatures politicized women's organizations and inspired women to become candidates. The National Organization for Women (NOW) and the Women's Campaign Fund gave a total of $2.5 million in cash and services to women, and to a few men, in the 1982 off-year congressional races. NOW supported 109 candidates, of which 60 percent were elected. NOW also raised more funds in 1983 than the Democratic National Committee. Geraldine Ferraro proved to be an excellent fund-raiser for the Democratic party in 1984.

The figures describing the gains made by women seeking elective office sound impressive. In the years between 1975 and 1980 the percentage of women holding elective offices across the country more than doubled, for a total of 9 percent of these offices. There were some gains in 1982 and 1984, but a missing piece of the puzzle is that there are so few women candidates. Women in America remain marginal in holding elite political posts.

Thus, we have shown that the emergence of the gender gap in the 1980s marked a milestone for the recognition of women in American politics. Since the reasons for this difference in attitude and behavior between men and women are anchored in long-run variables, it would appear that the gender gap will remain.

Several conditions must be met, however, for the gender gap to continue. There must be a clear choice of issues as presented by the candidates. Since candidates often seek the middle ground on issues so as not to alienate voters on either end of a left-right continuum, it is not always possible for the voter to find alternative positions on issues. The 1980 election was classic in meeting this condition. The gender gap would disappear also if peace became the world picture, if America returned to a prosperous, booming economy, and if discrimination against women no longer existed. The leading candidates presented clear choices of issues in 1984, but the failure of the Democratic candidate, Walter Mondale, to present alternatives as a qualified leader apparently led to an immense victory for Ronald Reagan. The gender gap did not withstand the peace and prosperity image that was presented by the Republican candidate. However, most observers join Theodore H. White, a foremost expert on U.S. politics, in assessing the 1984 election in the post-election issue of *Time* magazine. He described "the two largest underswells of 1984 . . ." as being "the outbursts of women and the grotesque debate on church and state." He noted that "Women come first—for no one can talk realistically of American politics today without recognizing them as a new, distinct and independent force."

We turn now to examine the effects of the women's movement on public policy.

The Impact of the Women's Movement on Economic and Social Policy

In the last few decades, changes in the social and economic status of women together with the women's movement have influenced public attitudes. Both men and women are more apt to support improvements in the status of women than they have been in the past. As women have pushed for autonomy and opportunity, the public has slowly come around to support their efforts. By 1980 a majority of both sexes supported the so-called feminist agenda, including sensitive and controversial issues such as abortion and the Equal Rights Amendment. As Table 7.2 suggests, by 1980 the differences between men and women on these issues were minimal.

These changes in attitude had an impact on public policy. John Kingdon has written of the links between public opinion and policy:

> People in and around government sense a national mood. They are comfortable discussing its content, and believe that they know when the mood shifts. The idea goes by different names— the national mood, the climate in the country, changes in public opinion, or broad social movements. But common to all these labels is the notion that a rather large number of people out in the country are thinking along certain common lines, that this national mood changes from one time to another in discernible ways, and that these changes in mood or climate have important impacts on policy agendas and policy outcomes.[4]

What is public policy? Carl J. Freidrich defines it as "a proposed course of action of a person, group or government within a given environment providing obstacles and opportunities which the policy was proposed to utilize and overcome in an effort to reach a goal or realise an objective or purpose."[5] There is little systematic knowledge of the impact of policies. In America, if a policy is a statute enacted by Congress, its impact depends entirely on the appropriation of funds attached to the statute, and its enforcement is further enhanced or hindered by the regulations or administrative laws of the executive bureaucracy of the federal or state governments. In some cases the impact of the policy is highly dependent on the philosophy and attitudes of the American president. A signal from the White House can either make or break a federal program. The same is true for state policy. Over time, public attitudes do translate into policy; whether those policies come to be fully implemented is another question.

Public policy in America has traditionally sought to protect women, not to accord them equal rights. This goal both reflected and

TABLE 7.2

Support for Feminist Issues, 1980

	WOMEN	MEN
Do you approve or disapprove of the proposed Equal Rights Amendment to the Constitution, sometimes called the ERA Amendment? (Approve)	63%	60%
In general, do you agree or disagree with the following statement: Our society discriminates against women? (Agree)	56	55
There's been some discussion about abortion during recent years. Which of these opinions best agrees with your view?		
Abortion should never be permitted.	10	9
Abortion should be permitted only if the life and health of the woman is in danger.	44	44
Abortion should be permitted if due to personal reasons, the woman would have difficulty in caring for the child.	16	20
Abortion should never be forbidden, since one should not require a woman to have a child she doesn't want.	29	24

Source of Data: Center for Political Studies, American National Election Studies, 1980, University of Michigan.

reinforced the nineteenth-century concern to protect the role of motherhood and preserve the family, and thus the moral fabric of the country. In fact, protectionism has perpetuated sexual inequality. Further, the three principal policy-makers—the president, Congress, and the courts—have been virtually a patriarchy since colonial times.

It is because of the magnitude of this opposition that the gains of the women's movement up to 1975 are so impressive. It achieved unprecedented legislative acts, executive orders, and court decisions. Milestones include the Equal Pay Act of 1963, the Civil Rights Act of 1964, Congressional support for the ERA and the pro-abortion decision by the Supreme Court in *Roe* v. *Wade* in 1973.

From 1975, internal conflict made the women's movement resemble the fictional Dr. Dolittle's Pushmi-Pullyu, an animal moving in two different directions. Forces on the Left crusaded for the feminist agenda. They were led by the National Organization for Women, a militant group formed in 1966 as a national action group. By 1984 NOW pressed most actively for ratification of the ERA, for equal pay, and to mobilize women to register and vote. This agenda was directly opposed by women on the Right, primarily under the leadership of Phyllis Schlafly. This group tried to hold the line on these social issues, opposing the ERA and seeking a pro-life amendment. In general, they sought a return to a policy of protectionism.

Another reason for the setbacks experienced by women in this period is that the women's movement struck hard times. The U.S. economy underwent its most devastating unemployment since the major economic depression of 1929. Business and industry, universities, medical institutions, city and state governments coped with inflation and slow economic growth. It was in this poor economic climate that women sought to implement policies like equal pay and affirmative action, and often were successful. The Reagan administration, elected in 1980 and reelected in 1984, has lowered inflation rates, and economic recovery has been underway. However, these benefits have been indirect as they affect the status of women.

A point-by-point review of policies related to status of women in the decade will make these points clear. We will look first at the policy, and then at the measures of its impacts.

The Lessons of the Equal Rights Amendment Fight

For the advocates of women's rights the most dramatic victory in the 1970s occurred in 1972 when the Equal Rights Amendment, almost a half-century after it was introduced, received the needed two-thirds vote of Congress and was ready for ratification by three-fourths of the state legislatures. Initially ERA had easy sailing at the state level, with 28 legislatures ratifying it during the first year. However in 1973 a "Stop ERA" campaign came to life, organized by Phyllis Schlafly. Her efforts were joined by many women, various conservative churches, and business groups who persuaded legislatures in three states to vote down ratification in 1983.

This amendment would have prohibited the denial of equality of rights under the law on account of sex. It was an omnibus bill providing an umbrella under which the state legislatures and Congress would have been given two years to bring legislation into line to correct discriminatory features in many areas, such as social security, insurance, pensions, and credit. The ratification campaign stalled because of disagreement as to the meaning of the amendment, and the answers that might eventually be given by the courts. Particularly effective in the campaign against the amendment were the arguments that it might require drafting women for combat in war, or that it might undermine laws that protected women on the job.[6] As the years went by, the issue came also to symbolize a struggle over a wide range of cultural issues.

While the defeat of the Equal Rights Amendment in 1983 was a setback for the feminist movement, it did not show a lack of support for equal rights for women in the United States. Not only did 35 states ratify the proposed amendment, lacking only 3 states for ratification, which would have meant success, but most people seemed to agree that women should have equal rights. As noted in Table 7.2, a majority of women and men favor this amendment. Second only to the crusade for the suffrage amendment fought in the nineteenth and early twentieth century, the fight for passage of the Equal Rights Amendment turned out to be the proving ground for the women's movement to develop maturity in playing the political game in a professional manner. The advocates lost the war, but won the battle. Women learned that they had to be insiders at the state house. Women learned that they had to raise money and follow traditional methods of electing candidates to office. Women learned that they had to go beyond being volunteers in political campaigns. The slogan "Run for office, not for coffee" became popular. In addition to developing sophisticated skills in lobbying and running for elective office, the fight over the ERA produced a skilled leadership that built networks to many women's organizations that had never cooperated before. This unification of the women's movement through consciousness raising, educating women about discrimination, and developing new political skills undoubtedly contributed to the emergence of the gender gap in the elections of the 1980s.

Despite the outcome of the 1984 elections, the Equal Rights Amendment will continue to be in the forefront of the women's movement. However, many of the goals of the ERA have already been achieved by legislative or court actions, thus suggesting that it may not be necessary to go the route of a constitutional amendment.

Job Opportunity and Access to Influential Position

The emphasis of the women's movement from the beginning has been to improve the economic status of women. More than 20 years have passed since passage of the Equal Pay Act of 1963, and Title VII of the Civil Rights Act of 1964 was enacted to prevent discrimination by sex. In 1972 the Equal Employment Opportunity Act extended the provisions of the 1964 Act to educational institutions, state and local governments. Title IX of the Educational Amendments Act attempted to open up opportunities for women in federally-aided education programs.

Milda K. Hedblom in 1983 evaluated the response of institutions to these public policies. She drew on two recent studies that measure the success of efforts to improve women's access to institutional centers of power. Hedblom summarized,

> Women continue as a tiny minority of those at the top despite specific goals of access. Women may be influenced in social, economic or political life in a variety of ways, but that influence is not primarily exercised through direct occupation of positions vested with power.

Hedblom cited the research of Dye and Strickland, who looked at 12 separate sectors of society in the United States. Their conclusion was that women were found to occupy about 4.1 percent of top institutional positions or 318 of 7,783 positions in 1980. Despite these small numbers, this represented nearly a doubling of the proportion of women in top institutional positions since 1970, when it was 1.9 percent.[7] Table 7.3 describes women's efforts to gain access and the variation of achievement in sectors.

The Wage Gap

The continuing inequality in the earnings of men and women remains a puzzle. During the 1970s women belonging to such organizations as the National Women's Organization wore green and white buttons that read 59¢. This underscored the fact that for every dollar a man was paid, a woman was paid only 59¢. This was part of an ongoing crusade to correct the disparity in wages between working men and women. Two legislative acts were intended to correct the wage gap. The Equal Pay Act of 1963 had been a significant victory for labor, civil rights, and women's organizations, who worked for 17 years for its passage. The Equal Pay Act provided equal pay for equal work and responsibility on jobs performed under similar working conditions. The passage of this act resulted in payment of 314 million dollars in back pay for women because of individual and class action suits in courts of law. Other major pieces of federal legislation in the area of pay equity included Title VII of the Civil Rights Act of 1964, which presumably was enforced by a federal agency known as the Equal Opportunity Commission. However, as stated earlier, the regulation and enforcement of this type of legislation depends greatly on the intention of the president and his administration. After the election of Ronald Reagan in 1980, the signal from the White House was counter to the best economic interests of women.

TABLE 7.3

Women in Institutional Leadership Positions, 1970 and 1980

	TOTAL NUMBER OF POSITIONS[a]		NUMBER OF WOMEN		PERCENTAGE OF WOMEN	
	1970	1980	1970	1980	1970	1980
Industry	1,543	1,499	3	36	0.2	2.4
Banking	1,189	1,095	2	25	0.2	2.3
Utilities	476	668	0	29	0	4.3
Insurance	362	783	3	9	0.8	1.1
Law	1,076	1,259	12	23	1.1	1.8
Investments	417	550	3	5	0.7	0.9
Mass media	213	235	9	16	4.2	6.8
Foundations	121	402	9	59	7.4	14.7
Universities	656	481	11	51	2.1	10.6
Civic and Cultural	438	536	70	45	16.0	9.0
Government	227	258	10	20	2.5	7.7
Military	24	17	0	0	0	0
Total	6,733	7,783	132	318	1.9	4.1

Source: Dye and Strickland, "Women at the Top: A Note on Institutional Leadership," *Social Science Quarterly* 63 (1982), 335.

[a]Presidents, all corporate directors including officer-directors; senior partners in law and investment firms; governing trustees of foundations, universities, and civic and cultural organizations; secretaries, undersecretaries and assistant secretaries of federal executive branch, senior White House advisors, congressional leaders, and Supreme Court justices; four-star generals and admirals on active duty.

There have been factors above and beyond presidential influence. A comprehensive study by Mary J. Corcoran and Greg J. Duncan concluded that the wage gap has not narrowed in recent decades, and that most of the wage gap is not justified by differences in qualifications. Further, a key conclusion was that the wage gap may simply reflect bias against women in the working world. They wrote:

> Essentially we are left with two alternative explanations of the persistent wage gap between men and women: (1) socialization effects may lead women to aspire to lower-paying jobs in the so-called 'pink-collar ghetto', and (2) institutionalized sex discrimination in the labor market may obstruct women's access to the 'better' jobs through hiring or promotion, or may simply mean less pay for women than men in any job.

Contrary to the prevailing view among feminists, this study found that the so-called old-boy network did not give men an advantage in finding better jobs. Men were somewhat more likely than women to obtain their jobs through an influential contact, but data on actual earnings turned up little evidence that using the influential connections led substantially to higher pay for either sex. Corcoran and Duncan went further:

> More than half the earnings gap remained unexplainable suggesting that we need to turn more attention toward the alternative explanations of socialization effects and discrimination. . . . It appears that we need the kinds of policies that attack discrimination directly by enforcing strict guidelines to ensure that equally qualified women and men receive equal treatment in hiring, pay and promotion.[8]

In the face of the continuing wage gap, women's leadership has developed a new legislative goal they describe as the fairness doctrine. The new concept is known as comparable worth, and is based on the assumption that women who work in jobs stereotyped as "women's work" are paid low wages and have little advancement opportunities. This concept is new because it operates on the basis of job value rather than labor market value. Traditional job evaluation systems by which wage rates are determined are viewed as maintaining and contributing to the wage gap between men and women. However, an equitable pay policy considers the value of the job to an employer rather than the market value of the same job. The concept of comparable worth does not require immediate increases to achieve pay equity, but calls for a reexamination of the causes of wage discrimination and the development of a pay equity process.

Critics have argued that comparable worth would be difficult to implement, that it would disrupt the workplace, and that some of the underlying premises of pro-worth advocacy are invalid. Nevertheless women's organizations are lobbying state legislatures and Congress for action on comparable worth, which appears to be the pay equity and civil rights issue of the 1980s.

In Congress, a growing number of men as well as women have shown new interest in the special economic problems of women. The fight has been led by the Congressional Caucus for Women's Issues. "Obviously, the members of the House of Representatives have to be more responsive to so-called women's issues," said Representative Marge Roukema, a New Jersey Republican. "There's growing recognition that the reward for a lifetime of homemaking can be an old age of poverty." But the women in Congress say their male colleagues are not acting entirely out of altruistic motives. Representatives Geraldine Ferraro, a New York Democrat, and Walter Mondale's choice for vice-presidential candidate in 1984, commented: "Quite frankly, they're worried about the gender gap, and I'm delighted it's there. We'll take support for whatever reason it's given."[9] An omnibus bill, known as the Economic Equity Act, should produce battles on Capitol Hill in the mid-1980s. Its provisions include tougher procedures for collecting court-ordered child support payments, reforms in pension and insurance benefits for women, tax credits to companies that hire displaced homemakers, and increased tax deductions for child care expenses. The act is part of a new feminist strategy developed after the defeat of the ERA, which would have ended discrimination in many of these areas.

Will comparable worth and the various provisions of the Economic Equity Act be implemented? The outlook depends on the direction of the economy, on the national mood, and on the occupants of the White House and Capitol Hill. But Representative Ferraro seemed to express the sentiments of the women's movement when she remarked "We're patient. If we don't get it all through this time (session of Congress in 1984), we'll just put our bill in again next time."

The Social Issues

One of the most volatile issues in American politics is abortion. Surveys taken during the 1975–1985 decade showed that a majority of men and women favored the rights of women to have control of their reproductive function. However, pro-life groups, aided by the rise of the Christian right, have worked vigorously in Congress to overturn the Supreme Court rulings by amending the Constitution to prohibit abortions. The women's movement had scored a remarkable victory in 1973 when the Supreme Court ruled in the 7 to 2 *Roe* v. *Wade* decision that no state may interfere with a woman's right to have an abortion during the first trimester of pregnancy. Since 1973 it is estimated that 1.3 million women terminated pregnancies by abortion each year.

Abortion became legal in 1973, but the Supreme Court decision did not settle the question of who should pay for abortions. The backlash from the pro-life supporters succeeded in passing the controversial amendment, sponsored by Henry J. Hyde, an Illinois Republican, that banned federal Medicaid payments for abortions even though medically necessary, except in cases of incest, rape, or where the mother's life was endangered. This worked against already disadvantaged women, since Medicaid had been paying for an estimated 300,000 abortions a year.

Pro-life supporters have vigorously lobbied members of Congress and state legislatures, which in the 1980s became the battlegound for disputes over funding. In 1980, 19 of the 34 states needed had passed resolutions calling for a constitutional convention to consider an anti-abortion amendment.

Pro-choice activists continue to support the 1973 Supreme Court decision, the principle of sex education in the public schools, and increased funding for research into both contraception and infertility. Again, the outcome will depend on the national mood, and more particularly on the philosophies of the new members of the Supreme Court who were likely to replace five members who were over 70 years of age in the mid 1980s, and who were seeking retirement.

EDUCATION

By the 1970s, women had significantly increased their level of education, as we discussed earlier. Twice as many women had some college training than was true in the 1950s. Almost one-third of all women aged 25– 29 continued their education beyond high school; among those aged 45– 64 fewer than 17 percent did so. In effect, the average woman today is far better educated than her mother.

These gains were encouraged by Title IX, a part of the Education Amendment of 1972, a federal law designed to prohibit discrimination on the basis of sex in all institutions receiving federal funds. This applied to all aspects of the schools' programs, not simply athletics. Title IX provided a tough enforcement mechanism: the withholding of all federal funds from discriminatory schools.

Women's gains in education have been threatened in 1975–1985 by the drift of the Supreme Court toward conservatism. One example is the showdown between equal educational rights and "education as usual" in the 1984 *Grove City* vs. *Bell* case. In a 6– 3 decision, the Court ruled that an educational institution could only be denied federal funds for specific programs that were found to be discriminatory, and not its entire federal funding. Feminist leaders believed that this decision gutted the spirit and enforcement power of Title IX.

One significant gain in education is the increased enrollment of women in professional training. By 1980 women were 12.8 percent of the one-half million lawyers in the United States. In 1975 women comprised 15.1 percent of law school graduates. By 1980 women had doubled that number, comprising some 31 percent. Further, by 1975 women constituted over 50 percent of the entering classes at several prestigious law schools.

This is an important development for the future of electing women to high office. More than half of the members of the U.S. Senate are lawyers, a profession that has dominated the halls of Congress and state legislatures from the days of colonial America.

Females were admitted to law schools in very few numbers until the last quarter of the century, with the rise of the women's movement. That barrier has been broken down. The entry of women into the legal profession portends a brighter future in winning elective posts.

POVERTY AS WOMAN'S ISSUE

The impact of public policy by the mid-1980s appeared to work toward the feminization of poverty, as described by the leadership of the women's movement. With the election of Ronald Reagan as president in 1980, the federal government engaged in cutting back assistance programs that had their origins in the New Deal in the 1930s under Franklin Delano Roosevelt. These programs had been implemented under Democratic presidents following Roosevelt, and were greatly accelerated under the Great Society program of President Lyndon B. Johnson. President Reagan had campaigned on a platform of cutting programs associated with the welfare state economy, and proceeded at once in his administration to roll back the clock on federal assistance to disadvantaged people. As described earlier in this chapter in looking at the demographics of women, many more women than men were vulnerable to these cutbacks. By mid-1980 almost 80 percent of poor people were women and children. Some 42 percent of all female single-parent households with children under 18 lived in poverty. Fifty percent of all minority female single-parent households with children under 18 lived in poverty, and two of three poor persons who were more than 65 years of age lived in poverty. Poverty had become a woman's issue and would accelerate in the future unless there was a return to a more prosperous economy and a continuation of federal and state assistance programs for disadvantaged people.

Thus, altogether there have been major changes in the life-styles of women during the decade under study. The response to the women's movement by the major policy-makers has been an uneven record.

OUTLOOK

For the first time during the decade under study American women became a force in American politics because of the emergence of the gender gap. Until then, women had been an invisible political majority with little influence over governmental policy and selection and election of candidates. Also, during this decade issues of particular interest to women gained remarkable acceptance across the country. According to various public opinion surveys, every major issue supported by the women's movement had found majority support from men and women. The explanation for this new visibility of women voters is found in the profound changes taking place in the roles of women in American society. The significant increase in women's socioeconomic status has given them background, resources, and interest in playing a more influential role in exercising influence in public policy.

What then is the outlook for the year 2000?

The women's movement in America is entering what can be described as the third wave. This development had its origins in the historical struggle of women in the nineteenth and twentieth century to secure the right to vote for women. The women's movement of the 1960s was the second wave. It rose as a protest movement in a world of rapid, large-scale changes in societies, technologies, cultures, and politics. Women now constitute a force in America that is comparable to the organized labor movement of the early twentieth century. What began as a special interest protest has emerged into a cohesive group, loosely organized, highly individualistic, and composed of women bearing left and right ideologies.

The decade under review makes a paradoxical case for women. The record is uneven, but despite setbacks women have the best opportunity since winning the right to vote to exercise political clout. Perhaps most important for the future is that a survey taken in mid-1984 by Louis Harris found a full 57 percent of American women nationwide believing that the women's movement "has just begun."[10]

The gains made in this decade are anchored in long-run variables that cannot vanish in the short run. At the same time external forces can intervene. The women's movement in its crusade for comparable worth, a shorter workweek, job security, and other measures is highly dependent on a growth economy and the philosophy of the major decision-makers. The women's movement must have a sympathetic Supreme Court that recognizes sex as a classification under the Constitution, a president and Congress who support the feminist agenda as well as friendly governors and state legislators. Whatever happens there is no going back to the status quo ante. American women will continue to become cosigners of the social contract.

NOTES

1. For an extensive analysis of the gender gap, see chapters 9 and 10 of Sandra Baxter and Marjorie Lansing, *Women and Politics: The Visible Majority* (Ann Arbor: University of Michigan Press, 1983).

2. Ibid., Chapter 2.

3. Ruth B. Mandel, *In the Running: The New Woman Candidate* (New Haven, CT: Ticknor & Fields, 1981).

4. John W. Kingdon, *Agendas, Alternatives, and Public Policies* (Boston: Little, Brown, 1984), 153.

5. Carl J. Freidrich, *Man and His Government* (New York: McGraw-Hill, 1963), 212.

6. Janet Boles, *The Politics of the Equal Rights Amendment: Conflict and the Decision Process* (New York: Longman).

7. Milda K. Hedblom, "Women and American Political Organizations and Institutions" (American Political Science Association, July 1983), 11.

8. This analysis was based on 13 years of data obtained from an ongoing Panel Study of Income Dynamics, The Institute for Social Research, *Newsletter* (Spring-Summer, 1983), 4, 5, 8.

9. *The New York Times*, May 6, 1984, EY 9.

10. The survey was commissioned by *MS* magazine, July 1984, 54.

RECOMMENDED READINGS

Baxter, Sandra, and Marjorie Lansing. *Women and Politics: The Visible Majority*. Ann Arbor: University of Michigan Press, 1983. This revision of the 1980 edition adds analysis of the 1980 and 1982 elections.

Frankovic, Kathleen A. "Sex and Politics—New Alignments, Old Issues," *Political Science* 15 (Summer 1982). This data-based analysis links the gender gap to women's aversion to war, among other issues.

Githens, Marianne, and Jewel L. Prestage, eds. *A Portrait of Marginality: The Political Behavior of the American Woman*. New York: David McKay, 1977. A reader with studies and commentary on women and politics, looking at the conflicting roles for the woman activist.

Klein, Ethel. *Gender Politics*. Cambridge, MA: Harvard University Press, 1984. A psychological explanation for the preferences of men and women for political issues and candidates.

Mandel, Ruth B. *In the Running: The New Woman Candidate*. New Haven, CT: Ticknor & Fields, 1981. A commentary on the campaign experiences of female candidates.

Sapiro, Virginia. *The Political Integration of Women: Roles, Socialization and Politics*. Urbana: University of Illinois Press, 1983. This study explores the socialization and private roles of women in relation to the integration of women into politics.

Part Two

Developing Countries

THE EIGHT CHAPTERS ON developing countries literally span the globe—Africa, the Middle East, Latin America, Asia, and India. A common theme throughout each is the continuing presence of a patriarchal culture in spite of moves toward urbanization, industrialization, and greater educational opportunities. The first three chapters discuss the varied effects of Muslim culture on women in Nigeria, Iran, and Egypt. The next three chapters, on Latin America, analyze recent trends in feminist research and the status of women in Colombia and in Mexico. This section concludes with a chapter on women in three traditional Chinese societies, Hong Kong, Taiwan, and Singapore, and a chapter on India.

The largest subnational ethnic group in West Africa is the Hausa Muslims of Nigeria. In their chapter, "Law, Education, and Social Change: Implications for Hausa Muslim Women in Nigeria," Barbara Callaway and Enid Schildkrout analyze the interactions among Hausa culture, Islamic beliefs, and modern secular law in Kano City. They discuss the recent constitutional changes that create the coexistence of Islamic and Western legal codes, but create contradictory provisions relating to women in the Sharia and in the fundamental human rights clauses. The authors argue that the legal system will never be effective in introducing reforms in Islamic sections of Nigeria. In the past decade, changes have occurred in women's political participation and in education, but the authors note that the prevalent desire to modernize without challenging the teachings of Islam leaves intact the fundamental family structures, authority relationships, and socialization patterns.

In Iran, the 1979 establishment of the Islamic Republic reinstated
religious fundamentalism and eliminated women's political role.
Eliz Sanasarian's chapter, "Political Activism and Islamic Identity
in Iran," focuses on the regime's limitations on women's status
through the laws and the pronouncements of the present leaders,
and the impact these have had on activists who endorsed women's
rights. She describes the emergence of the fundamentalist state and
identifies three strategies the regime has used to shape an Islamic
identity: radical changes in the educational system, domestication
of women by reenforcing their primary roles as wives and mothers,
and the promotion of the symbolic ideal woman. Two distinct wom-
en's groups have evolved: the reformists, who believe in a progressive Islam and who engage in social welfare activities, and the
traditionalists, who are more closely tied to the male fundamentalists in government. She notes evidence of a decline in the influence of reformists and questions the potential for development of a
genuine pro–women's rights group.

Fadwa El Guindi, in "The Egyptian Woman: Trends Today, Alternatives Tomorrow," discusses the importance of centuries of cultural traditions that form the contemporary Egyptian woman. She
traces two equally important identities, one as part of a kinship
group, and the other as an Arab woman. She says these can create a
culturally reenforced self-confidence in accepting changes, and recent trends in education and employment reflect this. She notes a
shift in attitudes toward working in urban areas rather than in
agriculture, and an increase in the literacy rate and a shift of some
women into professional college majors. A current trend among the
young, professionally educated women is identification with the
Islamic movement, which is seen as an avenue of legitimate access
to a major force in their lives.

In her overview of "Female Political Participation in Latin
America: Raising Feminist Issues," Jane Jaquette discusses the
growing concentration of research on the legal and economic status
of women, but the paucity of studies on political involvement. While
feminist research has grown since the early 1970s, the resurgence of
military regimes has legitimized corporatist theories, which emphasize the control of participation by channeling it through state-
authorized group access and representation, making this more
important than voting in determining government policies. She
argues that the concentration on economic rather than voting
studies also stems from a Marxist orientation to Latin American
social science and from the background experiences in leftist groups
and political parties of most feminists. In her article, Jaquette

analyzes research on women's political participation among female elites, in mass participation, among women's groups and networks, on the human rights issue, and in revolutionary movements. She concludes that feminist research in Latin America is having an impact, but analysts need to link that research more closely to mainstream issues such as capital movements, the debt crisis, interdependence, and new innovations in development theory.

Steffan Schmidt in "Women in Colombia" discusses recent political history in the context of the major historic forces in the country, and notes the persistent impact of social and economic class stratification. He discusses women's informal political participation, such as in villages and small towns, and in formal terms of the vote and in elective office. Although there is little evidence that women have defined a policy agenda, Schmidt cites a number of factors that led to 1974 reforms that improved women's legal position and revised labor law and social security. As in other developing nations, he notes that the status of women is highly dependent upon the viability of the economy, but anticipates increasing involvement of women in policy-making roles.

In "The Status of Women in Mexico: The Impact of the 'International Year of the Woman,'" Adaljiza Riddell argues that Mexico was strongly influenced by hosting the United Nations world conference in 1975 because it furthered an increase in awareness and writing from a feminist perspective. These studies, however, focus on problems and document limited positive changes. Riddell feels that it is the entrenchment of the male government leaders, rather than reluctance or inability of women, that has hindered legal and social equality. She focuses on three major unresolved Mexican issues, juridical equality of women with men, decriminalization of abortion, and reform of the rape laws. The dominant PRI party tries to control women's policies by integrating them into its sectors, while the views of feminists in the other parties have very little impact on public policy. In her conclusions, she notes that the most important impact of IWY was its contribution to the development and politicization of women, and the establishment of independent organizations. These groups are in their best position since the 1920s to enact reforms, she feels. IWY, however, did not change the male-dominated power structure.

Three traditional Chinese areas, Hong Kong, Singapore, and Taiwan, have experienced rapid economic growth since the early 1970s. Janet Salaff discusses the position of Chinese women in her chapter, "Women, the Family, and the State: Hong Kong, Taiwan, Singapore—Newly Industrialized Countries in Asia." She compares some of the geopolitical and program features they hold in common and discusses how their development strategies and dependence on world capitalist economies have incorporated women. All three societies have developed similar family strategies in response to employment opportunities. Economic necessity forces families to send their members into the wage-earning economy, and unmarried women dominate the female labor force. Patrilinial kinship continues to be the family core, and the birth of sons is crucial to the future of the family, while daughters still are expected to sever their parental ties on marriage. The domestic or immediate economic family, and the bonds of sentiment between women and their children may come into conflict with the patrilinial line. Her case study examples document the effects of the emotional stresses of these somewhat contradictory types of family units among unmarried working women in the three countries.

In "Women in India: The Reality," Neela D'Souza and Ramani Natarajan discuss women's expectations when India acquired independence from Great Britain in 1947, and the studies of the 1970s that document their deteriorating position. Despite the legal and constitutional guarantees of the Hindu Code Bill giving women rights of inheritance, divorce, and adoption, recent studies show that women's condition has worsened; the population proportion of women to men is steadily dropping, and life expectancy is lower for women than for men. They note that life for a girl is hard, but paradoxically there is a sprinkling of highly visible educated women, surrounded by masses of the most backward. Dowry has spread from the upper classes to all castes, which suggests it is a form of compensation for women's low economic value. They discuss the types of women's employment, but their high degree of illiteracy and industrial modernization is resulting in displacement. Although the total female electorate is increasing, the numbers of women in the state legislature is decreasing, in spite of the 16-year political domination of Prime Minister Indira Gandhi. They conclude that there is an increase in the number of women's organizations and movements, and more government sensitivity to women's issues, but that women's organizations must be more politically active if women are to gain the power and ability to shape their own lives.

8

Law, Education, and Social Change: Implications for Hausa Muslim Women in Nigeria

Barbara J. Callaway
Rutgers University
Enid Schildkrout
American Museum of Natural History

Nearly 50 percent of West Africa below the Sahara is Islamic, and Islam appears to be gaining adherents throughout much of Africa. The Hausa, a majority of whom live in northern Nigeria and adjacent territories, are the largest subnational ethnic group in West Africa. Thus, a discussion of the situation of Hausa Muslim women in Nigeria in the 1980s and of the interaction among Hausa culture, Islamic beliefs, and modern secular law as they affect women's status is relevant to an understanding of the status of Islamic women in much of Africa. Because many non-Hausa Muslims look to Hausa Muslim scholars for their interpretations of Islamic law, the Hausa case can be viewed as representing a "model" or paradigm of Islamic life in this region. However, it must be noted that in many respects the Hausa interpretation of Islamic doctrine is more conservative than elsewhere in Africa, particularly with regard to the question of the seclusion of women.

In this context a discussion of Islamic law *(Sharia)* and its implications for the rights, privileges, and obligations of women is appropriate. These rights, privileges, and obligations are contained under those parts of the Sharia popularly referred to as "Islamic personal law." In 1979, Nigeria adopted a new Constitution, which protected the position of Sharia law in the predominantly Muslim parts of the country. The debates about this very significant provision of the Constitution are enlightening, as they reflect profound anxiety over the nature and direction of social change. A discussion of both the limitations of legal reform and the potential of the constitutionally guaranteed right to free primary education for affecting, perhaps ambivalently, the dependence and subordination of women vis-à-vis men is germane to assessing the prospects for change in the lives of African Muslim women.

This analysis is based on a case study of women in Kano City, Kano State, Nigeria.[1] With 10 million people, Kano State is the most populous state in Nigeria, itself the most populous country in Africa. Kano City is the largest city in the ten northern states of Nigeria that together encompass an area that contains more than half of the country's population. The city is estimated to contain 2.5 million people, while the Kano metropolitan area is estimated at 5 million people, the vast majority of whom are Hausa and Muslim.

Since the early nineteenth century, Kano City has been the predominant urban site in the western-central Sudan. It is also a major center for Islamic learning and reformism in Nigeria, as well as the northern center of commerce and industry. Today, Kano is second only to the capital city of Lagos in its level of industrialization. As the most populous urban center in northern Nigeria, Kano City and metropolitan area harbor many immigrants from rural areas who, having abandoned their rural homes, struggle to eke out a subsistence in the city. Kano suffers from all the problems that plague other densely populated African cities: poor sanitation, cramped and expensive living quarters, inadequate water and electricity supplies, high food costs, and inadequate medical and educational facilities. All of these factors disproportionately affect women. A 1982 UNICEF study indicates that female children in Kano are the most undernourished in Nigeria. The infant mortality rate is still around 50 percent, and the average life expectancy for women is only 36 years.[2]

The Position of Women in Kano

In Hausa society great emphasis is placed on inherited family status, stratification of ascribed and achieved statuses (including rather strict stratification according to age, sex, and occupational criteria), continuity of institutions, and conformity of behavior to the prevailing interpretations of Islamic doctrine. In this scheme of life, women are defined as the minor wards of their fathers and husbands, are induced to marry by the onset of puberty, to confine their activities to the domestic sphere of social relationships and functions, and to observe postures of deference and service toward men.

Insofar as women are defined as dependent minors, men must be protectors and providers. The interpretations of Islam followed by the Hausa of Kano make it incumbent upon the male head of household to be morally, legally, and economically responsible for the welfare of his family. The age of marriage for men and the size of families depend upon men's economic success; wealthy males marry earlier and have larger families than poor men.

Adult status for women is conferred by marriage, for which girls are eligible before puberty. Once married, girls are considered to be adults regardless of their age; thenceforth they live in varying degrees of *kulle*, or seclusion. The overwhelming majority of Hausa women do not go out to shop or trade. At night they may visit relatives, but are always accompanied by an escort, who is usually a child. Even highly educated women in "modern" marriages go out only with their husbands' permission and only to approved destinations.

Hausa women have not yet been drawn into the wage economy, notwithstanding the fact that Kano is the second most industrialized city in Nigeria. However, there is ample evidence that secluded Hausa women make extraordinary efforts to be economically active.[3] Of 82 women interviewed by Schildkrout in two contrasting Kano City wards in 1977, 93 percent engaged in income-earning activities. Of the six women who did not report occupations, one had a substantial income from a house she owned, two were very old, and two were young and had five and six young children, respectively. The great majority of women engaged in petty trade, while a few engaged in occupations such as embroidery, machine sewing, hairdressing, and pounding grain. Many women prepared cooked food for sale. Selling cooked food and selling commodities such as cooking ingredients both require the assistance of people who are not in seclusion and who can act as intermediaries between secluded women and the outside world. In most cases this role is performed by children. Secluded women who have children helping them earn higher incomes than women who do not have such assistance. However, most secluded Hausa women operate with very little capital and remain at the very low end of the income scale in Kano as a whole. Very few earn as much as the lowest-paid wage laborers. Women who are not secluded—divorcees and widows—participate in the market economy more fully and sometimes are able to amass significant amounts of capital; enough, for example, to pay for pilgrimages to Mecca for themselves and their relatives.[4]

While most women do earn money, many of them do not directly contribute to the subsistence of their families. Theoretically supported by men, women are able to keep their own earnings separate from those of men, and women are able to use their income at their own discretion. Economic hardship often impinges upon this ideal, however, and many women do contribute to subsistence by buying some of their own and their children's food and clothing. Otherwise, women invest their money in durable goods, which are passed on to their daughters in the form of dowries. These dowries represent a kind of insurance for women in the event of widowhood or divorce, since they can usually be converted to cash.

While rural women in northern Nigeria are very much involved in household industry and production, they are almost totally uninvolved in traditional African women's work—farming. Even where their labor is badly needed and economic logic would suggest women's participation, women are absent. Studies of three villages in Zaria (to the immediate south of Kano) between 1975 and 1976 found no women active in agriculture because they were all living in strict seclusion.[5] Scholars of the area have noted with interest that in contrast to other parts of West Africa and other areas of Nigeria itself, women in rural Hausa communities are excluded from direct farm operations as a result of the constraining influence of Islam.[6]

Growing Up Female

In Hausa society girls are taught to be submissive and deferential to men, and boys are taught that they are innately superior to girls. A girl's lower status vis-à-vis her brothers, father, or male kin is emphasized early in her life. By six or seven years she is told to *"ki kinga yin abu kamar mace"* ("behave like a woman"), i.e., to sit like a woman, to lower her voice and talk softly, to cover her head, and never to contradict a man. From her earliest years she is taught that being a female means being inferior. One of our informants remembers being told, *"ba ki ganin ke mace ce, she namiji ne"* ("can't you see that you are a woman while he is a man?") and *"komai abinki, gidan wani zaki"* ("no matter what you do, you are going to someone else's house").[7] Finally, girls are repeatedly told that *"duk mace a bayan namiji take,"* meaning "every woman is inferior to a man."[8]

These Hausa maxims are reinforced by the formal teachings of Islam. Passages from the Qur'an are frequently cited in local papers along with commentary that sanctifies the superior position of men: "The Imam is the guardian of his people and is responsible for them. A man is guardian of his family and is responsible for them. A woman is guardian of her husband's house and is responsible for it."[9] "Men have authority over women, because Allah has made the one superior to the other and because they spend their wealth to maintain them. Good women are obedient. They guard their unseen parts because Allah has guarded them. . . . As for those women from whom you fear disobedience, admonish them and boycott their beds and beat them. If they obey you, do not seek a way against them."[10]

While girls are expected to marry by the time they are of child-bearing age, the introduction of "Western" education is beginning to postpone the age of marriage for girls. But even for girls who attend school, there is still pressure to marry early. Girls who are not engaged while in secondary school complain of being viewed with suspicion and having people say *"an gama da ita,"* "they have finished with her," implying that she is no longer a virgin and therefore not a good candidate for a first wife.[11] There are some indications that these attitudes are changing, however.

Because of the severity with which seclusion is enforced, the options of married Hausa women for defining their roles and activities are limited. Although they engage in economic activities, they are dependent upon children for carrying out these activities. While Western education is gradually increasing, there are virtually no opportunities for secluded Hausa women to utilize new skills within the confines of *purdah*. Also, the pro-natalist orientation of Hausa society means that fertile, married women are actively engaged in child bearing and child rearing from puberty to menopause. While there are great variations in fertility rates, due to a high incidence of secondary infertility,[12] many women have six or more living children, and many more births.

The role restrictions incumbent upon married women can be said to account for two frequently noted characteristics of Hausa society: the importance of the role of the "prostitute" or *karuwa*, and the frequency of divorce. In both urban and rural Hausa society the prostitute, or courtesan, is a recognized and common role. Prostitutes sometimes move in and out of marriage, and sometimes remain in enduring relationships with the same lover. While most move to towns away from their families, they are a frequent presence even in small villages. They are both scorned and envied by married Hausa women. They lack the respectability of married women, but their freedom is seen as desirable.[13] Aside from the *karuwai*, only children and elderly widows have the freedom to move in an out of the domestic world of women and the more public world of men.

Many Hausa women have been divorced at least once, and some have been divorced and remarried several times. Divorces occur most frequently early in marriage, in the first year or two, most often before any children are born. This is due to the fact that many girls' first marriages are compulsory unions arranged by the girls' families. While parents usually want their daughters to marry early, before they have had an opportunity to lose their virginity outside of marriage, they do not strongly object to the dissolution of unhappy first marriages. The loss of virginity is not a hindrance in contracting a second marriage, and men often marry divorced women as their second, third, and fourth wives. The expenses in contracting a marriage to a divorcee are less than those incurred in marrying a young virgin.

There is therefore both opportunity to remarry and great pressure to do so. While the options open to women within marriage are limited by the institution of *purdah*, the opportunities open to single women are also limited. Single women are freer than married women to go to market, but they face great competition from men in a male-dominated economy. Unlike the non-Muslim parts of Nigeria where women are a formidable market presence, in the north women's market activities are centered on house trade. In addition to the difficulty single women face in supporting themselves, they also encounter a certain amount of scorn from their families and other married women.

A further reason most divorced or widowed Hausa women remarry, despite the restrictive nature of Hausa marriage, is that the laws and customs surrounding divorce and widowhood are disadvantageous to women. Divorcees receive no continuing financial support from their husbands while widows receive only a tiny share of their husband's estate: one quarter if there are no children and one-eighth if there are children or grandchildren—and this portion is shared by all of the deceased's wives. What is even more significant is that divorcees lose all practical claims to their children. Once the children are weaned, they go to live with their father or someone he delegates; they are usually cared for by one of his other wives or by a female relative. Occasionally a man will allow his wife to keep one daughter with her, but this is not the woman's "right." It is not clear that this feature of Hausa culture is an Islamic injunction, however. In some Islamic traditions, children are allowed to remain with their mother until puberty, when they will choose with which parent to stay.[14] Strictly speaking, a widow's children also belong to her husband's kin, and if she remarries she cannot usually take her children with her. In many cases these children are at a severe disadvantage; in the worst cases they are treated as servants to the husband's other wives. This situation is feared by all Hausa women, and it is one reason why women will sometimes withstand unhappy marital situations once they have children.

The right of divorce for both men and women is available in Islamic law, but the circumstances by which it may be obtained differ according to sex. Women may obtain divorce in court and only on specified grounds, whereas a man can divorce his wife by *talaq*—by simply proclaiming three times in front of witnesses that he divorces her (or by doing the same thing in writing).

While men have the right to obtain divorce through renunciation and women do not, an actual examination of divorce cases in two courts in Hausa cities indicates that women seeking divorce generally get it. Such research further indicates that talaq is often initiated or instigated at the behest of women.[15] Reforms in other Muslim countries, such as Morocco, Singapore, Malaysia, Pakistan, Algeria, Iraq, Iran, and Somalia have eliminated or greatly restricted the use of talaq.[16] Although Hausa women who seek divorce generally get it,[17] many women try to stay in a marriage, no matter how unsatisfactory, because they do not want to lose their children, because they have difficulty supporting themselves outside of marriage, and because there is enormous family pressure to remain married.

The subordinate position of Muslim women in northern Nigeria is evident in a number of regulations that restrict women's participation in public life. In Kano, a Hausa woman cannot be employed by a public agency without the written permission of her husband. She cannot travel or apply for a passport, without his written consent.[18] In spite of the unanimous United Nations Declaration of Rights for Women in 1967, which included the right to vote, hold office, and have equal access to education, it was not until nine years later, in 1976, that the Nigerian military regime granted such rights to Muslim women. No woman can be a judge in an Islamic court, and while a woman can plead her own case in court, the testimony of two female witnesses is equal to that of one male witness. Although

Hausa women frequently visit relatives and neighbors, and have long-standing friendships with other women,[19] there are no formal women's associations to which they belong. The National Council of Women's Societies, the federally recognized umbrella organization for women's associations, has no branch in Kano. There are no northern Nigerian women on the faculty of the Bayero University in Kano. Women do not generally participate in university-sponsored conferences or symposia, and the university has never sponsored a program dealing with women's issues or concerns.

Despite all this, survey research in Kano clearly establishes that women support the "Islamic way of life."[20] Most women do not perceive an independent right to obtain an education, work, travel, postpone marriage, practice birth control, or have custody of children in the event of divorce. The vast majority of women are unaware that the Nigerian constitution grants them a legal status that differs from that defined in the Qur'an. What an outsider might consider *prima facie* evidence of inferior status is perceived as a divinely ordained differentiation in sex roles. Where women are deprived of opportunities for self-assertion and self-development outside the home, as in northern Nigeria, they do not easily perceive alternatives.

Islamic and Secular Law in Nigeria

Is legal reform and consequent public policy an effective means of changing this pervasive socialization process and the entrenched cultural values that result? As others have pointed out in studies done elsewhere in the Islamic world, the imposition of a secular legal code in personal matters may be inadequate for promoting change in norms and behavior.[21] In such societies secular law may be officially in force, but the Sharia continues to inform behavior, particularly in matters of family behavior and morality. During the colonial period of Nigeria (1902–1966), the British revamped the legal system in much of the country and sporadically tried to introduce legislation to promote change in the north, but for the most part the policy of indirect rule meant that the British did not attempt to interfere with Islamic law. This meant that while British common law had been incorporated into the Nigerian legal system in many parts of the country, in the north Sharia law remained essentially intact.

Although parts of the 1979 Constitution were suspended in 1983 when the elected government of Alhaji Shehu Shagari was overthrown by military action, the debate that took place during the drafting of the Constitution is most informative on the question of the place of Islamic law in the Nigerian legal system. In the Spring of 1978, elected representatives from Nigeria's 19 states met to debate and approve a Constitution drafted by a Constitutional Drafting Committee (CDC) appointed by the military government. The appointment of the CDC was an important step on the road to returning Nigeria to civilian rule after more than a decade of military government. The Constituent Assembly, however, floundered over the issue of the creation of a Federal Sharia Court of Appeal, which would review cases of Islamic law heard at the state level. The CDC had included a provision for such a court in the Constitutional Draft. After much debate, a compromise was reached wherein the Federal Court of Appeal would include judges versed in Islamic law who would, when the occasion arose, form a subunit of the court in order to hear such cases. This compromise was reached over strong objections from the northern Muslim members of the Assembly.[22]

During the course of these debates, several important issues were raised, including that of the nature of the relationship between sacred and secular law in general, the position of Islamic law in a secular state, and the separation of Islamic personal law out of the general body of Islamic law. As was made clear in the Nigerian Constituent Assembly Debates, Islamic law is regarded as revealed law derived from the word of Allah through the Prophet. "The rights which have been sanctioned by God are permanent, perpetual and eternal. They are not subject to any alterations or modifications, and there is no scope for any change or abrogation."[23] Any challenge to the Sharia is seen as a challenge to Islam itself; and since the Sharia is sacred, law cannot be used as an instrument of social change.[24] The Sharia is comprehensive in that prescriptions affecting religion, morals, politics, commerce, and family life are addressed. It includes criminal law, law of contracts and property, land tenure and succession, and law of evidence and procedure. The family is believed to be at the center of Islamic order, and approximately one-third of the *ahkam* (legal injunctions of the Qur'an) relate to the family. Hence, for Muslim women, the Sharia is of vital relevance and importance.

While it was stressed in the debates that Islam is a "total way of life" and the Sharia sacred in its totality, the Muslims compromised in order to make a separate Islamic court system acceptable to non-Muslim members of the CDC. They argued that the Sharia courts would deal only with Islamic personal law, except where the parties concerned voluntarily submitted other issues to these courts, as stipulated under the provisions regarding "customary" law in the new Constitution. Personal law was described as law dealing with marriage, divorce, legitimation and custody of children, and inheritance. The final version of the Constitution established a Sharia Court of Appeal in each predominantly Muslim state.[25] The Sharia courts were given explicit jurisdiction over matters relating to Islamic personal law, defined as (1) "marriage, divorce, family relationships or the guardianship of an infant,"[26] (2) "any question of Islamic personal law,"[27] and (3) "any quesiton of Islamic personal law regarding an infant, prodigal [sic] or person of unsound mind."[28]

The debate on the establishment of Sharia courts was acrimonious. Concern for women's rights *per se* did not feature in these debates, even though they are the persons most affected by the protections for Islamic personal law ultimately incorporated into the Constitution. It is significant that although five of the delegates to the CDC were women (all Christian), not a single one of them took part in these debates. Objections to providing special protection for the Sharia were made by men and concerned the wisdom of establishing what, in effect, was a dual system of justice in a large part of the country. There were reservations expressed about elevating Islam above other religions practiced in Nigeria by giving it a special place in the Constitution through the provision of the Federal Sharia Court of Appeal. It was also pointed out that the Sharia has been abolished in many Muslim countries with Muslim majority populations—for example, Egypt, which is 98.8 percent Muslim, abolished Sharia on August 21, 1956; and Turkey, which is 98.8 percent Muslim, abolished Sharia in 1924.[29] Nonetheless, after much discussion concerning the exact wording, the Assembly enshrined in the Constitution the provision that Section 150(5)(ii) of the Nigerian Constitution should read: ". . . that the President in exercising his power to appoint the Justices of the Supreme Court and the Federal Court of Appeal, shall include in his appointees persons learned in Islamic law and these persons shall sit and determine appeals relating to Islamic law."

It is interesting that only that part of the Sharia law most affecting women was emphasized by the proponents of the Sharia. As stated by a Muslim member of the Assembly, "Muslims want only a few matters concerning Muslim Personal Law to come under this provision . . . marriage, divorce, will or succession, guardianship of infants, endowments and gifts."[30] Despite this, when Justice Udo

Udoma referred to these matters as trivial, the Muslims took strong offence. Justice Udoma had said:

> There is nothing very important about it. After all it is about a right of succession of an average man and woman who is a Moslem: it is a right of marriage and dissolution of marriage which is open to the average Moslem, woman or man. The question of all these is to my mind very, very minor. And I can assure you that I would be the last person to sit down and allow the reputation of Nigeria to be jeopardised because of what I consider a very minor question. . . . Let us not make ourselves a laughing stock because if people outside, beyond the boundaries of this country, were to hear that a galaxy of intelligent people who had gathered here were not able to decide reasonably something dealing with this sort of matter I have been discussing, I think it would be a disgrace to Nigeria."[31]

In protest to this address, the Muslim delegates walked out of the Assembly, thus threatening the whole proceeding. In announcing the walkout, Alhaji Kam Selem stated explicitly that "we do not agree that any constitutional issue affecting the lives of millions of citizens of any country can be said to be very, very minor. We also disagree that matters affecting the family or succession can be said to be of no importance."[32]

It is evident that in order to insert provisions protecting Sharia law into the Constitution, the Muslims were willing to downplay the importance of the matters concerned, but when non-Muslims accepted this assertion at face value, it was clear that, in fact, Muslim men regarded these matters as of vital concern.

By passing the provisions the Muslims insisted upon, the Nigerian Constitution incorporated a blatant conflict between the provisions relating to women in the Sharia and the "Fundamental Human Rights" provisions found elsewhere in the Constitution. Section II(1)(a) stated that "every citizen shall have equality of rights, obligations, and opportunities before the law." Despite the fact that Islam "recognizes equality of all human beings regardless of race, color or nationality,"[33] the provisions in the Sharia that render a woman's testimony equal to one-half that of a man, or decree that women's property rights are less than those of men, imply that this equality does not apply to women.

Paradoxically, since Muslims are not a majority of the population in Nigeria, but rather represent Nigeria's largest minority (Nigeria is approximately 38 percent Islamic), the Sharia, with all its enshrined inequality, has come to be a symbol of minority "rights" and identity. It is important to bear this in mind in any attempt to understand the limited effectiveness of federal law to bring about change on the local level. In a federal system such as Nigeria, or the United States for that matter, law is easily rendered ineffective when government officials are unwilling, for political reasons, to confront special and sectarian interests. The dilemma presented by the coexistence of Islamic and Western legal codes in the same society is particularly difficult, and evidence from other such societies, India, for example, suggests that such conflicts are capable of arousing dangerous passions.

Chaper IV of the 1979 Constitution did contain guarantees of fundamental human rights that, if ever invoked, could have significantly extended women's rights. These constitutionally guaranteed rights included rights to the dignity of the human person, liberty, a fair hearing, privacy, freedom of thought, conscience and religion, freedom of speech and of the press, peaceful assembly and association, freedom of movement, freedom from discrimination, and property. The Constitution prohibited discrimination on grounds of belonging to a particular community, ethnic group, place of origin, or sex.[34]

Clearly, a Muslim woman would have a most challenging and interesting case should she ever contest the restrictions of the Sharia under the constitutionally guaranteed human rights clauses. To date, however, in Nigerian constitutional law and history, there does not appear to be any specific case brought on behalf of a woman (or a man) on grounds of discrimination. In order to illustrate how discrimination may occasion relief, cases from American constitutional law are cited in Nigerian law schools. The one case that might be applicable does not set an encouraging precedent. The Children and Young Persons Law of 1958 prohibited children under 18 from participating in politics. This feature of the law was in specific response to protests against the use of children in northern political campaigns during the 1950s. Both northern political parties at that time (Northern People's Congress and Northern Elements Progressive Union) complained that the other party was organizing children, aged 8 to 12, into bands to shout abusive slogans at opposition politicians. Under laws existing at that time, neither the children, nor their parents under Islamic law, could be prosecuted. In *Cheranci* v. *Cheranci* the constitutionality of this act was challenged.[35] Lawyers for the defendants argued that those sections of the act that made it an offense to admit a juvenile into membership in a political party violated the guarantees of freedom of association extant in the Constitution. The court ruled affirmatively that sections of the act did violate sections of the Constitution, but it did not strike them down; it rather ruled that those sections of the Children and Young Persons Law were "justifiable and reasonable in the society and justifiable in the interests of public morality." If appeals to cultural and moral arguments override legal arguments, as in this case, it is unlikely that the guarantees of fundamental human rights in the Constitution will have much meaning for Muslim women in Nigeria.

In a situation where sectarian political concerns override legal issues, it is difficult for law to be a catalyst for social change or even a correction for perceived social maladies. Two other examples from Nigerian legal history illustrate this. During the 1950s the colonial government was concerned about the dangers that young girls engaged in street trading incurred from older men who often sexually molested them. In response, the Sokoto Native Authority issued the Juveniles and Young Females Street Trading Prohibition Rules. "Street trading" included hawking goods, playing, singing, or performing for profit, or any other occupation practiced in the street. The rules were drawn up by a committee appointed by the Sultan of Sokoto in order to deal with the problem of child prostitution. These rules were meant to be models for other provinces, but in the correspondence that followed, the view was strongly expressed that the rules were not enforceable, partly because they were "contrary to Islamic custom."[36] Rules against child employment and street trading exist today throughout Nigeria, but have not been enforced, at least not in the informal sector. In the formal sector, the employment of children is limited both by labor law[37] and the 1979 Constitution,[38] which expressly prohibits exploitation of children and the aged. These protections have never been utilized in court, however.

The second example concerns a father's right to arrange or compel his child's marriage *(jabr)*, which Nigerian Muslims believe the Sharia protects. The effectiveness of fathers' ability to control their daughters' marriages is limited in practice by the option of divorce, which is often instigated by women. Nevertheless, the continuing practice of jabr accounts for and justifies the early age of marriage in the north. The authority of men increases with wealth, and girls in wealthy families often marry much earlier than do daughters of poverty. Although many of these marriages do not last, girls are still being married at age ten and sometimes younger. The major objection to early marriage within the society comes from those persons who are concerned about the physical dangers of very early childbirth. The age of marriage became an issue of legal conflict in 1950 and 1951 when an attempt was made to amend the criminal code to prosecute child prostitution. This reform would have raised the "age of consent" from 13 to 15 years of age. Although some of the traditional rulers approved of this effort, the Northern House of Assembly defeated the bill on the grounds that it would cover married girls under the age of 15. The proposed code defined rape as including any intercourse with girls less than 14 years of age and provided no exceptions, even if she was the man's wife.

In summary, although the 1979 Constitution provided potentially significant protections to women and children, their effectiveness was questionable. Before the 1979 Constitution, when legislation appeared to override the Sharia, or when it went against customary law, tradition and Islamic custom have prevailed. If this pattern continues, we cannot expect Muslims in northern Nigeria to accept legal reforms in regard to inheritance, divorce, custody rights, and freedom of movement and association. The important question then becomes the political one of whether the federal government will enforce the Constitution in opposition to sectional interests. Given the protections granted to the Sharia we have discussed, such a development seems unlikely in Nigeria in the foreseeable future. It is interesting to note that in a number of other countries where Muslims are not a minority, which are historically much more theocratic than Nigeria, legal reform for women's rights is far more advanced.[39]

Focus on Education

It is our contention that the legal system itself will never be effective in introducing reform in the life options of women in the Islamic parts of Nigeria. Quite the contrary, law in the Islamic north is a force of conservatism. It is controlled by men and used to enforce both Islamic and customary rules and traditions. It is not through the courts, therefore, that the position or status of women can be expected to change. This is, as we have said, even more true in Nigeria, where the Muslims are a minority in a secular state, than it is in states officially designated "Islamic." This is so precisely because it is the legal system itself, the Sharia, that is seen as the symbol of "minority rights" and regional identity. Given this reality, one must look elsewhere for pressures for change in the lives of women. Legislation about compulsory primary education is the most significant potential source of change in northern Nigeria and perhaps in the rest of the Islamic world.

The Constitution states that the government should seek to eradicate illiteracy, promote science and technology, and where practicable, provide compulsory and universal free primary, secondary, university, and adult education.[40] Universal free primary education has now (1984) been introduced in all 19 Nigerian states, including Kano State, although it is not yet compulsory.

Research elsewhere has shown that there is a definite correlation between women's education, higher levels of female employment, and greater awareness of women's issues such as the practice of purdah, age of marriage, consent for marriage, and the rate of child bearing.[41] Thus, education can be the catalyst for radical changes in women's consciousness and for major changes in their status.

The number of children in school has greatly increased in Kano since the introduction of Universal Primary Education (UPE) in 1976. Table 8.1 shows the dramatic increase in the number of children in school. While the percentage of girls in school has not increased significantly during this period, the increase in their absolute number is dramatic.

We contend that the position of women will be changed in this society not through confrontation with women's issues *per se*, but through legislation that affects the lives of children, particularly the legislation conerning UPE. This legislation affects women in two ways: at present, school attendance removes children from the home and changes the position of secluded women who rely on chidren to help them perform domestic chores; in the future, it may change the attitudes toward marriage and employment of those women who have gone to school.

In both rural and urban settings, women in purdah are unable to carry on their daily domestic responsibilities without the help of children.[42] In wealthier families, servants (or family retainers) do the chores children might be expected to perform, but in middle- and lower-income families, children perform most of the household labor. Children do the daily shopping; they take out trash; they fetch water; they deliver food and messages to neighbors and friends; and they escort women when they go out. In their income-producing activities, women are also dependent on children. Children buy supplies and sell the products women produce. Women with children to help them earn, on the average, three times as much as women who do not have children helping them.[43] Although both girls and boys have long been expected to receive a minimal Qur'anic education in northern Nigeria, Qur'anic education for girls usually does not take up a great deal of time. Most girls attend Qur'anic school for less than an hour a day and, at most, two hours a day. Boys often attend for longer periods and also do somewhat less

TABLE 8.1

School Attendance by Sex, 1976–1981

YEAR	MALES	%	FEMALES	%	TOTAL
1976	254,385	74	87,421	26	341,806
1977	340,000	72	132,274	28	472,413
1978	469,570	71	190,358	29	659,928
1979	601,219	70	253,420	30	854,639
1980	726,753	71	299,677	29	1,026,430
1981	843,514	70	356,828	30	1,200,342

Source: Ministry of Education, *Statistical Yearbooks* (Kano: Kano State Government, 1976–1981).

housework. The long hours required for attendance at UPE schools are in addition to time spent in Qur'anic school, and thus remove children from the domestic domain for a larger portion of the day. This makes life in purdah much more difficult for women, and explains in part the reluctance of many people to send their daughters to school.

In the long run Western education may equip women for new occupational roles and may make them less than enthusiastic about living in seclusion. One dramatic effect of UPE that can already be documented is that it alters the age of marriage. In a longitudinal study of Kano children between 1976 and 1981, we found that all the girls who entered primary school postponed marriage beyond the traditional age of 11 or 12 in order to at least complete primary school. In the first few years after UPE was started, the federal and state governments actively campaigned to enroll girls in primary school. They built a number of secondary schools with the intention of making parents feel that their daughters could both attend school and protect their "virtue." This policy seemed to work: In our study, of 15 girls who began school in 1976–1977, only one had left school to be married by 1981, and this girl had completed primary school. All the other girls had gone on to secondary school. Of the 28 school-age girls who did not attend school, all were married in 1981, by age 14. It is too early to predict the effect of schooling on these girls' attitudes to marriage, child bearing and career, but we feel confident that there will be some dramatic and significant changes in their expectations and behavior.

The state's commitment to provide free primary education is of vital importance to women, both as potential students and as secluded wives dependent on child labor. The issue of Western education for women in the north is not a simple one, and it is a goal that has met with opposition from many northern conservatives.[44] However, the overriding need to equalize the distribution of education throughout Nigeria has profound implications and is not an issue on which the north can afford to compromise. Recognizing that regional differences in the distribution of education are so great that they pose a political liability, most northern politicians welcomed UPE and the government's efforts to correct these disparities. In equalizing educational opportunities throughout the country, women have been slowly, and inevitably, included.

There already exists a small but growing number of professional women who have benefited from the provision of free university education in Kano State. Note, however, that the ratio of women to men has deteriorated at Kano's state university (Bayero) since the provision of free university education. As more girls graduate from the newly created girls' secondary schools in Kano State, there will likely be more female students at the university. In recent years the proportion of women from states other than Kano has declined, largely accounting for the decline in the number of female students (see Table 8.2).

There is evidence that female university students, at Bayero University at least, favor legal reforms that have occurred in other less conservative Islamic societies—limitations on polygamy, an end to arranged and early marriages, an end to talag, the right of child custody, and requirements for the provision of support for women and children after divorce. In 1982, women students at Ahamdu Bello University in Zaria (a city 100 miles south of Kano) formed a new organization, Women in Nigeria (WIN), to address (among other things) the nature of women's rights, particularly in Islam.

Reflections on Social Change and Hausa Women

When the military government extended the right to vote to all women in 1976, northern political parties had to court the women's vote by organizing "women's wings" and expressing concern about women's issues—at the time limited to praising Islamic "protections" while encouraging education for women. Although no specific legislation pertaining to women was proposed, the subject of women's status was at least considered. The most distressing aspect of all the debates in the Constitutional Drafting Committee about the Sharia was that one of the underlying issues—the systematic sexual inequality inherent in Sharia law—was never challenged. One can only surmise that this may have been because there

TABLE 8.2

Sex Ratio of University Students, Bayero University, Kano, 1977–1982

YEAR	MALE	FEMALE	TOTAL	% FEMALE
1977–1978	1,632	261	1,893	14
1978–1979	2,094	194	2,288	8
1980–1981	2,745	251	2,996	8
1981–1982	3,147	282	3,429	8

Source: *The Registrar, Annual Reports, 1976–1982,* Bayero University, Kano.

was, after all, a certain amount of sympathy (and therefore complicity) on the part of those very men who advocated the protection of "fundamental human rights." The non-Muslims were willing to challenge the protection of a separate legal system, but consistently stayed away from discussing the content of that law and the way in which it conflicted with other constitutional proposals pertaining to women.

At present, while social life for northern Nigerian women is profoundly restricted, they do have control over their own destinies in a very limited sphere: They control the allocation of labor in the household; they have control over their own incomes; and they have learned to rely upon and support one another. Due to this autonomy and the rigid segregation of men and women in daily life, most women are not emotionally dependent on men. Rather they depend upon other women and their children for daily emotional support. In this respect northern Nigerian women are far more "liberated" than many of their Western counterparts. However, Hausa society does not place a high priority on personal autonomy and individualism *per se,* and Hausa women may not be psychologically prepared to deal with the plethora of choices "liberation" implies.

Legal reform in Nigeria as a whole, in the Constitution or in statute law, has had little effect in the north for reasons we have discussed. A direct legal attack on the unequal treatment of women in Sharia law would be an attack on a whole set of interlocking ascribed roles. To overtly challenge the position and status of women would be to question the distinctive characteristics defining maleness itself and hence not just the superordinate position of men vis-à-vis women, but male self-image, self-definition, and self-esteem.[45] Moreover, the subordination of women has increasingly become a major symbol of cultural identity for many Muslims. A challenge to female roles or status through political action or policy initiatives thus threatens men's self-perception and their group identity. Women too are likely to feel threatened by such initiatives and, preferring the security they know to opportunities not understood, many will likely oppose such initiatives (just as women in the United States opposed efforts to enact the Equal Rights Amendment to the U.S. Constitution).

In the absence of official programs and stimuli, there is unlikely to be spontaneous support for women's concerns. As examples from other Muslim countries suggest, the development and aggressive pursuit of such programs and reforms can engender profound resistance from both men and women. Support for reform then becomes a symbol of support for "Western values," which increases the isolation and alienation of those advocating change. In response, in many Muslim countries there has been a resurgence of traditional values. Although reforms in Nigeria itself have not been significant, there is a feeling of vulnerability on the part of many orthodox Muslims. The emergence of strong Islamic students' associations on northern Nigerian university campuses is one manifestation of this. The resurgence of extreme forms of Islamic fundamentalism in major northern Nigerian cities, including Kano, also suggests that the most conservative forces are finding fertile ground.[46]

Gradually, in the West, in both Christianity and Judaism, images of male and female complementarity came to be in conflict with universalistic norms associated with the more general quest for increasing social equality. It is this quest that is reflected in the United Nations Declaration of the Decade for Women. Changing perceptions and values have given rise to a gradual liberalization of religious teachings and acceptance of social movements that questioned prevailing arrangements and pressed for the extension of egalitarian principles into new arenas. The women's movement, where it has taken root, calls for a fundamental transformation of economic and social institutions as well as religious beliefs and psychological understandings. Historically, however, women were the last social group to respond to the egalitarian ethic in the West. While some women began to realize the political implications of democratic values by the end of the eighteenth century, for another whole century the political role of women was restricted to raising children rather than practicing citizenship.[47]

Is there reason to believe these transformations will be more rapid in Nigeria than they have been in the West? This is a difficult question, and, given the faltering course of the fight for women's issues worldwide, it is presumptuous to use Western industrialized societies as models for the rest of the world. Nevertheless, even

though there are still battles to be won in the United States and
Europe, the point is that many women are fighting them. Progress
may be slow, but the goals have been articulated. We believe these
developments may occur in Nigeria as well, but only after the level
of education increases and Muslim women themselves begin to
question their subordinate status. What happens once they do ask
these questions depends in part on the reaction of men and the
opportunities open to women at the time. In Nigeria, as elsewhere,
"liberation" as an abstraction is meaningless to most people;
women have to see the reason for having freedom of choice in regard
to marriage, child bearing, education, and employment.[48]

Despite the enormous obstacles, there has already been some
change in the lives of women in northern Nigeria. Women voted
in large numbers in 1979; universal primary education was
implemented in Kano State in 1977; and women began to go to
secondary schools and universities for the first time. A few new
opportunities for women exist, in teaching and health care, and
women are allowed and sometimes encouraged to pursue them.
But, in one crucial area there has been little progress. Islamic
personal codes and family laws governing marriage, child bearing,
divorce, custody, and property are viewed as being the foundation
and root of Islamic tradition and thus above challenge. Until Islamic law as applied here is challenged, it will be difficult for most
women to take advantage of the limited legal reforms that have
occurred.[49]

The desire to modernize without challenging the teachings of
Islam—an attitude prevalent among many articulate and educated
Nigerians—leaves intact fundamental family structures, authority
relationships, and socialization patterns. The accepted view of sexual inequality in Nigeria, as elsewhere, is that it has its origins in the
hierarchy of nature itself. Only after this traditional view of reality
is called into question, as it has been in the Judeo-Christian world,
can sexual inequality be seen as convention rather than inherent in
the nature of a divinely created world.

Although educated Nigerian women feel that values regarding
relations between the sexes are too deeply imbedded to be overcome
any time soon, surveys nevertheless reveal that female students
believe life will be better for their daughters than it is for them.[50] In
line with the hopes of this small vanguard of educated women, we
predict that as the level of education increases, new patterns of
interaction between men and women and new aspirations on the
part of women will emerge. As far as law is concerned, it is legislation in areas such as education, rather than legislation directly

bearing on women's legal status, that will be the most powerful catalyst of change in the future. For major changes to be generally accepted, however, a new generation of women must reach maturity—women whose horizons extend beyond the confines of their compounds and neighborhood and women who trust that they can find security and satisfaction through a more "liberal" interpretation of Islamic doctrine.

NOTES

1. Barbara J. Callaway was visiting Fulbright professor at Bayero University in Kano, Nigeria, during 1981–1983. Enid Schildkrout worked in two wards of Kano City during 1976–1978 and, with Carol Gelber, did a brief follow up study in 1981. Dr. Schildkrout's research has been supported by the American Museum of Natural History, the National Science Foundation, and the Wenner-Gren Foundation for Anthropological Research. We wish to thank Carol Gelber for substantial research and editorial help.

2. *Nutritional Status of Children in Nigeria (A Study Prepared for the UNICEF Nutrition Project)* (New York: United Nations, 1982); World Health Organization, *Demographic Yearbook, 1978* (New York: United Nations, 1979, tables 8, 10.

3. Kabir Bashir, *The Economic Activities of Secluded Married Women in Kurawa and Lallokion Lemu, Kano City* (Zaria: B.Sc. Thesis, Ahmadu Bello University, 1972); Polly Hill, "Two Types of West African House Trade," in Claude Meillassoux, *The Development of Indigenous Trade and Markets in West Africa* (London: Oxford University Press, 1971), 303–318; Renee Pitten, "Sex Role Stereotypes and the Behavior of Women: The Ideal/Real Dichotomy" (Benin: Proceedings of the National Conference on Women in Development, September 22–26, 1980), 886–903; Enid Schildkrout, "Dependency and Autonomy: The Economic Activities of Secluded Hausa Women in Kano," in Edna G. Bay, ed., *Women and Work in Africa* (Denver: Westview Press, 1982), 57–82.

4. Schildkrout, "Women's Work and Children's Work: Variations among Moslems in Kano," in Sandra Wallman, ed., *Social Anthropology of Work* (London: Academic Press, 1979), 69–85.

5. M. M. Konan, *Occupational and Family Patterns among the Hausa in the North of Nigeria* (Zaria: Institute for Agricultural Research, Samaru Miscellaneous Paper 52, Ahmadu Bello University, 1975), 14; Emmy B. Simmons, *Economic Research on Women in Rural Development in Northern Nigeria* (Washington, DC: Overseas Liaison Committee, American Council on Education Paper No. 10, n.d.), 10, 17.

6. H. C. Abell, *Report to the Government of Nigeria (Northern Region) on Home Economics Aspects of the F.A.O. Socio-Economic Survey of*

Peasant Agriculture in Northern Nigeria: The Role of Women in Farm and Home Life (Rome: F.A.O., 1962), mimeo; Hill, *Rural Hausa: A Village and a Setting* (London: Cambridge University Press, 1972); Michael G. Smith, *The Economy of the Hausa Communities of Zaria* (London: Her Majesty's Stationery Office, Colonial Research Studies, 16, 1955.)

7. Zainab Sa'd Kabir, "The Silent Oppression: Male-Female Relationship in Kano," seminar paper given at Bayero University Faculty Seminar, Kano, May 1981 (mimeo, Department of Sociology).

8. Callaway Interviews 6 and 21, Kano, April and July, 1982.

9. Ahmed Khurshid, *Family Life in Islam* (Leicester, England: Islamic Foundation, 1974), 16.

10. The Qur'an, 4:34. A. J. Arberry (translator) (London: Penguin Books, 1955 ed.).

11. Callaway Interviews 9– 12, Bayero University students, February 1982.

12. This is a common problem of women who have had their first child at a very early age; they are often plagued with a variety of gynecological problems including fistulas and infections. Infertility has been viewed as a regional problem in Africa by some authors; in areas of Cameroon, Chad, Sudan, and Gabon as many as 20 to 30 percent of women are infertile. Anne Retel-Laurentin, "Problèmes sociaux et familiaux des régions africaines à faibles fécondité," in Christine Oppong and Gemma Adaba, Manga Bekombo-Priso, John Mogey, eds., *Marriage, Fertility and Parenthood in West Africa* (Canberra: Australian National University, 1978), 507– 521. As far as we know, there has been no comparable study for northern Nigeria, but empirical evidence we have would suggest that the rate may be high there also.

13. Renee Pittin, "Houses of Women: A Focus on Alternative Life-Styles in Katsina City," in Christine Oppong, ed., *Female and Male in West Africa* (London: Allen and Unwin, 1983), 291 – 303; Enid Schildkrout, "Age and Gender in Hausa society: Socio-economic Roles of Children in Urban Kano," in Jean S. LaFontaine, ed., *Sex and Age as Principles of Social Differentiation* (New York: Academic Press, 1978), 109– 137.

14. In fact, one recognized scholar of Islam asserts that the texts "provide that boys should remain in the custody of their mothers, unless the latter remarry outside the immediate family, etc., until they reach puberty; after which they are given an option as to which parent they will live with; whereas girls should stay with their mothers, on the same conditions, until they go to their husband's houses." J. M. D. Anderson, *Islamic Law in Africa* (London: Frank Cass, 1970), 214.

15. Renee Pittin, "Hausa Women and Islamic Law: Is Reform Necessary?" *Proceedings*, Twenty-second Annual Meeting of the African Studies Association (Los Angeles, CA: October 31– November 3, 1979).

16. See Neil Coulson and Doreen Hinchcliffe, "Women and Law Reform in Contemporary Islam," in Lois Beck and Nikki Keddie, eds., *Women in the Muslim World* (Cambridge, MA: Harvard University Press, 1978).

17. Margaret O. Saunders, *Marriage and Divorce in a Muslim Hausa Town* (Ann Arbor, MI: University Microfilms, 1978).

18. The 1960 Constitution reserved to the states the power of enfranchisement. The eastern and western state governments granted the right to vote to all persons over 21, but the north enfranchised only men. The region's premier at the time, Sir Ahmadu Bello, states: "Female suffrage is inimical to the customs and feelings of the great part of the men in this region." *My Life* (London: Cambridge University Press, 1962), 233.

19. See Mary F. Smith, *Baba of Karo: A Woman of the Muslim Hausa* (London: Faber, 1954).

20. Only 2 of 154 women students surveyed at Bayero University in 1982 believed that Islam made life "more difficult" for women. The rest responded that Islam provided a "good" life for women.

21. See Haeri Shahla, "Women, Law and Social Change in Iran," in Jane Smith, ed., *Women in Contemporary Muslim Societies* (Lewisburg, PA: Bucknell University Press; London: Associated University Presses, 1980).

22. See *Proceedings of the Constituent Assembly, Official Report,* Vol. III, April 3–May 30, 1979 (Lagos: Government Printing Office).

23. Al' Mawdudi, *Human Rights in Islam* (Leicester, England: Islamic Foundation, 1976), 14.

24. Nigerian Muslim scholars are more conservative in regard to this matter than some other Islamic scholars. It has been asserted by one such authority that "Islam does not offer a ready-made rigid body politic—but, rather a dynamic polity sensitive to change in social, physical, environment, and developmental fabric of society." Sadiq El Madi, "Islam's Moral Appeal to Mankind," in *Arabia: Islamic World Review* 8 (April 1982), 34.

25. *Nigerian Constitution,* S. 240 (1) (Lagos: Government Printing Office, 1979).

26. Ibid., S. 242.

27. Ibid., S. 243.

28. Ibid., S. 241 (4).

29. *Proceedings, Constituent Assembly Debates,* Vol. III, J. O. J. Okezie, 2049–2051.

30. Ibid., Alhaji Gaba Ja Abdulkadir, 2020.

31. Ibid., Mr. Justice Udo Udoma, Chairman, Constituent Assembly, 2047.

32. Ibid., Alhaji Kam Salem, 2077.

33. Ibid.

34. *Nigerian Constitution,* ibid., S. 38.

35. File N.R.N.L.R. 24, 1960, Nigeria National Archives, Kaduna.

36. File M.S.W.C. 1088, Nigeria National Archives, Kaduna.

37. Section 17 (3) (F), Labor Decree of 1974 (Lagos: Government Printing Office).

38. *Nigerian Constitution,* 1979, S. 17 (3) (f).

39. Elizabeth White, "Legal Reform as an indicator of Women's Status in Muslim Nations," in Lois Beck and Nikki Keddie, eds. *Women in the Muslim World* (Cambridge, MA: Harvard University Press, 1978), 52–68.

40. *Nigerian Constitution, S. 17.*

41. See for example, William J. Goode, ed. *World Revolution and Family Patterns* (New York: Free Press, 1970); Michael Gordon, ed., *The American Family in Social-Historical Perspective* (New York: St. Martin's Press, 1973); Tamara K. Hareven, *Transitions: The Family and the Life Course in Historical Perspective* (New York: Academic Press, 1978); Neil J. Smelser, *Social Change in the Industrial Revolution* (Chicago: University Press, 1959); Louise A. Tilly and Joan W. Scott, *Women, Work and Family* (New York: Holt, Rinehart and Winston, 1978).

42. Schildkrout, 1978, 1982.

43. Schildkrout, 1979.

44. Mervyn Hiskett, "Islamic Education in the Traditional and State Systems in Northern Nigeria," in Godfrey N. Brown and Mervyn Hiskett, eds., *Conflict and Harmony in Education in Tropical Africa* (London: Allen and Unwin, 1975), 134–151; J. P. Hubbard, "Government and Islamic Education in Northern Nigeria (1900–1940)," in Brown and Hiskett, 1975, 152–167; Schildkrout, 1982, 68.

45. Studies in other Islamic societies underscore this interdependence. See, for example, Horace M. Miner and Gary DeVos, *Oasis and Casbah* (Ann Arbor: University of Michigan Press, 1960); Douglas C. Gordon, *Women of Algeria: An Essay on Change* (Cambridge, MA: Harvard University Press, 1968); Fatima Mernissi, *Beyond the Veil: Male-Female Dynamics in a Modern Muslim Society* (Cambridge, MA: Schenkman, 1975).

46. Since 1979 a number of northern Nigerian cities, including Kano, Kaduna, Maiduguri, and Yola have been troubled by uprisings by followers of a self-proclaimed fundamentalist prophet called Maitatsine. Although the Maitatsine was killed by government forces in Kano in 1981, the sect has continued to exist. Its followers are from the poorest segment of the society and many are said to be migrants from outside Nigeria.

47. See Sheila Rowbotham, *Women, Resistance, Revolution* (New York: Vantage Books, 1972).

48. Of 180 Kano City women interviewed by Callaway's students in 1981–1982, 134 replied "yes" when asked if they had heard of "women's liberation." Of these 134, only one could discuss the concept in terms of her own society. The others all replied that it was "not applicable" to their lives or to women in their culture.

49. In Kano and Kaduna states, the Peoples Redemption party (PRP) controlled the state governorships from 1979 to 1983, and in Kano State the PRP controlled the state legislature as well. The PRP represented itself as the party opposed to status and privilege. It was the only one of Nigeria's five political parties to have had a platform plank calling for increased educational opportunities and increased social equality for

women. While the party did greatly increase educational opportunities for women and did appoint two women as state commissioners in the governor's cabinet, no direct campaign to confront women's disabilities was either developed or contemplated. Callaway Interview 29, April 1983.

50. Of 240 female secondary school students surveyed in 1982–1983, 98 percent believed that life would be better for their daughters than it was for their mothers or will be for them.

RECOMMENDED READINGS

Anderson, J. M. D. *Islamic Law in Africa*. London: Frank Cass, 1970.
The standard work on Islamic law in Africa. Somewhat dated.

Bello, Sir Ahmadu. *My Life*. London: Cambridge University Press,
1962.
The autobiography of Northern Nigeria's first premier, the Sar-
dauna of Sokoto. An excellent representation of conservative,
Northern Nigerian, Islamic thinking.

Hill, Polly. *Rural Hausa: A Village and a Setting*. London: Cambridge
University Press, 1972.
An excellent ethnographic work with a wealth of detail and much
information concerning the lives of rural Hausa women.

Hiskett, Mervyn. *Conflict and Harmony in Education in Tropical
Africa*. London: Allen and Unwin, 1975.
Reflections on Islamic education in African states, including
northern Nigerian states by a long-time British education officer
in Northern Nigeria.

Mernissi, Fatima. *Beyond the Veil*. Cambridge, MA: Schenkman,
1975.
A harsh critique of male/female relationships in modern Egypt.

Smith, Mary. *Baba of Kara: A Woman of the Muslim Hausa*. London:
Faber, 1954.
A beautifully written biography of a rural Hausa woman. Consid-
ered a classic.

9

Political Activism and Islamic Identity in Iran

Eliz Sanasarian
University of Southern California

T he establishment of an Islamic regime in Iran in 1979 had a devastating effect on the status of women. The retrogressive policies of the Islamic Republic were focused and consistent. The religious fundamentalists dominated the all-male political leadership through elections, politico-religious appointments, and coercion. Their traditional views on women were directly translated into laws. Despite this, masses of Muslim women rallied behind these clerics, and became the spokespersons as well as the implementors of the fundamentalists' views on women.

In the complicated milieu of Iranian politics, utilization of women by the *ulama* (religious leaders) was not new. What was unique in this case was the strong support of educated women who, with deep conviction, embraced Islam. They came to identify Ayatollah Khomeini as a leader, and the regime as an extension of their religious beliefs.

This chapter focuses on the Islamic Republic's policies concerning women as well as the pro-regime position of women. The limitations of female political activism and the reinforced Islamic identity are discussed through an analysis of laws affecting women, the pronouncements of religous-political leaders in power, and the reactions of pro-regime organized women. Singling out the philosophy of those Muslim female activists who endorsed women's rights, this study assesses their viability as a political force in Iranian politics.[1]

A Brief Look at the Past

Although there had been a loosely structured women's rights movement in the 1920s and the early 1930s, under the reign of the Pahlavis no independent activities were allowed. The Women's Organization of Iran (WOI) was a pro-establishment entity whose various branches throughout the country were manipulated by the wives and female relatives of local leaders. The WOI's small circle of Tehran leadership, however, was instrumental in the passage of a few measures supporting women's rights. The Family Protection Acts of 1967 and 1975, addressing marriage and divorce, custody of children, and family relations in general, and the liberalization of abortion in 1977 were the highlights of legislative changes concerning women.

Women's ignorance about the existence of these laws, arbitrary rulings by male judges in favor of men, the lack of connections and economic clout by the individual woman and her family, and the judicial system's general disinterest in enforcement were some of the problems plaguing the implementation of these laws. The most critical problem with family laws was that they had remained in the realm of *Sharia* (Islamic religious law). Consequently, many rules governing women were based on a traditionalist literal interpretation of the Qur'an. Polygamy, for instance, was never outlawed, but through hideous bureaucratic procedures its practice was discouraged. Most of the negative laws against women were never changed.[2]

Going beyond legislation, the status of women in Iran in the 1970s was uncertain. Despite the apparent freedom in apparel, women were continuously harassed by males in public. Pseudo-Westernized Iranians of the middle to the upper classes were typically obsessed with fashion, life-style, and any other superficial association with the West, especially the United States.[3] Although the educational level of women increased, their traditional value system did not undergo a major change. They still adhered to their customary roles as mothers and wives. By the end of the Mohammed Reza Shah's reign, however, the majority of women were illiterate and lived in poverty in villages and urban slums.[4]

The Emergence of a Fundamentalist Islamic State

The Islamic government of Iran has not always been a coherent political and centralized unit. From 1979 to the present, those in important decision-making positions have changed continuously.

By the end of the first year, it was clear that the Islamic elements had achieved full control, and by 1982 most of the Islamic reformists were eliminated. As the Islamic Republican party gradually dominated the political leadership, the fundamentalists gained increasing power. Among this group there were differing points of view on economic and foreign policy issues; however, on women's issues there was more widespread consensus. By 1984, there was still a limited number of clerical leaders who voiced their opposition to women's involvement in any activity outside the household including religious affairs and the right to vote or to be elected to public office. Yet they were ignored by other fundamentalists who saw controlled female activism as a major political advantage for the Islamic regime.

Having gradually dominated the main decision-making channels, the fundamentalist elements institutionalized their power base. The influential leaders in government proposed legislating their interpretation of Islamic rules concerning women. One by one their personal declarations were transformed into laws. The signs of repression appeared within a few months after Khomeini's return to Iran; the Family Protection Acts were dismantled, and abortion was declared illegal. Gradually, masses of women were removed from the workforce, including professional women as well as the unskilled factory workers. The *hejab* (veil) became a national obsession;[5] its use first became compulsory in government offices, and later all women were forced to cover themselves whenever in public. The minimum marriage age for girls was reduced to puberty, and divorce rights for women became extremely limited.[6] Polygamy was tolerated and even encouraged by the Islamic Republican regime until 1984, when clear disagreements emerged among the clergy. It was then declared by the Ministry of Justice that the husband must seek the permission of the wife (or wives) and the court before seeking an additional spouse. This declaration was not prompted because of a concern for women but was an acknowledgement that the state ends up with the costs of supporting the wives and children neglected by the polygamous man.[7]

Within the first two years of the revolution large numbers of women who had been staunch supporters of the uprising turned away from Ayatollah Khomeini, but many more continued to back him and the fundamentalist elements in government. On the surface they appeared to comprise one entity based on their observance of the veil and strong pro-regime slogans. However, in terms of their ideological position on women's rights, these women could be divided into two distinct groups: the reformists and the traditionalists.

The reformists consisted of well-educated and often Western-educated women who believed in an enlightened and progressive Islam. This group was predominantly represented in the Women's Society of Islamic Revolution (WSIR). Being the largest women's organization in the country, WSIR neither endorsed a special party nor was controlled by the state. It "was not a centrally organized body, but a loose association, with fragmentary activities, the most important of which were conducted by and under the name of individual Muslim women members."[8] WSIR did not have any specific goals, but its activites consisted of organizing seminars on women's issues, conducting literacy classes, and engaging in general social welfare activities.

The traditionalists consisted of a much larger group of women, ideologically less sophisticated and with much closer ties to the male fundamentalist elements in government. This group was not represented by any single organization. These were individual women as well as small units organized on the local level or by the government to perform specific "Islamic" tasks. *Setad-e Hejab* (Headquarters of Hejab), for example, was founded in 1982 to combat unveiling in society and demonstrate the true Islamic status of the Muslim woman. Although its structure of activities underwent various changes, many women either worked there or volunteered their services. Saralahis were another example, comprised of the female and male Hezbolahis.[9] They were basically a public vigilante group who would roam the streets in search of improperly covered women. If spotted, a woman was at the mercy of an individual Saralahi or Hezbolahi. Treatments could range anywhere from instruction and advice to harassment, threat, flagellation, imprisonment, and hard labor. Also, individual women, without consistently participating in organized and active groups, took part in demonstrations, served as informers, and volunteered their services to the state on various occasions.

Legislation negatively affecting women was not the only way in which women's issues were dealt with under the Islamic Republican regime. If anything, these laws were an extension of a state-endorsed Islamic identity for women.

State-Sponsored Islamic Identity

Despite controversy and political stifling among various factions of Islamic elites, three strategies, each with widespread consensus and state support, were employed to shape a coherent "Islamic" identity among women in accordance with government needs. First was the uprooting of the Pahlavi educational system and substitution of an Islamic one, geared toward intensive socialization beginning in primary schools. Within the first two years, large numbers of female teachers and principals of girls' schools were dismissed on various falsified charges of prostitution, moral misconduct, and nonobservance of the proper hejab. They were replaced by the clergy and pro-government Islamic women. Educational opportunities for women were tremendously reduced by banning coeducation, disallowing young married women to attend high school, reducing the number of female teachers, changing textbooks, and imposing the wearing of the hejab. Banning coeducation had a major negative effect at the university level; in any gathering, women were made to sit behind men, and a curtain separated them from the male students. Female students were not allowed to directly question the professor; they would write their questions and hand them to a female inspector who would then pass them to the instructor. In order to control fields of study, the government announced in late 1982 that female students, because of their "physical condition," would not be permitted to continue their studies in the field of agriculture. Women were encouraged, instead, to change their major to fields more "appropriate" for their sex, namely, laboratory sciences, radiology, nursing, and midwifery.[10]

Young children have been affected more than any other group by these changes. Forced recitation of daily prayers mixed with an intense repetition of certain codes of dress and conduct are reshaping a new generation of Iranian men and women. A child eight years old at the start of the new regime is now in his or her mid-teens; there is much that he or she has learned and internalized about his or her role in society. The enforcement of strict norms of behavior has progressed too far among the youth to be erased overnight. Young women are urged to take lessons in the use of weapons in schools and mosques. These lessons are often accompanied by "ideology" classes where pro-regime Islamic precepts are instructed. Such preparations are viewed as a struggle against *kofar* (disbelievers) and for the defense of Islam. The war with Iraq has helped to propagate this view, but Iraq is seen only as an instrument of the United States against which the main crusade is under way.[11]

The second strategy employed by the Islamic Republic to implant an "Islamic" identity in women focuses on women's roles in the family and the workforce. Undoubtedly, women's primary role as mothers and wives has been at the forefront of the regime's ideologues. However, the tension between the more extremist elements and the state's needs plus the overall knowledge of the utility of women has prompted an added dimension: encouraging women to be active outside the household in affairs benefiting the state. The pronouncements of the political elites as well as the legislative measures undertaken by the regime clearly demonstrate this combined push in both directions.

The Constitution of 1979 viewed women primarily in the context of family, and women's rights were assured only in conformity with Islamic law.[12] The Constitution was merely a reflection of the clerical leaders' perspective on women. Ayatollah Khomeini has been a strong opponent of day-care centers for children. He has argued that the shah's regime, by allowing the operation of such centers, has promoted the separation of mothers and children and the corruption of society. He sees mothers as solely responsible for raising true Islamic believers.[13] As a result, the few day-care centers operating before the revolution have practically disappeared.

In December 1983, as a reflection of this belief, a legislative measure on women's part-time work went into effect. The measure states that if a woman's demand for reducing her work hours to half-time is approved by her supervisor, she may continue in that position with certain benefits for a duration of no more than five years. The chair of the Islamic Assembly's Commission on Work and Employment (which oversees the law) announced that since women become pregnant, are responsible for running the household and raising of children, it is unfair to make them work like the men outside the house. However, if women must work because of financial hardship, they should divide their time between the house and the workplace.[14]

In addition to the policy of domestication of women, there have been continuous efforts to involve them in a particular type of outside work. Earlier, Ayatollah Rafsanjani, the head of the Iranian Majlis (Islamic Assembly) had favored women's role in the family and the importance of motherhood.[15] Yet in a recent interview he condemned "women's imprisonment in the house and their exclusion from social work. . . . We should not let women feel wasted in the house." He blasted the so-called extremists who had questioned women's suffrage and expressed a desire to see women active in "those endeavors needed in the country."[16] In line with this perspective, the training of female preachers has been expanded, based on the belief that in order to export Islam to the rest of the world, preachers of both sexes are needed. Also, women were permitted and even encouraged to form their own groups in support of the government and especially the Iran-Iraq war efforts.

A typical example of traditional women's involvement in public work has been the establishment of social work organizations. Many such groups (including the largest women's organization, the WOI) existed during the rule of the Pahlavis. It was considered, in fact, chic for upper-middle to upper-class women (especially the wives of public officials) to take part in social welfare activities. Under the Islamic Republican regime, many Islamic women's welfare groups sprung up throughout the country, including one founded by Khomeini's daughter. It was funded by various state agencies, such as the Revolutionary Guard and the Ministry of Education, to form Qur'an and literacy classes and to teach women sewing and other domestic duties.

The third major strategy to impart an "Islamic" identity on women has been the development and promotion of an ideal symbol of a Muslim woman through glorification of the kinswomen of the Prophet Mohammed. The most distinguished among them are: Khadijeh, the first wife of the Prophet; Fatima, the Prophet's daughter who married Ali (whom the Shi'ites consider to be the successor to the Prophet Mohammed); their daughter Zeinab; and Somayyieh, known as the first martyr of Islam.

Attributes bestowed upon these women emphasize familiar themes such as their great devotion and obedience to their fathers, husbands, and sons, and their instinctive willingness to sacrifice themselves for their men and Islam. They possess the double qualities of domesticated heroines and activists in defense of Islam.[17] The appearance of the ideal woman is a crucial component of this symbol. She is clad head to toe in a black veil and carries a rifle. The Islamic Republic has been a staunch promoter of the hejab for women, both through socialization and coercion. A woman without cover can receive a one-month to a year prison sentence. A whole political ideology has been formed around the use of the hejab. Some of its components are: The hejab of a Muslim woman annoys Westerners, therefore, it is a strong weapon to be used against the West; those who refuse to cover themselves are the enemies of Islam in collaboration with the West; and the veil represents the superior traits of courage and strength in a Muslim woman compared to other women. To uproot past practices and reinstitute new ones, the Islamic Republic denounced the celebration of International Women's Day and declared the birthday of Fatima, the Prophet's daughter, the new Women's Day in Iran.

An Assessment of Reformist Reaction

The "Islamic" identity promoted by the regime embodied a political and patriarchal definition of femaleness in society. Two major ideological components of this identity were readily accepted and endorsed by Islamic women of both reformist and fundamentalist persuasions: (1) Women are equal to but dissimilar from men, and (2) Western values are a corruptive menace to be avoided by women. Since the latter group did not attempt to, in any way, deviate from or alter the official stand, the following discussion concentrates mainly on the reformists' interpretation of several women's issues.

A commonly voiced opinion by many Islamic clerics is that women and men are equal but dissimilar in nature and temperament.[18] Ayatollah Morteza Motahhari, a Shi'i scholar, has written extensively about women. From his philosophical standpoint, in their humanity men and women are equal, but discoveries in biological and psychological sciences have made it clear that the two sexes are different. Their differences are innate, and sociohistorical factors do not play any role in causing them. When women's natural disposition is ignored, their rights are violated. Nature has bestowed upon women a monthly period, pregnancy, nurturing of children, and less labor and productive strength. Because of this, she has naturally been put under the protection of the male; having more rights than he but fewer responsibilities. This corresponds with the animal kingdom where male species instinctively protect females. Thus, men and women have equal but not identical rights since their natural disposition is different.[19]

The reformists endorse this view but attach additional precepts. Differences between men and women are complementary and not the sign of superiority or inferiority of either sex. They insist that Islam should be understood in its totality, otherwise it will be applied out of context. Society at large and not its individual members (e.g., women) is the main concern of Islamic doctrine. Using specific examples, the reformists maintain that Islam's position on women has been misunderstood. For instance, according to the Qur'an a woman inherits half of what a man inherits. The reformists explain this rule by asserting that women have the right to keep their own money and dispose of it as they please. Women can engage in economic activities but do not have the obligation to support a family. The financial support of the family (and its female members) is the primary responsibility of the man; therefore, it is only sensible for the male to inherit twice as much as the female. This indicates why both sexes have equal but dissimilar economic rights.[20]

The concept of equal but different is reflected in most of the stands of Islamic reformers. The Islamic Republican regime does not allow females to be judges, asserting that, being emotional, women are not fit to serve in the field of jurisprudence. Female reformers have responded that exemption from jurisprudence is not "deprivation of a right" but exclusion from "a burdensome responsibility." However, they still demand that women be allowed to serve as judges on the ground that through "education, exercise, and experience" women "can learn to control themselves." Moreover, Muslim women would be able to take their legal problems to female judges, a condition corresponding to having female doctors for women. And since the Qur'an does not object to having female judges, they ask that the condition of sexuality be replaced by the condition of competence.[21]

In addition, on another related issue, the Qur'an states explicitly that two female witnesses equal one male witness in testimony. The reformists accept (or pretend to accept) the traditional male argument that women's emotionalism caused by their menstrual cycle is responsible for this law. Although men also might face the problems of emotionalism, reformists believe that this characteristic is more prominent in women. Therefore, while asserting that the law is intended to protect people's rights, they contend that if a judge considers the testimony of one woman sufficient, then this rule may be abandoned.[22]

On the question of polygamy, specifically endorsed in the Qur'an, the reformists assert that the doctrine was intended to protect orphans as a social necessity and not for "someone's fancy and indulgence." However, the determination as to whether polygamy, at a particular time in history, is a social necessity must be decided by an Islamic community that understands Islamic laws. The present society does not comprehend these laws and, hence, misuses the prescript to the disadvantage of women. They argue that before Islam, men had an unlimited number of wives; Islam limited the number to four under certain circumstances. Also, the Qur'an clearly suggests that if a man cannot do justice to all four equally, he should be content with only one wife. Since feelings cannot always be controlled by reason, then the Qur'an endorses marrying only one.[23]

On the whole, the reformists' acceptance of the notion of equal but dissimilar implies adherence to the concept of equal but separate. Perhaps an argument in defense of this position is that, in societies segregated by sex in the Middle East, the proponents of women's rights would advance faster if they took stands that did not violate the existing norms of their societies. However, this raises many questions. Racial separation has never led to equality in any community; why should sexual segregation be an exception? In a patriarchal system, can separate be equal? Even if this system comes to endorse a female judge for women only, is it not suggesting that emotional and imbalanced creatures should judge only their own kind? What about the large number of legal cases involving both sexes? Undoubtedly, a male judge would preside over them, and a separate judge for women would make a direct statement that women are not fit to judge men.

Futhermore, the reformists make the most destructive compromise to a male hierarchy by accepting the primary reasoning for certain discriminatory laws and practices against women. As was shown in the cases of providing testimony and the operation of the judicial system, the reformists abide by the chauvinistic traditional perspective that women are naturally more emotional and that menstruation is a deficiency. No true believer in women's rights will ever yield to this, the argument most often used against women. The Muslim reformists, by not departing form the equal but dissimilar stand, have put themselves in an impugnant position of dispute, compromise, and justification in dealing with the authorities.

The second ideological component of the "Islamic" identity also voiced by the reformists was condemnation of the West. During the celebration of the Islamic Republic's Women's Day in 1983, Ayatollah Montazeri, the predicted successor to Ayatollah Khomeini, in his message to women stated: "Pull yourselves away from Western society where women are used to satisfy the lust of men, to sell expensive products and to show themselves off which only serves to corrupt society."[24] Similar sentiments have been expressed by Ayatollah Khomeini before, during, and after the 1979 Revolution.[25] The Islamic reformists also condemned the West (and the East to a lesser degree) and denied the existence of equality, equating women's freedom in the West with the expansion of corruption. The reformist perspective on the status of women in the West is best exemplified in the following paragraph, describing the Iranian woman's search for her own identity after the Revolution:

> Behind her she sees years of repression and traditional male chauvinistic society where she was looked upon only as a child-bearer, sex object and a slave of man. This certainly is not her choice! She looks at the West and their 'democratic system' where women are encouraged to get out of their home. She studies hard and works very hard too. Yet she doesn't find the

equality or happiness that she is after, and she turns to tran-
quilizers and pills. She is turned into a sex object and multinational corporations exploit her sexuality for more benefit in a
consumerized society. She is beaten by her husband and beats
her children in frustration. She turns to alcohol and cigarettes
and starts giving birth to defective children. Her body is being
sold and subjected to inhuman abuses in the new slave markets
of pornographic movies. The family bonds get looser and the
children pour into the streets where they get into alcohol and
drugs as early as eight to ten years of age, looking for something
and never finding it, seeking refuge in strange cults and man-
made religions. The Iranian woman can't choose this model in ·
spite of Western insistence and feminists.[26]

The work from which this paragraph is taken also condemns the
Communist Eastern bloc for turning woman into a tool of production and taking away her humanity.

The paragraph above raises points with which most social critics
will agree; it focuses attention on problems facing women in
capitalistic and communist societies. However, as a serious
perspective it contains two major fallacies: (1) equating capitalistic
exploitation of women with feminism, and (2) disregarding
feminism as an ideology of human liberation. Here, the inadequacies of Western societies are viewed as the result of a vague
concept of liberation advocated by feminists. Issues raised in the
paragraph, such as pornography, wife beating, and drug abuse by
women are realities Western feminists have defied and challenged.

Ironically, the Islamic reformists have borrowed much from the
feminists. Their writings and claims show a great deal of conceptual
reliance on feminism, but then they bend backwards to adjust these
concepts to Islamic codes. When the use of the hejab was made
compulsory in government offices and strongly recommended in
public, in spite of their own observance of the hejab, most reformists
opposed legislation on forced veiling. One of the major points was
that men, too, should cover themselves according to the Qu'ran,
otherwise the government decree violates Islamic doctrine and is
discriminatory. On the issue of custody of children a similar stance
was taken. Custody of children (boys older than two and girls older
than seven) goes directly to the male. The reformists have raised
strong objections declaring that the rule is unjust and cruel to both
the mother and the children. On the important point of women's
role as a nurturer and caretaker of the household, reformists have
relied heavily on the regime's symbols of womanhood. They view
the woman's physical ability to procreate as a significant gift; her
role in the family as an undisputed virtue; and her societal role as
one of political activism without restraints.

The Islamic Republic's dualistic policy of domestication and activism of women has had positive and negative consequences for the
reformists. They have focused on the activist part in the hope of
increasing women's rights. They insist that a woman's sexuality can
serve as no excuse for her lack of involvement in all kinds of national
affairs. They have relied heavily on the role of the Islamic heroines,
comments of the clerical leadership, and detailed interpretations of
the Qur'anic verses to galvanize this point. The reformists argue
that God and the Prophet have given women the right to become
active in *any* sphere they choose and men cannot deprive them of
this right. However, this view is different from the official one in
that the authorities have limited women's activism to social work
and those occupations considered fit by the clerical leadership. The
reformists' lack of success in, at least, their dialectical disputes with
the authorities, stems from a crucial distinction: From the Islamic
leaders' standpoint, the role of women as defenders of Islam (the
avenue of activism) derives from and is directly tied to their primary roles as nurturers of children and caretakers of the household.
The former is only an extension of the latter and not an independent
thought as the reformists maintain.

It is easy to draw on many more examples to demonstrate the
extent to which feminist ideas have been incorporated in the formulation of positions on women's issues, a factor leading some to call
the reformists "Muslim feminists." The continuous undercurrents
of contradictions and justifications inherent in the arguments
raised by this small group of Islamic intellectual women make it
extremely difficult to view them as feminists. While they claim that
Islam does not acknowledge separate rights for women (or any other
category of people), they have focused on women's issues, negating
their own stand. The attempt to fit in their desires and demands
within a state framework is bound to fail since it ignores the inflexi-
ble all-male power structure in the Islamic Republic. Their efforts
have clashed with the realities of masculine power politics, which
will not compromise unless forced to do so. In the face of theocratic
dictatorship, these women are doomed to failure. The recent elections demonstrated this fact.

Evidence of Reformists' Decline

Until the 1984 elections four women served in the Majlis, all representatives from Tehran province. In order of their support for wom-
en's rights they were: Azam Taleghani (head of the WSIR, a staunch

reformist); Mariam Behroozi (reformist bent on conservatism, pro–forced hejab but endorsing the working rights of women); Gohar Dastgheib (less reformist than the latter, critical of divorce laws); and Ategheh Sedighi (wife of the assassinated ex-prime minister Rajai, conservative, endorsing harsh treatment of women without the Islamic hejab). During the 1984 elections for the Islamic Assembly, all of the above with the exception of Azam Taleghani were reelected. An active member of the Islamic Republican party, Marzieh Hadidchi Dabagh replaced Taleghani in the Majlis. Taleghani's loss in the election was significant since she was the most outspoken female member of the Islamic Assembly between 1980 and 1984. A staunch reformist, she had condemned forced hejab for women, discriminatory divorce laws, and illegal arrests, imprisonments, and executions in Iran. During May 1981 she raised the possibility of official involvement in the attack on the Women's Society of Islamic Revolution branch in Isfahan. She was often excluded from various decision-making platforms for her outspoken remarks. At one point, the right-wing fundamentalists in the Majlis asked for her dismissal from the Assembly.

The other three female members of the Majlis were not controversial figures. Two of them, Gohar Dastgheib and Mariam Behroozi, were mildly reformist on women's issues but staunch conservatives on other issues. The fourth member, Ategheh Sedighi, gained popularity and recognition because of her dead husband, ex-prime minister Rajai. She remains a strong conservative on women's and other issues. Marzieh Hadidchi Dabagh, who replaced Taleghani in the 1984 election, was the leader of the women's section of the Islamic Republican party (IRP) and one of Khomeini's companions while he lived in Paris. It is to be noted that all these women, except Taleghani, ran on the IRP slate. Taleghani was allowed to run for the Majlis but reportedly did not win enough votes. The only reformist and truly independent female politician was removed from office.

Prospects for the Future

Iran's war with Iraq has put the country in a state of emergency; the war has been used as an excuse to strengthen the roots of the Islamic Republican party. The pseudo-Westernism of the Pahlavis has been replaced by the pseudo-Islamism of this regime; the reformists have succumbed to the latter. The point is not to deny thoroughly the probability of reformism on women's issues in Islam. A similar effort has been pursued by religious Christian and Jewish women in

the West. However, despite attempts to restore some rights to
women and despite their criticisms of the authorities, the Iranian
reformists have remained generally silent on numerous violations
of human rights in Iran. There are thousands of female prisioners,
including many teenagers accused of moral and political crimes,
and many have been tortured and executed.

Beyond the hypocrisy that accompanies the reformists' allegiance to the Islamic regime, they face serious conceptual and
dogmatic problems. Basic to these contradictions and distortions is
a crucial socio-historical factor. Many of the reformists were exposed to the West either by residing there or through the mass
media. In face of the lack of a genuine nativistic identity, Islam has
become a solid identity through which everything is explained and
redefined. Cultural capitalism and unpopular Western (particularly
American economic and foreign) policies have put even the pro–
women's rights elements on a defensive. This is an ironic development not limited to the Iranian case. The women's liberation
movement in the West was confronted only by the patriarchal men
and women opposing women's rights. Today, while the expanding
communication network has made the discussion of women's issues
easier cross-nationally, it has facilitated misperceptions of feminist
ideology. The linkages between women's issues and other issues
(e.g., religious and national) have intensified to the point of serious
distortion of the idea and practice of feminism. The Western
capitalist penetration, mixed with Western feminists' general lack of
interest in or knowledge of the developing nations, have put Third
World women on the defensive, therefore stifling the pure development of feminism as in the West.

Under the present Iranian regime, there is no chance for the
development of any genuine pro–women's rights group. However,
among the millions of Iranian exiles, there are positive signs of a
rebirth of feminism. Already, there are small independent women's
groups active in France, England, and the United States. Facing the
temptation of cultural assimilation, these groups are trying to form
their own "nativistic" feminist ideology. This is a very recent effort,
and any assessment of their work at this time would be premature.
But one point is clear; for any feminist group to be successful, it
must penetrate the masses of traditional women in Iran. It should
attempt the difficult task of translating feminism into an indigenous
ideology attractive to women without compromising its basic
principles.

NOTES

1. Access to sources and knowledgeable individuals is limited under present conditions but not impossible. This study relies on the objective news reports published outside Iran, and editorials and commentaries published inside the country. Some of the written materials were substantiated by eyewitness accounts of friends and colleagues who have recently visited Iran. I am especially grateful to S. H. for her insightful comments.

2. For instance, one of the worst laws closely identified with Sharia (Islamic religious laws), which practically encouraged crimes against women, was never changed. The law allowed a man to kill his wife, sister, or mother if he witnessed either one having sex with a man. This law was to protect the "honor" of the man and his family; however, in practice the murder was committed merely on the basis of suspicion. Refer to Reza Mazlooman, *Zankoshy dar Lava-ye Qanoon* [Female-killing under the protection of the law] (Tehran: Sazeman Zanan Iran, 1352/1974).

3. In critical works by either the secular or the religious elements on this topic, especially in the anti-Pahlavi opposition literature, Iranian women were condemned for their fashion obsessiveness. What most of the political groups and individual commentators conveniently missed was the Iranian males' equivalent preoccupation with Western fashions and life-style. For one of the classical works on this topic refer to Jalal Al-Ahmad, *Gharbzadegi* [Weststricken] (Tehran: 1962).

4. For a comprehensive analysis of the effect of Mohammed Reza Shah's regime on women see Eliz Sanasarian, *The Women's Rights Movement in Iran: Mutiny, Appeasement, and Repression from 1900 to Khomeni* (New York: Praeger, 1982), chapters 5 and 6.

5. Hejab is the Muslim term for the practice of covering women. The type of cover may differ from one community to another, ranging anywhere from a simple scarf to a long head-to-toe traditional veil with a hood.

6. Women's divorce rights under the FPA were abolished in 1979. In 1981 and 1983 they were replaced by other measures that amounted to no rights at all. In 1984 a series of new laws were enacted that were more a reflection of the regime's needs rather than anything even approaching the rights of women in divorce. Refer to *Iran Times*, September 11, 1981, 5; April 1, 1983, 1; and July 13, 1984, 15. For an analysis of women's divorce rights until 1982, refer to Sanasarian, 94–97, 139. For an analysis of marriage and especially child-marriages, refer to Haleh Afshar, "Khomeini's Teachings and their Implications for Iranian Women," in *In the Shadow of Islam: The Women's Movement in Iran*, compiled by Azar Tabari and Nahid Yeganeh (London: Zed Press, 1982), 82–84.

7. Refer to *Iran Times*, April 27, 1984, 1, for a summary interview of the *Zan-e Ruz* magazine with the chief prosecutor of Iran, Yousef Sanei.

8. *In the Shadow of Islam*, 224.

9. Literally known as Hezb Allah (the Party of God), the group is made up of religious fanatics who resort to violence against an individual or

group whom they identify as anti-Islamic. Their organizers are not known but they have very close ties with the government.

10. *Iran Times*, December 3, 1982, 2.

11. An example of this position can be found in *Banovan: Pooieandegan Rah Zeinab* 20 (18 Azar 1359/December 1980), 26.

12. Refer to the text of the 1979 Constitution, *Qanoon Assasi Jomhoori-ye Islami Iran*, especially articles 20 and 21, which directly address women. For an analysis of these articles see Sanasarian, 131–133.

13. "Mothers Are the Source of Goodness," *Mahjubah* 2:8/9 (Muharram–Safar 1403/November 1982–January 1983), 4–5.

14. This information was reported in a number of issues of *Iran Times:* January 21, 1983, 4; February 11, 1983, 2; and December 16, 1983, 2.

15. An interview with Rafsanjani reported in *Mahjubah* 1, 2, 3 (Rajab–Ramadhan 1403/May–July 1983), 10–13.

16. Reported in *Iran Times*, May 11, 1984, p. 14.

17. Writings on the biography and astute qualities of these women are mainly being published in magazines and books. A series of paperback books published by Amir Kabir publishers in Tehran, entitled *The Great Women of Islam Series*, discusses the lives of each of these women, separately.

18. The view concerning the equality of men and women (without either the definition of equality or a discussion of the essence of dissimilarity) was often voiced by Ayatollah Khomeini before his return to Iran. See Ali-Reza Nobari, ed., *Iran Erupts* (Stanford, CA: Iran-American Group, December 1978), 9–17. This interview with Khomeini was first published in *Le Monde*, May 6, 1978. Its English translation was published in the *Manchester Guardian*, May 21, 1978.

19. Ayatollah Morteza Motahhari, "The Rights of Women in Islam," *Message of Revolution* 17 (March–April 1983), 32–37. This is a preface to one of his works written in 1974, entitled *Nexam Hoquq Zan dar Islam* [The rights of women in Islam] (Tehran: Daftar Nashr Farhang Islami, 1353 Khorsheedi, 1394 Qamari). Considering himself an expert on women, Ayatollah Mutahhari has written extensively on the subject. Refer to *Akhlagh Jensee dar Islam va Jahan Gharb* [Sexuality in Islam and the Western world] (Qom: Intesharat Sadra); *Hoquq Zan, Ta'adoddi Zojat, Izdevaj Movaghat* [Women's rights, polygamy, temporary marriage] (Qom: Intesharat Ahli Bait); and *Masale-ye Hejab* [The question of hejab] (Qom: Intesharat Sadra). Also, his articles and parts of his books have appeared in *Zan-e Ruz* magazine.

20. Shanin Etezadi Tabatabai, "Understanding Islam in Its Totality Is the Only Way To Understand Women's Role," in *In the Shadow of Islam*, 176.

21. Fereshti Hashemi, "Proposal for the Legal Revival of the Rights of Women," ibid., 187–188.

22. Fereshti Hashemi, "Women in an Islamic Versus Women in a Muslim View," ibid., 182.

23. Ibid., 181; Fereshti Hashemi, "Polygamy and Social Justice," *Mahjubah* 2:3 (Sha'ban 1402/May–June 1982), 45.

24. Ayatollah Montazeri, "Learn from Fatima Zahra," *Mahjubah* 1, 2, 3 (Rajab–Ramadhan 1403/May–July 1983), 9.

25. Ayatollah Khomeini's position on women has appeared in numerous publications after the revolution. For an example of his views refer to *Dar Jostejoo-ye Rah az Kelam Imam (daftar sevom): Zan: Az Bayanot va Ilamieh-ha-ye Imam Khomeini az Sal 1341–1361* [In search of the path from Iman's words (third book): Women: From the statements and announcements of Imam Khomeini from 1341 to 1361] (Tehran: Intesharat Amir Kabir, first printing, 1361/1982). Also refer to Oriana Fallaci, "An Interview with Khomeini," *New York Times Magazine*, October 7, 1979, 29–31.

26. Tabatabai, *In the Shadow of Islam*, 176.

RECOMMENDED READINGS

Bamdad, Badr ol-Moluk. *From Darkness into Light: Women's Emancipation in Iran.* Trans. and ed. by F. R. C. Bagley. Smithtown, NY: Exposition Press, 1977.

Beck, Lois, and Nikki Keddie, eds. *Women in the Muslim World.* Cambridge, MA: Harvard University Press, 1978.

Nashat, Guity, ed. *Women and Revolution in Iran.* Boulder, CO: Westview Press, 1983.

Sanasarian, Eliz. *The Women's Rights Movement in Iran: Mutiny, Appeasement, and Repression from 1900 to Khomeini.* New York: Praeger, 1982.

Tabari, Azar, and Nahid Yeganeh, compilers. *In the Shadow of Islam: The Women's Movement in Iran.* London: Zed Press, 1982.

10

The Egyptian Woman:
Trends Today, Alternatives Tomorrow

Fadwa El Guindi
University of Southern California

T he analysis presented in this chapter focuses on the development of women's status in Egypt in the context of cultural processes interweaving traditions over centuries of modern history.

A cultural framework is proposed within which the nature of gender, the meaning of being men and women, and the actual relation between the sexes are understood in terms of institutionalized interpretive structures woven into shape as culture-bearers, who construct reality out of a universe formed through cultures of Arab Islamic traditions.[1] The goal here is to assess the contemporary situation of women in Egypt and perhaps postulate alternative trends for the future.

Egyptian Women in Arab-Islamic Tradition

It is postulated in this analysis that the construction of Egyptian sexual identity in relation to the social world has been in formation for at least 13 centuries of the developmental history of Arab Islamic tradition in Egypt. As reality is socially constructed in this process, sexual identity is simultaneously scripted.[2] Through socialization, social constructions are internalized, and, as experience is

reaffirmed in symbol and ritual, one's individual identity is gradually formed.

Accordingly, it is essential to identify the characteristics of Arab
Islamic tradition considered most dominant in scripting the identity of individuals as men and women. Toward this goal a culture-
based framework is more productive than the universalistic
frameworks contrasting culture/nature, public/private, or domes-
tic/extradomestic for describing Egyptian women's status and role.
It is my contention that the most adequate framework for understanding Egyptian sexual identity in particular, and Arab sexual
identity in general, is one based on cultural content organized into
two worlds equally relevant to the understanding of both sexes.
These two worlds—one's separate sexual world and one's kinship
world—cutting across public and private domains,[3] more significantly than any other factor shape individual identities.

Translated in terms of individual experience, an individual is
born into either a women's world or a men's world on the one hand,
and into a world of kinfolk on the other. In the case of a woman, a
newborn female joins two ready-made existing worlds—one of
women and another of kinship, both crucial in determining her
identity and self-image as a culture-bearer and central in providing
support for her and controls over her as a member of society.

The World of Kinfolk

In addition to determining her identity, the kinship world provides
a woman with support, protection, and security. Both sexes are
relationally defined vis-à-vis this universe of kinfolk and are identified permanently by it.

The importance of kinship for one's identity in Arab culture can
be seen in the naming pattern for both sexes alike. Last names of
large important families are often preceded by *al-* (as, for example,
al-Khalifa, al-Sabbah, al-Saud, which are the names of the ruling
families of Bahrain, Kuwait, and Saudi Arabia, respectively), or by
bin, bani, or *awlad* (meaning "offspring of"). Both uses signify identification with a larger body of kin through ascent or descent, reinforcing one's identity not as an autonomous individual but as
member of a kin group. Perhaps only a few centuries before Islam a
transition began to occur from a previous rule of matriliny (as
shown in Egypt and also believed to have existed throughout the
Peninsula) to the contemporary form of patriliny, according to
which both sexes (unlike name patriliny in the U.S., to which only

males subscribe) officially acquire and maintain for life the patrilineal family name, irrespective of marital affiliation. This continuity of one's identity with the natal kin group throughout the life
cycle expresses and reinforces the consanguineal tie for men and
women alike. No official name transfer after marriage occurs in the
case of Egyptian (and by extension all Arab) women. Affiliation with
one's kin is unambiguously defined at ritual birth for both sexes and
remains as a determinant of one's identity forever.

Within the larger world of kinship a narrower circle of kinsmen is
directly significant in the life of every woman. For it is these
kinsmen who share the risk of reputation with her, who hold controls over her, and who are obligated to protect her and provide her
with tangible and intangible forms of security irrespective of her
marital or financial status. It is in the context of this set of man-to-
woman obligations that sexual asymmetry in inheritance rules in
Islam (e.g., that a man's share in inheritance is twice the size of the
woman's) is justified by the interdependent obligations binding the
man to financially support his wife, daughter, mother, sister, or any
other dependent female relative. For the women, perhaps more in
ideal terms, but supported by law, these kinsmen are required to
provide the equivalent of modern institutionalized plans of lifetime
support, insurance, pension, retirement, unemployment, disability—all in one package. Quality of support is also part of this
obligation. The husband is required to maintain the standard of
living his wife was accustomed to in her father's home, which may
include an obligation to provide domestic help, child care, or even a
wet nurse should the wife so desire. She has no similar financial
obligations to her husband, and, consistent with her premarital
status, may not be required to perform domestic labor nor even
nurse her own babies. Rather, upon marriage she becomes *Sitt
el-bait* or the lady of the house—a term that corresponds with the
reality of her autonomous managerial role as head manager of the
household.

Extending the premise further, this same man can prevent a
woman from *needing* to participate in employment by virtue of his
continued financial responsibility to support her. This latter factor
alone minimizes Arab Eastern women's need to work for wages.[4] In
wealthy families this need is completely eliminated. In fact it would
be a stigma for a woman to work for wages. Traditionally the stigma
applied irrespective of financial position or economic status, since it
was culturally interpreted to mean that her kinsmen are either
unable to support her or are not meeting their obligation to support
her. Such factors serve as social pressures directly affecting one's

reputation and ability to function in society. It must be emphasized, however, that the stigma is not as much about work as about *paid* work. And it is worse if the work is culturally devalued or is held in low esteem.

Moreover, the protective nature of kinsmen's relation toward a kinswoman translates in terms of employment opportunity into preventing her from being in a situation in which a nonkinsman is in a position superior to hers with power over her. This constraint does not apply to employment in which she is in a superior position to strange men. Taking these factors together, we can account for certain patterns in employment for Egyptian women, particularly in the 1950s and 1960s, when women visibly began to join the public force.

Traditionally, elite women all over the modern Arab East performed public social services on a volunteer basis. The early feminist movement of 1919 in Egypt was run by a group of such gentlewomen.[5] In contrast to wage employment, voluntary work was not disapproved of. As a result, it was not in the too distant past in the Arab East that the positions usually associated with females in industrial societies such as secretary, typist, and nurse were exclusively male or foreign women's jobs. Only recently are these jobs being filled by native women in the less wealthy countries. No observer traveling on an Arab airline will fail to notice the absence of native women stewardesses. Either all-male stewards, as on Air Algerie, or foreign stewardesses mostly from Europe occupy these positions. As in the case of the airline stewardess, in wealthy Arab countries domestic jobs are generally filled by imported labor. The idea of stigma from paid employment and the goal of protecting women from being in subordinate positions to strange men as well as from low-status positions are key factors that have been acting as constraints on women's employment, significantly affecting its pervasive patterns. These factors are particularly evident today in the oil-rich Arab countries where kinsmen can and do afford to pay the price of protectiveness. Contemporary economic and population pressures in Egypt make it difficult to sustain these desired patterns. With its population size expanding exponentially, Egypt cannot afford the luxury of absolute control over women.

The World of Women

Arab Eastern conceptualization of the sociomoral world is in terms of two sexes, male and female, unambiguously defined, clearly demarcated, and separate. The conceptual boundary between the two is expressed symbolically, ritually, as well as directly, at all times throughout an individual's lifetime.

Just as a person is born into a kinship universe, if female she is simultaneously born into an already existing world of women, cross-cutting age groups and unbound by kinship. Her identification with this world of women is immediately and permanently established and continues to be reaffirmed throughout her lifetime.

Underlying the conceptual division of society into two separate sexual worlds is the sociomoral Islamic community, which recognizes the disruptive nature of strong active sexuality uncontrollably characteristic of both sexes. Strong sexuality is considered to be positive and desirable in Islam, but must be harnessed and subjected to controls so that temptation will not lead to a chaotic society. In cross-sex interaction between marriageables desexualization becomes necessary. One way is to desexualize social space by enforcing *de facto* physical segregation.

While effective, this extreme separation is neither possible in rapidly changing societies that are not wealthy and do not have space, nor is it required by Islam. Alternatively, desexualization can be achieved by interacting with *maharim* (those male kin who are bound by the incest taboo and are hence eliminated from a woman's spouse pool) or if a *mahram* (singular form) accompanies a woman as occurs in sacred spaces such as the *Hajj* (pilgrimage to Mecca). A third means of achieving desexualization is expressed among the college women today in most of the Arab and Islamic East who are part of the growing Islamic movement. These young women voluntarily choose to dress conservatively in such a way that not only their bodies are desexualized but also the cross-sex interactive space. Their style of talking, choice of vocabulary, tone of voice, and facial expressions are all consistent with the desexualized nature of their interaction.

The two aspects—identification with one's gender and separateness from the opposite sex—are closely linked. A close association with the world of women is simultaneously a separateness from the world of men. This separateness is expressed and reinforced in modern Arab societies through ways ranging from partial to total and from cultural to physical separation between the sexes. Saudi Arabia is usually the popular example given for a society that successfully continues to rigidly enforce a total physical segregation between the sexes in social and architectural space, in education as well as in public employment.

However, even in the least physically segregated Arab societies

such as Egypt, sexual integration is more apparent than real, because whether it is replicated on the physical plane or not, the
feature of separateness is pervasive and expresses a dominant cultural premise that continues to define relative sexual identities and
relations between the sexes. For example, in Egypt there is an
apparent absence of sex segregation that tends to be positively
perceived in terms of Western standards as an index of progressiveness. Perhaps in some way it does reflect superficial progressiveness. Nevertheless one should not disregard the subtle ways by
which separateness is expressed and continues to persist widely.
This is so not because it is externally enforced by authority, but
rather because it is compatible with the cultural configuration.

It is this cultural dimension of separateness that can account for
the ease with which public sexual separation is voluntarily adopted
today, for the sense of comfort felt by women with other women, and
for the tendency among women to seek support from female friends
unrelated to them by kinship rather than confide in their own
husbands.

When women are alone, the pressure for desexualization is eliminated and they comfortably socialize, seductively dance, deveil (if
veiled) revealing their high-style clothes, freely exchange confiden-
tial information, laugh loudly, and express unrestrained femininity.
As a result, a same-sex solidarity develops that is neither sexual
(that is lesbian) in nature nor feminist. Rather, the consciousness
that binds these women is one of strong womanhood.

Being with other women becomes for each woman a matter of
privacy. She is assertive in defending the privacy of her sexual
space. In some situations this develops as a strategy by which
women protect themselves from harassment by strange men. For
example, it is not uncommon to observe in Egypt today situations
requiring queuing, as for example outside a food cooperative or
bakery, where men and women automatically form two queues, one
for each sex. Invariably, women appear more jealous about their
separate lines, assertively and even aggressively preventing male
intrusion, intentional or accidental. Today's college women who are
in the movement to restore traditional values are choosing a literal
public separation between the sexes that, as is known from Egypt's
past, is an institution that is not indigenous to Egypt. But this
should not detract from the fact that a strong sense of gender
separateness does exist today among both sexes at all levels, outside
the context of the recent Islamic movement, even though it may not
be accompanied by physical sexual separation.

Nor is this separateness to be confused with antagonism between the sexes. Egypt, and Arab-Islamic culture in general, is not characterized by cross-sex antagonism in attitude or in institutionalized social form as in the ethnographic cases of New Guinea and South America, and increasingly in U.S. society as well. Rather, the phenomenon conveyed is one of a deep-rooted, historically supported, ideologically reinforced gender self-sufficiency, autonomy, and completeness translated in a woman's character into a strong sense of self and a positive self-image as a person and as a woman. Institutions of separate naming, independent economic status, and autonomous identity reinforce this self-image and strengthen it.

In a world in which kinship and marriage alliances are intertwined, women associating with each other ultimately hold valuable information about potential brides for their sons, brothers, and in certain cases husbands or fathers. Given the significance of marital networks in countries in which not only business (as in Lebanon) but even governments (as in Saudi Arabia) are run along kinship lines, women are able to acquire a large degree of control and power through this "natural" identification and association with other women, a power that can have implications beyond their separate space and domestic world, into the wider political and economic arena.

Therefore, observations frequently made that automatically link segregation with subordination and weakness of women are challenged, since it is this very institution—sex segregation—that inevitably becomes the source of their strength, their autonomy, their assured self-image, and power. This is not to minimize the potential abuse that can result from the same source of women's strength, hence becoming their source of oppressiveness. Therefore, a negative association between segregation and women's status is not automatic, even though situations exist in which the group of kinsmen who hold all the controls over a woman in order to ideally provide her with support and protection may be the same ones that oppress her, exploit her, or hinder her chances of participation in public life.

The difference is important. It is neither the idea of gender separateness nor the institution of sex segregation *per se* that are oppressive, but their manipulation and abuse. Nor is it the case that men in general subordinate women. Rather it is the woman's protectors who can become her worst oppressors. In the same vein, if barriers at the kinship level are absent, the woman will face no serious obstacles at the level of society. Accordingly, given the culturally reinforced self-confidence built into her about herself and her ability, which as shown, is deeply rooted in history, an absence of

primary barriers (by her kinfolk) can and does result in an overwhelming embrace by her of opportunities continually opening to
her because of revolutionary change. This is clearly demonstrated
in the area of education, in which a dramatic increase can be seen in
women's presence at all levels. Less dramatic but equally impressive is the extent and distribution of their participation in the labor
force, the area in which the constraints identified in this analysis are
most applicable.

Current Trends in Education and Employment

In modern Egypt the first school for girls was opened in 1856,[6]
offering general education and some vocational training. It is revealing to consider the differential response to this opportunity by
upper-class and middle-class families. Upper-class families ignored
it, and middle-class families resisted it even though both considered
the opportunity it provided for girls' education to be highly desirable. The reasons are different in the two cases and illustrate the
complexity that needs to be taken into consideration in any analysis
of Arab women's situation. The reason why upper-class women did
not join the school is that in those days they received private tutor-
ing in the luxurious seclusion of their homes or were sent abroad to
Europe for proper education.[7]

The situation for middle-class families was different: They considered the opportunity offered through the school for girls' education to be positive but that the inclusion of vocational training that
linked education with employment prevented them from enrolling
daughters and sisters. They feared that the implied association
between education and vocation was intended to prepare women to
seek income-earning jobs, which would reflect negatively on their
families and particularly on their protective male relatives.

In other words, it was not education for women that was resisted
but possible employment, and what women were being protected
from was not work *per se* but paid work and low-status jobs. In
terms of upper-class women, clearly there was no resistance to
women's education since they received exclusively tailored tutor-
ing. Rather they were being protected from ordinary education and
from mingling with commoners.

The advent of the Egyptian Revolution of 1952 with the subsequent revolutionary reform launched in the area of education was
the single most marked factor bringing about change in Egypt at the
populist level. From a situation of approximately 96 percent illiter-

acy among both sexes in colonial days, Egypt saw a "stampeding" to educational institutions made available to them since the Revolution. Trends were set in the 1950s and continued in the 1960s and 1970s that reflected a quantitative and qualitative change for both sexes. While population increased at the rate of about 2.4 percent per year over the time period of 1952–1976, student enrollments in higher education, for example, increased at the rate of 7.5 percent per year, with a fivefold increase in just over two decades, far exceeding the rate of general population increase.

The educational situation of women as Egypt entered the 1980s demonstrated a dramatically different picture from that in 1856 when the first girls' school was opened to the public. An examination of women's proportional distribution at the various education levels based on enrollment data by sex for 1979/1980 points to the relatively large proportion of women—48.5 percent—in vocational training. This observation can be related to three factors: First, there is a shift in attitude toward work for women, particularly in the face of rising inflation and population. Second, whereas in 1961 43 percent of working women were in agricultural labor, we find that a decade later only 25 percent of working women were in that sector, shifting instead to alternative urban vocations such as factory work and industrial labor. Third, the steady decline in women's illiteracy from 82.4 percent in 1961 to 54.1 percent in 1971 influenced the kinds of jobs women were moving into and hence the need for vocational training.

In colonial Egypt, the largest sector for women's employment other than agricultural labor was that of services, which in 1947 constituted 90.6 percent of women's labor, declining to 27.6 percent in 1961 and to 17.1 percent in 1971. Within the services sector 89.3 percent constituted domestic labor in 1960. Therefore, the factors are all interrelated: With a decline in women's illiteracy, a rise in inflation, a more diversified job opportunity for women, and a change in attitudes toward work, a shift occurred away from illiteracy-related labor (agriculture and services) more to semi-skilled and increasingly to skilled labor that became available to women since the Revolution. These observations can be seen in Table 10.1, which shows the percentage distribution of females among working women in the different categories of employment on the basis of available data in the two years 1961 and 1971.

There are additional patterns discernible from this summary. First, other than the categories of services, agriculture, and sales, all three showing a statistically significant decline, all other categories of employment (the remaining five in the table) show statistically

TABLE 10.1

Percentage Distribution of Females in the Female Labor Force in the Years 1961 and 1971

CATEGORY OF EMPLOYMENT	1961	1971
Technical-Scientific-Professional	8.3%	19.3%
Clerical	2.5	10.7
Managerial, Executive	.9	1.4
Production and Manufacture	6.7	9.6
Uncategorized Labor	2.3	9.4
Agriculture, Fishing, Forestry	43.0	25.1
Services	27.6	17.1
Sales	7.7	7.4

Source: Abdul Baqui Zaydan, *al-Mar'a baynal-Din wal-Mujtama'* (Cairo, Egypt: Maktabit al-Nahda al-Misriyya, 1977), 254–255.

significant percentage increases. Second, of those showing an increase, the two categories of relatively high significance are the technical-scientific-professional, in which women increased from 8.3 percent in 1961 to 19.3 percent by 1971, and the clerical, in which the increase was from 2.5 percent in 1961 to 10.7 percent in 1971.

This suggests that two patterns were simultaneously occurring: First, women at the bottom of the status/income scale are increasingly moving out of agriculture and services and up the scale as illiteracy decreases. At the same time women are significantly increasing at those levels of employment requiring college education. Interestingly in this regard, male-female ratios on the basis of data for 1974, from CAPMAS 1979 (al-Tawathuf wal-'Ugur wa Sa'at al"Amal) are approximately 17.3:1 for labor and 3.5:1 for technical-managerial-professional-clerical combined. In other words, the higher the level of employment the closer is the ratio of females to males, which suggests a system favoring a high level of work for women.

Education at all levels seems to be sought by women entering the labor force. Examination of a percentage distribution of females according to level of education shows that in one decade a significant decrease in illiteracy occurred among working women. Also significant is the increase demonstrated for working women at every level of education, although the relatively least dramatic is that at the graduate degree level.

Furthermore, a look at university educational patterns with a focus on the fields in which men and women major in preparation for their careers leads to interesting observations.

Clearly, male/female ratios have been shifting toward a closer correspondence with the overall university ratio of males to females. The Western trend of women going to "soft" fields or home economics and men to "hard" fields does not seem to occur in Egypt. Egyptian women tend to be evenly distributed in all coeducational majors.

Of particular significance are the five professional majors. According to the Egyptian system of higher education, the practical (professional) division requires much higher scores for entry in the national high school examination than do other fields. Within the professional majors, medicine and engineering alternate in requiring the highest scores—95 or 96 percent—followed by dentistry, pharmacy, and veterinary medicine. In 1960/1961 the gender gap in these professional majors is reflected in the male/female ratio of 8.8:1, while in 1975/1976 the ratio became 3.4:1. Clearly, the wide gap between the sexes previously characterizing the professional fields has been narrowing as more women are invading these specializations traditionally considered the most prestigious majors and careers and that continue to require stiff national competition at entry level.

A summary of enrollment data by sex for these difficult majors in Table 10.2 shows the shift in the enrollment of women since 1952. Data for the most demanding majors, as shown in Table 10.2, show that the percentage increase from 1960/1961 in medicine-pharmacy-dentistry was 748 percent for females and 448 percent for males; in engineering, 1,420 percent for females and 270 percent for males; in veterinary medicine, 1,414 percent for females and 387 percent for males. All in all, by 1979/1980 the most recent available population census shows men increasing at the rate of 3 percent and women at 4 percent at the university in general.[8]

Decade for Women and Beyond

It should be pointed out that for the purpose of an adequate understanding of the dynamics of women's changing roles in Egypt, as elsewhere in the Arab Islamic tradition, it would be useful to make an analytic separation between education and employment. This is not to say that a linkage between the two is absent in the Arab East. Rather, as the present analysis indicates, certain factors at the cultural level operate as constraints in the area of employment and not as much in education. For example, family-based constraints seem to be stronger against women's employment. By separating

TABLE 10.2

Enrollment by Sex in Five Practical (Professional) Colleges (Majors)

YEAR	MEDICINE, PHARMACY, AND DENTISTRY		ENGINEERING		VETERINARY MEDICINE	
	Females	Males	Females	Males	Females	Males
1952–1953	603	5,093	9	5,203	29	439
1956–1957	932	7,116	35	6,970	30	557
1960–1961	1,626	8,221	386	10,920	72	1,055
1964–1965	3,855	12,412	1,347	18,576	212	2,048
1968–1969	6,768	19,662	2,041	20,451	312	2,071
1972–1973	8,364	27,415	2,816	20,144	541	3,647
1975–1976	12,171	38,814	5,480	29,555	1,018	4,078

Sources: *Annuaire Statistique* (various years), Imprimerie Nationale, Cairo. *Statistical Abstract of the United Arab Republique* (various years), Campas, Cairo. *al-Kitab al-Ihsa'l al-Thanawi* (Statistical Yearbook), (1952–1974; 1977), Campas, Cairo. *al-Ti'dad al-'Am lil-Sukkan wal-Iskan 1976* (General Census for Population and Housing, 1976), 1978, Campas, Cairo.

the two areas, then examining each in the context of cultural premises, it is possible not only to discern subtle and unexpected patterns but also to account for them.

Clearly, even barriers at the familial level are currently being transcended, perhaps because Egypt, unlike Saudi Arabia and the Gulf, in the face of inflationary economic conditions worsened by exponential population increase, cannot afford the luxury of male protectiveness or any self-imposed female leisure. As a consequence we are witnessing strides in education and employment of significant impact. Today women in Egypt are visible in all corners of public life.

Simultaneously, during the decade for women another dominant force emerged in Egypt parallel to these modernizing trends and with potentially equal impact for the coming decade. This force is the contemporary Islamic movement, which showed visible signs in Egypt at the beginning of the 1970s and which continues to grow today. For the first time in similar movements of this kind we find women having a strong presence. What seems ironical is the fact that the women who show assertive identification with, and who are most activist in, the movement are the young, college-educated women, particularly those majoring in professional fields for careers in medicine, engineering, dentistry, or pharmacy.

While ostensibly this movement is conservative and can be regressive, the voluntary participation of young Muslim women on such a visible scale suggests a more complex picture. The fact that women at the populist level are acquiring Islamic literacy for the first time since the days of the birth of Islam in the seventh century in Arabia has significant implications. Since those early days Muslim women gradually moved inward, giving up their right and obligation to public active participation in Islam. They stopped acquiring firsthand knowledge of Islam and participating in Friday public prayer in Mosques. As a consequence, Muslim women adopted a passive, dependent posture in which immediate practical Islamic information was "lectured" to them situationally by their kinsmen, and the ultimate legal authority over issues of their concern was (and still is) dictated by the men of Islamic learning who are in control of al-Azhar and Islamic teaching and legislation. Al-Azhar came to represent the bastion of male dominance in Muslims' affairs.

Therefore, while women were left out of the major force in their lives, men were increasingly dominating Islam and its translation into daily reality. And while Islam has released its grip on many domains, it has persistently clung to personal status, which is the area holding most controls over women—marriage, divorce, inheritance, custody of children, among other areas. By holding on to personal status/family issues, Islam is essentially reasserting the right and obligation of kinsmen to remain in charge of their women. While this can and often does entail tremendous advantages for the woman as discussed earlier, it simultaneously insulates exploitation and prevents abuse from being subjected to external protection and justice.

This was the justification behind Mrs. Jihan Sadat's initiative introduced to reform the family code in such a way as to ensure a higher degree of protection for economically dependent women. Its two central points stipulated that permission from the first wife would be required before a husband acquired another wife, and in the case of unilateral divorce by the husband, it is the husband who would leave the house while the wife and children remain.

Interestingly, since this reform in 1979, coupled with an intense housing shortage in Egypt, it has been reported that there was a visible decline in divorce during this period. Yet, conservative forces within the Islamic establishment are strongly in opposition to this reform and are now attempting to introduce modifications to it. This issue exemplifies the kinds of issues within the Islamic fold that are central to women. Without access to literacy and education women are blind to rights and privileges intended originally to protect them but evolved over the ages into mechanisms controlling them and often oppressing them. Women's participation in this contemporary Islamic movement can provide them with the opportunity to acquire a legitimate role in matters that will make the difference in the quality of their lives.

To many women this movement offers avenues of legitimate access to the force previously inaccessible to them. The concern that this movement may be regressive for women is not completely without justification. However, the activism expressed among the young women in Egypt today does not seem to be accompanied by any *de facto* regressive steps for women. There is no indication of retreat into seclusion; the college activists are both in the movement and in public life. A fear expressed by their mothers who experienced the women's liberation in the 1920s is mostly based on disapproval of conservative symbols of modesty adopted by the young women (and men) in the movement. Today the same mothers who objected to their daughters' new modesty are themselves acquiring their own secularized version of modesty, and a general mood of conservatism is prevailing in Egypt outside the Islamic movement.

This is only one example of the movement's impact on existing structures. The women in particular are posing a new challenge to the Islamic establishment. By adopting the "Islamic dress" college women succeeded in putting al-Azhar on the defensive since such "movements" are expected to come from the establishment downward, not the other way around. When al-Azhar (the only segregated university in Egypt) approved the Islamic dress invented by the young women and enforced it in identical form (style, fabric, colors) on the female students in al-Azhar college for women they were also providing legitimacy to the young Muslim women's pioneering movement.

Could such a challenge to traditional structures at various levels translate into a larger share of active participation in the Islamic process? It is possible that the new Islamic consciousness emerging at the populist level among nonelitist educated women will lead them to a direct and legitimate participation in the tradition that is most vital for their lives for the first time since the days of Muhammad, when women held sessions educating men about Islam. Should they succeed in invading this sanctuary as they have the university, perhaps a step backward is a giant step upward. The next decade will tell.

The data upon which this analysis is based were collected from many years of anthropological fieldwork in Egypt (1961– 1965; 1976– 1982), from existing sources, and from the experience of growing up Egyptian until adulthood. Funding support was provided by a faculty grant from UCLA African Studies Center (1976), by Ford Foundation grant no. 770– 0651 (1979– 1980), and the Fulbright Fellowship (Islamic Civilization Senior Research Scholarship) grant no. 80-006-IC (1981– 1982).

NOTES

1. Judith D. Laws and Pepper Schwartz, *Sexual Scripts: The Social Construction of Female Sexuality* (Hinsdale, ILL: Dryden Pres, 1977), 1– 8.
2. See Laws and Schwartz above, 1– 8; S. B. Ortner and H. Whitehead, eds., *Sexual Meanings: The Cultural Construction of Gender and Sexuality* (Cambridge, England: Cambridge University Press, 1981).
3. The use of domestic/extra-domestic distinction for the description of women's activities is associated with Rosaldo and Lamphere, culture/nature with Sherry Ortner, and public/private, specifically in the case of Middle Eastern women, with Cynthia Nelson.

4. N. Youssef, "Women in the Muslim World," in Lynne B. Iglitzin and Ruth Ross, eds., *Women in the World* (Santa Barbara, CA: ABC-Clio, 1976), 203–217.

5. F. El Guindi, "Veiling Infitah with Muslim Ethic: Egypt's Contemporary Islamic Movment," *Social Problems* 28:4 (1981), 465–485.

6. Zaydan Abdul Baqui, *al-Mar'a baynal-Din wal-Mujtama'* (Cairo, Egypt: Maktabit al-Nahda al-Misriyya, 1977), 221. It is interesting to see the different years in which formal schooling for girls was first introduced in the different Arab countries. For example, in Sudan private al-Ahfad schools for girls were founded in 1903; in Kuwait the first private primary school for girls opened in 1921; in Bahrain 1928 and Saudi Arabia women's education began in 1960.

7. For the attitude of aristocratic Egyptians regarding women's education see A. Marsot, "The Revolutionary Gentlewomen in Egypt," in L. Beck and N. Keddie, eds., *Women in the Muslim World* (Cambridge, MA: Harvard University Press, 1978), 261–276.

8. F. El Guindi, "Veiled Activism: Egyptian Women in the Contemporary Islamic Movement," *Femmes de la Mediterranée, Peuples Meditèrranéans* 22–23 (1983), 79–89.

RECOMMENDED READINGS

El Guindi, Fadwa. "Veiled Activism: Egyptian Women in the Contemporary Islamic Movement," *Femmes de la Mediterranée— Peuples Meditèrranéans* 22–23 (1983), 79–89.

————. "Veiling Infitah with Muslim Ethic: Egypt's Contemporary Islamic Movement," *Social Problems* 28:4 (1981), 465–485.
These two works are the first and only analyses on Egypt's contemporary Islamic movement based on original and systematic field research with a balanced approach to the role of both sexes in the movement.

Fernea, Elizabeth W. *Guests of the Sheik.* New York: Doubleday/ Anchor, 1965.
A sensitive, personal ethnographic account written by a wife of an anthropologist about her encounter with Shi'a Muslim women in a rural community in Iraq.

Hansen, Henny Harald. *Investigations in a Shi'a Village in Bahrain.* Copenhagen: National Museum of Denmark, 1967.
A historical-sociological account of rural Shi'a Muslim women in Bahrain.

Lancaster, William. *The Rwala Bedouin Today.* Cambridge, England: Cambridge University Press, 1981.
A competent ethnographic account of bedouin life with a balanced unbiased depiction of the roles, position, activities, and attitudes of both sexes.

Marsot, Afaf. "The Revolutionary Gentlewomen in Egypt," in L. Beck and N. Keddie, eds., *Women in the Muslim World* (Cambridge, MA: Harvard University Press, 1978), 261–276.
A fascinating analysis of upper-class urban Egyptian women and their role in both feminism and society.

Mernissi, Fatima. *Beyond the Veil.* Cambridge, MA: Schenkman, 1975.
An original challenging approach to the study of Muslim women that bases its analysis on the analytic separation between ideology and institutions vis-à-vis the position of women in society.

Nelson, Cynthia. "Public and Private Politics: Women in the Middle Eastern World," *American Ethnologist* 1 (1974), 551–563.
This analysis challenges the literature describing Middle Eastern women as powerless and submissive and demonstrates the way in which women are able to become powerful persons.

El Saadawi, Nawal. *The Hidden Face of Eve.* London: Zed Press, 1980.

An angry Egyptian feminist voice against women's oppression by their kinfolk maintained by tradition.

Youssef, Nadia. "Social Structure and the Female Labor Force: The Case of Women Workers in Muslim Middle Eastern Countries," *Demography* 8:4 (1971), 427–439.

A classic quantitative account tying employment patterns of women to factors of social structure.

11

Female Political Participation in Latin America: Raising Feminist Issues

Jane S. Jaquette
Occidental College

> "Mother, what do men talk about?"
> "About women, dear, they talk about women and about politics. And you know why they talk about politics? Because *la política* is a feminine word, they think they can go to bed with her and become eternal fathers."
>
> — *Carmen Naranjo*, Diario de una multitud, quoted in an interview with Lourdes Arizpe, *Signs, Autumn 1979*

The two most common generalizations to date about research on women and politics in Latin America—that there is little and that what does exist is not feminist—are no longer valid. Today there is a rich and growing variety of studies—on the legal and economic status of women, on male/female power relations in the family, and on sexuality. The past, present, and future potential political role of women is the object of lively discussion and debate. Further, contrary to Marysa Navarro's observation in 1979 that scholars writing on women refuse to call themselves feminists,[1] both scholars and activists are increasingly declaring themselves and their goals as feminist, although almost always within a theoretical framework that recognizes the primacy of class conflict and links the liberation of women to the liberation of the whole working class.

A decade ago, in a similar review of the literature, I found very little research on women in Latin America and even less on political participation.[2] From the studies then available, I hazarded a few generalizations: that lower rates of female political participation could better be explained by factors such as literacy, level of industrialization and urbanization, not by gender itself; that women tended to vote for more conservative parties, but that their conservatism could be attributed to female self-interest rather than "woman's nature"; and that the importance of the family as a continuing source of power for Latin American women, even those in the modern sector, made it unlikely that Anglo-American-style feminist revolution would take root there. Paradoxically, these same "traditional" values did not prevent the emergence of powerful female political figures, Eva Perón being only the most obvious example.

Some of these generalizations have held up well. Fortunately for the future of feminist politics in Latin America, others have proven too pessimistic. For this reason alone, an update of the earlier study is justified.

In the earlier review, two studies proved particularly important. The first, by Armand and Michelle Mattelart, was an extensive survey of male and female attitudes toward political change in Chile, looking at urban rule and class differences.[3] The impetus for the study was the push toward change during the Allende period and the fear that women might prove to be a conservative force—which they ultimately were, but not along the lines predicted by the study. It was middle-class urban women, not poor rural women, who helped to bring about the military coup and the end of the socialist experiment. The second study, Elsa Chaney's survey of women elected officials in Chile and Peru, was then available only as a dissertation but has since been published.[4] It concluded that female elites viewed their political roles as extensions of their domestic roles; hence the book's title, *Supermadre*.

Both these studies provide invaluable benchmark data for new efforts, yet nothing comparable to them has since emerged, despite a veritable explosion of feminist research in the region. The reasons for this lack of new survey research and the relative lack of interest in topics such as voting and the behavior of elected women, which are standard fare for feminist political researchers in the United States, are complex. They illustrate the barriers to research on comparative political participation and the subtleties required of comparative analysis in this field.

On the surface, the lack of voting and attitudinal studies can be explained by the replacement of democratic governments with "bureaucratic authoritarian" regimes in some of the most industrialized and populous nations of the continent: Brazil, Argentina,

Uruguay, and Chile. However, this is only the empirical tip of a large theoretical iceberg. The resurgence of military regimes in the last two decades has been accompanied, even legitimized, by the emergence of corporatist theories of Latin American politics. In corporatist theory and practice, the state is seen not as an umpire, but as an active mediator among the various social interests, acting in order to contain class conflict. Scholars have argued that individualistic, democratic forms are inconsistent with Latin traditions and political culture and that corporatist forms fit the region's political culture.[5]

The definition of corporatism is broad enough to include systems as divergent as military authoritarian regimes in Latin America and liberal capitalist states in Europe. What corporatist systems share is the tendency to control participation by channeling it through groups authorized by the state. Thus group access and representation are more important than voting in determining government policies, though women are rarely organized around their interests or recognized as a legitimate representative group by the state. This in turn makes voting and attitudinal studies less central to research on participation.

A more significant reason for the lack of survey research on female participation may stem from a tendency among Latin American scholars to reject behaviorism, the methodology associated with "pluralism," considered by many as an inappropriate political model for a Latin America characterized by class polarization and international dependency. These critics would argue that the study of politics cannot be compartmentalized or separated from economics and sociology, and that an ideal of politics that reinforces an (unjust) status quo is suspect. Political events are often seen as epiphenomena, the result of deeper forces. In the more prevalent Marxist view, deeper forces are economic, but the more recent popularity of Gramsci's work in Latin America has given cultural factors more weight. The Marxist orientation of much of Latin American social science has produced numerous studies of the economic conditions under which women labor, from female contributions to family income to analyses of labor force participation, the informal sector, and work in the new export-oriented electronics and textile factories. By contrast, "value-free" studies of voting and attitudes are seen as superficial and are rejected as underwriting a liberal capitalist system that is exploitative and degrading to the majority of the population.

But there is yet another reason for the concentration on economic analysis. Most Latin American feminists gained their political experiences and commitments in leftist groups and political parties. On the one hand, this background frees them from loyalties to traditional institutions of social control; on the other, it makes feminist scholars and activists very vulnerable to criticism from the Left. The most common of these is that feminism diverts attention from the "real" issue: class conflict. Feminists have had to respond not only at the level of practice but of theory: Are sex and class equally valid analytical categories?

The position of a growing number of Latin American feminists is to declare both categories valid, and to argue that efforts to liberate women are consistent with and reinforce the class struggle. They observe that the oppression of women antedates capitalism and postdates socialist revolutionary transformation. They have defended *"doble militancia,"* double commitment both to the class struggle and to the struggle against patriarchy. In fact, as Julieta Kirkwood argues, it is only with a feminist consciousness that women can develop class consiousness and a radical political stance. Under patriarchy, the congruence between the hierarchical relations of everyday life and the hierarchical order of authoritarianism will inevitably tend to make women vote and act conservatively.[6] And the fact that women are not seen (and do not see themselves) as "productive" means that they cannot be organized as workers.

However, the Left, to varying degrees, continues to maintain the position that gender exploitation can be accounted for by class analysis and accuses Latin American feminists of becoming the unwitting tools of North American cultural "hegemony." Feminism is seen as one more imperialist export.[7] Against this line of attack, leftist feminists have held their ground with increasing success, but the controversy is still heated and the battle is far from won. Under these circumstances, feminist research can be expected to emphasize the economic dimensions of women's oppression, for that is the arena in which the issue must be raised for feminists to gain intellectual respect and ideological clout.

There is one major exception to this generalization: the rapid growth of research and analysis of sexuality, which is one category of human experience that cannot be completely subsumed under economics. Women's personal knowledge of sexual power relations cuts across class divisions, provides a new source of insights into the perpetuation of all social hierarchies, and can provide a radical agenda.[8] Here again, though, the "dependency" relationship between Latin America and the United States is a hobbling factor. Women cannot simply demand reproductive freedom, for example, because heavy-handed U.S. population policies have associated contraception and abortion rights with U.S. pressure for "control" of Third World populations.[9]

Finally, though commitment to social change may require research, the legitimate purpose of social analysis in the Latin American context is to facilitate action, not simply to feed academic presses. As a result, university-educated women who are aware of their privileged status feel the need to organize across class lines. Researchers inside and outside of academia are committed to reaching out to poor women, urban and rural. The report of the first Latin American Conference on Women's Studies held in Rio de Janeiro in 1981 illustrates this concern. It recommends sensitivity to the differences among women of different classes, warns of the pitfalls of "traditional" (i.e., behavioral) methodologies, and seeks "pragmatic" goals based on research and the sharing of research results with the women under study.[10]

Groups in Brazil, Peru, and Mexico share the position articulated by Mexico's CIDHAL (Communication, Interchange and Development in Latin America): Forming women's groups among the poor can

> provide an arena for women to collectively discuss their problems in a supportive environment, and to gain confidence in their ability to take action . . . [to] raise their political consciousness both as women and as members of an exploited class. By asking women why they in particular are so concerned with water, sewage, and education for the community, women can easily proceed to explore the central and exclusive role they play in housekeeping and child-rearing. They can then examine how the lack of services in their community reflects their role in the broader social and economic structure.[11]

For all these reasons it is difficult to construct a tidy, "objective" survey of female political participation in Latin America in this era of rising feminist awareness. There is no help to be had from the mainstream literature, which, with few exceptions, does not see female political participation as a significant issue.[12]

The following discussion emphasizes the surprising variety of ways in which female political participation has been conceived and studied. It is organized under the following general categories: (1) female elites; (2) mass participation; (3) women in groups; (4) women and human rights; and (5) women in revolutionary movements. The conclusion examines the international dimension of feminist political mobilization and identifies areas for future research.

Female Political Elites

There is very little work on female elites, and the existing studies emphasize the degree to which the women who do make their way into elected or appointed jobs tend to support the status quo. Earlier research, such as Elsa Chaney's study of Peruvian and Chilean elected officials,[13] found that women consider their political roles as extensions of their household roles. They were unwilling to raise feminist issues and portrayed themselves as traditionally feminine.

More recent studies, such as work by Eva Alterman Blay and Fanny Tabak, do not offer a major challenge to Chaney's view. Alterman's study of female mayors in Brazil shows, paradoxically, that women are more likely to be elected in the "poorest, least industrialized and least urbanized states,"[14] where they are members of the rural power elite. Fanny Tabak also finds that more women are elected to the local and national legislative bodies in Brazil in the least industrialized states, though the coincidence of redemocratization and feminism in Brazil may change that pattern in the future.[15]

Tabak's research underscores the slow progress of women into the political elite. At the national level it took 30 years from the date when women received the vote to elect women to the Chamber of Deputies (two were elected in 1966), and the first woman senator was elected in 1979. During the 1960s and 1970s, when male deputies were removed from office by the military government, their wives were occasionally elected to fill their places,[16] a Brazilian variant of the "widow's succession."

In the 1978 elections there was a major departure from this pattern, both as a result of the political "opening" (partial redemocratization) in Brazilian politics and the impact of International Women's Year in 1975, which had "made women's themes the order of the day and which led to the creation of feminist organizations throughout the country...."[17] In that year, three women were elected to the state legislature of Rio de Janeiro, one of whom was a militant feminist. Tabak's brief examination of the legislative records of female representatives, however, indicates that women's issues are still not being introduced into the political agenda.

A study of recent elections in Peru by Victor Lora shows changes in the number of females elected to the Chamber of Deputies, from 8 in 1956 (just after women got the vote) to 2 in 1963 (an era of liberal reform) to 12 in 1980, when the military government turned power back to the civilians. The level of female representation in the

Senate is even lower, but shows a similar pattern. Lora argues, not without some justification in comparative research,[18] that the increase should be attributed to a switch in voting rules, from single-member districts to proportional representation. For Lora, this is no cause for celebration:

> In past elections, voters elected specific persons: [but] proportional representation was used in 1980. No party put a woman before the tenth place for Senator or Deputy of Lima. No party inscribed a woman before fourth place for Deputy anywhere. As we can see, if some women are in Congress now it is not because people wanted to elect them specifically nor because parties are encouraging their participation in politics. The real reason that the parties felt compelled to inscribe women is because a few women's organizations managed to raise a fuss.[19]

Of course, other groups have historically achieved political representation in just this way, but when women agitate for a position on a slate they are "raising a fuss."

Discussions of political participation at the elite level posit various barriers that are common to women elsewhere: lack of time and familial support, relative lack of access to professional careers that commonly become feeder routes to political careers, and lack of public or party "acceptability," which in turn leads to lack of organizational and financial support. Latin American women face some special obstacles as well. Colombian analyst Esmerelda Arboleda Cuevas has argued that women encounter a "double standard of moral values": "standards of behavior are required of women which are never required of men, and conduct which in women is considered inadmissable is all too often lightly dismissed in the case of men."[20] She offers the example of a woman appointed to a governorship by the president who had to leave the office when it was discovered that she had remarried outside of Colombia, a common practice in a country that forbids divorce. Many male politicians have similarly remarried, but it is not a public issue for them.

Cornelia Flora and Nora Cebotarev have both argued that a failure to understand the social constraints on female sexuality could imperil development projects that attempt to include women.[21] It seems clear that almost any political activity will involve behavior on the part of women that is still considered unacceptable to many sectors of society in Latin America, such as travel alone or in the company of non-kin males, meetings at night, and access to power resources that challenge male authority within the family. Females who violate these rules may be subject to personal abuse. More importantly, their families may experience loss of status, which can create a direct but often unrecognized conflict between family loyalties and political participation for many women.

Further, insofar as increased status is connected with an increased capacity of the family to protect its women from the vicissitudes of the labor market and "the street," the women who have more time and greater financial resources may be less likely to devote their energies to political participation, which yields negative status returns. This constraint probably does not operate as strongly among modern urban upper- and upper-middle-class women as it did a decade ago, but it is still important at other class levels and for rural women.

Another barrier is guilt. A Peruvian researcher, Carolina Carlessi, argues that guilt is the primary barrier to female participation: guilt over time not devoted to one's family, guilt for the working woman unable to be both a good worker and a good mother, with no time left for politics; guilt for fear that work on feminist issues may detract from class conflict; guilt for "not having the answers."[22]

I have attempted elsewhere to gauge the changing environment of public acceptability for female elites in the last decade by reviewing the way they are presented in the Latin American media. Looking at both women's magazines and news weeklies, I found that women are now much more visible and accepted in political roles, but that the feminist agenda had still not acquired legitimacy. National styles of female integration varied markedly, ranging from the openly cooptive approach of President Lopez Portillo in Mexico to the delinking of female elites from feminist issues in Chile. One common element, particularly among appointed women, was the disavowal of any competition with men. As Rusa Luz Alegria, named as minister of tourism in Mexico, put it in 1980: "As women, our intention must never be to compete with men but to work together, because together we will do it better." Female equality was not a political agenda item for these women nor for their constituencies.[23]

In fact, some Latin American feminists have argued that a politics based on female *differences* is as important as the demand for equality Alaíde Foppa (an internationally renowned feminist who "disappeared" in Guatemala in 1981 and is now presumed dead) argued in the Mexican feminist journal, *fem*, that equality for women must arise out of both types of claims:

> Today, things have changed and that is why I speak of a cultural revolution. In the past we spoke of the "feminine nature" in

another context, and the peculiarity of feminism is that it will be arguing for difference. It was logical to argue for equality when difference meant less. Before women were much given to arguing "We are the same, we can do everything, we are equal to men." Now it represents a position of strength to say "We aren't equal to men; we want to be different, we are capable of being different." When it was good to be male and the female was seen as incapable, she said, "We're equal. . . ." [Now women workers can say] "this weighs too much, we want more time, we should have maternity rights," etc. It was logical to fight for equality first, and later for rights that come from difference."[24]

Mass Participation

The best work being done on female participation involves sophisticated efforts to link female participation in the division of labor, class analysis, family politics, and cultural ideologies of female subordination. As noted earlier, social sanctions against behavior inappropriate to women can be more effective than legal barriers in preventing political action on the part of women. Studies have shown that, although these sets of rules vary across cultures, they are quite consistent within cultures, even when there are deep class divisions.[25]

Bourque and Warren's study of women in two different villages of Andean Peru[26] illustrates the way in which women adapt to changing economic circumstances. By comparing life in an agricultural village to that in a commercial town, they show that, although women in the town may take jobs formerly reserved to men in the village, they are now excluded from a new set of economic mechanisms that endow work with both profit and prestige. Thus, changing economic roles may not change the distribution of power resources.

Bourque and Warren also launch an effective attack against those who would romanticize male/female differences as a significant source of power for women. Women may have *influence*, but men have power:

> Influence . . . represents the development of strategies by groups (or by individuals) to limit the exercise of power on oneself and on others. Cross-culturally, men's power is insitutionally based; that is, embedded in and derived from important political, economic and religious institutions. To the extent that women are excluded from key institutions, they must depend, more exclusively than men, on strategies of influence . . . Women's influence involves culturally formalized strategies which are generally recognized as legitimate by both sexes.

> ... The chief contrast between power and influence, which we
> stress in this context, is that they emanate from structurally
> different positions in the institutionally perpetuated social
> order.[27]

Nearly all social ideologies restrict women's access to public and
religious institutions. This becomes a more onerous barrier as modernization breaks down the kinship networks through which
women traditionally exercise what influence they have.

The evidence indicates that women pursue more effective economic strategies than political ones, but that they are still economically marginalized, and perhaps increasingly so. Cross-cultural
studies show, however, that women do not perceive themselves as
subordinate to a patriarchy or as oppressed by a system of class
dominance. Women do persist in trying to find an economic niche;
they are much less consistently focused on gaining access to political forms of power. The studies of labor force participation so
prevalent in the literature may thus reflect important aspects of
women's reality, but they do not of themselves reveal the linkages
between class and gender hierarchies, or between social ideologies
(internalized by women themselves) and institutional exclusion.

Verona Stolke has argued that one of the most difficult issues is
"consciousness," i.e., the causes of "subordination by women themselves":

> How can we grasp women's particular experience as gendered
> beings and as members of a class ... obstacles and forces that
> may induce women to endorse in practice the social system
> despite their consciousness of class equality and gender subor-
> dination?[28]

Feminists may differ cross-culturally in their answer to this question, but the possible answers range along a spectrum. First, there
are the theories, typical of mainstream feminism, that argue that
women are in fact not conscious of class and gender
subordination—because they are socialized to believe otherwise.
Alternatively, it is possible to argue, as is common on the Left, that
women are profoundly aware of their condition and fighting for
their rights, but that they are coerced by an oppressive system.
Between these conflicting positions are theories that see women as
having some or even an acute awareness of gender inequalities but
argue that women perceive either too little stake or too much
risk—well short of "repression" as conventionally understood—in
pursuing political means to redistribute power.

Most Latin American writers agree that socialization plays some
role, and there are important instances of government coercion of

women activists. Feminist organizations in authoritarian regimes fear the possibility of government repression. If we look more closely at the socialization explanation, however, it may converge with the perspective of a rational risk aversion (or female stake in the status quo). Distinctions between the sexes are heightened by an ideology of *machismo* and *marianismo*,[29] in which *marianismo* is the view that women gain respect and influence from their adherence to a chaste, home-bound, and thus apolitical existence. Thus women gain some benefit from the existing system, which they are unwilling or fearful of exchanging for the higher-risk strategies and negative social sanctions of the public sphere. Esmerelda Arboleda Cuevas makes this point in the UNESCO study:

> It is not surprising that Latin American women are very apathetic toward political parties, nor should we be surprised that statistics show a considerable lack of enthusiasm among women with regard to the exercise of long-recognized political rights. There is a lack of attainable objectives which are of interest to women voters: there is thus a large "floating" sector which falls an easy prey to agitators, as in the "march of the empty cooking pots" which contributed to the *coup d'état* (against Allende) in Chile. . . . On the other hand, when traditional parties make bold to appeal to women voters, the results can be extraordinary; this occurred in the Colombian elections of 1974 when the number of women voters exceeded all forecasts and gave victory to the Liberal Party by a large margin.[30]

When issues are raised that *are* salient to women, levels of voter participation increase and "gender gaps" appear in Latin America as well as in the United States. Argentina is a case in point. Women voted in greater numbers than men in 1983 for Radical candidate Raul Alfonsín, who won the election, and not only against the military authoritarianisms of the Right but against the violence associated with the strategy of the Peronists on the Left.[31]

To the question of general *levels* of female participation must be added the question of the content of such mobilization. Can women voters develop a stake in supporting leftist parties? This issue motivates much of the research currently under review. Cornelia Flora's work on *fotonovelas* and female self-concepts shows that these printed "soap operas" socialize female readers to find individual solutions to their problems—usually marriage. There is almost a total absence of group cooperation to reach goals, and the structures that create poverty are never questioned.[32] A recent study in Peru by Zoila Hernandez, who researched the responses of urban women to the economic crisis of recent years, reinforces points made earlier in a classic study of women's attitudes in Chile by Armand and Michelle Mattelart:[33] that women put employment issues first (availability, stability, and remuneration of jobs), that they lack knowledge of their legal rights as women or as workers, that they do not question the justice of the social system nor do they reject their sexual subordination.[34] Similar patterns emerge from the personal histories recorded in June Turner's edited collection, *Latin American Women: The Meek Speak Out.*[35] Are these patterns due to women's ignorance or to some degree of self-conscious choice?

A decade ago, I argued that women were likely to be put off by leftist parties:

> One factor which may affect female resistance to "radical struc-tural change" is women's attachment to the institution of the family ... [W]omen have a stake in the family as a strong in-stitution in which they have power—in terms of socialization of children, the enforcement of social sanctions ... and the preser-vation of moral and spiritual values which are still a part of the Latin American cultural heritage.
>   The importance of the Latin American family as an effective agent of social control makes it the perennial target of attack by radical political movements. Yet, by opposing the family, these movements shift the focus of power from the private, informal sphere, where women have maintained considerable influence, to the public, formal sphere, where men dominate.[36]

Steven Neuse's study of female participation in Chile during the Allende period shows that participation in government programs related to their needs increased support for Allende among lower-class women. Once women had experience with and a stake in progressive government, they could no longer "necessarily" be ex-pected to "provide the margin of victory for non-Marxist candi-dates," as had been assumed.[37]

Kathryn Burns' historical study of women's experiences in the Peruvian APRA party during the 1940s gives us a fascinating insight into female recruitment into a radical party.[38] In an earlier phase of Peruvian feminism, Burns writes, women pressed for legal equality, access to education, and changes in the labor laws to assist women in the modern sector. But, as one feminist writer of the time felt it necessary to emphasize: "We are not fighters." Burns comments:

> Although [this writer] clearly had a great deal of respect for North American feminists, nevertheless she proposed a dif-ferent tactic for Peruvian feminists: *la gentil persuasion.* She did not want anything to do with aggressive tactics for masculine goals; she avoided confrontation between the sexes.[39]

In contrast to the liberal or *civilista* approach of the earlier feminists, the women who joined the APRA party were committed to a radical critique of existing social and economic institutions. A combination of Marxist and indigenous elements, *aprismo* represented a sufficient threat to the Peruvian oligarchy and to the military to provoke decades of often bloody conflict, and the persecution of party members. Nonetheless, women joined APRA, and one woman, Magda Portal, was named the party's first secretary general. Magda Portal never considered herself to be acting as a "feminist," and she supported suffrage only for working women, recognizing that the vote itself had little meaning in a society characterized by profound economic inequalities. Portal controlled APRA's *Comando Feminino*, but few women were put up for political office. APRA's program for women centered around "civic and moral education and domestic economy."[40]

The charismatic, almost legendary figure of Victor Raul Haya de la Torre dominated the party. Haya saw the *aprista* home as central to the party's goals:

> The *Aprista* Woman must realize that *aprismo* begins in the *Aprista* Home, in the way that children are prepared, corrected and guided. Because our party is not only a Political Party but also a norm of conduct. For this we need the help of the Woman in order to convert the *aprista* conscience into a principle of action and a principle of life within the Home. . . .[41]

Portal broke with the party when the national convention of 1948 declared that "women are not active members of the party but only comrades, because they are not qualified citizens," that is, because they had not received the vote.

Portal was a member of the elite, and thus belongs to a Latin American "tradition" of radical elite women.[42] But the party also attracted many women from the popular classes, despite the hierarchical structure of the party itself and the danger of government repression. Burns argues that an important factor in APRA's ability to recruit women was its emphasis on the family and its image of the APRA party as a family-like structure. In an era of urbanization and social breakdown, APRA reinforced family norms, with Haya in the role of a father figure. APRA did not alienate women by attacking the family or by forcing women to choose a life governed solely by public political norms; instead, their feminine roles as wives and mothers were explicitly encouraged and valued by the party.[43]

The challenge to feminist utopia-builders is to go beyond the glorification of the family or the female sphere to a creative dialogue between public and private, an interchange that would transform both. Julieta Kirkwood argues that "negation"—an emotion

women are not supposed to feel—is necessary to liberation: negation of violence, of the perception of the female condition as "unproductive," of "dependency," and, although she does not say it directly, the negation of guilt.[44]

Women's Groups, Networks, and Female Politicization

The relative marginalization of women from the formal political
system and long periods of depoliticization during periods of authoritarian rule have combined to turn the attention of researchers
to different levels of the political system. Larissa Lomnitz's pioneering look at female networks in a poor neighborhood in Mexico[45] has
been followed by other studies. Lynn Bolles has looked at linkages
among kin and extended families in Kingston, Jamaica, noting that
both urban and rural linkages are key to the survival strategies of
these women. Bolles describes the responses of wage-earning
women to the reduction of factory jobs and wages as a result of
international capital movements and policies of economic stabili-
zation imposed by the International Monetary Fund. These women
are well aware of the role of international and domestic policies in
their plight, but Bolles does not draw the implications of this
awareness for political mobilization.[46]

Jeanine Velasco's study of survival strategies in poor neighborhoods of Lima also shows the significance of personal networks, and
emphasizes that they are the crucial means of gaining access to
outside resources, ranging from municipal services to emergency
health care. Velasco finds that "heterogeneous"networks (i.e., those
not composed entirely of women or of one's relatives) are the most
reliable, that interchanges among women are not as carefully calculated or utilitarian as Lomnitz's research had shown, and that
women in squatter settlements are more likely than women in
slums to use such networks. Velasco concludes that, as a political
strategy, networking may actually limit radical changes because,
"to accept a new way of doing things or thinking requires that the
new approach be accepted by everyone in the network."[47]

Marianne Schmink has done an extensive review of the participation of women in various kinds of groups in Brazil during the recent
period of *abertura* or "opening" toward democratic politics. Many of
these groups in working-class neighborhoods have existed for many
years, such as the Association of Housewives Against the High Cost
of Living, which began in the postwar period, as did the Brazilian
Federation of Women. Schmink observes that these groups

are unique among "political organizations" in having a residen-
tial basis, and focusing on demands related to daily basic needs
(infrastructural facilities, services, and most frequently, the
high cost of living) which are not commonly considered to be
part of the political realm.[48]

These groups virtually disappeared after the military takeover in
1964, but new groups of housewives' associations have been formed
to press for similar goals. Some have been active in helping women
adjust to the new phase of democratization, providing political
education on voting and representation and supporting political
slates.[49]

Mothers' clubs have also played a similar role, not only pressing
for improvements in education, but also for price controls and wage
increases. These groups are most visible in São Paulo, but are also
active in Rio, Belo Horizonte, and other major cities. Relations with
the political parties are far from satisfactory, however: "They are
either ignored or co-opted by more general movements who then
abandon their specific demands." There have been successful attempts to organize such groups into federations, to increase political visibility and clout, and to mount public demonstrations, a key
power currency in Latin American political systems. However, divisions among and within these groups have made these efforts less
effective than their potential.

In describing these movements, Schmink makes some key observations of female politicization at this level. First, mobilization has
occurred based on neighborhood residence, not workplace, and on
women's familial responsibilities.[50] Second, women's participation
is legitimate when it is organized around clear attempts to improve
the family's welfare. Such activities should be recognized as *political*: "These organizations are not merely secondary, back-up groups
for the 'real' political mobilization that goes on in union and party
organizations."[51] Third, women organize *despite* severe constraints
on their time, although there is a generally held image of women
that they have "free time" that can be used for "voluntary work" in
party organizations and even for development schemes.

Finally, looking from Brazil to Chile, Schmink argues (in contrast
to Neuse) that it was the failure of leftist and working-class parties
to include women's groups in their generally successful mobilization of the working class that made women responsive to "rightist"
efforts to mobilize them against Allende. Those who would organize
women must also remain aware of the split between elite women
and working-class women on the issue of the family: Elite women
are mobilized to seek independence from the family, but working-

class women are mobilized to ensure the economic survival of the family, "a crucial instrument for solidarity."[52]

Often women's organizations with ostensibly social goals may develop political roles as well. Rosemary Brana-Shute has looked at the politicization of "street" and "dance" clubs in Suriname. Here religious and social groups have become not only mutual support networks for their members, but "broker institutions tying various domestic and neighborhood networks into the national political parties favored by Creoles."[53]

Women who join such groups are older, have stabilized their financial situations, and have developed a core of friends on whom they draw for support. The political function of these groups arises out of the overlap between them and the political clubs (kernen), which have both male and female members, but which are dominated by older Creole women from their base in the social clubs. The kernen organize support for political candidates very effectively, but women rarely run for office, and women's issues " have not been sufficiently strong to organize women as a constituency." These groups have "influence," in this case the ability "to affect the proportion of attention given issues such as prices, jobs for the young and women, and expanded health and educational services."[54]

The activity of such groups was redirected by the military coup of 1980. As Brana-Shute describes it, the older Creole women organized passive resistance against the revolutionary pretensions of the young men who had directed the coup:

> In sum, the failure of the People's Committees is the best held secret in Paramaibo, and not only for ideological reasons. In the military's attempt to de- (or re-) politicize citizens and court the support of fellowers of old parties, they have bypassed the very groups that lend structure and cohesion to working class, urban Creole neighborhoods.[55]

Middle- and upper-middle-class groups of women have not received research attention in North America because they are not seen as political in the North American context. In Latin America, and elsewhere in countries where democratic participation may be the exception rather than the norm, women's groups with formal or informal links to powerful institutions like the church and the army may have significant influence. Linda Miller has done a pioneering study of women teachers and educational administrators in a county seat in Brazil that has undergone rapid change since the arrival of the TransAmazonian Highway in the early 1970s. She describes how these women gain access to new resources to "advance their careers and serve their schools,"[56] contrasting the strategies used by different groups of women educators to tie into the existing power structure and illustrating both the importance of "influence" and the significance of an institutional base. "Success" can be measured in terms of funds raised, and groups vary in terms of initial access to resources, status, geographical location, and fund-raising strategies.

This study also shows the importance of two other "women's groups": nuns and army wives. In many states under military rule, army wives are an important pressure group that has received little attention. In this Brazilian county,

> [n]uns and military wives represent, respectively, the "local" and the "outsiders" in the schools. The political power of the "locals" has been diluted by the arrival of the "outsiders," especially the new middle class agency staffs and commercial entrepreneurs. The mayor and the nuns have tried to preserve their traditional power in the face of a rapidly expanding school system dominated by the army and agency wives . . .[57]

Miller concludes that female educators use strategies that gain support from both groups, that they have power over resources and outputs of the system, and they they increase that power through personal networks that are political and can be extensive. These women also have power in their own families, where their education and steady income give them leverage.

From this review of the growing literature on the political mobilization of women's groups, it is possible to see not only the wide variation in the power of such groups, but also the scope of their power (or influence), ranging from issues such as neighborhood services and infrastructure to school financing and national economic policy.

Women and Human Rights

The human rights issue has mobilized hundreds, perhaps thousands of women who would never have been politicized for any other cause and whose very image as "traditional women" gives them and their cause additional legitimacy. Although very little has been written on such women,[58] the most well known example is the Mothers of the Plaza de Mayo in Buenos Aires, who, when protests were forbidden by the military regime, circled repeatedly around the Plaza to protest the loss of their children, the young men and women who were among the "disappeared." These women were housewives without previous political experience, and at the time they received little support in Argentina, although they did attract international attention and support from abroad, which was crucial to their survival.

The strength of this movement lay in its demand for the preservation of life, which "is prior to politics."[59] When the military regime stepped down in 1983, after its defeat in the Falklands/Malvinas War, the Mothers of the Plaza de Mayo continued to demonstrate in order to demand that the military leaders responsible for the abduction and even the murder of their sons and daughters be brought to justice.

Julia Guivant has argued that these women have had an impact that goes well beyond human rights narrowly conceived: They have brought ethical criteria to bear on Argentine politics in this redemocratization period and, along with other groups including feminists and the ecology movement, they are an important factor contributing to the legitimacy of democratic politics and to the creation of a new set of political rules. But, as Guivant notes, their strength is also a weakness. They are a single-issue group maintaining their legitimacy in part because they are "nonpolitical." Assuming that a democratic order continues and that the military is increasingly under civilian control, by their own definition of the terms of their participation, it will be very difficult for them to redirect their political resources toward new political goals.

Yet the long-run and the indirect effect of this group's emergence on the Argentine political landscape (and of other groups like it elsewhere in Latin America) may be that traditional women will be more able to enter political life. The view that all political activity is inappropriate for women will have eroded a bit, and along with it the view that only women who are "modern" can be politically active. Their experience also challenges the view that, when traditional women are mobilized, the results are inevitably politically conservative. In Mexico, participation in a group similar to the Mothers of the Plaza de Mayo turned a housewife into an activist. When Rosario Ibarra de Piedra ran as an opposition candidate for the presidency against Miguel de la Madrid, her campaign drew record crowds and received international attention.[60]

Women in Revolutionary Movements

There is a great deal of literature on this subject already available in English. North American observers tend to be sympathetic to the argument that revolutionary change is necessary and to identify with the important role women have played in Cuba and to a greater degree in Nicaragua. But most of these accounts are more laudatory than analytical, which makes it difficult to assess the real impact of revolutionary change on women's political roles.

Cuba has been the focus of much praise and some criticism for the way in which women have been mobilized. Praise for the Family Law, which posits that men share responsibility for domestic tasks, has been matched by criticism of the Castro regime for mobilizing women only to the extent they are needed by the national economy.[61] There is a leftist critique of the Cuban experience centering on the issue of whether the Cuban Federation of Women is truly a mass organization, with input from below, or whether it is primarily an arm of the government, which uses it to promote decisions made at the top. Cuba is no longer the unique revolutionary experience in the hemisphere; its practices can now be compared with the brief period of radical change in Chile under Allende (1970–1973), and with the five-year-old revolution in Nicaragua.

The Nicaraguan Revolution is a significant departure from the Cuban case in that women were directly involved in large numbers during the guerrilla phase of the revolution and had their own organization (AMPRONAC) from that phase through the establishment of the Sandinist government to the formation of AMLAE, the revolutionary mass organization that succeeded it. Norma Chinchilla has argued that the Nicaraguan Revolution has been more effective at mobilizing women than the Cuban:

> The ability of the *Sandinista* movement to organize one of the first mass women's movements in the history of Latin America is directly related to its break with economistic, dogmatic, and mechanical conceptions of Marxism and the revolutionary strategy. When they founded AMPRONAC (the women's organization) they broke with the sectarianism that demands that women's organizations be composed only of party members or working class women or that they be totally subordinate to the party organization. It was able to break with the "liquidationist" approach to problems of working class women which sees them only in their class aspect and not in the combination of class and gender exploitation. AMPRONAC succeeded where other organizations had failed because it was truly an organization where the masses of women could participate, obtain political education, and learn leadership skills.[62]

Women took up arms to fight for the Sandinista cause, and one of the most powerful images of the Nicaraguan revolution abroad is that of a woman with a rifle in one hand and a baby in the other. But the increasing trend toward militarization of society (which can be attributed in part to U.S. policy), and the active role women are playing in that process, is raising doubts among feminist observers elsewhere in Latin America who associate feminist politics with resistance to military rule and to militarization itself.

Women who have joined the revolutionary movement in El Salvador and who might be expected to have an influence on post-revolutionary policies should the leftists win, have the experience of Cuba and Nicaragua to draw upon. A document prepared by the Association of El Salvadoran women (AMES), affiliated with the Democratic Revolutionary Front (the political arm of the leftist coalition), shows that the El Salvadoran female revolutionary leadership is aware of the new currents of political mobilization and of feminist analysis in Latin America, and that it is trying to define its own feminist revolutionary goals, making choices among some of the themes we have been reviewing here. The document, "Participation of Women in Social and Political Organizations,"[63] begins by confronting the issue of class versus gender, then moves abruptly to an attack on marriage as an escape valve:

> Latin American women, who face double oppression, have not been exempt from [permanent economic, political and social crisis]. Although the principal source of our subjugation is capitalism, even before its advent feudal society had already assigned a subordinate role to women.... As Simone de Beauvoir has pointed out, 'One is not born, but rather learns to be, a woman.' We Latin American women have undoubtedly been learning: learning *not* to be accomplices of the myth of Cinderella, who waited for Prince Charming to free her from misery and convert her into the happy mother of numerous little princes; learning to take to the streets to fight for the elimination of poverty; learning to be active protagonists in the forging of our destiny.[64]

AMES argues that capitalism survives because of women's unpaid labor in the home, but wages for housework can only be a "remote goal" until prior issues are resolved: the need for jobs and the exploitation of the "principal wage earner." The struggle for reproductive freedom may be significant in the "developed countries," but "in Latin America we must also fight against forced sterilization" and the kinds of birth control projects "which some governments have agreed to under pressure from the United States."[65] In a further attempt to distance themselves from "bourgeois" feminist goals, AMES maintains that:

> For us women, it is not a question of demanding collective services such as day care centers or laundries, but rather of demanding general community services such as water, light, housing and health care.[66]

Yet, as we have seen, these are precisely the services urban, working-class women are demanding elsewhere. There is no doubt that they are needed—and the women of El Salvador, if consulted, might want day care as well. But there is little evidence that support for these issues entails a broader politicization, either socialist or feminist.

AMES dismisses the "alleged separation between 'public' and 'private'" as merely a "sophism," apparently to strengthen its case that socialism entails the emancipation of women. And, although the Left customarily hails all peasant and working-class mobilization as progressive, AMES sees feminist movements elsewhere in Latin America as merely reformist and thus counterrevolutionary.

> Conceived within a liberal context and subject to penetration by bourgeois ideology, the defense of women's traditional role is the precondition for women's mobilization (in capitalist regimes). It is not easy for the state to repress those who, as mothers, wives, daughters, confront it in the very roles which constitute the pillar and foundation of domination.
>
> When the private realm is altered from outside, Latin American women come out of their homes and take to the streets. . . . They have pressured the authorities and employers to demand wage increases or jobs for family members, or their release from prison. That is to say, their demands are not their own, but familial . . .[67]

In their attempt to create an ideological space distinct from all forms of "bourgeois" feminism, AMES has climbed out onto what all the evidence from this survey indicates is an untenable limb. If commitment to radical goals requires that peasant and working class women abandon "familial demands," the prospects of mass support for AMES seem dim. AMES may win the battle—it may create a sufficiently different approach to a feminist program to win a place among those who would outline a postrevolutionary agenda—but it could lose the war.

Conclusion

What is the significance of the research reviewed here? What are the priorities for additional research? The rapidity with which feminist thought has been absorbed and reworked by Latin American scholars to reflect Latin American realities is striking. Latin American feminists are at the point of making substantial contributions to feminist theory, as is the case in Foppa's discussion of the politics of difference, Kirkwood's call for a political analysis of the private sphere, and Muraro's and Barrig's use of sexuality to begin to redefine politics itself, to name just a few examples. But there are larger gaps. It would be useful to have more research on the influence of international feminism, particularly the United Nations Decade for Women meetings in 1975 and 1980, and the two Latin American feminist conferences held in Colombia in 1981 and in Peru in 1983. What is the influence of the exile community? Many women who have now returned to their native countries spent key years in Europe, the United States, or in Mexico and Brazil, where Latin American feminism has been a significant force. There is already a growing literature on another international influence: the attempt to promote "women in development" by international and bilateral development agencies.[68] What role have the major private foundations played in promoting women's studies programs, research and action programs? How has Latin American participation in these international fora helped mold new agendas?[69]

A second observation would be that the feminist attempt to raise women's issues, though often viewed with distrust by governments, has created a new political space in a wide variety of political systems ranging from the one-party-dominant system in Mexico, to corporatist, revolutionary, and democratizing regimes. In democratizing regimes, the role of women's groups and feminist issues has become an important focus for research, but their role in a given system may be ambiguous. In some cases, feminist activism may be one of the independent sources of pressure for authentic forms of participation. In others, women's groups may provide a convenient means for the regime to coopt women, though a revolution of rising feminist expectations makes this more difficult. Individual women have been used by regimes trying to soften their authoritarian images. "It has become fashionable," as Carmen Naranjo has pointed out, to use women for "political decor."[70] Yet even cooptive integration creates new possibilities for female participation in the future, and can increase public acceptance of women candidates and women's issues. These possibilities can be built upon when authoritarian regimes yield to demands for democracy.

Third, within the context of redemocratization itself, female images of politics can play a role in structuring the new "rules of the game." In Argentina, the increased participation of women has been associated with antimilitarism and a shift toward a more ethical politics. This can be a trap, as the history of early feminists in the United States illustrates, but it is also a major opportunity, particularly when a broad consensus is emerging in a society to move toward these values. Women's groups can join with other new social movements that share a similar vision of the future to accelerate the pace.[71]

Finally, feminist analysts need to do a better job of linking our work to mainstream issues: capital movements and changes in the international division of labor, the debt crisis, interdependence, and the new innovations in development theory that are affecting governments' policies.[72] Feminist theory purports to change the content of politics, but to do so it must also make itself accessible, even indispensable, to the analysis of major economic and political trends. Otherwise, women will continue to be denied a stake in the politics of the future. There is still much work to be done.

NOTES

1. Marysa Navarro, "Review Essay: Research on Latin American Women," *Signs: Journal of Women in Culture and Society* 1:5 (Autumn 1979), 113.

2. Jane S. Jaquette, "Female Political Participation in Latin America," in Lynne B. Iglitzin and Ruth Ross, eds., *Women in the World* (Santa Barbara, CA: ABC-Clio, 1976), 55 – 74.

3. Armand and Michele Mattelart, *La Mujer chilena en la nueva sociedad* (Santiago: Editorial del Pacifico, 1968).

4. Elsa Chaney, *Supermadre: Women in Politics in Latin America* (Austin: University of Texas Press, 1979).

5. See, for example, Frederick Pike and Thomas Stritch, eds., *The New Corporatism* (Notre Dame, IN: University of Notre Dame Press, 1974); Howard Wiarda, ed., *Politics and Social Change in Latin America: The Distinct Tradition* (Amherst: University of Massachusetts Press, 1974); James M. Malloy, ed., *Authoritarianism and Corporatism in Latin America* (Pittsburgh: University of Pittsburgh Press, 1977); David Collier, ed., *The New Authoritarianism in Latin America* (Princeton, NJ: Princeton University Press, 1979). This interpretation is also found at the level of popular journalism. See Michael Novak, "Why Latin America is Poor," *Atlantic* 249:3 (March 1982).

6. Julieta Kirkwood, "El Feminismo como negación del authoritarismo," FLACSO Discussion Paper #52, Santiago, Chile, 1983, 4–8 and *passim*.

7. One of the ways in which Latin American feminists can distinguish themselves from North American feminists, at least from the mainstream or liberal feminism, is by labelling. Liberal feminism, calling for a "piece of the pie" and, from the Latin perspective, associated with sexual "liberation" and the emancipation from household responsibilities, can be seen as "hedonistic," which makes it possible to distinguish the "serious" social goals of Latin American activists from the more selfish, classist goals of their North American counterparts.

8. See, for example, Maruja Barrig, *Cinturon de Castidad* (Lima: Mosca Azul, 1979); Rose Marie Muraro, *Sexualidade da mulher brasileria* (Petrópolis, Brazil: Vozes, 1983), now in its fourth edition.

9. Helen Shapiro, "Women Challenge the Myth," from "The Many Realities," *NACLA Report on the Americas* 14:5 (September–October 1980), 24.

10. Seminario latinamericano de programas de estudios sobre la mujer, "Notas de relatorias," Rio de Janeiro, November 1981.

11. Shapiro, 25.

12. Notably an article each in two volumes on political participation in Latin America edited by John Booth and Mitchell Seligson: *Political Participation in Latin America*, Volumes I and II (New York: Holmes and Meier, 1978).

13. Elsa Chaney.

14. Eva Alterman Blay, "The Political Participation of Women in Brazil: Female Mayors," *Signs* 5:1 (Autumn 1979), 45–46.

15. Fanny Tabak, "Exercicio do voto e atuacao parlamentar da mulher no Brasil," paper presented at the meeting of the "Women and Politics" Working Group, National Association of Graduate Studies and Research in Social Science, Frieburg, Germany, 1982, 22.

16. Tabak, 10.

17. Tabak, 22 and *passim*.

18. See, among a number of studies that have made this observation, Karen Beckwith, "Structural Barriers to Women's Access to Office: The Cases of France, Italy, and the United States," paper presented at the American Political Science Association Meetings, Washington, DC, 1984.

19. Victor Lora, "Women and Politics in Peru," paper presented at the Yale University Council on Latin American Studies, January 28, 1984, 4.

20. Esmeralda Arboleda Cuevas, "Women in Latin America," paper written for UNESCO for the International Women's Year (mimeo, n.d.), English version, 25.

21. Cornelia Butler Flora, "Social Policy and Women in Latin America: The Need for a New Model," in Sandra F. McGee, ed., *Women and Politics in Twentieth Century Latin America*, a special issue of *Studies in Third World Societies*, Publication 15 (March 1981). E. A. Cebotarev, "Rural Women in Non-Familial Activities," paper presented at the Wellesley Conference on Women in Development, June 1976.

22. Carolina Carlessi, "La culpa como factor desmovilizador de los grupos de mujeres," Serie Cuadernos Feminismo 1. (Lima: Lilith Ediciones, 1983).

23. Jane S. Jaquette, "Legitimizing Political Woman: Expanding the Options for Female Political Elites in Latin America," in Jean F. O'Barr, ed., *Perspectives on Power: Women in Africa, Asia, and Latin America* (Durham, NC: Duke University Center for International Studies, 1982).

24. Alaíde Foppa's remarks are taken from a debate on "Feminism and

Political Organizations of the Left," published in *fem* (Mexico City) 4:17 (February – March 1981), 45. My translation.

25. For a review, see Edwin D. Driver and Aloo E. Driver, "Gender, Society, and Self Conceptions: India, Iran, Trinidad-Tobago, and the United States," *International Journal of Comparative Sociology* 24:3–4 (1983).

26. Susan C. Bourque and Kay Barbara Warren, *Women of the Andes: Patriarchy and Social Change in Two Peruvian Towns* (Ann Arbor: University of Michigan Press, 1981).

27. Bourque and Warren, 53–54.

28. Verona Stolke, "Social Inequality and Gender Hierarchy in Latin America," unpublished manuscript (mimeo, n.d.), Social Science Research Council.

29. Evelyn P. Stevens, "*Marianismo:* The Other Face of *Machismo* in Latin America," in Ann Pescatello, ed., *Female and Male in Latin America* (Pittsburgh: Pittsburgh University Press, 1973).

30. Arboleda Cuevas, 23.

31. Julia Guivant, "Women and Politics in the Americas," presentation at the American Friends Service Committee's Institute for International Understanding, Whittier College, July 2, 1984.

32. Cornelia Butler Flora, "Integration into the World System and Mass Culture: Symbolic Manifestations of the *Fotonovela*," paper presented at the Latin American Studies Association Meeting, Pittsburgh, April 1979.

33. Armand and Michele Mattelart, *La mujer chilena en la nueva sociedad* (Santiago: Editorial del Pacifico, 1968).

34. Zoila Hernández, "Comportamiento de la mujer peruana en período de crisis económica," paper presented at the Congreso de Investigacion acerca de la Mujer en la Región Andina, Lima, Peru, June 7–10, 1982. For a review of the papers and conference discussions, see the *Informe Final* (Lima: Asociación Peru-Mujer, 1983).

35. Jane Turner, ed., *Latin American Women: The Meek Speak Out* (Silver Spring, MD: International Educational Development, 1980).

36. Jane S. Jaquette, "Female Political Participation in Latin America," 61.

37. Steven M. Neuse, "Voting in Chile: The Feminine Response," in John A. Booth and Mitchell A. Seligson, eds., *Political Participation in Latin America*, Vol. I: *Citizen and State* (New York: Holmes and Meier, 1978).

38. Kathryn J. Burns, "Mas alla de 'ese esencial feminino': el desarrollo feminista en el Peru, 1900–1950," paper presented at the Congreso de Investigacion acerca de la Mujer in la Región Andina, Lima, Peru, June 7–10, 1982.

39. Burns, 5.

40. Burns, 10.

41. Haya de la Torre, from *La Tribuna*, November 16, 1946. Quoted in Burns, 11.

42. Jane S. Jaquette, "Women in Revolutionary Movements in Latin America," *Journal of Marriage and the Family* (May 1973).

43. Burns, 17–18.
44. Kirkwood, 16–17. See also Jose Joaquin Brunner's argument that the identification of the public with the "rational" and the private with the emotional/irrational must also be changed in a feminist politics. In "La Mujer y lo privado en la communicacion social," *Zona Abierta* (Chile), (July–December 1983), 147–153.
45. Larissa Lomnitz, *Networks and Marginality: Life in a Mexican Shantytown* (New York: Academic Press, 1977).
46. Lynn Bolles, "Kitchens Hit by Priorities," paper presented at the Latin American Studies Association Meeting, Pittsburgh, April 1979.
47. Jeanine Anderson de Velasco, "La red informal en las estrategias de supervivencia de familias limeñas," paper presented at the Congreso de Investigacion acerca de la Mujer en la Región Andina, June 7–10, 1982.
48. Mariana Schmink, "Women in Brazilian *Abertura* Politics," paper presented at the Latin American Studies Association Meeting, October 1980.
49. Schmink, 10.
50. Schmink, 21–22.
51. Schmink, 23.
52. Schmink, 27.
53. Rosemary Brana-Shute, "Working Class Afro-Surinamese Women and National Politics: Traditions and Changes in an Independent State," in McGee, 35.
54. Shute, 38.
55. Shute, 49.
56. Linda Miller, "Patrons, Politics, and Schools: An Arena for Brazilian Women," in McGee, 67.
57. Miller, 85.
58. For an interesting literary treatment of the theme, see Ariel Dorfman, *Widows* (New York: Pantheon, 1983).
59. Guivant.
60. Rosario Ibarra de Piedra (Frente Nacional Contra la Represión), lecture at Occidental College, April 16, 1984.
61. Susan Kaufman Purcell, "Modernizing Women for a Modern Society: The Cuban Case," in Ann Pescatello, ed., *Female and Male in Latin America* (Pittsburgh: University of Pittsburgh Press, 1973), 257–272.
62. Norma Stoltz Chinchilla, "Women in Revolutionary Movements: The Case of Nicaragua" (mimeo, 1981), 24–25. For an additional study of Nicaragua, see Elizabeth Maier, *Nicaragua, la mujer en la revolución* (Mexico City: Ediciones de Cultura Popular, 1980).
63. The Association of Salvadoran Women (AMES), "Participation of Latin American Women in Social and Political Organizations," paper presented at the First Latin American Research Seminar on Women, San Jose, Costa Rica (November 1981). Published in *Monthly Review* 34 (June 1982).

64. AMES, 11–12.

65. AMES, 12.

66. AMES, 12–13.

67. AMES, 17. Italics mine.

68. For a discussion of women in development from a critical Latin American perspective, see Lourdes Beneria and Gita Sen, "Class and Gender Inequalities and Women's Role in Economic Development: Theoretical and Practical Implications," *Feminist Studies* 8 (Spring 1982), 157–176. See also Flora, in McGee; Patricia Maguire, "Women in Development: An Alternative Analysis" (Amherst, MA: Center for International Education, 1984).

69. On the history of international women's movements in the hemisphere, see Francesca Miller, "The International Relations of Women of the Americas, 1890–1930," paper presented at the American Historical Association Meeting, San Francisco, December 1983. On recent international meetings, see *fem*, 8:31 (December 1983 – January 1984).

70. Lourdes Arizpe, "Interview with Carmen Naranjo," *Signs* 5:1, 105.

71. Eduardo Viola, personal communication.

72. Cornelia Butler Flora, "Socialist Feminism in Latin America," Michigan State University, Women in International Development Working Paper 14 (November 1982). For a discussion of feminism and authoritarian regimes, see Fanny Tabak, "Women and Authoritarian Regimes," in Judith H. Stiehm, ed., *Women's Views of the Political World of Men* (Dobbs Ferry, NY: Transnational Publishers, 1984); and Kirkwood.

RECOMMENDED READINGS

There are very few books in English. The only monograph directly on the topic is:

Elsa Chaney. *Supermadre: Women in Politics in Latin America*. Austin: University of Texas Press, 1979.
    Based on interviews of women politicians in Peru and Chile in the early 1970s, *Supermadre* explores the constraints on female political participation in the Latin American context, recruitment and career patterns represented among these women. The fact that these politicians tend to view their political roles as an extension of their domestic roles provides the title of the book.

In addition, there are two books that shed light on female politicization at the mass level in two very different contexts:

Susan C. Bourque and Kay Barbara Warren. *Women of the Andes: Patriarchy and Social Change in Two Peruvian Towns*. Ann Arbor: University of Michigan Press, 1981.
    Bourque and Warren contrast the economic and social conditions of two Peruvian towns, one a traditional farming village and one a commercial center, with an eye to the impact of economic change on the political and familial power of women.

Oscar Lewis, Ruth M. Lewis, and Susan M. Rigdon. *Four Women: Living the Revolution; An Oral History of Contemporary Cuba*. Urbana: University of Illinois Press, 1977.
    Four Women was compiled from data collected in Cuba under a project directed by Oscar Lewis before his death in 1970. The book chronicles the lives of four women in very different social classes and with different responses to revolutionary mobilization and change; it is particularly interesting for gauging the changing (and stable) boundaries between the public and private spheres for women in a society committed to socialist transformation.

Finally, sections of various journals have been devoted to issues of women and politics in Latin America. Of these the most important are:

"Women in Latin America," *Signs: Journal of Women in Culture and Society* 5:1.
    Includes a review essay by Marysa Navarro, who has written on Eva Peron, an article on women mayors in Brazil by Eva Alterman Blay, plus a number of essays on socioeconomic themes relating to political participation and ideology.

"Women and Politics in Twentieth Century Latin America," a special issue of *Studies in Third World Societies* (March 1981), edited by Sandra McGee.

Includes articles by Cornelia Flora, Steffan Schmidt, Rosemary Brana-Shute, and others. The most up-to-date collection.

12

Women in Colombia

Steffen W. Schmidt
Iowa State University

olombia represents a particularly fruitful environment for
the investigation of women in politics and society because
for most of its history it has been a relatively open system.
Political parties have competed for power and control over policy-
making mechanisms. A diverse and uncensored press and the existence of multiple interest groups, unions, and other autonomous
structures have contributed to a lively discussion of the national
agenda.

Moreover, Colombia is fairly representative of the ethnic and
cultural composition of Latin America; of the economic forces that
have gradually transformed a monoculture, rural economy into a
mixed system; of the migratory processes from countryside to
towns and cities; of the relatively inequitable distribution of income
and social opportunities and of the gradual entry of women into the
national political process. Colombia is the "mean" between extremes in Latin America and thus offers a useful starting point from
which to further study and understand the reality of woman in
Latin America.

This chapter describes and explains several forces affecting
women in Colombia: the formal and informal participation of
women in the last decades, the political and policy conflicts affecting women, and the role and impact of women for the future.

The scholar investigating women in Colombia or anywhere else
must attempt to treat distinctly the *description* and *discussion* of

women, on the one hand, and on the other, the *critique* and *prescription* of women's reality. We are reminded, as W. H. Auden wrote, that all "the judgements, aesthetic or moral," and we assume scholarly and political as well, "however objective we try to make them, are in part a rationalization and in part a corrective discipline of our subjective wishes."[1] With that human limitation in mind, we have reconstructed in this chapter the reality of women as clearly and directly as possible, well aware that the normative pitfalls lurk in the background.

The Stream of History

In order to more accurately describe, dissect, and interpret the contemporary political and policy issues relating to women in Colombia, it is useful to remind ourselves that woman's reality in 1985 or 1990 is the cumulative effect of at least six forces that have shaped events—in other words, six streams of history. These are:

First, the social structure and values of pre-Columbian Indian civilizations, which occupied the territory now called Colombia for thousands of years before the Spanish arrived.

Second, the Spanish, who discovered and conquered the Indians, settled and colonized these lands and who brought with them both Iberian and North African values (Iberia was occupied by the Moors for over 500 years).

Third, the substantial influence of nineteenth- and early twentieth-century European values. These were directly transferred through immigration to Colombia during this time. They were also indirectly imported because Colombians studying in France, England, Germany, Italy, Spain, and other European nations were exposed to the intense debates over women's roles and rights that were sweeping through the intellectual community of these countries, which they brought back as topics for debate and discussion.

Fourth, the impact of the United States, especially from the second decade of the twentieth century on, an impact that commingled capitalist, industrial, Anglo-Saxon, urban, materialist, feminist, consumerist, and other values over the course of the past 60 or so years.

Fifth, the impact of socialism, Marxism, the Russian Revolution, and the intense radical feminism associated with Communist international women's peace movements and other revolutionary tendencies, which worked their way into the Colombian national political stream primarily through the Socialist party, Marxist movements, and the Communist party (PC).

Sixth, the persistent impact of social and economic class stratification on Colombian society as a whole and on women's status within it.

A complete discussion of these aspects of women's history in Colombia is well beyond the scope of this analysis; however, it must be at the very least a backdrop against which to discuss contemporary events.

More important than the historical events themselves is the theoretical matrix or model by which one explains the dynamics of history (i.e., how the historical currents flow into, over, and across each other) and its contemporary sociopolitical meaning. In the Colombian case several models have proven to be useful reference points for focusing on women.

1. *The Organic Society Model* posits that society is like a living organism, which depends on its parts being positioned and performing specific functions in order for the total organism and its individual parts to survive. Thus, the place of men, women, and all other groups and institutions should not be rearranged nor the logic of their place questioned, because they are part of a complex whole with systemic unity. While often not explicitly stated, this model certainly affected women during parts of Colombia's early history when this orderly, frozen view of society was more popular. No doubt, however, even today the idea that there is a specific "place" for women in society and thus the notion that the Colombian woman should "stay in her place," is a residue of the organic theory.[2]

2. *The Incremental Model* assumes that as different subcultures, classes, and economic forces have interacted over time, some parts of each were transferred to a slowly changing women's reality. Thus, according to this explanation, woman in Colombia today is an amalgam of many bits and pieces "collected" by history.

3. *The Transformation Model* suggests that in each historical phase of Colombia, the old reality is in effect destroyed and replaced with a new situation that is *not* simply the sum of the parts of changing conditions, but instead is a new whole, different in its own right. There is, however, little or no presupposed direction of the transformation. It is viewed as a more or less eclectic, haphazard, spontaneous process.

4. *The Dialectic Model* differs from the transformation model in that it presumes several systematic conditions and processes premised on Marxism and the concept of class conflict. The Marxist analysis of woman in Colombia explains conditions and events within the larger framework of exploitation, dependency, international imperialism, colonialism/neocolonialism, and capitalist exploitation affecting not just women but all persons.

   Specific indigenous, national factors are quite coincidental in this model, and the explanatory power of universal, historical-dialectic, and materialist forces is what supposedly provides clarity and accuracy to the analysis of women's roles in Colombia.[3]

5. *The Dual-Society Model* disaggregates women into essentially two categories—traditional and modern. Often this implies rural and urban, rich and poor and suggests a society divided into a dichotomy. In the case of Colombia this model also assumes that "development" has something to do with women's status and that conditions improve as more modern forces make themselves felt in the woman's environment. Lacking the Marxist ideological framework, this model is incremental, reformist, and evolutionary.

6. *The "Imperialist" Model* should not be confused with the political or global imperialism of Marxist or nationalist thought. Instead, it refers to the cultural imperialism of certain values that continuously absorb, coopt, or destroy alternative norms, and that thus survive from period to period *regardless* of the political ideology, infrastructure, economic forces, and so forth. The tremendous staying power of patriarchy and the consequent belief in male

superiority and female inferiority is one such "imperialist" tendency.[4]
7. *The Pluralist Multi-Subculture Model* is a sort of classic liberal explanation of women. It states that women exist in a great variety of ethnic, religious, educational, class, regional, marital, and ideological miniclusters. Each combination of woman's characteristics differs from others. Woman's reality and contributions to society cannot be generalized. One must single out specific situations and the women existing in them, and this is the only logical way of describing and analyzing women in Colombia.

I shall not attempt to resolve here the validity of these models. However, it is important to understand that much of the analytical as well as political debate about women in Colombia today stems from differing interpretations about the best way of explaining the role of women in Colombia. Moreover, concrete, policy-oriented disagreements regarding changes in Colombian society that would benefit women are also better understood with these fundamental interpretative frameworks in mind.

The roots of these disagreements require a brief overview of the background and political history of Colombia; it is in the changing alignments and the clashes of groups that the formula for defining all groups (women included) can be discovered.

While little systematic work has been done on women in the pre-Columbian period, it is clear that women were an integral part of the productive systems of society. Moreover, when the Spaniards encountered women, they were often also on the "front lines" of battle. A 1510 commentary on northern Colombia noted, "... women were noted as warriors but were somewhat immodestly dressed 'their hair long and ... dressed in cotton from the waist down.'"[5]

Later, during the revolutionary war against the Spaniards, Kathleen Romoli reports that when Spanish Commander Warleta arrived in the city of Cali, to carry on his campaigns, "he did not find one able-bodied man in Cali: all of them had gone to the war." However, "he found a remarkably stubborn lot of women, who did everything in their power to hamper the Spaniards. When news came through of the victory of Boyacá, it was 'a guerrilla largely composed of women determined to give no quarter' that waylaid the Spanish governor as he marched from Popayán, killing him and routing his escort."[6]

Other fragments of evidence from that period suggest that women were active in a variety of ways. Ann Twinam[7] writes about Don Mateo Molina, a merchant in the city of Medellin, who looking out of his store in 1810 "... might see his wife, Maria, who usually worked side-by-side with him in the shop, as she hurried off on an errand." She also describes the numerous feasts of Medellin, among which the most prestigious was the feast of Nuestra Señora de la Candelaria (the patroness of Medellin). Each feast was headed by an alférez who "... had to be wealthy, since they had to plan, organize, and most important, subsidize an eight-day town celebration." Twinam notes that being selected as alférez for a festivity "... was one of the few ways that existed for women to distinguish themselves. Barbara Posada, for example, as the inheritor of a mine, served as an alférez." Twinam also says, "the most famous woman miner in Antioquia was Doña Bárbara Caballero y Alzáta, who registered titles to a placer mine in 1817 and to a lode mine in 1825."[8]

This is fascinating because if she was "the *most* famous" this means that there were other less famous women miners in Colombia during the nineteenth century, a matter that certainly deserves extensive further investigation.

During the wars of independence, Colombian women appear to have played a significant role as suppliers, informants, companions, and even as spies in the struggle against Spain.

These fragments of information on women in Colombia during the early periods are important clues that suggest that already in 1510 women were actively involved in the political struggles of their lands. They are also reminders that the paucity of information on women during the early centuries may be more a function of scholarly neglect, and of the values that served as blinders to persons documenting those epochs, than of the lack of participation by women.

Political History

Since independence in 1819, Colombia has been characterized by an intensely competitive, factionalized and often violent two-party system dominated to this day by the Liberals and Conservatives.[9] The original differences centered primarily on the preference for almost anarchic federalism (often confederationalism) and Jacobin anticlericalism on the part of the Liberal party and a predilection for strong, centralized unitary government coupled with close church-state relations on the part of the Conservatives.

For students of Colombian women, this early period is frustrating because there is little documentation of formal political participation by women. However, one must assume that women contributed in many informal ways to the political struggles of the times. An interesting footnote is that during the Federalist period, women's suffrage was guaranteed in the province of Vélez by the 1853 Constitution; however, the record shows that no women actually voted. Later, in the 1886 Constitution, women were barred from holding public office and denied the legal guarantees of citizenship. This condition survived until the middle of the next century.

The clear distinctions between the two political parties declined after they fought each other in the debilitating Thousand Day's War at the end of the nineteenth century. Women played an important role during this war. Bergquist[10] describes one battle in 1901 in which "... in their unsuccessful efforts to control the coffee zones, [Conservative] military commanders resorted to mass arrests of both men and women considered Liberal sympathizers *or potential guerrillas"* (emphasis mine). After capturing hundreds of men and women, one commander wrote to the minister of war,

> [B]oth the men and the women are accomplices and auxiliaries of ... bandits who they hide in their houses; as a result I am sending all of them to Bogota believing that the men should be sent as recruits to the coast and the women punished as Your Excellency sees fit, since they are a very bad breed.

Later that same day the commander changed his mind and decided to send the 200 women "... to the coffee groves warning them that they will be severely punished if they aid the guerrillas."[11]

At the end of this war, Conservatives established a hegemony that finally crumbled in the late 1920s. The mainstream elite leaders of both parties were unable to contain a reformist, quasirevolutionary swing to the left by the Liberal party under the dynamic leadership of Jorge Eliécer Gaitán. He represented an outlet for social and economic frustrations and inequities. He also projected an appealing ideological sharpness, distinct from the increasing sameness of the mainstream Liberal and Conservative parties and their oligarchies. When the Liberals were in power, they pushed through reforms in 1936 by which women obtained the right of appointment to public office, and in 1945 women were granted the legal rights of citizenship (*not* including the right to vote).

While these reforms are evidence of the increasing progressiveness of the Liberals in a period of intense change, Gaitán was a

leader who sought quasirevolutionary transformation and the displacement of the existing reformist Liberal elite. Gaitán was murdered in 1948, allegedly by a Conservative party gunman. In the
wake of his assassination and the almost uncontrolled rioting, burning, and looting that followed (the so-called *Bogotázo*), the leadership of the two parties permitted or even encouraged extremists to
carry the battle between the two camps to civil war.

This period, called generically *La Violéncia*, raged on from
roughly 1949 until the early 1960s, costing as many as 300,000 lives,
mostly in the rural areas. This violence seriously affected women. It
was an intensely brutal experience in which not only politically
active leaders or militants fought but indeed the civilian population
was the primary target of violence. The incidence of rape was extremely widespread, and reports of intrauterine infanticide (in
which women's bellies were slashed open and the exposed fetus,
together with the mother, was massacred) were widespread.

The impact of *La Violéncia* on families and children was horren-
dous. Large masses of rural peasants were displaced from the land
and became refugees in town and cities. Accompanying this dias-
pora was a plague of profound social and economic problems from
which the country is still recovering.

The explosion of homeless and parentless children created a
seedbed for criminality that tested to the limits the social and law
enforcement agencies of Colombia. In the definitive book *La Violéncia en Colombia*[12] the authors devote an entire chapter to this crisis,
saying,

> A high percentage of the current perpetrators of horrible crimes
> are part of the so-called "children of *la violéncia*." We are har-
> vesting what a few years ago was criminally planted.[13]

It also resulted in an explosion of the street urchins *(gamines)*,
who formed nomadic bands that roamed and lived on the streets of
major cities. Attacks by guerrillas, bandits, partisans, or military
patrols affected thousands of other children who fled or hid from the
fighting but saw and heard the massacre of their siblings, parents,
grandparents, family, and/or friends. The long-term consequences
of experiencing such brutality have been profound.

These conditions obviously created a devastating situation for
Colombian families. Of direct impact on women was the economic
displacement they suffered and the attending necessity for many of
them to become full- or part-time prostitutes in order to survive. In
short, while the impact of *La Violéncia* on women and families is
by itself the subject of a substantial study, suffice it to say that

the consequences for Colombian women and their families were profound.

The peak of the fighting was briefly curbed in 1953 when the chieftans of the two parties informally agreed to allow a military man, General Gustavo Rojas Pinilla, to take over the government. Rojas Pinilla, having aspirations of becoming a Colombian Perón and leading the soldiers and workers in a new populist cum fascist movement, soon found the Liberals and Conservatives driven into each other's arms against him. In his attempt to construct a Perón-like power base, Pinilla instructed his Constituent Assembly to grant women full rights including suffrage. However, this process was never completed. In the wake of increasing human rights violations, corruption, and a renewed civil war, the underpinnings of his regime washed away. Rojas Pinilla was overthrown in 1957, and a National Front coalition government, with power sharing and an alternation of the presidency between the two parties, replaced him. It was then that the women's rights initiatives Pinilla wanted were actually ratified, legalized, and institutionalized.

Rojas Pinilla, again emulating Perón's regime and Eva Perón's prominent role in Argentina, had given his daughter, Maria Eugenia, a visible position in politics and in social welfare. Maria Eugenia later headed a movement and "third" political party (ANAPO) made up of her father's supporters. Indeed she later became a political force in her own right, sitting in Congress and running as a presidential candidate on the ANAPO party ticket.

While she certainly served as a role model for many Colombian women, her connection with the dictatorship and the allegations of corruption surrounding her activities during that time (in particular the misuse of funds from a charitable foundation she headed) appear to have discouraged many women from following in her footsteps.

The social costs and terrible suffering brought to light during the period of violence and the struggle for human rights and civil freedoms necessitated by the dictatorship politically mobilized a great many Colombians. This new consciousness was accompanied by a restlessness and reformism within the Catholic church. The socioeconomic inequities that in part were singled out as causes of the violence were seeds that later gave birth to Colombia's "rebel priests" (the *Golconda Movement*) and "liberation theology." Women were largely on the periphery of this, as it was identified primarily with so-called rebel priests, not nuns. Given the male domination of the Catholic church, women (especially lower-class women) have been the indirect beneficiaries of the debate on social justice but are not directly identified as leaders in that movement.

The National Front coalition succeeded in ending the civil war, reestablishing the normal electoral procedures and the hegemony of the two traditional parties. It has led to the restoration of competitive politics in which factions of both political parties have managed, in more or less honest elections, to turn over the presidency at the voters' preference. So it was not until the post-dictatorship period, starting in 1958, that women began to directly participate in the political process by voting, being elected and appointed to political office, and joining political parties. And it was the 1974 reforms, discussed further on, that at least statutorily fundamentally redefined women's rights.

However, socially, Colombia has remained an inequitable society with skewed land and income distribution, a resilient class system, and serious structural economic problems similar to those of the rest of Latin America.

The residue of guerrilla and bandit violence, surviving outside the law and in constant conflict with the military, lasted until 1984, when many of the groups laid down arms and negotiated for a reincorporation into national life. However, several Marxist revolutionary guerrilla organizations pressed on with their battle for fundamental revolution in Colombia.

Moreover, in the late 1970s and the 1980s, a drug "Mafia" trafficking in marijuana, cocaine, and amphetamines (primarily for export to the U.S. but also locally consumed) came into prominence and even into direct and violent conflict with the government. Interestingly, several of the top drug lords of Colombia have been women.

While this brief review of the political evolution of Colombia sheds light on the dynamics of politics and conflict, we must turn to religion to find additional clues about the formation and transformation of social norms.

The Church and Religion

The Roman Catholic church has been a very important factor in the life of Colombia, and it is of great significance in understanding the role of women.

Kline says, "The Colombian Roman Catholic church has long been considered one of the 'strongest' in Latin America...."[14] It has also been extraordinarily political, with the top hierarchy often supporting the Conservative party. The link between church and state has been quite explicit for most of Colombia's history, and, as Kline says, it is not lost on the observer that the National Congress and the National Cathedral share space on the Plaza Bolivar in Bogotá, the nation's capital.[15]

This institutional connection was formalized with the 1887 Concordat signed with the Vatican. The Concordat established that

1. The church was an "essential element in the social order" of Colombia.
2. Education was to conform to the theological and moral prescriptions of Catholicism.
3. The church became the major bureaucracy for registering births and recording deaths.
4. Marriage was placed under church authority.
5. Because of the church's dogma "civil divorce did not exist; civil marriage for baptized Catholics was made contingent on a declaration of abandonment of the faith, to be made before a judge, posted publicly, and communicated to the local bishop."
6. Over 60 percent of the national territory was placed under the administrative jurisdiction of the church in the form of "mission territories."[16]

Quite obviously many of these areas of church jurisdiction profoundly affected women and families. Perhaps most importantly the church's control over national education, its right to censure films, its power of *imprimatur* over books, and the norms it promoted had a tremendous impact on the socialization of Colombians, and in particular, the socialization of young girls and women. As recently as 1949 a statement by the National Bishops' Conference prohibited Catholics from voting for Liberal party candidates who would "... wish to implant civil marriage, divorce, and co-education, which would open the doors to immorality and Communism."[17]

A 1973 renegotiation of the Concordat allowed civil marriage, while the missionary jurisdictions of the church actually were expanded. However, in the last 20 years, the "official" church has been challenged. The church has become divided between conservatives, liberals, and radicals or revolutionary priests like Camilo Torres, who died in a battle after joining Marxist guerrillas. Torres' "Message to Women," published in *Frénte Unido* on October 14, 1965,[18] was a scathing, succinct, urgent, Marxist critique of sexism and class discrimination against women in Colombia. Torres writes,

Colombian women, like the women of all underdeveloped countries, have always been in an inferior position to men and
society.

This is followed by an enumeration of the ways in which women
in the four major social classes are exploited. Those of the *popular
class* through illiteracy, hard chores ("the garden, pigs, chickens,
dogs and so forth . . .") with no time for the ". . . problems and
responsibilities of motherhood." *Working-class* women by having no
legal protection or supportive social programs to help them when
the husband ". . . plagued by misery and unemployment, faced with
the overwhelming responsibilities of a large family, takes refuge in
vice and abandons his family." *Middle-class* women because ". . .
these families could not survive if the women did not work, and we
know that the working woman, the office girl, suffers all types of
exploitation and pressure from the boss." *Upper-class* women because they lack intellectual and professional opportunities in Colombia and are thus ". . . relegated to leisure, to card games and social
affairs." Moreover, ". . . marital fidelity is required only of the
woman. Censorship falls only on her when she commits an error of
this type."

Given this reality as Torres described it, how can women break
out of the bonds that oppress them? Not through politics as usual,
which Torres condemned as controlled and dictated by the ". . .
caprice of the oligarchy." Moreover, women should be especially
wary because the oligarchy ". . . like an octopus, is beginning to
extend its tentacles to the Colombian women. Men of this class
[oligarchy] have given them the right to vote in order to continue
using them as an instrument."

Instead, Torres asserted, "the Colombian woman is readying herself for the revolution. She has been and will be the support of the
revolutionary man. She has to be the heart of the revolution."

Not all of Colombia's radical clergy have been as revolutionary as
Camilo Torres. However, this diversity has produced pressures on
the church to take a more progressive position on social issues and a
more outspoken stand on human rights. Nonetheless, its official
view on many issues of importance to women remains consistent
with its relatively conservative past and with Vatican dictums.
Kline quotes a statement by Colombia's bishops in response to a
1982 presidential campaign statement by one of the candidates
(López) that divorce should be easier. It said in part,

> One who might not wish to commit treason to his faith cannot
> favor electoral platforms that include sharp blows to mat-
> rimony and to the family, that propose divorce in sacred mat-

rimony, that intend to legalize the crime of abortion, that favor sterilization, that support antinatalist campaigns which include methods that contradict the teaching of the Church. . . ."[19]

The attitudes of the church as reflected in government policy, laws, and values clearly discriminated between men and women and for several centuries thus institutionalized a two-track system. This resulted in girls receiving less access to education, and it placed women at a distinct disadvantage when it came to property rights. Moreover, it was the influence of the church and its social as well as moral priorities that helped define for centuries which were the "women's issues" in Colombian society, government, and politics.

The values that determine a society's institutional structures and processes are, of course, not only religious but also the result of economics and public policy. To understand these better we must look at two areas: labor and education.[20]

The Status of Women

Labor Participation

If we look very briefly at the labor participation levels of men and women, we can understand more clearly the evolution of Colombian women in the economy. Table 12.1 expresses this process.

In Table 12.1 we see a fairly high participation rate for women (49.8 percent) in the first census figure (1870) followed by a steeply declining rate in subsequent decades (1938, 23.9 percent; 1951, 20.0 percent; 1964, 18.8 percent). This trend line begins to reverse itself in the 1973 census figures (23.4 percent) and in our projection for 1983 (27.4 percent).

What does this mean?

The most reliable analysis is that the early census reflects an economic system in which production is carried out by a relatively wide spectrum of the population, since this period is characterized by a "precapitalist" economy. In this system, most members of the family performed economic activities (agricultural, artisan, service, and so forth). These activities included women in fairly large proportions to their numbers in the population.

As this traditional economy eroded, larger and larger ratios of the population shifted over into employment anchored in the agricultural and manufacturing sectors of a capitalist production mode. Here greater labor specialization and formal working relationships

TABLE 12.1

Rates of Participation in the Labor Force: 1870–1983 (percentages)

	1870	1938	1951	1964	1973	1983 (ESTIMATED)
MALE	90.2	82.4	91.4	79.6	73.5	67.5
FEMALE	49.8	23.9	20.0	18.8	23.4	27.4

Source: ACEP figures, census data, and extrapolations. Participation is defined as the global rates within each gender group.

(as opposed to the informal family labor division) came into existence, and in these women were gradually squeezed into the margins of the system.

Women are especially disadvantaged as a result of two factors. First, hard manual labor (such as construction and sugar cane cutting) favors males, who are employed in these activities in greater numbers than women. Second, employment requiring more formal skill training and education also favors males, who tend to continue their studies for longer periods. Moreover, as more lucrative formal work opportunities present themselves, and as work away from the place of residence grows, two trends enter the picture:

1. Larger incomes mean that in some sectors of the population the male is now able to support the entire household with his paycheck; this leads often to a desire by males to serve as the family "breadwinner." Moreover, given this possibility of a single source of income, many women also choose not to work.

2. Work away from the home, coupled with a lack of institutional child care and the erosion of the extended family (by migration and greater mobility) in which grandparents and others could care for the young, forced a new division of labor: the male working and the woman forced to stay at home to take care of domestic chores.

This trend begins to reverse itself as the capitalist production system expands, providing more jobs women can fill. The reversal grows with the gradual expansion of education in which women are increasingly trained for new skilled jobs. Greater women's participation rates also result from the demands of a larger service sector, from the increased educational facilities for the children in families, and last but not least from increasing need for both men and women to work in order to satisfy family needs and to fulfill expectations of an increased standard of living. The choice to remain single, late marriage, separation or divorce, and the entry of young women contribute further to this.

Attention should also be called to the prevalence of female-headed households, which come under great pressure for the woman to find formal work to sustain the family out of pure necessity. In a nation where common law relationships, casual and informal partnerships, and male abandonment are quite widespread, this is a very significant factor.

This process can be called a *developmental model* of women in Colombia (see Figure 12.1).

FIGURE 12.1

Hypothetical Developmental Model: Woman in Colombia

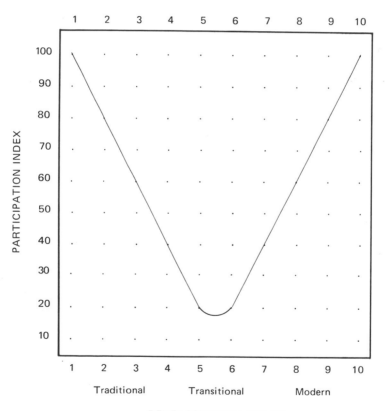

DEVELOPMENTAL STAGE

Hypothesis: Women in *traditional*, agrarian/artesan society are full (index = 100) participants in productive functions of society. Women in *transitional* societies are displaced from economic functions and become dependent low-production (index = 20) citizens. Women in *modern* societies attain new productivity from expanded economic activity and new educational and career opportunities.

A more detailed picture of these processes emerges when we analyze the sectorial trends of women and men in the labor force (see Table 12.2).

The stereotype of women as homebodies, relegated to the care of children and domestic chores, is clearly not now, nor has it ever been, an accurate picture of women in Colombia. Instead, Colombian women have been productive contributors to their personal, family household and to the national economy and have shifted their labors in response to economic and social pressures. In the last decade, no less than in previous ones, women in Colombia have been a critical factor in the nation's outputs of goods and services.

These changes in the context of work for women have pushed job-related issues to the forefront of the women's agenda since the period of the mid-1970s. As more and more women chose or were forced to enter the job market, requiring regular work away from their homes, these issues have included: child care, job security, availability and reasonable pricing of public transportion, housing, job-related safety, social security, public health services and insurance, as well as issues somewhat more tangential to work itself, namely, decent housing, public safety, water, sewage, and electricity, pest control, and a host of other urban quality-of-life needs.

Women and Education

A second important factor in understanding women in Colombia is education.[21]

Until the end of the eighteenth century, females in Colombia did not attend school but were instead taught by their parents, or in the upper classes by female tutors at home. Gradually, female education became a recognized and acceptable part of Colombian public policy objectives. Separate classes and sometimes schools for boys and girls gradually expanded the opportunities for females. By 1935 females made up 46 percent of primary school students; by 1974 that had risen to 51 percent, approximately where it currently stands.

Progress in education, however, does not mean that Colombian society took good care of its children. As late as 1938, 57.1 percent of males and 59.1 percent of females were still illiterate. This began to decline as increased numbers of people moved to the cities, where more and better schools were available, and as more resources were invested in the rural areas. By 1951 male illiteracy had declined to 41.1 percent and female to 44.0 percent; this was further reduced so

TABLE 12.2

Economically Active Population by Type of Occupation (percentage by gender)

OCCUPATION	GENDER	1870	1938	1951	1964	1973
Professional, technical, administration, public functionaries	M	0.5	6.9	9.9	9.1	10.3
	F	0.3	8.3	12.9	19.3	22.6
Sales and commerce	M	3.6	5.1	1.4	5.2	8.7
	F	1.3	4.3	2.8	7.1	8.4
Service	M	8.4	3.4	2.7	3.6	4.3
	F	25.8	28.6	44.7	41.5	36.0
Agricultural labor, hunting, foresters	M	75.5	70.3	63.5	57.4	39.6
	F	28.3	17.7	14.5	11.4	3.9
Laborer, machine operators, drivers	M	10.8	12.4	18.1	21.1	26.9
	F	42.5	38.4	24.1	17.8	14.8
Armed forces, other	M	1.2	1.9	4.4	3.6	10.5
	F	1.8	2.7	1.0	2.9	14.3

Source: Magdalena León de Leál, *La Mujer y El Desarrollo en Colombia (Bogotá:* ACEP, 1977), 197. Translated by the author.

that in 1964 illiteracy accounted for 29.8 percent of males and 31.4 percent of females.

These relative gains in at least minimal education are counterbalanced by the fact that a rapidly growing population (as much as 3 percent per year) has pressured the educational system, so that in absolute terms there has been little change for several decades. In 1950 there were 1.3 million women and a little over 1 million illiterate males. By 1970 those figures remained virtually unchanged, as Figure 12.2 graphically demonstrates.

Beyond the most basic levels, education expanded, with females accounting again for roughly half of middle school students. Finally, at the higher university level, women have gone from being 16 percent of the student population as recently as 1960 to 26 percent in 1973 and projected to over 35 percent by the early 1980s.[22]

These changes have been important and have demonstrated a gradual incorporation of women into the educational structures of the country. It should be added that women still predominate in "female" careers such as teaching, nursing, and fine arts, probably due to a combination of various forms of discrimination in some of the "male" professions, notably engineering, agricultural sciences, and medicine, as well as women's socialization, which steers them in greater numbers to those areas considered favorable for women.

FIGURE 12.2

Illiteracy, 1950—1970

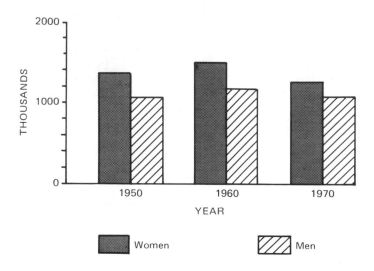

Political Participation and Policy

Work and education are indeed important and basic indices of gender status and participation in society. However, there is a larger and more complex universe which we must briefly review to fully understand the context within which the Women's Decade has unfolded in Colombia.

To gain a better perspective on the concept of "participation," it is useful to divide women's activities in Colombia into informal and formal participation. A brief discussion of each will help clarify the political experience and impact of women on policy.

INFORMAL PARTICIPATION

I have argued elsewhere[23] that to understand fully the impact of women on politics, especially in rural Colombia, it may be necessary to investigate informal networking and mobilization structures. In particular I found that in villages and small towns, women may use social structures (such as community welfare societies) as vehicles for political work. I described the case of one woman who used her access to town prisoners to whom her organization provides charitable services (reading material, clothes, etc.) as an opportunity to work on behalf of the town's Liberal party. I argued that, while this activity is functionally undifferentiated and can be called *parapolitical*, it nonetheless is an important element in the political outcomes of local communities.

A second form this "informal" political activity takes is the much-debated "great woman behind the man" process. While this is a less-than-ideal context for women to exercise political influence, it warrants consideration, especially in Latin America, where some notable women politicians, such as Eva Perón, have indeed accumulated their political capital from or together with a male political figure. In Colombia, the two most visible female political figures, Bertha Hernández de Ospina and Maria Eugenia Rojas de Moreno, were identified with male politicians (Mrs. Ospina's husband was president; Mrs. Rojas de Moreno's father was General Rojas Pinilla, president and dictator in the early 1950s).

Even in Cuba, the only revolutionary state in Latin America and a socialist, Marxist-Leninist country, this is part of the political reality. In spite of the official policy of fully incorporating women into the national life, and despite impressive social and economic gains for women, they constitute only a miniscule proportion of the top power structure (only 3 in 1983 out of 101 top positions). Moreover, the "top" women in Cuba, Vilma Espín, head of the Federation of Cuban Women, alternate member of the Polit Bureau of the Cuban Communist party, and member of the Council of State, is the *wife* of Raul Castro.[24] It is, one would have to argue, highly likely that if his fortunes were to change (if he were to lose the five second-tier positions he holds in Cuba—his brother Fidel holding all five top positions), Vilma Espín would probably also disappear from the power structure.

I stress the idea of women achieving power "together with" a male counterpart because one might argue that, in the cases noted and in many other cases that are less well known, the assets, energy, and political acumen of women may actually constitute a critical component in the success of the male politician. Over the past decade in Colombia it was alleged by informants in my research that many prominent male politicians may indeed "owe" their career and success to women who are not formally visible, but who range from spouses to mothers and grandmothers. Their impact includes providing financial resources to fund a political career, using family connections, behind the scenes manipulation, and pushing for action on policy issues of interest to women. We also recorded numerous comments to the effect that "she is the one with brains."[25]

I am not arguing for surrogate politics or indirect women's political influence as desirable. I *am* suggesting that its role and significance should be studied because it may tell us a great deal about the prevailing norms on women's participation in politics or about women's own preferences in terms of how they (as individual women) choose to inject themselves into the political process, albeit indirectly. It may also provide interesting information on the *origins* of policy that was debated or implemented. Finally, it would be a useful strategy for estimating the "policy leverage" women may have been able to exercise during periods of history when they were not legally, institutionally, or normatively permitted to directly inject themselves into political activities. As we saw earlier, these periods cover a considerable time frame in Colombia.

In another area—jobs and work—women's reality is also difficult to identify. This is a function of the skewed system for gathering census data and national statistics. The failure to include informal work, to include women as agriculturalists in categories not specified by the census, and the myriad of employment categories in services, small-scale production and marketing, in which women are active, produces a highly biased and inaccurate picture of the productivity of women in Colombia.

FORMAL PARTICIPATION

Formal participation is generally measured in terms of voter participation and women in elected or appointed political and governmental positions. The following conclusions can be drawn from a review of the existing evidence on Colombia.[26]

First, Colombian women have significantly lower political participation rates than men. On average over the past decade, there is roughly a 15 percent gap between male and female voter participation (see Figure 12.3).

Second, women have held a very small slice of national elected positions, approximately 3.5 percent of congressional seats (see Figure 12.4).

Third, women's political opinions and attitudes correspond more closely than men's to the parents' or head of household's political views. For example, one Colombian study showed that 71 percent of the women identified with their husband's political preference.[27] In that same study women indicated the following sources of their political ideas: mate/head of household, 28 percent; a relative, 30 percent; mass media, 27 percent; other, 15 percent.

Fourth, women seem to score higher than men on the conservative end of the liberal (radical)/conservative scale.

FIGURE 12.3

Voter Participation.

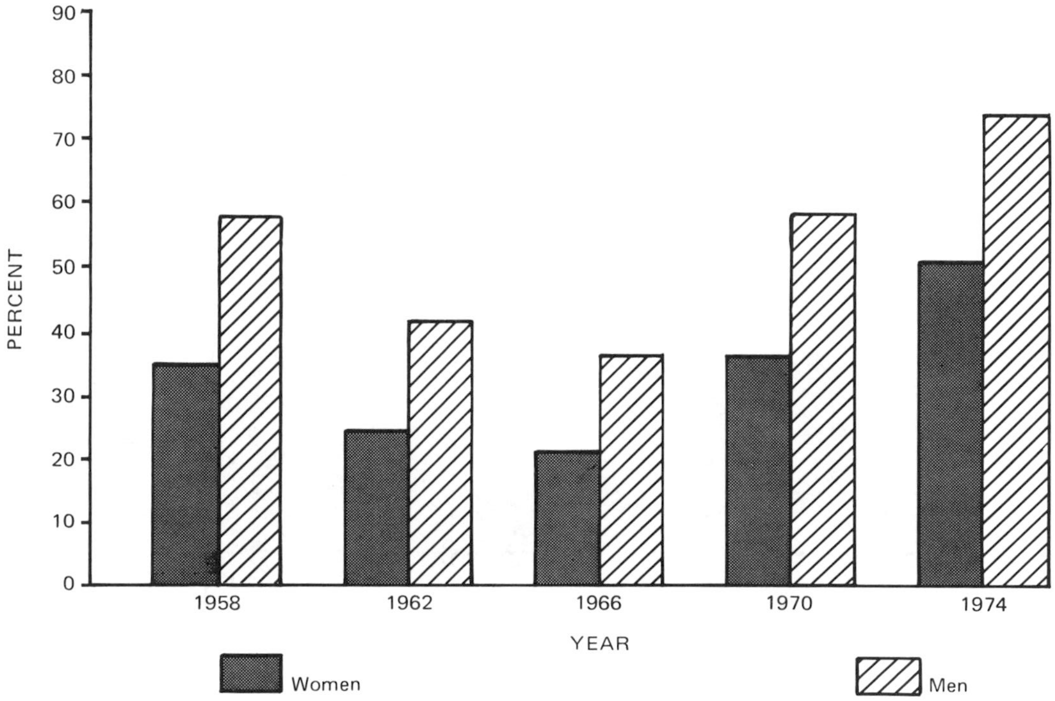

FIGURE 12.4

Representation in the Lower Chamber of Congress

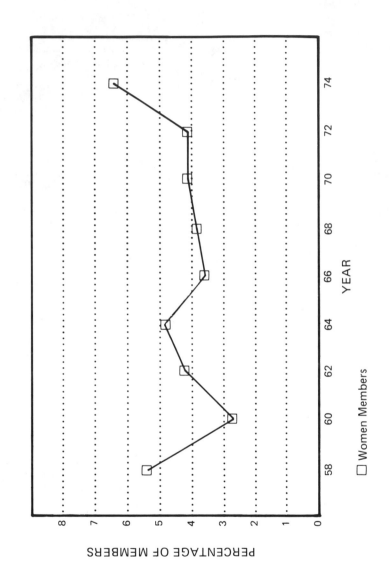

Fifth, women's political action organizations or a women's movement appear to have some impact on national politics, but there is agreement that the women's movement is divided by ideological differences and by the divergent models discussed earlier. Moreover, some of these groups have been controlled by women of relatively high social status who have used these organizations to advocate their pet projects or have gained personal leverage and visibility through them. In other instances, women have been mobilized into more diffuse struggles, that is to say, those that are not gender-specific, for example, women in the antigovernment guerrillas and women in the labor movement.

These characteristics are not surprising; in fact, they represent a profile that is fairly representative of women's formal political participation in most nations. However, according to a recent inventory compiled by JoAnn Fagot Aviel,[28] Colombia ranks third of 19 Latin American countries for which she compiled data on the number of women in high government posts (the Dominican Republic ranks first with 27; Mexico second with 18, and Colombia follows with 17). However, quite clearly women in Colombia have occupied a rather insignificant absolute number of positions in the formal power structure, and women have constituted a very small relative proportion of these positions within Colombia as well.

Policy Impacts

Given these background characteristics, what implications are there for policy making in areas of interest to women, and, more generally, what impact do women have on policy?

Clearly, from a "representativeness" perspective, women in Colombia cannot rely on other women in policy positions to speak for them or to advocate their causes. The Colombian political elite at all levels is male-dominated. If we use a strict definition of representativeness—i.e., that a given group controls positions of power, authority, and influence equal to their numbers in the general population—Colombia, as most countries, fails miserably.

A somewhat different measure of policy influence might be the role interest groups play in pressuring the policy formation institutions (such as legislatures) into considering certain policy needs.

A 1976 study of Colombian legislative behavior[29] provides some interesting facts on the role of pressure groups in the Colombian Congress. When they asked members of Congress which general (categorical) groups of constituents had visited them in their offices

the survey showed that *Acción Comunal* (a community action organization set up by the government), representatives of municipal
government, peasants, clergy, labor unions, departmental (state)
governments, teachers, and representatives of a variety of economic
organizations (industrial, agricultural, etc.), in that order, passed
through the offices of members of Congress.

When we attempt to evaluate the degree to which this inventory
of groups represented "women's issues," it becomes clear that we do
not have a conceptual instrument with which to differentiate
"women's issues" from others. Neither the list of organizational
contacts nor the narrative by the authors of the study from which
this information comes allows us to make a judgment as to which
are primarily (or intensely) women's concerns. Only teachers, a
large percentage of whom are women, suggest themselves as potentially a group contacting members of Congress with so-called wom-
en's issues. It is important to note that the authors of this study on
the Colombian Congress were not interested in disagregating and
discussing women and women's roles or policy interests.

Moreover, in Colombia, both male and female have low participation rates; the 1977 ACEP study data, for example, shows only 5
percent of women saying they belong to a political group.[30]

The 1974 Reforms

While we have very little evidence that women *per se* have defined a
policy agenda and while women do not occupy positions of power
and influence in great numbers, the status of women in fact worked
itself into the national agenda of Colombia. It did so during a period
characterized by.

1. A heightened awareness of women's issues stimulated by the
feminist movement's new aggressiveness in the 1970s

2. The commitment of international organisms such as the
United Nations and the Organization of American States to women
through the UN and OAS commissions on women

3. The designation of 1975 as International Women's Year

4. The declaration of the 1975–1985 period as the Women's
Decade

5. The World Conference on International Women's Year held in
Mexico City

6. A growing awareness that women play a key role in the development of Third World nations

7. The ever growing concern with population policy and the
attendant issues of women's control over their bodies

8. A surge of scholarly and applied work on women in Colombia, accompanied by the growth of new cadres of men and women interested in and knowledgeable about women's issues and problems

These factors were pressures that led to the passage in December 1974 of a new 71-article law on the family, the purpose of which was "improving the judicial status of the family and eliminating various odious and ancestral types of discrimination between the sexes."[31]

While only one woman lawyer participated in the drafting of the law, it did represent a major revision of women's status in order, as President López Michelsen said, "to eliminate all forms of discrimination against women." The law specifically accomplished the following. It

1. Repealed Article 1504, which declared women to be "legal incapables"—those who are under someone else's legal guardianship such as children, the mentally ill, etc.
2. Revised the double standard on adultery in which male adultery was legitimized while female adultery was grounds for divorce. (Men had to move out and actually live with their mistress before their behavior became grounds for separation.)
3. Laid the groundwork for legalized divorce (which came with the revision of the Concordat with the Vatican).
4. Entrusted both spouses with the responsibility of guiding and educating children.
5. Mandated that the obligation of bringing up children, choosing a place to live, organizing the family budget, and so forth should be shared equally between the parents.
6. Stipulated that husbands and wives must each contribute to the upkeep of the family if, for example, they should keep separate financial accounts.
7. Holds that children owe respect to both parents (not just the father, as was previously mandated).
8. Stipulates that the parents of children who are born out of wedlock enjoy the same rights as parents of "legitimate" children, if the family lives together.

These reforms, coupled with revisions of labor law, social security legislation, and other policy areas, represent a major course correction for Colombia. They do not mean that women's status *has*

changed. "Progressive as they were, the new measures did not completely eradicate the old situation."[32] In fact, according to one
source, "At the moment, the majority of Colombian women still
bear the full brunt of a repressive cultural tradition and even
greater burden of economic exploitation.[33]

In some instances the impact of Colombian law on women is
puzzling. This is especially true in labor legislation because it is
gender- and age-differentiated. Decker and Durán[34] report,

> Colombian labor legislation distinguishes between minors
> under fourteen, minors under eighteen, and women. Minors
> under fourteen are prohibited from working in mines, sand and
> gravel pits, manufacturing, and construction. They are allowed
> to work in agriculture only if their work does not prevent their
> attendance at school. Minors under eighteen and women are
> prohibited from working at night in jobs that are banned on a
> regular basis to persons under fourteen. They are also banned
> from work in underground mines.
>
> The labor law provides for special privileges to pregnant
> women. At the time of birth, women are entitled to an eight-
> week paid leave. The rest period is shortened to between two
> and four weeks in the case of abortion or miscarriage.

Is this special legislative consideration an advantage or a disadvantage to women and children (perhaps because of employer
reluctance to hire them)? Terry Jean Rosenberg, in a study of protective labor legislation, concludes, "There is no evidence in my findings to support the contention that protective labor legislation has
hindered female industrial employment."[35] She adds, however, that
were the appropriate laws enforced more consistently, the conclusion might be different.

The new laws provide an arena and a legal reference point for
women to exercise their clout and articulate their needs and expectations, even though equality and full implementation of women's
rights has not been achieved. The Women's Decade of 1975–1985 in
Colombia can most accurately be described as a vigorous and growing effort to actualize and institutionalize the principles laid down
in the 1974 reforms.

Prospects for the Future

It has been alleged that to understand the role of women in Colombia one must take into account the stream of history and the
peculiarities of domestic subcultures and social classes in order to
understand the dynamics of the process. With that in mind, what

are the forces and factors that will affect political and policy-making institutions in Colombia in the next two decades?

Overall, one has to distinguish between revolutionary change (such as was advocated by Camilo Torres) and incremental change, which would take place under governments controlled by bourgeois parties (such as the Liberals and Conservatives.) One cannot underestimate the determination of revolutionary politics, which draws much of its inspiration, rhetoric, and political methodology from the Cuban and Nicaraguan revolutions. However, the existence of relatively free and honest elections, a vigorous mass media, and a persistent commitment to gradualist reforms has resulted in relatively little apparent support for the revolutionary approach. Thus, I will limit my discussion to scenarios under a continuation of hegemony by the Liberal and Conservative parties.

First, it seems quite evident that Colombian women are highly dependent on the overall viability of the Colombian economy, its growth or stagnation, and the impact global economic conditions have on the system. Progress for women and new or increased opportunities are apparently a function of Colombia's economic health, of economic growth in a mixed, predominantly capitalist system. High oil prices, costly credits, a large foreign debt, and stagnation of exports have all hurt women in the past decade.

Second, a continued emphasis on the role of women in society will most likely result in the growth of women's organizations in Colombia, which to date appear not to have materialized into powerful organizations. However, the general tendency in Colombia (as well as the rest of Latin America) has been for the "women's movement" to be highly fragmented. Radical feminist groups play a relatively minor role, and women tend to mobilize around more functionally specific issues.

Third, the legal foundations laid by the 1974 reforms will continue to challenge the system to live up to those new expectations. In a host of policy areas related to women, children, families, work, and health among others, but especially in women's and family law, one can expect a new intensity of effort as well as competition for an increasing share of the national budget.

Fifth, as Rosenberg indicates,[36] ". . . provision of adequate day care services and the expansion of technical training programs for women are potentially the most effective means of promoting female industrial employment in Colombia." We can expect renewed emphasis here as well as pressure for wage parity and other benefits.

Sixth, as far as rural women are concerned, it seems likely that they will continue to suffer from the pressures that have adversely affected their status as a result of the decline of traditional agriculture and the growth of commercial or capitalist production. Thus, rural social services and new training or educational programs for rural women are a high priority.

Seventh, there is evidence that a renewed effort to expand education in selected areas (by hiring more teachers, most of whom would be female, for example) would add significantly to the employment opportunities of many women.[37]

Finally, one can expect a gradual increase in the number of women running for public office and attaining appointed positions in the policy-making establishment, as the old patriarchal norms gradually give way to a model of woman as a coequal and vital participant in the national life of Colombia and as more women present themselves as candidates for public posts. However, one would not expect dramatic changes in this regard, as the experience of most other nations suggests.

The author wishes to thank the Political Science Department, and the Graduate College of Iowa State University, and in particular Prof. Victor Olorunsola for support that made possible research on which this chapter is based. Also thanks to the staff of the Library of Congress.

The level of research on women in Colombia seems to be levelling off from a peak in the mid-1970s. A recent survey of the journals *Signs*, *Feminist Studies*, and *Connexion* and the newspaper *New Directions for Women*, "International Roundup" section showed no information on women in Colombia. *The Latin American Research Review* in the past three to four years has also had a greatly diminished number of fresh references to research on women in Colombia. Moreover, there is still a serious lack of public opinion poll and other systematic survey research of a general nature on women's attitudes and views. Finally, difficult economic conditions and budget problems in Colombia have adversely affected census taking and other publicly funded investigations.

NOTES

1. *Harper's*, May 1984, 38.
2. Some very interesting material can be found in Ofelia Uribe de Acosta, *Una Vóz Insurgente* (Bogotá: Ed. Guadalupe, 1963).
3. *De Donde Venimos, Hacia Donde Vamos, Hacia Donde Debemos Ir?: Proletarizacion* (Medellin: Ocho de Junio, 1875).
4. For an excellent discussion, see Lynne B. Iglitzin, "The Patriarchal Heritage," in Lynne B. Iglitzin and Ruth Ross, eds., *Women in the World*

(Santa Barbara, CA: ABC-Clio, 1976), 7 – 24.

5. Ann M. Pescatello, *Power and Pawn: The Female in Iberian Families, Societies and Cultures* (Westport, CT: Greenwood Press, 1976), 135.

6. Kathleen Romoli, *Colombia: Gateway to South America* (Garden City, NJ: Doubleday, Doran and Co., 1941), 177.

7. Ann Twinam, *Miners, Merchants, and Farmers in Colonial Colombia* (Austin: University of Texas Press, 1982), 125, 175.

8. Ibid.

9. A useful, concise review of Colombian parties and political history on which this discussion is based is Robert J. Alexander, ed., *Political Parties of the Americas* (Westport, CT: Greenwood Press, 1980).

10. Charles W. Bergquist, *Coffee and Conflict in Colombia: 1886 – 1910* (Durham, NC: Duke University Press, 1978), 158 – 161.

11. Ibid.

12. German Guzmán Campos, Orlando Fals Borda, and Eduardo Umana Luna, *La Violéncia en Colombia, Tomo II* (Bogotá: Ed. Tercer Mundo, 1964).

13. Guzman Campos, 205.

14. Harvey F. Kline, *Colombia: Portrait of Unity and Diversity* (Boulder, CO: Westview Press, 1983), 87.

15. Kline, 89.

16. Kline, 88 – 89.

17. John Martz, cited in Kline, 88.

18. John Gerassi, *Revolutionary Priest* (NY: Random House, 1971), 397 – 399. All quotes from Torres are from this source.

19. Kline, 91.

20. See Magdalena León de Leál, ed., *La Mujer y el Desarrollo en Colombia* (Bogotá: ACEP, 1977).

21. The following information on education comes from the Departamento Administrativo Nacional de Estradística, Resúmenes de Censos, Bogotá.

22. Data from Ministerio de Educación Nacional. Planeamientos Estadísticos.

23. Steffen W. Schmidt, "Women's Changing Roles in Colombia," in Lynne B. Iglitzen and Ruth Ross, eds., *Women in the World: A Comparative Study* (Santa Barbara, CA: ABC-Clio, 1976), 243 – 255.

24. JoAnn Fagot Aviel, "Political Participation of Women in Latin America," *Western Political Quarterly* 24:1 (March 1981), 156 – 173.

25. Notes from interviews in Bogotá, Cali, Pereira, Buga, and Popayán.

26. See the discussion in Steffen W. Schmidt, "Women in Colombia: Attitudes and Future Perspectives in the Political System," *Journal of Interamerican Studies and World Affairs* 17:4 (November 1975), 465 – 489.

27. Patricia Pinzón de Lewin and Dora Rothlisberger, "Participación

Política de la Mujer," in León de Leál, 36–37.

28. Aviel.

29. Gary Hoskin, Franscisco Leal, and Harvey Kline, *Legislative Behavior in Colombia*, Vol. II, Council on International Studies, State University of New York at Buffalo, 1976.

30. León de Leál.

31. Information on the 1974 reform used here comes from "Colombia: Family Law and Legal Reform," in *Slaves of Slaves: The Challenge of Latin American Women* (London: Zed Press, 1977), 82–95.

32. Ibid.

33. Ibid.

34. David R. Decker and Ignacio Durán, *The Political, Economic, and Labor Climate in Colombia*, Multinational Industrial Relations Series, No. 4, Wharton School, 1982, 67–68.

35. Terry Jean Rosenberg, "Female Industrial Employment and Protective Labor Legislation in Bogota, Colombia," *Journal of Interamerican Studies and World Affairs* 24:1 (February 1982), 59–80.

36. Rosenberg, "Female Industrial . . .," 79.

37. Terry J. Rosenberg, "Individual and Regional Influences on the Employment of Colombian Women," *Journal of Marriage and the Family* (May 1976), 339–353.

RECOMMENDED READINGS

(Note: There are no books in English on women in Colombia. The non-Spanish speaking reader will have to refer to selected journal articles in English which summarize, review or critique these works. The *Latin American Research Review*, *Signs*, *Journal of Marriage and the Family*, and the *Journal of Interamerican Studies and World Affairs* are especially recommended.)

Acosta, Ofelia Uribe de. *Una Vóz Insurgente*. Bogotá: Editorial Guadalupe, 1963.
This book covers in its 20 short, narrative essays a great deal of Colombian women's experience. The author, a feminist and founder of the *Agitación Femenina*, the first feminist magazine in Colombia, pulls together her panoramic and richly interpretive perspective. The essays are evenly divided between politics or law and social problems and policies. Originally, these pieces were a seminar on women in Colombia organized by the author. As a source of direct quotations and newspaper excerpts of the most crudely offensive sexist views throughout Colombia's history, this book is priceless. It should be translated into English!

Amezquita de Almeyda, Josefina. *Law and the Status of Colombian Women*. Medford, MA: Law and Population Program, Fletcher School of Law and Diplomacy, 1975.
This is a useful resource book that provides the reader with exactly what the title says.

León de Leál, Magdalena, ed. *La Mujer y el Desarrollo en Colombia*. Bogotá: ACEP, 1977.
This is an excellent eight-chapter, multi-authored survey of woman in Colombia, the product of a two-year research effort coordinated and funded by the Colombian Association for the Study of Population (ACEP). Strongest chapters are the ones on health, women in the labor force, and education. One of the problems (common to all research on Colombia) is that fresh, reliable, and extensive *data* are very hard to come by.

León de Leál, Magdalena, Carmen Diana Deere, et al. *Mujer y Capitalismo Agrario: Estudio de Cuatro Regiones Colombianas*. Bogatá: ACEP, 1980.
A largely sociological study of rural, peasant women in four regions of Colombia, this book traces the effects of "capitalist agriculture" on the female labor force. It finds the effects generally disruptive. It also concludes that conventional census and survey

techniques *greatly* underestimate the productivity and labor force participation of women in Colombia. The book is very hard to read because conclusions and significant points are lost in a veritable blizzard of tables and data.

Osorno Cardenas, Marta Cecilia. *La Mujer Colombiana y Latino-Americana.* Medellin, Colombia: Tipografia Italiana, 1974.
This is an extraordinarily interesting but frustrating book written by Sister Osorno as a doctoral thesis in education in Paris, France. It is terribly eclectic and unorganized but contains everything from a short history of women in Colombia to interviews with widows, divorcees, a chapter on prostitutes, and a section on women and voting. The principal objective is, however, to design a model for the "new" family in Colombia in light of the breakdown of the old and to develop a pedagogical framework for educating couples and members of these future families.

13

The Status of Women in Mexico: The Impact of the "International Year of the Woman"

Adaljiza Sosa Riddell
University of California, Davis

Introduction

The International Women's Year World Conference sponsored by the United Nations and held in Mexico City from June 19 to July 2, 1975, has left an indelible mark upon women throughout the world, but more so on Mexican women. The simple fact that the Mexican government agreed to host the conference and that a major address was given by President Echeverría must have been a great surprise to all of those observers and scholars who consider Mexico to epitomize a patriarchal regime. Yet, Mexico played host to women from all over the world, women of color, women of poverty. President Echeverría's speech, interestingly, did not focus exclusively on women. He argued that "the essential problem of our times was no longer the achievement of equal rights, imperative and indispensable though this was. The hope of the modern age is the liberation of all people from institutions and patterns of conduct imposed in the interests of the great majority." In this cause, he said, the women of developed countries should "use their potent moral force to support the poor nations of the world."[1] President Echeverría also "proposed a constitutional amendment to open avenues for incorporating women into the political, social, and economic life, which required the recognition that their *de jure* and *de facto* capability lay behind a continuous social effort that had to be stimulated in all sectors."[2] In short, President Echeverría was arguing that concerns for equal rights were secondary to economic issues. The situation for women in Mexico could not improve substantially unless there was a commensurate improvement in all sectors of Mexican life. Women could, presumably, benefit from the IWY *after* the economic and political situation for all of Mexico improved drastically. This sentiment was far from new; it had been echoed and re-echoed by Mexican leaders throughout the decades of the twentieth century.

While the lofty goals called for by ex-President Echeverría have not been fulfilled in Mexico, one of the many positive results of the International Women's Year Conference has assuredly been an increased concern for, awareness of, and interest in writing on the status of women in Mexico. This interest is obvious in the writings by Mexican scholars as well as scholars in the United States, many of whom have taken a renewed interest in events in Mexico. This situation is a major change from the literature available when the previous article on women in Mexico was undertaken for the first edition of this volume in 1974. The 1974 article, entitled "Female Political Elites in Mexico: 1974," criticized the majority of the literature on Mexican women because it was either nonexistent, ethnocentric when written by scholars from the United States, or male-centered.[3] The major works cited in the 1974 article included Gabriel Almond and Sidney Verba's *The Civic Culture*, Ward Morton's *Woman Suffrage in Mexico*, and an article by William Blough, "Political Attitudes of Mexican Women."[4] Mexican periodicals reviewed included the *Revista Mexicana de Sociologia*, *La Revista Mexicana de Sciencia Política*, and *Hispano-Americano*. These periodicals yielded less than half a dozen articles altogether. The only exception to this paucity of writing on Mexican women was one Mexicana scholar, María Antonieta Rascón, who remains today one of the most important feminist writers on women's issues.

By contrast, the literature that has emerged in the last decade represents a very different political perspective on the history of political participation of Mexican women in Mexico. That perspective can best be described as a feminist one. Among the most recent and thorough of this genre is the book *Against All Odds* by Anna Macias, published in 1982 in the United States. Dr. Macias documents Mexican women's steps toward acquiring an education as early as 1869, when the first secondary school for girls opened in Mexico. She describes women's participation in activities directed at the overthrow of Porfirio Díaz in Mexico City as early as 1904, and, in the state of Yucatán, as early as 1910. That is, activities directed at the emancipation and/or enfranchisement of women occurred in Mexico at approximately the same time that advocates for similar women's rights were mobilizing in the United States.[5] Many women were in leadership positions within the organizations attempting to educate the Mexican populace about the need to overthrow the regime of Porfirio Díaz. Author Macias has completely dispelled all myths of nonparticipation by Mexican women in pre-Revolutionary Mexico. The problem, as she boldly notes, has been that male scholars have chosen to ignore the role of women and have instead focused on the male revolutionary heros. The book by Macias also contains an extensive bibliographic study of works by several other authors on the same topic, thus leading us to a rich body of literature on Mexican women.

Two other important developments in Mexicana scholarship have been that of the publication of feminist periodicals and contributions by male "feminist" writers. The most useful of these feminist periodicals is *fem* because it has been in continuous publication since 1981 and because it features articles almost exclusively by women about women. Among the major writers for *fem* are María Antonieta Rascón, Marta Acevedo, Esperanza Tuñon, Elena Urrutia, and, especially interesting, several Chicana (Mexican-American female) writers. Male writers who are currently attempting to focus on "women's" issues include Carlos Monsivais, Ramón Márquez, and Ignacio Ramirez. Overall, these authors provide us with a view of Mexican women as women who have been, and continue to be, an integral part of a worldwide move among women to define their own role in society. It is no longer possible to view Mexican women as "passive" or "antirevolutionary," as had too often been done in the past. Rather, we find that there have been constant changes, *de jure* and *de facto*, in Mexican society, as there have been in many other parts of the world, and that Mexican women have been in the forefront of the movements to implement change. Based upon this recent literature, this study attempts to document those changes that have occurred since the International Women's Year World Conference in Mexico City. Understanding and documenting these changes enables us to better assess, without the constraints of antifeminist bias, the status of women in Mexico today.

Hypothesis and Research Methods

Working with the premise substantiated by the research of such writers as Anna Macias, María Antonieta Rascón, and Luisa María Leal that women in Mexico have sought changes in their political and economic structure and that these changes are in line with the many reforms sought by feminist women in other nations, my hypothesis for this study is that women in Mexico have not achieved the juridical nor social equality they have sought more because of the entrenchment of the male leadership of the Mexican government than because of any inability or unwillingness of the women to deal with the issues. There have been some changes, and those changes have come as a result of political pressure from women and their organizations. The issues that concern women in Mexico are similar to those that concern women in the U.S. Yet there are several unresolved problems similar to those in any magazine or newspaper in the U.S., including such problems as the decriminalization of abortion, rape and all its attendant problems, lack of women's organizations for women's rights, lack of equal rights legislation, concern over working conditions, maternity benefits, unemployment, on-the-job discrimination, and the lack of adequate day care centers.

It has not been as easy to document actual positive changes as it has been to find the problem areas that needed much work. The focus of this study, therefore, is to discuss the major issues outlined above, to assess them in terms of progress made since the IWY, and to explain the role of Mexican women in the battle for reforms on these issues. Research methods included a review of several Mexican periodicals including *Proceso, Plural, Nexus, Revista Mexicana de Sociología*, and *UAM-Azcapotzalco*, from 1976 to 1984. Literature on women included a review of *fem*, 1980–1984, a review of literature specifically on women in Mexico, and finally some discussions with several female researchers at the Centro de Estudios Fronterizos del Norte de México (CEFNOMEX), a research institute established by Colegio de Mexico, based in Tijuana, Baja California. My purpose for these discussions at CEFNOMEX was to assess changes for women in Mexico from the perspective of those people who theoretically could be the most critical, women working and residing in the border areas who have intensive and extensive contact with women in the United States. The chapter first presents a brief outline of the demographic and economic situation for women followed by a discussion of the history of contemporary women's organizations and their major concerns. The next section discusses three issues that appear to be most significant to Mexican women, abortion, rape, and equal rights, including such related concerns as maternity benefits, working conditions, child care, on-the-job gender discrimination, and some comments on the special case of *las maquiladoras* (assembling plants owned by foreign companies located in border cities). Finally, I shall conclude with my own observations on women in Mexico ten years after IWY.

Women and the Mexican Nation

The realities of life for the majority of Mexican women are harsh, restricted, and often beyond their control. One cannot ignore the realities of life in Mexico: the flight of rural campesinos to the urban areas, where they live in overcrowded, poverty-stricken conditions; the drastic devaluation of the Mexican peso and its accompanying economic hardships; high unemployment rates; the constant stream of migration to the northern border and then to the U.S.; the recurring plunders of the national treasury by former government officials; the penetration of foreign capital and accompanying extraction of the wealth of the land. Mexican women are equally represented in sharing the hardships resulting from these conditions. They share all of these conditions, sometimes to an even greater degree than their male counterparts, since women have outnumbered men in Mexico since at least 1900. In 1900, women constituted 51 percent of the population, while in 1970, they were 50 percent.[6] Certainly, one must be cautious about statistics available in the years prior to the Mexican Revolution, since the methods of census taking in the earlier part of the century were admittedly crude, but the population trends are quite clear. There are more females than males in the urban areas, 51 percent, and more men than women in the rural areas, 49 percent. Statistics also demonstrate that this trend continues into the 1980s and that there will be no drastic changes in the ratio of women to men in Mexico, 50.1 percent to 49.9 percent.[7]

Another obvious trend in these figures is the very high rate of population growth due to several factors, including a high fertility rate and a sharp drop in the mortality rate.[8] This high fertility rate has, of course, concerned Mexico's and the United States' policymakers to the extent that during the 1970s the Mexican government adopted several measures designed to reduce this population growth. These policies came at the same time (1974) that ex-President Echeverría (1970–1976) extended Mexico's invitation to the United Nations for hosting the IWY. These simultaneous actions can lead to the conclusion that there is some relationship between population growth limitations and juridical changes in the status of women. This relationship has been noted by some Mexican scholars, in particular, M. Teresita de Barbieri. She writes that "basically, the right to [regulate] family is reformed and the idea of protecting women and mothers is abandoned in favor of societal responsibility over maternity."[9] Barbieri implies that governmental policies on population control are important to women not only because of their direct impact on them as women but also because of their relationship to other policies that have the potential to render women more vulnerable as well as more equal. Barbieri also notes concern over the long-term effect both types of policies will have on male-female relationships.[10] In economic terms, women in Mexico suffer more economic deprivation and hardships than their male counterparts, difficult as that may seem. Statistics on the economic status of women demonstrate that although the population is nearly evenly distributed, women's share of the national income is about 10 percent.[11] This low share of the income continues in spite of the fact that 23 percent of the population that is economically active are women, and in some industries, notably *las maquiladoras*, women represent 77 percent of the workforce.[12] The official position of the Mexican government on this issue is that this is due to the fact that women hold a marginal position in society. Male critics of this official line, including people like Carlos Monsivais and Ignacio Ramírez, disagree with the government. Ignacio Ramírez, writing in *Proceso*, argues that this situation is due to the second-class status to which women are relegated, the lack of equal rights, and the resulting exploitation and discrimination.[13]

The status of women in Mexico, then, has been determined, to a very large degree, by the economic and demographic situation. For some observers of the Mexican milieu, the causal factor for the extremely depressed social, economic, and political status of women should more accurately be attributed to the lack of equality between men and women rather than to Mexico's overall economically depressed conditions. The IWY did contribute to some juridical changes in the direction of greater equality, in particular the types of changes called for by then-President Echeverría in the speech described earlier. Unfortunately, Echeverría called for the integration of women in the economic life of the country, not equal rights, thus setting the stage for what was to continue through Lopez Portillo's administration (1976–1982) and into the administration of Miguel de la Madrid (1982–1988) as official policy on the status of women in Mexico. This governmental response, however, does not reflect with any kind of accuracy the amount of effort that has been put forth to motivate the government as well as the society to respond positively to the needs and concerns of Mexican women. That activity has, to be sure, come from feminine and feminist groups[14] that reflect a diverse political spectrum. In order to comprehend the scope and scale of the activities of these groups, it is useful, at this point, to present a brief historical outline of their activities, issues, and types of organizations.

Feminist Organizations and Their Major Concerns

The important work by Macias, *Against All Odds*, as noted earlier, is the best contemporary summary work, available in English, on Mexican feminine and feminist organizations. In Spanish, several works have been authored by María Antonieta Rascón. These works chronicle certain facts about the women's movement in Mexico. It seems quite clear that the earliest expressions of feminism appeared beginning in approximately the 1870s. These early writings appeared mostly in such women's periodicals as *La Mujer Mexicana* and advocated a secular, vocational, and academic education for all classes of Mexican women. The majority of women who allied themselves with feminist writings and other feminists were well educated, working in white-collar jobs, and thus concerned with the social and economic problems throughout Mexico.[15]

During the first two decades of the twentieth century, Mexican women were involved in the Mexican Revolution in several capacities as soldaderas and as participants in the organizations and groups that opposed the Porfiriato (regime of Porfirio Díaz). Individual women participated in such organizations as the Partido Liberal Mexicano, "Ponciano Arriaga" Confederation of Liberal Clubs, and, of course, the Zapatistas. These organizations were clearly those supportive of Madero's democratic ideals, or committed to the overthrow of the Porfiriato. Additionally, women formed their own feminist organizations. Between 1900 and 1920, women in and around Mexico City and in the state of Yucatán organized Amigas del Pueblo, Hijas de Cuauhtemoc, Sociedad Protectora de la Mujer, and the Ligas de Orientación Femenina, among many other groups.[16]

The situation in Yucatán was most interesting because of the unique combination of leadership and ideology that existed there during the military governorship of Salvador Alvarado. According

to Macias, General Alvarado "alone among his revolutionary colleagues, viewed the struggle for woman's emancipation as integral
to aiding the weak and oppressed."[17] Alvarado not only implemented social reforms for women but encouraged women to
organize and to develop a feminist consciousness. As a result of
these efforts on the part of Governor Alvarado, the state of Yucatán
has the distinction of holding the first feminist congress in all of
Mexico in 1916, although an article in *fem* mentions a conference in
1915, El Primer Congreso Feminista Nacional.[18] Nevertheless, the
Primer Congreso Feminista de Yucatán was a very important event
because: (1) It was the first of its kind; (2) it was organized primarily
by women; (3) it was well attended; (4) it articulated some of the
most important concerns for women at that time; and (5) it proposed suffrage for women over 21 in local elections. General Alvarado, not quite satisfied, called a second feminist congress for the
end of the year, 1916. His purposes for this included the fact that he
wanted support for his gubernatorial candidacy in the first elections
to be held in Yucatán. Thus, he encouraged resolutions endorsing
women's suffrage at least at the local level, a position urged by the
most radical of the delegates. Although the results were negative,
feminist activities in Yucatán set the stage for further action there
under the leadership of Felipe Carillo Puerto, first governor-elect,
and the Yucatecan Socialist party.[19]

The second period in Yucatecan feminism merits some discussion
because it supports one of the central hypotheses of this chapter,
that Mexican women have sought reforms generally similar to those
desired by other feminist women in other nations and at similar
times although with varying results. Macias describes events at the
conference in Mexico City held by the Mexican Branch of the Pan
American League for the Elevation of Women, May 1923. Apparently, Carillo Puerto's radical feminist ideas were shared by the
feminist organizations and their participants in Yucatán because at
the conference they advocated discussion of "such controversial
issues as female sexuality, birth control, 'free love,' and sex education in the public schools."[20] These views seem not to have been
shared by the majority of feminists throughout Mexico since most of
the arguments of the Yucatecan radical socialist feminists were
rejected. Instead, other positions were supported, including wom-
en's suffrage in Mexico.

The uneven results of the efforts of Yucatecan feminists lead us to
conclude that Mexican women, particularly the middle-class supporters of the new government in power, were not ready for socialist
feminism. Whether this was right or wrong, beneficial or harmful, is

certainly interesting and debatable, but it is not the subject of this study. Rather, it is important to note that radical feminist ideas, radical for that era as well as the modern era, were advocated by at least some women, and some limited results were achieved. Macias appropriately notes all of the contradictions present in Mexican society during the 1920s, many of which continue to confront feminists as they continue their efforts for reform.

During the next decade, feminist organizing continued as women attempted to reform more aspects of Mexico's social and legal structure. Perhaps the most important of these organizations was El Frente Único Pro Derechos de la Mujer (FUPDM, Unique Front for the Rights of Women). Writing in *fem*, E. Tunón considers FUPDM the single most important experience in feminist struggle and organizing in the history of women in Mexico[21] despite the fact that FUPDM, although it was the most forceful and almost successful advocate for women's suffrage, was not able to secure that suffrage by 1940. What is especially interesting about FUPDM is that it was able to unify women throughout Mexico and represent a wide spectrum of "feminist" positions. At its zenith, FUPDM included 50,000 women representing about 25 organizations from all over Mexico.

One of the most interesting of the Mexican feminist organizations was the República Femenina, by far the most visionary of the groups. La República Femenina recognized that the elimination of oppression for the working class would not bring liberation for women nor could women's liberation only be achieved after the liberation of workers. This group also recognized the limitations of seeking the right to vote as the sole effort of FUPDM. Concha Michel stated that "the problem for women is not solely one of class: with the working class, we women have cause in common and a different cause. The common cause is that the majority of women live exploited by the capitalists, and the different cause is [the need for] the reconquest of our autonomy in relationship with the social responsibility we have as mothers or as producers of the human species."[22] For República Femenina, at least, the contradictions in Mexican society described by Macias were contradictions in the structure of capitalism and not in the causes espoused by women of different classes. Tuñon concludes that FUPDM actually failed in its mission of espousing women's rights and the right to vote not because of those contradictions, but because FUPDM was coopted by becoming a part of the newly formed official government party, the Partido Revolucionario Mexicano (PRM), previously the Partido Nacional Revolucionario (PNR) and precursor to the contemporary Partido Revolucionario Institucional (PRI).[23]

Perhaps it is this final situation that accounts for the paucity of
feminist organizations and advocacy groups during the next three
decades—that women were lulled into thinking that they could
better achieve their ends by working through the feminine auxil-
iaries of the established political parties. By the time the right to
vote in national elections was granted to women in Mexico, the
FUPDM, the República Femenina, its leaders, and all of their efforts
toward that end were all but forgotten. From the evidence presented
by Macias and Rascón, one can conclude that women were denied
the right to vote not because they were conservative, as many people
claimed, but because the male power-holders were afraid that they
might be too radical.

Thus by the1970s, what was in place were the women's branches
of the major parties. For PRI, there was the ANFER, Asociación
Nacional Femenil Revolucionaria, and other parties either professed to integrate women into their ranks or had a similar *grupo
femenil* (women's group).[24] The 1970s, however, was a period of
intense organizing of women's groups separate from the groups that
to date had achieved few changes from the early postrevolutionary
years. Many groups formed that focused on specific "women's"
issues, organized women exclusively, and involved themselves in
the politics of the Left. By the 1980s, some of the major organizations included the Coalición de Mujeres Feministas, Nueva Cultura
Feminista, Centro de Promoción de Mujeres en América Latina,
Centro de Orientación de la Mujer Obrera, Centro de Apoyo a Mujeres Violadas (rape), Unión de Mujeres, Lucha Feminista, and
many more. Organizing was done in the major cities and in the
countryside, in the ejidos and in the industries where women
were employed. Conferences were called in many areas and for a
multitude of reasons. On the border where *las maquiladoras* with its
predominantly female workforce are located, women organized the
Colectivo de Mujeres Xochiquetzal in Tijuana and sponsored the
Primer Encuentro Sobre la Identidad de la Mujer (First Encounter
on the Identity of the Woman). Similar activites occurred throughout the border cities of Ciudad Juarez, Matamoros, Mexicali, and
others.

The issues with which these organizations concern themselves
bear much similarity to the concerns of the 1920s and 1930s, with
the sole exception of the right to vote and equal rights to the land. Of
the nine (or so) points contained in the program of the FUPDM in
1935,[25] only the right to vote and run for office and the right to own
land were a reality by the 1970s, while the other seven points continued to be very important to women. One point in the program

was the juridical equality of women; three items were concerned with working conditions; and the remaining three included protection of children, cultural programs for women, and the incorporation of indigenous women in the social-political life of the nation.[26] The last statement sounds very much like lines in Echeverría's speech at IWY, and it is echoed in the name of the PRONAM, Programa Nacional para la Incorporación de la Mujer al Desarrollo (development). After 30 years, many of the major concerns of women have yet to be addressed in a meaningful way, and two new items have been added, the decriminalization of abortion and reform on laws involving rape (violación). These are not all that new, since they were issues raised in the internal debates of all of the women's organizations, past and present, already discussed, but they have taken on a new urgency in this decade.

In a series of interviews in 1981, *fem* asked each of the major political parties in Mexico several questions about that party's stand on "women's" issues. PRI focuses on "integration" of women and their issues into the party both through the three sectors—peasants, workers, and popular sector—and through ANFER. The role of women is seen more as a problem of management than one of meeting anyone's needs. Women seem to gain recognition only as a part of someone else, as mothers, daughters, or wives.[27] The PRI official line on abortion was evident when, in 1979 and again in 1982, the national Cámara de Diputados (Chamber of Deputies) refused to decriminalize abortion.[28] PAN, Partido Acción Nacional, is even more unresponsive to the concerns of the women's groups, arguing instead that PAN considers women as equal to men and an integral part of the party. However, this is dependent upon women fulfilling their role as mothers. On the question of abortion, PAN advocated pro-life legislation during the 1979 effort by the Partido Comunista Mexicano to decriminalize abortion in the National Congress.[29]

The parties of the Left do not have a much better record than PRI and PAN on responding to the concerns of feminist organizations. The PCM (Partido Comunista Mexicano), for example, introduced legislation into the Cámara de Diputados in 1979 to decriminalize abortion; but this came after much internal struggle, with many PCM members voting against the resolution.[30] The PST (Partido Socialista de los Trabajadores) offers a very confusing scenario, proposing on the one hand that "the specific role of woman in society is to be a mother," and, on the other, claiming that this is due to the exploitation of society. Further, the PST does not support the decriminalization of abortion because the issue tends to be divisive.[31] Finally, a PST female member spoke against feminism, arguing that "it is a current created by imperialism itself to distract women from the main battle."[32] One other party, the PDM (Partido Demócrata Mexicano) was equally out of tune with women and their concerns. The PDM seems most concerned with the role of women as housewives. Two other parties did seem to hold positions more in proper alignment with feminist organization positions, the PPS (Partido Popular Socialista) and the PRT (Partido Revolucionario de los Trabajadores). However, this discussion of the positions of the political parties must be analyzed in the context of Mexican politics, where the PRI has virtual control over the presidency, the Chamber of Deputies, and the government bureaucracy overall. The fact that several of the "leftist"organizations supported some of the issues as defined by feminist organizations means very little in terms of public policy implementation.

Three Major Issues

The preceding discussion introduced the three major issues that seem to dominate the writings by advocates of women's rights: juridical equality of women with men, decriminalization (despenalización) of abortion, and reform of the rape (violación) laws. At a unification conference held in August 1981, the delegates representing the Partido Comunista Mexicano, Partido Mexicano de los Trabajadores, Partido Socialista Revolucionario, Movimiento de Acción y Unidad Socialista, and Partido del Pueblo Mexicano attempted to unify the several parties of the Left on women's issues. The result was a platform that called for the following:

1. The renewal of improved social conditions and passage of legislation necessary to guarantee the juridical equality of women. . . .;
2. The decriminalization of abortion with the provision of free medical care by the State; forbid employers to ask for proof of non-pregnancy for employment . . .;
3. Equality of women with men in rights to the land, and to organize into syndicates (unions); and
4. Creation of day care centers, nurseries, public restaurants, public laundries, and other services which help liberate women from domestic work.[33]

In this platform, we see two other issues raised, concern over specific requirements for employment and an interest in the establishment of systems that will assist women in holding jobs. This platform very appropriately sets forth the major concerns of women's groups, along with those already specified, which merit further discussion.

The issue of women's juridical equality with men is quite confusing in Mexico. On the one hand there is the 1975 law that recognizes, but does not guarantee the juridical equality of men and women.[34] On the other hand, there are the constant concerns of feminist writers and male "feminist" writers that women are not in fact equal to men in Mexican society. Carlos Monsivais argues that women occupy a worse situation than second-class citizenship and that they actually constitute a nation outside of the Mexican nation.[35] This seems an interesting metaphor, but does not reflect the fact that women are very much a part of the Mexican nation, but a part that must be controlled in order to maintain the patriarchal social order. In this somewhat contradictory situation, the only conclusion one can come to is that there is a huge gap between what is legal and what is the reality of life. However, this concern for equal rights is not an uncommon one in other countries. Mexico is not so different from the U.S.A. in its refusal to guarantee equal rights to women in any specific manner that can be enforced.

Perhaps the most extensive and important issues directly related to equal rights for women are those relating to their role as workers outside the home. As long as equal rights are not guaranteed, women will have to deal with gender discrimination and sexual harassment as an individual matter and with a case-by-case approach. Yet it is precisely in her role as a worker, *trabajadora*, that the Mexican woman faces sex discrimination, sexual harassment, conditions not conducive to her good health, and conditions of work incompatible with a family life. First, it should be noted that most of the women who work outside the home work in factories and they earn considerably less than their male counterparts. In interviews, it was learned that, understandably, women were very concerned with earning higher salaries, having collective bargaining through the *sindicatos* (unions), less hours per work shift, better work conditions on the site, job-related health problems, and lastly, an interest in on-site day care centers, *guarderias*.[36] There are many rules, which vary from industry to industry, but taken together they constitute sexual discrimination. For example, a woman is often disqualified for work if she is pregnant. Women are black-listed for a multitude of reasons, including participation in syndicates (unions). Then they must deal with their own personal feelings about working outside the home. Women workers are often convinced that they should be at home in order to be good wives and good mothers. Yet the reality of the situation is that they have no other choice. They must work in order to survive.

The case of Mexican women working in *las maquiladoras* serves to illustrate the points of discussion. In the *maquiladoras*, factories that constitute the Border Industrialization Program (BIP) in the cities of Mexicali, San Luis, Nogales, Agua Prieta, and Ciudad Juarez, women are well represented. Figures range from 70 percent on the average up to 90 percent in some industries. These women workers are also very young, 16 to 26 years old, fairly well educated, and either the sole supporters or important contributors to the support of the family. They are evenly divided between single and married status. They earn slightly better wages than other industries, and they experience lower unemployment rates.[37] Still, because this is a specific program where the companies are owned by the United States and decisions are made outside of Mexico, the industries and thus the workers are always in a tenuous situation. If capital decides to relocate, there is a high unemployment rate. If the governments decide to cancel the international agreements that allow the *maquiladoras* to exist, workers will lose their jobs completely. Decisions that are oppressive to workers are made in the U.S. Conditions such as the requirement of pregnancy testing, which are not usually tolerated in the U.S., are tolerated in Mexico. Wages are much lower than minimum wages just across the border. This situation illustrates the point that the BIP companies are exploiting Mexican female workers to a far greater degree in Mexico than they could do if they operated in the United States. This is indeed an irony, since the United States is considered to be much more advanced in its legal and social liberation of women than Mexico.

The issue of abortion is as difficult to unravel as the issue of juridical equality, since there are some sections of the Constitution and the Penal Code that seem to allow women control over their own bodies. The reforms of 1975 also include a statement that recognized the right of individuals to control family size and spacing. Yet Luisa María Leal, writing on abortion, argues that the Penal Codes of the states and the Federal District have not changed since 1931 on the issue of abortion, and these codes clearly render abortion, for any reason, a criminal act.[38] One problem appears to be that women cannot obtain an abortion on demand but that they must obtain permission for it. It is this permission that is nearly impossible to obtain, and there is no protection from prosecution for doctors who perform abortions without that official permission nor for the women who receive them. Therefore, only women who can pay for medical care and permission have access to abortion. Clandestine abortions continue to be extremely dangerous and contribute to a higher mortality rate among women of child-bearing age. Ana Laura Nettel cites figures of actual abortions performed ranging anywhere from 600,000 to 800,000 per year, with a mortality of 50,000 women per year directly related to abortions performed under poor medical conditions.[39] This is the issue that unites almost all women's and feminist groups. What women's groups appear to be advocating, at the very least, is a situation similar to that which exists in the USA as a result of *Roe* v. *Wade*, the 1974 U.S. Supreme Court decision that found that the states could not deny women abortion on demand in the first trimester (first three months) of pregnancy. Of course, it should be recognized that there is a very strong possibility that abortion on demand may once again be outlawed in the U.S., since it has never actually been written into the law. Rather, it has existed as law because of a court decision. There is little evidence that the U.S. would pass laws any different from the situation in Mexico in a male-dominated administration. As of this writing, all attempts to decriminalize abortion in Mexico have failed, but feminist and other women's groups continue to advocate this as one of their main concerns.

A different but related issue is that of the manner in which the state handles rape cases. This issue is important simply because of the manner in which rape and rape laws tend to victimize women. Additionally, there is concern with the fact that women cannot obtain permission to receive abortions in case of pregnancy resulting from rape. This is another issue over which women have successfully organized for reform advocacy. There are several dimensions to this problem. First there is the sheer size of the problem. Centro de Apoyo a Mujeres Violadas (COMVAC), the most important organization in the area of dealing with rape victims, reported that there are about 100,000 cases annually of reported rape, 10 percent of which occur in the Federal District. Contrary to any popular notion that rape laws favor women, COMVAC notes that for every 100 rapes reported, 25 come to trial, 5 actually serve their sentence, and not a single case served more than one year.[40] There is also concern by women over what rape represents and why it is treated so lightly by the judicial system. To women, rape represents control over their body by a male; it represents power over them. Fear of rape keeps women imprisoned and victimized. It renders them nonpersons, simply physical entities—bodies. When the very system that is supposed to protect women appears to side with the perpetrator of violence, it is a signal to women that the society does not value them as much as it values a male, any male, even a criminal male. Thus, as in the United States, women are agitating for reform of the penal codes applicable to rape. There is a very long way to go, as COM-VAC's Beatriz Saucedo explains, because the entire Mexican social and political system is pervaded by the ideology that offers a woman validity only when she is someone else's property.[41]

Conclusions

The original hypothesis that women in Mexico have pursued changes in their political, social, and economic structure, and that these changes have been in line with the many reforms sought by feminist women in other nations, is certainly plausible in light of all the historical and contemporary evidence presented. Mexican women have been their own strongest advocates, but they have not always achieved that for which they have struggled. Many times it has seemed that they were only able to win concessions from the male power-holders when there was a male who could also advocate their cause, as was the case with the military governor of Yucatán, Alvarado, and his elected successor, Governor Felipe Carillo Puerto. Yet, when President Lazaro Cárdenas advocated, in 1938, before the Chamber of Deputies that women should have the right to vote, success did not follow. The women, having been all but guaranteed the right to vote since they had the support of the president, were betrayed at the last moment and forced to wait more than ten years for their suffrage. Perhaps this was because Cárdenas did not advocate ardently enough, or perhaps he did not have a strong following on the issues. Altogether, most results of women's advocacy have been uneven, and women in Mexico find themselves constantly having to renew their struggles for causes that have long been of interest to women's advocates in Mexico. Although class divisions have been a serious problem, they do not appear to be as strong an impediment to change as a patriarchal political structure. Perhaps it is the interstice of these two situations, class and gender oppression, that has made it so difficult for Mexican women to make even the smallest gains.

How then can we access the role of the IWY in bringing about change for women in Mexico? From the preceding argument, it is evident that the most important impact of IWY was not directly upon the Mexican political system. Rather, the important result of

IWY is that it contributed to the development and politicization of the women themselves. IWY encouraged women to organize as women, to develop a feminist perspective, and to advocate for issues that had been too conveniently forgotten. Mexican women were again able, after several decades, to proclaim themselves feminists. They were able to begin developing the structures that would ensure that their efforts of the 1960s and 1970s would not be forgotten and ignored as were the groups involved in the FUPDM of the 1930s, the efforts of the Yucatecan feminists in the 1920s, and the female supporters of the Mexican Revolution. At this point in time, Mexican women are in a better position for effecting reform than they have been since the 1920s because they have so many independent organizations in place. They continue to face the immense problems of the Mexican nation. There is, however, no evidence to support the notion that women will be better off once the entire nation improves its socioeconomic condition. The evidence is quite the contrary, since Mexico's leaders have advocated that position since the years of the Porfiriato at the very least. Although at times the socioeconomic climate has improved, there has been no commensurate improvement in the conditions for women. Women, therefore, will need to advocate the resolution of the questions of their own liberation if there is to be that reform. If not, then they are going to have to wait many more decades before the Mexican nation is in a healthy state, and much more than strong advocacy by women's groups will be needed to bring any degree of prosperity. Since socioeconomic power appears to be firmly fixed in the hands of the male power-holders of Mexico, it is highly unlikely that anything short of a complete overhaul of that system will significantly improve Mexico's economic status and thus the quality of life for the majority of its residents.

Perhaps what Mexico needs is to sponsor another International Women's Year very soon as a means of forcing Mexico's president and other members of the PRI and the government to deal with the issues raised by the women. Another IWY could also serve to raise the level of consciousness of people in the U.S. on the role and status of women in Mexico. IWY can also serve to highlight the international aspects of the problems of Mexican women as workers in the *maquiladoras* and other industries in the border towns. The importance of women in the border areas of Mexico cannot be ignored, for there they are not only the major wage-earning group, but they are also developing strong feminist and workers' organizations which have close ties with their counterparts in the U.S. An IWY hosted by the border city of Tijuana or Ciudad Juarez would certainly be a major step in the future empowerment of Mexican women as they learn the lessons that women all over the world are learning, that positive change for women will only come when the women organize themselves, advocate for themselves, and gain decision-making power.

This research was made possible by an Inter-campus Travel Research Grant from the Committee on Research, University of California, Davis, CA. Special thanks go to the editors of this current volume, to Amelia Malagamba, and to the entire staff of the Centro Fronterizo del Norte de Mexico, CEFNOMEX, Tijuana, Baja California, Mexico.

NOTES

1. *Action Survey of IWY, Part I* (New York: UNIFO Publishers, 1976), 9.

2. Ibid., 43.

3. See article by Adaljiza Sosa Riddell, "Female Political Elites in Mexico: 1974," in Lynne B. Iglitzin and Ruth Ross, eds., *Women in the World* (Santa Barbara, CA: ABC-Clio, 1976), 257.

4. Ibid., 257–258.

5. Anna Macias, *Against All Odds* (Westport, CT: Greenwood Press, 1982). In a chapter entitled "The Roots of Feminism in Mexico," Macias discusses the dealings of Mexican "Liberals" with the educational system as early as the 1850s, when the goal was to promote public coed education. Two chapters of this work deal extensively with Mexican women in the Revolution and women's organizing in the state of Yucatán. The final bibliographic essay, pp. 159–181, provides a useful guide to both general works on Mexico and works on Mexican women in relationship to specific time periods.

6. *Agenda Estadistica, 1983* (Mexico City: Secretaria de Programacion y Presupuesto, Instituto Nacional de Estadistica, Geografia, e Informative, 1984), 6.

7. Ibid., 7.

8. M. Teresita de Barbieri, "Politicas de poblacion y la mujer. Antecedentes para su estudio," *Revista Mexicana de Sociologia* 45:1 (January–March 1983), 293–388, 293.

9. Ibid., 296.

10. Ibid.

11. Ignacio Ramirez, "Plan para otorgar a la mujer autentica condicion de ser humano," *Proceso* 301 (August 1982), 18–21, 18.

12. Ibid., 19.

13. Ibid., 18.

14. Feminine and feminist organizations are distinguished from one another in that a *feminine* organization has all female membership but

does not necessarily advocate for "women's" issues. *Feminist* groups have all female membership *and* advocate for women's issues. In this paper, the majority of groups discussed are feminist, but they are often mixed in their major concerns. There is no attempt to judge organizations according to their degree of "feminism."

15. Macias, 12–13.

16. Ibid., 25–49.

17. Ibid., 66.

18. Anonymous editorial, *fem* 8:30 (October–November 1983), 2–4.

19. Macias, 76–80. This paragraph briefly summarizes many important events described very well by Macias. My intent here is to support my hypothesis that any reforms from women in Mexico came about as a result of their own activism rather than because the men in power granted them those rights.

20. Ibid., 97.

21. Esperanza Tuñon, "El Frente Unico Pro Derechos de la Mujer, 1935-1938," *fem* 8:30 (October–November 1983), 19–23, 19.

22. Ibid., 21 (my own translation).

23. Ibid., 23 (my own translation).

24. *Feminil* is defined in Spanish as feminine or womanly, while *feminista* is defined as feminist. The terms selected for use by the political parties appropriately reflect the attitude of the patriarchal leadership within the parties that feminine is fine, but feminist is threatening.

25. Elena Urrutia, *Imagen y realidad de la mujer* (Mexico City: SEP Diana, Secretaria de Educacion Publica, 1979), from an article by María Antonieta Rascón.

26. Ibid.

27. "PRI-Patriarcado politico e integración femenina," *fem* 5:19 (June–July 1981), 19–23.

28. "El Consejo de Población Presenta el Plan que el PRI Rechazo al PCM," *Proceso* 290 (May 24, 1982), 6–10, 7.

29. "PAN," *fem* 5:19 (June–July 1981), 14–15.

30. "Arnoldo Martinez Verdugo aclara la relación del feminismo con la izquierda," *fem* 5:19 (June–July 1981), 10–12.

31. "Organización partidaria y federacion de mujeres, doble tarea para los militantes del PST," *fem* 5:19 (June–July 1981), 10–12.

32. "El feminismo y la revolución permanente," *fem* 5:19 (June–July 1981), 33–35. See also other articles in this issue of *fem*, 22–27, 37–38.

33. Marta Acevedo, "El Partido Socialista Unificado Mexicano y las mujeres," *fem* 5:21 (February–March 1982), 86.

34. Luisa María Leal, *El problema del aborto en Mexico* (Mexico City: Miguel Angel Porrua, 1980), 162.

35. Carlos Monsivais, "Notas sobre el estado, la cultura naciónal, y las culturas populares en Mexico," *Cuadernos Politicos* 30 (October–December 1981), 33–43, 38.

36. Interview with Norma Iglesias, investigadora de **CEFNOMEX**, August 1984.

37. Mitchell Seligson and Edward J. Williams, *Maquiladoras and Migration Workers in the Mexico-United States Border Industrialization Program* (Austin: University of Texas Press, 1981), 28. Also, see Centro de Orientacion de la Mujer Obrera, *Primer taller de analisis sobre aprendizaje en la produccion y transferencia de tecnologia en la industria de maquila de exportacion* (Juarez: Centro de Estudios Fronterizos del Norte de Mexico, 1982).

38. Luisa María Leal, xiii.

39. Laura Ana Nettel, "Aborto procurado y aborto consentido: analisis constitucional," *UAM-Azcapotzalco* 3:5 (January–April 1982), 187–191, 191.

40. Barbara Garcia, *Critica Politica* 5 (June 1–15, 1980), 12.

41. Ramon Marquez, *Uno Mas Uno* (May 5, 1984), from an interview with Beatriz Saucedo.

14

Women, the Family, and the State: Hong Kong, Taiwan, Singapore—Newly Industrialized Countries in Asia

Janet W. Salaff
University of Toronto

Hong Kong, Singapore, and Taiwan have since the early 1970s entered the ranks of the "newly industrialized countries,"[1] based on export-led manufacturing, in which women play key roles. Their successes are most impressive in an era when many Third World nations are, in contrast, suffering from a relative or even actual decline in their living standard compared with the developed nations.[2] This accomplishment warrants a closer look at the factors contributing to the industrialization of these three countries. They are grouped here because they bear many geopolitical and programmatic features in common. From them we can learn about one set of development strategies, and how these have incorporated women into the new economy, polity, and society.

This chapter will discuss the place of Chinese women in these three countries. The Chinese comprise 98 percent of the populations of Hong Kong and Taiwan, and 76 percent in Singapore, and so we are discussing the majority population. The three areas differ in size. Hong Kong and Singapore are city-states, with over 5 and nearly 3 million people, respectively, while Taiwan, a province of China, with nearly 19 million people, is "country" size, and has a sizable rural sector. However, all three areas suffer from limited natural resources and small populations. Half of Taiwan's 36,000 square kilometers is mountainous, and only one-quarter of the land is cultivated. To solve their developmental limitations, all three areas turned to foreign trade in their industrialization programs. Hong Kong was the earliest; Taiwan, and then Singapore followed to promote export-oriented industrialization.

They are similar in the magnitude of their economic change: All experienced an annual rate of 10 percent growth in their gross domestic products (GDP) during much of the 1960s and 1970s. Industry's share in the GDP ranged from 31 to 45 percent in the three countries in 1977, and the share of manufacturing exceeds 25 percent.[3] Manufacturing is an important asset, then, and women are central in that part of the labor force that manufactures for export. After the developmental strategy of export-related manufacturing was adopted, the proportion of women in the registered labor force grew rapidly. From 21 percent of the registered labor force in Hong Kong in 1931, 19 percent in Taiwan in 1956, and 18 percent in Singapore in 1957, women comprised around 34 percent of the labor force in each of the three countries in the 1970s. Approximately 47 percent of women in these countries now work for a wage full time.[4]

The constraints of the world capitalist economy shape the relationships among the state, economy, and society in each area. All three have strong, authoritarian states whose elites have engineered the labor force to supply relatively well educated and skilled, but low-paid labor, much of it female, to far-flung world markets. Within each nation, state social policies draw the populace deeper into the commodity economy. Yet all three exclude basic social insurance provisions, thereby subjecting families, newly dependent on selling their labor to the world market and buying goods with their wages, to extreme uncertainty. The outcome, as I detail it in this chapter, is a so-called family strategy, with families turning to their own means to ensure survival. Thus, state development strategies and the families' responses to them as they bear upon women are similar in the three countries, and form the topic of this chapter.

State Strategies in Promoting Export-led Industrialization

Three main sets of political strategies are common to the export-led industrialization programs of Hong Kong, Taiwan, and Singapore.

They first created a climate of political stability, based on insulating the state from competing claims of class politics.[5] The interests and ideologies of state elites consequently play a determining role in shaping possible investment strategies. In all three areas technocratic developmental views prevail. Women play little part in policy making as individuals or interest groups. This leads to their exploitation in the economic and social spheres.

Also important is the establishment of an economic infrastructure conducive to investment, and appropriate responses by elites to political-economic turning points. The governments perform the key functions required for investment: provision of low-cost loans, credit, encouragement of new markets, labor force training, among others. These economic institutions are often lacking in new nations. In establishing their industrial frameworks, the three countries put into place an economy that draws on female wage labor.

Finally, the countries provide quality labor force participation through policies that make it impossible for families to continue to perform many quasi-economic activities families may once have performed outside the money economy. Public policies further induct family members into the market to earn wages to meet old and new needs. And among the members that go out to work are young women. I turn now to the three sets of political strategies in each of the countries.

Hong Kong

Hong Kong is a colony of Britain with a highly centralized administrative machinery. Fundamental policies are formulated in London, which appoints the colonial administration, headed by the governor, who in turn chooses his advisors from men of industry and finance in Hong Kong. Local Chinese, until now barred from holding central office, have access solely to advisory channels to influence politics. Or, they become elected urban concillors, popularly referred to as the "garbage council," which oversee some urban services, half of whose 24 members are elected. Here one finds some women leaders.[6] The relatively passive indirect rule permits the Chinese to engage in economic activities, but not political activities that address political boundaries.[7] Top-down, essentially nonparticipatory rule remains in force.

Constrained by its colonial status, Hong Kong's geographical limitations, no natural resources, and an ambiguous, quasidependent political relationship with China, the authorities evolved a

laissez-faire approach to the economy. The public tenets of state
rule are: to encourage economic growth, to reflect agreed-upon
government policies, and to "rule in the interest of the people."

Undergirding laissez-faire market policies, the government provides a stable framework of laws, political controls, and fiscal and
public expenditure practices. Even corruption leads to dependable
outcomes for investors, e.g., cutting red tape. Municipal services are
competently performed. Employers can count on economic policy
outcomes: They know what to expect.[8]

Lacking universal franchise, the state is insulated from competing economic parties. Moreover, trade unionism is weak. About a
quarter of the labor force is unionized, but youths in general and the
light industrial manufacturing section where women predominate
are especially underrepresented. Strikes have varied over the years,
but they usually are of short duration. Among the causes of trade
union weakness is the government's disinterest in supporting
strong workers' groups. But even organized bodies have become de
facto voluntary welfare organizations, and an insignificant force in
industrial relations.[9]

Young adults claim to abhor politics due largely to a sense of
political powerlessness. They turn instead to individualistic material goals. Women, who elsewhere in the region are quite active in
the community, are uninvolved in Hong Kong.[10]

Government policies do not overtly control the economy. One
finds no five-year plans, state direct investment, minimum wage,
protection of local cottage industries, rent controls over commercial property, tax holidays, or investment allowances. The state
employs only 8 percent of the labor force. Nevertheless, there is no
institutional vacuum in the economy. Banks and experienced trading companies play the crucial institutional role in stimulating
local manufacturing, purchasing and providing specifications,
guaranteeing loans, and supplying credit and raw materials.
Moreover, although no protection of indigenous firms is practiced,
established industrialists enjoyed a protected period in China prior
to 1949, when they obtained knowhow, a market, connections, and
capital.[11]

The state's role is nonetheless significant, starting with the re-
clamation of land and control of the land market. When Hong Kong
experienced competition from other low-wage nations in the 1970s,
the administration helped industry upgrade quality and obtain new
markets. It selectively sold land to capital-intensive industry, such
as the Dow petrochemical plant, although previously it was unwill-

ing to court particular industrial sectors. It has established the statutory Vocational Training Centre to assist manpower training.

The Hong Kong state responds quickly to external shocks, which provides flexibility to its development strategies. After the 1949 Chinese revolution, the economic structure shifted from early economic ventures tied to shipping and the "entrepôt" economy, which had little place for women. In an *entrepôt*, goods from the place of origin are reshipped to their market. Hong Kong became instead an economy based on export-dominated manufacturing, which rests on low-cost labor, essentially of unmarried women. From 10 percent of all exports in 1947, locally manufactured exports soared to 70 percent in 1959. Transnational corporations became significant in key sectors of the economy in the 1960s, but local firms still dominate. With increased Third World competition, Hong Kong capitalists upgraded their products from transistor radio assembly to digital watches and to electronic circuits. Tourism and China entrepot trade regained importance in the late 1970s. Manufacturing, 40 percent of the labor force in 1966 and 50 percent in 1971, dropped to 33 percent in 1981. Women are so far underrepresented in such tertiary industries. But now that their part of the economy has been established, they may be able to sustain a high level of labor force participation despite the changing economic profile.

Public policies that create a quality labor force start with immigration regulation. While 57 percent of the population was born in Hong Kong, half the immigrants came from cities and towns in China; and even peasants from the Pearl River delta had long contact with commercial agriculture. Shanghai migrants were especially accustomed to cutthroat economic competition. Thus, the immigrant culture suited local industry.[12] It is further widely believed that manufacturers today convey their need for inexpensive labor to the government. Thus, at a time when Hong Kong women had had a low birthrate for years, and wages were high, the 1979 influx of boat people into the labor force dampened real manufacturing wage increases.[13]

Health care through government hospitals and outpatient dispensaries is low-cost, and basic care is adequate. The death rate is 5 per 1,000 people. Women and men expected to live 74 and 68 years, respectively (at birth) in 1973. Family-planning workers are active and reach all women. The crude birthrate dropped from 20 to 17 per 1,000 people in the decade before 1983. The age of marriage has risen, enabling women to receive more education and to work for a substantial period before marriage.

Full primary school education was guaranteed by the late 1960s, and three years of secondary education provided free in the late 1970s. Sixty-one percent of youths aged 16 and 17 continue at their families' cost, reflecting the necessity to develop marketable skills in Hong Kong's competitive economy. Girls attended nearly as long as boys. Most youths (89 percent) study in secondary schools where English is used, in response to the international nature of the Hong Kong economy. The government funds polytechnical institutes to upgrade technical skills, but limits college enrollment to about 5 percent of the age group in order to retain a technically skilled labor force. The government regulates hours of work, and provides some recreational facilities, but gives no minimum wage or unemployment insurance. It furnishes a modicum of public assistance to the needy, but the able-bodied are ineligible, and are forced to turn to kin, or must accept any work they find. In this way, shifts in demand for labor greatly affect people's lives.

The Hong Kong government carries out one of the largest resettlement and low-rent housing programs in the world. It dominates the housing market. Small, high-rise public housing apartments were home to 40 percent of the populace in 1979. Rents are low, though they provide only minute spaces. This large-scale housing program in "housing estates," or complexes, affects labor supply. Small factories and workshops obtain premises on the estates. Busses conduct the workforce to nearby factory districts. Women are likely to work near their homes, and local factories can draw on women as a labor source. Public housing also subsidizes low wages. Most important, squatters pay nothing for housing, but high-rise dwellers pay rent and utilities. Further, squatters engage in social exchange, but this declines greatly in the high-rise, where people are socially distant. Nor can they conduct subsistence economies in the high-rise as easily as they can in a squatter settlement. Resettlement thus places families in industrial time and space and propels them into the wage economy for their needs.[14]

The government does not enforce controls over wages and incomes, but the net effect of government spending is redistributive. Full employment exists, and the social services such as housing improve the living standards of the poorest sectors. Thus, it has been estimated that real wages increased by two-thirds in the 16 years up to 1978.[15]

Taiwan

Like Hong Kong, Taiwan is part of China, with an ambiguous political status. It is an island located off the southeastern coast of China mainland. The government has actively sought to build up the Taiwanese economy, and has turned to export-oriented manufacturing as the means to do so.

The "Nationalist" Kuomintang (KMT) party of Taiwan is also insulated from local social groups. Following defeat of its party and army in the Chinese civil war in 1949, the KMT regime fled to the island of Formosa, where they took over ex-colonial Japanese properties, and the assets of the modern sector. "Mainlanders," approximately 15 percent of the population, monopolize high political posts, and dominate the mighty military machine, excluding "local" Taiwanese from leadership posts. Considerable aid from the United States through 1965 enabled the KMT to maintain its huge government bureaucracy, and one of the highest soldier/civilian ratios in the world. Government consumed 31 percent of Taiwan's Gross National Product (GNP) in 1954, 25 percent in 1973, and 25 percent in 1983. Defense spending exceeds 10 percent of the GNP, and 8 percent of the population is in the armed forces. Control over funds and manpower, a measure of state power, insulates it from local groups. Leftists and nationalists have been kept out of politics due to the perpetual war footing. Martial law remains in effect.[16]

Taiwan does not have a strong labor movement. Unions were moribund for years, and today factory management head the unions in many companies.[17] The KMT has used the perpetual conflict with the Chinese Communists to declare strikes and other labor actions illegal. The lack of this vital bargaining weapon and labor surplus for years prevented workers from aggressively defending themselves. There is full employment today, but labor's impact on politics remains limited.

The Constitution and Civil Laws provide equality between the sexes in the spheres of politics, education, property and some areas of family formation. But these laws are imperfectly implemented. There are three women's organizations, whose programs stress political mobilization against communism, not sexual equality. They direct their actions to promote family life and motherhood, extolled as women's service to the country. The Constitution grants women a 10 percent quota of KMT posts and legislative positions. Women exceed this proportion in lower-level elected positions to the national assembly, Legislative and Central Yuans, prefectural and city councils, but there has never been a female cabinet minister.

Surveys find women today to be nearly as interested in political issues and to vote in equal numbers with men. But only 5 percent of women engage in community volunteer work.[18] Further, the government has recently affirmed the stress on motherhood as women's best way to make a national contribution. This emphasis may reflect the restructuring process and reduction of unskilled labor in the economy, which women provided, and a concern for women to serve as an unpaid labor force to raise quality children for the new economy. Nevertheless, women have gained a place even in managerial and administrative positions over the decades, and their economic momentum is likely to continue.

The economic ideology of the KMT elite, based on Sun Yat-sen's "Three Principles of the People," combines private ownership of the means of production and central planning in an eclectic mix. In the 1950s, import substitution strategies strengthened the private sector. The role of public enterprises was reduced in the economy. Significant land reforms extended the control of the state into the countryside. Local Taiwanese capitalists benefited from these industrial strategies, and continue to dominate manufacturing. In 1960, American advisors and Taiwanese liberal technocrats obtained policy reforms that integrated Taiwan into the international world economy on the basis of its comparative advantage in low-wage labor. Local firms began to export: 93 percent of the production of firms established after 1973 was exported. Investment policies are not left to the market, in contrast to Hong Kong. Investment incentives are governed by the Statute for the Engagement of Investment. Joint ventures and local content are promoted, in contrast to Hong Kong and Singapore, where local firms do not obtain special encouragement.[19]

Land reform placed a ceiling on investment in agriculture, and since political and military careers were blocked to them, propertied rural Taiwanese entered entrepreneurial careers. They reinvest profits in enterprise and commerce, not land. Industrial activities are widespread, and there is no economic dualism. Proto-industrial activities, such as electric looms and knitting machines in country homes and shops, are common. This decentralized pattern of economic development has shifted Taiwan's economy from agriculture to light industry, and industry is not confined to metropolitan enclaves. This strategy succeeded because colonial Japan built an infrastructure of communications and education, and it was spread afterwards. The labor-intensive nature of Taiwan development made it useful to locate near rural labor sources, aided by government incentives, thereby greatly affecting rural women.[20]

The free trade zones established in 1965, in which foreign firms bring in capital and raw materials, employ Taiwanese labor, and sell finished products overseas without having to pay the usual import duties and fees, hire mostly young rural women. However, the three zones account for only 289 factories and 5 percent of the workers in manufacturing in 1975. There is much labor mobility outside the zones, and women migrate to cities and towns to work, as much as the men do.[21] And thus the zones do not dominate the industrial picture.

The "second oil crisis" of 1978 had a severe impact on the three economies; although all three recovered, world recessions bear heavily on these export-oriented economies. To protect itself against a recurrence, the government is upgrading the capital and technology components of industry. Modern industrial parks, and the "10 major construction projects" reflect this transition. The impact of the oil shock led to a drop in female employment between 1975 and 1980, but women are reentering the labor force.[22] Nevertheless, the impact of restructuring on women's labor is not yet clear.

In this closed economy, rural to urban migration is the main source of new workers. Although women were legally granted inheritance under the land reform, informally they usually acquiesce to giving their brothers their proper share.[23] Thus, women were among the earliest factory applicants, leaving their brothers home to tend the small fields.

Health standards have been improved, and the expectation of life for women and men was 73 and 68 years, respectively, in 1975 and 75 and 70, respectively, in 1982. Literacy and educational levels have risen rapidly. In 1980 nearly all children completed primary school, and most then went on to junior high school. Three-fifths of junior high graduates entered senior high school.[24] While sex differences in education were sizable in the 1960s, by 1980 girls and boys received nearly the same years of schooling. However, by senior high and tertiary levels, they specialize in different types of training; girls in teacher's education, boys in university. And within university there is also gender-linked education.[25]

The Taiwan National Family Planning Association has been active for two decades, guided at the outset by American organizations. It disseminates birth control implements free of charge in the countryside. The crude birth rate fell from 47 per 1,000 people in 1952 to 26 in 1976, and to 22 in 1982, which is still higher than the crude rates of Hong Kong and Singapore (17 in both places in 1982), partly due to the agrarian component in the population. A rising age at marriage enables married women to work for wages for a longer period. As in Hong Kong and Singapore, due to women's low wages, married women are less likely to work: Over 80 percent of married Taiwan women are not economically active.

The government places the highest priority on economic growth, not income redistribution, and taxation, which has been on sales more than on firms or incomes, is regressive. Nevertheless, the rate of growth of the economy is so rapid and sustained that it has absorbed the unemployed, although underemployment is still a problem. Employers have to compete and offer slightly higher wages and fringe benefits than in the past, and even unskilled workers' wages have risen. Economic growth is considered responsible for the increased income equality over the past decades. As rural handicrafts declined, new outlets for jobs were sought. The proportion of net rural farm income derived from nonagricultural activities increased substantially, to 53 percent in 1972, and to 61 percent in 1979. The poorest families, with the least land, felt the need to earn supplementary wages first, and this has helped equalize income overall. Women's income contribution has been substantial. Women must continue to contribute because income is still unequally distributed: the lowest 40 percent of the population obtained only 22 percent of all personal income in 1982.[26]

Singapore

Singapore is comprised of Chinese (76 percent), and Malays and Tamil Indians form the remainder of the population. The Chinese left southeastern China in the nineteenth and twentieth centuries in search of jobs and hoped for wealth. A colony of Britain from 1819 to 1959, Singapore is now an independent republic. It is situated off the Malay archipelago, and Malaysia and Indonesia are its geophysical neighbors.

Singapore also has a highly centralized state machinery insulated from competing local interests. Even less than Taiwan, and much less than Hong Kong, the state does not let market forces take their course. It intervenes to attract the type of investment it wants. The government is a multiparty system, in which a single party, the People's Action Party (PAP) has since independence been constantly returned to office, and holds all but two seats in Parliament. There is an active, if controlled, political life. Sovereign independence provides a sense of national purpose. These integrating and loyalty-generating factors are used to enforce specific controls over wages and incomes on elites and people.[27] The state is led by a highly educated, technocratic elite, which claims to represent all major interests. Labor, management, and the state participate in "tripartite" political and economic policy-making bodies. This identification in structural terms dulls class conflict, and discourages interest group politics. The party-state thus retains hegemony.

The PAP encourages union recruitment of labor, and may require companies to recognize its unions. Included here are electronics firms, in which large numbers of women are employed. Despite this, however, only one-quarter of the labor force is unionized, the same as in Hong Kong. Ninety percent of these unionized workers are affiliated with the PAP-led National Trades Union Congress, which is headed by a government minister and run by government bureaucrats. The government has ensured labor peace, few days are lost through strikes, and other labor actions have become negligible.

Women once played a larger part in politics. Active in the anticolonial political struggle, several served in Parliament after independence in 1959. The Women's Charter of 1961, a forward-looking document, provides equal pay for equal work and outlaws polygamy. However, fewer women now enter the formal political arena. For a number of years no women were fielded as PAP candidates. Indeed, PAP spokesmen proposed recently that educated women should spend more time with their families. Minister Goh Chok Tong stated in 1980, "most women will not allow the men to do the housework" and "women play a more beneficial role at home" than in office. Feminists voiced concern over such public depreciation of their place, although they cannot express their concern through interest group politics. Some women are currently standing for election and will surely try to present their views.[28]

Of the three countries discussed here, Singapore has the largest component of foreign investment. Foreign investment fills a void, because local investors had dealt mainly in real estate prior to 1959. Foreign and jointly owned firms account for 92 percent of all exports by value. The government's macroeconomic management policy encourages foreign investment through incentives and labor controls. The state commits itself to stable, corruption-free administration, and further attracts investors, even though labor costs are high for the region.[29]

Key to Singapore's development program is the extensive network of statutory boards, government enterprises, and state participation in private enterprise.[30] A substantial development budget devoted to social and economic infrastructure aids the economy. Local savings in state financial institutions such as the Post

Office Savings Banks and Central Provident Fund help finance the development program. The government is the main actor in the land market, and has earmarked half the land for development. The government also accounts for 20 percent of total employment. The tripartite National Wages Council regulates wages, and the state invests in manpower training programs to benefit private industry. These policies give Singapore a comparative advantage in export manufacturing, which this small city-state would have lacked if market forces prevailed.

Government policies shifted Singapore from an entrepôt in the 1950s, in which women played small part, to a short period of labor-intensive import substitution in the early 1960s, and then to export-oriented industrialization after 1965. Women's role in the economy grew rapidly, especially in the manufacturing sector. Workers' wages were kept low at first, but in the early 1970s, however, full employment was reached, and since 1979 wages climbed to their market levels. With the resulting wage increases, government policies shifted to promote capital-intensive activities, with manufacturing still a leading sector. Towards this end, the state restructured investment incentives and set up a new national productivity council to oversee technical and skills upgrading and increase labor productivity.[31]

Women are moving forward in the new jobs and industries, but not as quickly as men. Even so, the labor shortage and women's access to education, including technical skills, creates a demand from which women cannot be easily excluded. The need for highly skilled labor, however, appears to underlie the new policy to return educated women to their homes to raise quality children for the more sophisticated industries.

Highly selective immigration policies fill labor force gaps. In the 1970s, a shortage of skilled labor led to immigrants on work permits. Today there are still 200,000 immigrant workers, but state policy opposes long-term immigration. It aims to restructure the economy to do without guest workers.

Medical and health care services have reduced mortality and greatly improved popular health. The expectation of life was 74 for women and 69 for men in 1980. The total fertility rate for the Chinese was 6.5 between 1947 and 1957. Then, post-1959 fertility controls brought down birthrates rapidly. At first voluntary, fertility limitation policy now is stringent. In 1973, with already a crude birthrate of around 20, the govenment strove to attain replacement-level fertility. It introduced the Social Disincentives Against Higher Order Births, which penalized parents for bearing many children.[32]

Since then the crude birthrate dropped to 17 in 1982. The age of marriage has also risen, allowing women to work longer before quitting the labor force soon after marriage. There is currently a backlash, however. The state is urging educated women to resist spinsterhood (which is anyway not common) and bear more than two children, to ensure that their so-called superior stock prevails. While dictated by eugenics, this policy is also related to the drive to raise the skill level of the populace, with middle-class women an unpaid labor force to rear their children for superior roles in society. This policy has incurred the most vocal reaction of women and men of any policy in recent years.[33]

In the mid-1970s, Singapore provided universal primary school, and by the late 1970s three years of secondary school. Education for girls and boys is nearly equal. Concern with the quality of the labor force has led to testing and streaming as early as age nine. Technical training in state-run or joint institutions follows junior high school. Higher education is not left to the market either, and is strictly regulated by national admissions policies. As in Hong Kong, only 5 percent of the college-age youths are in tertiary institutions. Women have nearly an equal share of education, but courses are linked to expected gender roles.

As in Hong Kong, high-rise housing greatly affects the supply of labor. The state-provided housing by the Housing and Development Board, called HDB housing estates, housed half the populace in the mid-1970s. Small factories are allotted space there, with electronics factories especially favored, which draw on women residents as a labor force. The removal of people from squatter or *kampong* settlements (village communities) concentrates them as a labor force, and causes the people to spend more on housing. Entry into the market economy is but the next step. Home industry has nearly disappeared, and even the shadow economy in the HDB estates serves the factory system directly. For example, instead of vending homemade food, women take in seaming for neighborhood factories.

As a result of these state policies, the standard of living in Singapore has improved, full employment exists, and real wages have risen. Women's role in the economy is essential in this new-found prosperity.[34]

Family Strategies in Encouraging Women To Work

Families in the three countries have developed similar strategies in response to opportunities for employment. Implied in the concept of family strategies is a corrective to individualistic views of women wage-earners, motivated by personal interest and gaining power as a result of access to wages. Instead, in these societies family roles propel women to work and reap the benefits of their employment. Families are not just attracted by wage work opportunities for their offspring, but also have been forced by necessity to send members to work. They are decreasingly able to live off the land, to grow or make goods themselves. The penetration of the money economy forces them to depend on earnings to survive. They must buy food, clothing, furnishings, education, and housing. Families thus exploit the environment to get cash, but do so within the bounds of social structure. The following discussion sets out the structures that influence families' strategies of encouraging daughters to work.

I now turn to the work experiences of women in Hong Kong, Taiwan, and Singapore in the mid-1970s, the height of the export-oriented industrial strategies in the three areas. I compare material from my in-depth study of 28 ummarried working- and middle-class women in Hong Kong with research by Linda Gail Arrigo and Lydia Kung on Taiwan factory women, the same ages, and with case histories by myself and Aline Wong of 100 young Singapore Chinese married women, from working- and middle-class backgrounds, half of whom were employed.[35] This comparison shows how state strategies and the survival and family upgrading strategies of Chinese families have led to similar patterns of women's work in the three areas. Unmarried women dominate the female labor force, and married women are unlikely to work in the formal sector. This single-peaked work pattern resembles that found in North America at the turn of the century.[36] North America today, in contrast, has a double-peaked work pattern, with women working during the periods after they leave school, and after their children are school-age. This is not the case for the Chinese women under study here.

Structural reasons for the single-peaked labor force pattern include demographic pressures, especially a high dependency ratio, the Chinese family type, and the family life cycle stage. These will be discussed in turn.

Demographic Pressures

The high post–World War II birthrates in the three areas, with improved health conditions, meant that women born ca. 1948 to 1960, and aged in the teens through their twenties in the mid-1970s, had many brothers and sisters. In Hong Kong, for example, women similar to the mothers of the young employed I studied in the 1970s, aged 40 to 44 in 1971, averaged 4.3 live births. Comparable large families are found among Singapore and Taiwanese mothers of the same age cohort. This demographic situation created a high dependency ratio, as measured by the ratio of wage-earners to dependents. In the families of my sample of 28 Hong Kong women, dependency ratios of over 1:4 to 1:9 were common when respondents were youngsters, ca. 1960 (Table 14.1). There was usually only the father as the single earner, and only when his contribution diminished—having become ill or having died, taken two wives or deserted the family—did the mother go to work. For another example, two-fifths of the fathers of men in the 100 Singapore couples we studied passed away or deserted their families before the lads were early teenagers, compelling their mothers, brothers and sisters, and themselves to work. Most mothers were burdened with many small children, labor-intensive household chores, and insufficient help at home, and they lacked education or industrial labor force experience. In Taiwan they had farm tasks to perform. Such mothers rarely worked for a wage outside the home.

In these states, which propelled the populace out of the subsistence economy, the high dependency ratio made the need to earn money overwhelming. The demographic situation also suggested the means to do so by sending children out to work. Thus, young women who went to work after primary school entered the new low-waged manufacturing work just then opening up in the 1960s, and the dependency ratio markedly improved. In my study of Hong Kong working daughters, I found that the dependency ratios improved to 2:4, and even 3:7 in 1965, because of the daughters' entry into the labor force (Table 14.1). Several years later, when unmarried working daughters were aged 25 or so, the dependency ratio even reversed itself, with more workers than nonworkers in many cases.

Although their wages were low, young women were able to support themselves, and as they gained work experience they could contribute more to the family coffers for survival, or even modest family prosperity (Table 14.2). The same was true for the unmarried Taiwanese women that Kung and Arrigo studied.

TABLE 14.1

Ratio of Wage Earners to Family Dependents, 1960 to 1974

RESPONDENTS	1960	1965	1970	1973	1974
Working Class					
A-li	1:8	3:7	3:7	4:6	4:6
I-ling	1:4	2:4	3:3	3:3	3:3
Mae-fun	1:7	3:5	4:3	4:3	3:3
Wai-gun	1:7	3:6	3:6	4:5	5:4
Upper Working Class					
Ming	1:6	1:7	3:5	3:5	3:5
Middle Class					
Ju-chen	1:9	2:7	3:7	4:6	3:6

When young women married, they typically entered the house-hold of their husband's parents, which created an extremely favorable dependency ratio, especially where the newlyweds lived patrilocally (with the husband's parents). In the family structure of married Singapore women, several adults were old enough to work. It was therefore usually unnecessary for the new bride with only a modest education to remain in the labor force since she could not earn much in the kinds of women's jobs that were available. She would be requested to quit her job and do the housework, and might, thereby, free other younger unmarried daughters to continue their employment. Married women might, however, continue to work if they had above-average education and could work in the slightly better paying women's jobs, so long as other women were willing to undertake the housework in their stead. Nevertheless, when young women had children, they found it difficult to remain at work in the prevailing low-paid women's jobs. They simply did not earn enough to justify giving their homemaking burdens and obligations to others.

Type of Family

Families long looked forward to the transition to an improved dependency ratio. Parents thus tried to stretch out the period, within limits. Their goals were structured by the type of family that prevailed.

Students of the Chinese family distinguish three conceptual units. The patriliny is the family core, composed of men linked by descent, and with equal rights to inherited property.[37] This family type is dominant in the three areas discussed here. It is true that few

TABLE 14.2

Occupational Profiles, Family Members and Income

OCCUPATION OF SEVERAL RESPONDENT'S FAMILY MEMBERS	HOUSEHOLD INCOME PER MONTH[a]		PERCENTAGE CONTRIBUTION OF ALL DAUGHTERS TO HOUSEHOLD INCOME, 1973
Mae-fun	**1963**	**1973**	
Father ———————	$ 85	$120	
Mother			
Sister ————	25	80	
Mae-fun ————	25	80	42%
Brother —————		100	
(seven members in family)	$135	$380	
Wai-gun			
Father —————	$ 50	$ 80▲	
Mother ————	30	60	
Wai-gun ————	20	80	52%
Sister ————		70	
(nine members in family)	$100	$290	
Suyin			
Father ———————	$ 15▲	$ 20▲	
Mother ————	30	60	
Suyin ————	30	120	73%
Sister ————	30	100	
(eight members in family)	$105	$300	
Chin-yiu			
Father ———————	$---▲	$200	
Mother			
Chin-yiu —————————	30	160	66%
Sister ———————	30	170	
Sister ————		70	
(seven members in family)	$ 60	$600	
I-ling			
Father —————————	$---▲	$200	
Mother ————	30	60	
I-ling ———————	30	100	28%
(six members in family)	$ 60	$360	

Never worked
———— Unskilled
—————— Semiskilled
—————— Skilled
—————————— Low-paid clerk
—————————— Well-paid clerk

▲ Father contributing little due to unemployment, layoffs, illness, or residence elsewhere

[a] All dollars are given in U.S. dollars, at the rate of $5 HK = 1 U.S.

families in the two city-states inherited land, and Taiwanese land-holdings are small. Immigrant families in Hong Kong, and to some extent, Singapore, grew up without a full set of paternal kin, and in Taiwan, rural to urban migrants might also leave their kin behind. High wartime levels of mortality also meant a low probability of survival of grandparents and parents in the three areas.

Even though an ideal form of patrilocal household cannot come into existence everywhere, the patriliny still remains a guiding goal for behavior, and so it is crucial for families to bear sons for eco-nomic reasons. In these industrial settings daughters earn less than sons, and only in Singapore do parents have some enforced con-tributory retirement savings. Parents also aim to continue the fam-ily line, and this further endears sons to them. In such a patrilineal family, ties of women to their kin cause potential loyalty conflicts, which the patriliny attempts to dilute. Daughters are expected to sever their ties with their parents on marriage, and so more fully turn their loyalty and energy to their husband's line.

The patrilineal concept affects strategies toward daughters' train-ing and employment. When the young women born in the post-World War II years were growing up there was rarely enough money to train both sons and daughters in these three societies. Looking toward the future, parents saw daughters as "goods upon which one loses," while boys were the future of the family. Thus, in the 1950s and 1960s, girls received less schooling than boys. Certain that they would work for only a few years until their marriage, with enough education to give them literacy, but not enough for them to enter skilled jobs with a future, young women were a prime labor force for low-waged export-oriented industries.

Turning to postmarital patterns, in Singapore patrilocal resi-dence was common for young couples in 1975, and three-fifths of the couples studied had once lived with kin, most with the husband's family. By the time one or two children were born, just under half of the families studied still lived with kin, and two-fifths of the couples studied lived with the husband's parents. They were not expected to remain there. The eldest son married first by custom, and brought his wife into the household of his parents. He usually had children soon after marriage. From a low dependency ratio, the family then had a higher dependency ratio. When the next son planned to marry, it was hard to put all couples under one roof in a high-rise flat. The first son and his wife and children typically moved out, and the newlyweds took their place, improving the dependency ratio once again.

The second conceptual family unit, the domestic unit or economic family *(chia)* focuses on present-day economic survival, rather than the line of inheritance. The domestic unit contributes to the common budget. Since it draws on all available labor power, it includes women in these efforts. Ties to women's kin are tolerated and even may be encouraged if they contribute to the well-being of the household. The family's drawing upon the labor of the children stems from the domestic family.

The third family unit is formed by the bonds of sentiment between women and their children. Since the mother lacks the same rights as her husband in the line, she compensates by building bonds of support with her children. Emotional exchanges underlie these bonds of support. Where the father is emotionally distant from his offspring, as is common in Chinese families, the mother can more easily build up these alliances. Based on her Taiwan research, and applicable to Hong Kong and Singapore, Margery Wolf calls the female-centered family the "uterine family."[38] The willingness of daughters to contribute to the economic family, despite their exclusion from the patriliny, family inheritance, and family future, is ensured by the sentimental bonds of support built in this family unit.

We can easily note that these several concepts of family can come into conflict. While people will attempt to minimize the conflict of expected behaviors,[39] at times conflict cannot be avoided, and the result may be particularly painful. An example is the case of a young Hong Kong working daughter, Wai-gun, depicted in Tables 14.1 and 14.2 above, who contributed her wage, first as an electronics assembler, then as a higher-paid garment seamstress, to the family budget since she was 12 years old. In 1971, when I first met her, she was only one of three contributors, and the only child to earn a living, in a family of nine members. By 1974, however, two younger siblings entered the labor force, and there were five wage-earners and four dependents. Wai-gun's place in the domestic economy was now becoming less essential. She was permitted to use more of her money for recreation and leisure time, and hobbies. She was also preparing to marry. Her intended was an eldest son whose father lived in the Philippines, and who lived with his mother in Hong Kong. The couple planned to marry in the near future, and saved money for the event. Unfortunately, Wai-gun's father became critically ill, and passed away, while her mother, whose health was never strong, also began to deteriorate. Soon neither parent earned money, and the family dependency ratio unexpectedly in 1976 took a turn for the worse. Three older children supported three younger children, and the ill mother. Now Wai-gun could not withdraw her earnings from the household, and thus she could not marry. On the other hand, her fiancé was under pressure by his own mother to further the family line. He was expected to marry and bear a son in the patrilineal tradition. Thus, the two potential partners were enmeshed in different family concepts. Wai-gun in the domestic circle, her fiancé in the patrilineal system. Their relationship predictably broke up under the conflicting definitions of family demands.

In sum, the young girl who matures into adolescence and then early adulthood finds her worklife determined by the demographic pressures of the period: The three types of family units form the bounds within which demography is defined. These are the long-term stress on males due to the line concept, the short-term stress on women's earnings due to the domestic economy concept, and the bonds of affection between mother and daughter that propel her to add to the household economy, due to the concept of the uterine family of affection.

The Family Life Cycle

The Division of Labor in the Household

The numbers of family members, and their contribution to the household division of labor vary by cycle of the family. Expected household tasks for the young unmarried women living at home in Hong Kong, Taiwan, and Singapore during the period under study are shaped by the large family size. William Goode notes that sheer size in an organization entails rules of interaction, authority, obedience, and emotional intimacy.[40] Robert Winch focuses on the number of functions the family fills: The more functions filled, the more need there is for a strict definition of roles by age, sex, generation, and lineage.[41] The family at the stage we are studying here is sizable enough to require a number of rules, which are generally accepted.

First was early training of children to participate in family tasks. By age 5 most learned many necessary tasks, and by age 12 on the eve of their entry to wage work, all hauled water, cooked, washed clothes. As they neared adolescence the older girls took in putting-out work (plastic flowers, transistor assembly, pressing metal eyelets, beading). They did this as part of a family-wide project, carried out in the home, and they received no individual wage or recognition. This was most common in Hong Kong, the earliest entrant to the international world economic order. In Taiwan, young girls often had tasks that were associated with their agricultural roots or housekeeping: They fed the pigs, nipped the ends off bean sprouts. Singapore girls similarly performed subsistence work, helped in family hawker enterprises, or did domestic work in other households.

With this bridge of hard work to perform household tasks and work in family putting-out projects, working-class Hong Kong daughters entered the paid labor force between ages 12 and 14. Their Taiwan counterparts similarly began work around age 14; the Singapore girls we studied started to work a few years later when factories began to reach out for them. Middle-class families were more likely to delay the entry of their daughters to the workforce until they completed some portion or all of high school, and they went to work at around age 16.

Not only were tasks divided by age, but sex roles marked different expectations. The daughters went to work after having completed primary school, so that their period during which they would contribute to the domestic economy would be a long one. They entered before reaching age 14, and were, in the accepted definition of the International Labour Organization (ILO), child labor. They would leave the domestic family upon marriage. Their brothers, however, were to be contributors to the domestic economy throughout their lives, albeit unevenly due to their own domestic economic burdens. If there were a sum of money available for only some of the children to study, the boys were therefore chosen. They could repay the family back at a higher rate of return.

The lengthening of the daughters' years of contribution to the domestic economy was accomplished not only by their early entry to the labor force, but parents might also postpone their daughters' exit through marriage. Hong Kong parents sought a full decade of daughters' income contribution, the number of years molded perhaps by the need to ensure younger siblings' completion of schooling at an ever higher rate. If the daughter was herself a younger sibling, the length of time she needed to contribute her wages to the household economy was reduced. Even so, younger daughters sought to repay their parents for the costs of their upbringing. Social class differences came into play. The lower-middle and middle-class daughters with the longest period of education

also entered the labor force at an older age. They then were expected
to contribute to the family budget, and as a result delayed marriage
past the period of working-class women.

Kung's study of Taiwanese factory women similarly stresses the
daughters' desire to repay their parents for the cost of their upbringing. Although Kung did not study middle-class women, the 1980
census of Taiwan reveals that marriage age is directly associated
with educational level in Taiwan.[42] Among the reasons for this delay
is undoubtedly the period of post-educational employment, much of
which aids the families.

A newly married woman's right to work is also decided upon as
part of a household-wide strategy. Here, too, the division of labor
takes its mark from the household size, where many people may be
accommodated and many functions performed. The older generation sets the division of labor. In situations of patrilocal residence,
where there are several adults in the household, the elders can
choose the women with the strongest wage-earning power to work.

Actually, few Singapore women in our study were in this happy
situation. Few could earn a wage that justified their leaving their
homemaking burdens to others. After all, women are designated to
take over men's homemaking burdens, and work for a wage lower
than would be charged if men paid full market value for the services
needed to support them.[43] Thus women's wages are set by the
presumption that they are dependents on others, and do not themselves support others. Women's wages are further depressed by the
large number of women who compete for a narrow range of jobs.
Consequently, only 18 percent of Singapore women with two children were still in the labor force in 1973, and similarly under 20
percent of ever-married Taiwan women were economically active in
1980.

In order to go out to work, women must find others to do the
household chores, child care, and other internal ministering of the
household for them. In a large household, there was considerable
work to do. However, a large household with a strong dependency
ratio also has the potential for a division of labor in which young
women can find backup services of others in their homes. Singapore
research of the mid-1970s showed that the factories' demand for
women was crucial in determining which would go to work, and
which would remain as backup workers in the home. Women with
above-average education, some technical skills, and longer industrial employment experience were most often chosen for better-
paying factory work. Thus, although most women in our sample had
worked prior to marriage, many had helped in traditional types of

TABLE 14.3

Comparison of the Residences of Full-time Wage-Earning Wives and Homemakers, Singapore ca. 1975

	WIVES' EMPLOYMENT STATUS					
Form of Residence	**Wage-Earners**		**Homemakers**		**Total**	
	%	(Number)	%	(Number)	%	(Number)
Stem or Extended	65		31		49	
Neolocal	35		69		51	
	100	(52)	100	(48)	100	(100)

Source of Data: See note 35 to text.

work, on farms, in workshops or small factories packaging peanuts, making gold paper used to burn for the dead, or in soy sauce factories. Their labor force experience could not command a good postmarital job. Those who worked were among the better-educated, the women with superior class backgrounds in our sample.

In addition, those women whose families were in great need, whose husbands were quite poor, might also work for a wage, but typically they could only get low-paid work. They were then highly subsidized by other women in the household, who responded to their great need. Alternatively, some of them might do nonindustrial work in the neighborhood, take in washing, wash floors part-time, which was not registered in labor force statistics, for neighborhood women.

That household support is key in aiding married women to work is seen in a comparison of full-time wage-earning women and homemakers in our study (Table 14.3). Women who lived in the same home with other kin (stem or extended households) were more likely to work than women who lived neolocally. In addition, however, a number of women carved out support systems that crossed household walls and drew upon several kin in a community area. These women are "interactors."[44] Thus, wage-earners invariably had kin-based support systems to help them out.

Women enter and create complex interpersonal relationships in order to stay in the labor force after marriage. One Singapore woman, Sim Soo Kee, seamed garments six days a week in a small, four-woman garment workshop located near her apartment. Her husband, Man Wah, operated a kiosk in the Golden Mile Shopping Center where he sold popular music cassettes and earned around S$400 a month.[45] The couple lived with their two children in a rented one-room HDB flat in the Bukit Ho Swee public housing unit.

TABLE 14.4

Interaction Patterns of Working Wives and Housewives, Phase 1, Singapore ca. 1975

	WIVES' EMPLOYMENT STATUS			
	Wage-Earners		**Homemakers**	
	%	(Number)	%	(Number)
Isolates	10		35	
Interactors	90		65	
	100	(52)	100	(48)

Source of Data: See note 35 to text.

Soo Kee earned $5.50 daily at her sewing machine. She obtained low-cost help with her children from her close kin while she worked. A typical day's chronology of family child care arrangements for Sim Soo Kee is given in Table 14.5. (Man Wah was, we note, not part of these intricate arrangements.) Many working women who lived in small households found it necessary to engineer child care arrangements of this type.

Soo Kee was thus enabled to put in a full working day, but the S$100 total she paid her mother and aunt for assistance in child care and the S$30 paid to a domestic servant who washed her laundry and floors every week exceeded 80 percent of her monthly income. Soo Kee explained,

> By working I can afford to pay people to do things for me, and I have a little left over for pocket money. I enjoy my work. It's easier to pass the day and I'm more relaxed than before. I've even put on a little weight.

The Sims told the interviewer that they were discussing the purchase of an apartment in a new housing estate, and Soo Kee's work might add a few dollars toward this goal. Without the help of kin, Soo Kee could not afford to work for the low wage she earned.

The Consequence of Their Work

Families reward women for their employment and their input to the household. Women get something out of their input, which keeps them in the exchange. Working Hong Kong daughters widened their sphere of decision making as it affected their social lives. So long as they could put in a good-sized proportion of their wages to their family budget, they kept a portion for their own spending money.

TABLE 14.5

Chronology of Family and Neighborhood Assistance for Sim Soo Kee, Phase 1.

TIME	ACTION	COST TO SOO KEE[a]
6:30	Soo Kee rises to prepare breakfast for her two sons (ages 6 and 3).	
7:30	Soo Kee and the two boys leave home and walk to the apartment of her parents in the adjacent housing block. 6-year-old is entrusted to Soo Kee's mother.	S$50/month
8:00	Soo Kee and 3-year-old walk to the apartment of one of her mother's sisters, who takes him for the day.	S$50/month
8:30	Soo Kee arrives at her garment workshop to begin work.	
8:45	Mother puts 6-year-old on school bus and proceeds to her neighborhood market for her daily food shopping.	
9:00	Laundress washes clothes and floors in the Sim's flat.	S$30/month
13:00	6-year-old returns to mother's house for lunch and spends the rest of the day with his grandmother.	
17:30	Soo Kee departs from work.	
17:45	Soo Kee fetches 3-year-old from her aunt.	
18:00	Soo Kee and her child arrive at her parents' home, where dinner is waiting for her and the two children.	
20:00	Soo Kee and her two children return home.	

[a]See note 45.

They could thereby join peer activities, dress better, and use their free time in ways decided upon by themselves.

Similarly, Taiwan daughters enjoyed a period of friends, participation in the newly expanding consumer culture, and group dates. These opportunities were more accessible when the working daughters lived in factory dormitories, and less accessible when the girl lived at home.[46] Working daughters could not greatly expand their input into decision-making processes in their families in either setting, and their wages did not confer upon them power to realign their dependence on the family itself.

In Hong Kong, opting out was limited by the expectation that women remain at home until marriage, despite their earning money. This expectation is reinforced by aspersions cast on the sexuality of women who leave home as loose women. But in addition, since the housing market is dominated by the state's public housing, given only to families by need criterion, plus a very expensive private housing market, it would be hard for most women earners to live alone or with other women. They cannot leave. Taiwan factory women lived in the main in tightly supervised dormitories, and the women who moved into private flats found it was too expensive to meet their obligations to their families. Those who could live at home and commute to work did so, to save money. Work did not confer a period of accepted physical independence from the family. However, women who lived apart from their families, in factory dormitories, had the greatest chance to choose recreational activities and friends of their own.

Although working daughters obtained a meaningful outcome from their employment, their employment cannot entirely be seen as a transaction, between two parties, in which they have equal power to work or not to work. Unmarried Hong Kong, Taiwan, and Singapore women have less power in their households than their parents. Too, married women are so closely dependent on others in their homes in order to work that they are not free agents either.[47]

Married Singapore women were unlikely to perceive their employment as a form of independence, since their money went to their families. Even middle-class women saw their work as only possible if they could successfully field their family obligations to others. They enjoyed an enlarged sphere of action due to having money of their own, it is true. With their funds they bought clothes for their children, rounded out the family budget, provided small sums to their mothers or other kin, which could not legitimately be drawn from their husband's or wider household budget. They could join peer outings with workmates on special occasions, and purchase presents with their earnings. However, in all cases studied, women placed the major part of their earnings at the disposal of their family, usually their nuclear family. The freedom gained was not an individual form of liberty. Rather, they obtained a widened sphere for their small nuclear unit in the extended, usually patrilineal, construct.[48]

The material consequences of women's work were crucial, much more so than a widening of their proper sphere. Purchases of the household varied by the dependency ratio, a product of the life cycle. When, as young unmarried daughters, women first entered the labor force within the context of a high dependency ratio, their wages helped their families buy necessities—rent, and food for the entire family. Medical care was an optional, but costly item, and families improved their care when extra money became available. Married Singapore women in the poorest households, typically those with a difficult dependency ratio, also placed their wages at the disposal of the family. Working women's income enabled extended education for younger siblings past the years provided by their governments. Married women could help pay for tutors for their own children, to improve their performance on competitive state examinations.

An example of the daughters' importance in this regard is the case of the eldest sister in a Hong Kong family of five girls. Still unmarried at age 29, she earmarked one-third of her factory earnings for the education of her youngest two sisters. All of her sisters had the opportunity to continue school past primary 6, the eldest had only reached primary 4. The youngest went further in her studies than the oldest girls. The eldest's economic assistance was to continue until the next two working sisters could assume the entire burden themselves.

As the dependency ratio improves, daughters in working-class families can contribute toward an improvement in the family living standard through the improved education of the younger sons. But since everyone in the society is in pursuit of more education, there is a spiralling of credentials, and youngsters must remain in school longer just to keep in the same place. Nevertheless, the ability to raise younger brothers' education was most feasible when daughters had been working for a decade. Telephones, televisions, small semiautomatic washing machines, and other goods add to household comforts, and are made possible by the combined earnings of the employed children, notably the working daughters.

Middle-class girls also contribute their earnings; for example, many help their parents launch a small business, such as hawking, or knitting or garment shops. The high savings propensity of the Chinese in Hong Kong has been documented, and their willingness to risk investment in the local economy.[49] Earnings of the children, added to the family budget, thus in turn boost the export-oriented manufacture economy. The extent to which children aid their parents in building capital in these areas is worthy of future study.

Thus, we have come full circle. The states of each of the three areas discussed here, Hong Kong, Taiwan, and Singapore, have boosted their economies, making crucial steps to develop export-oriented economies. They drew upon the inexpensive labor of unmarried women in the main, and to a small extent that of married women. They propelled the families into the money economy, which required families to increase their access to cash. Parents held control over their daughters' labor, and their daughters dutifully went to work in support of the families they would soon leave upon marriage. With the earnings, parents made ends meet, but eventually some could accumulate capital themselves to invest in small-scale enterprises, some of which served local populations and others of which formed part of the export businesses.

The working women of these three countries were conscious of their place as earners in the family economy. They knew their need to earn was due to family necessity, linked both with demographic demands—a large number of siblings—and with rising aspirations in the consumer economy. At the same time, they witnessed an explosion of wage-earning opportunities over their working life span. The ideology of market capitalism conveys the wish to be free. Since their households control their labor, these women did not enter the workforce as independent individuals, hence they do not internalize this wish to be free. They feel the surge of "freedom" in terms of consumer goods, and a widening sphere of choice, but at the same time they retain their sense of obligation to the family unit. Interest in political activities is not fueled by the state apparatus, and their sense of rights as individuals is not developed. Consequently, the overriding concern of many of these women is to promote their own interests within the family context. In such a setting, feminist concerns that ride on a sense of justice regarding formal rights and rights when compared with men is often not developed. But as I have tried to show, the lives of these women are undergoing great change, along with the economy and their position in a changing family unit. The outcome of these forces is a dynamic vitality which, while not the same as that felt by middle-class Western women, is nonetheless profound.

NOTES

1. The three areas discussed, in association with the Republic of Korea, are commonly referred to as the "newly industrialized countries" of Asia. Strictly speaking the areas discussed here include only one country, Singapore, while Hong Kong is a colony, which will revert to the People's Republic of China in 1997. Taiwan's political status is still in dispute, and is usually referred to as Taiwan province or the Republic of China. As shorthand I will refer to these places as "countries."

2. International Labour Office, *World Labour Report, 1: Employment, Incomes, Social Protection, New Information Technology* (Geneva: author, 1984), Chapter 1.

3. *World Bank Report* (Washington, DC: World Bank, various years).

4. Hong Kong Housing and Population Census, 1931, unpublished statistics, *Hong Kong Housing and Population Census* (Hong Kong: Hong Kong Government, Census and Statistics Department, 1971); S. C. Chua, *State of Singapore: Report on the Census of Population, 1957;*

Report on the Labour Force Survey of Singapore 1979 (Singapore: Research and Statistics Division Ministry of Labour, 1980); *An Exact Report on the 1980 Census of Population and Housing,* Taiwan-Fukien Area, Republic of China (Taipei: Census Office of the Executive Yuan, R.O.C., 1982; Directorate-General of Budget, Accounting, and Statistics, *Year Book of Labor Statistics* (Taipei: Executive Yuan, R.O.C., 1958–1960).

5. Bruce Cumings, "The Origins and Development of the Northeast Asian Political Economy: Industrial Sectors, Product Cycles, and Political Consequences," *International Organization* 38:1 (Winter 1984); 1–40; Stephan Haggard and Chen Tun-jen, "State Strategies, Local and Foreign Capital in the Gang of Four," Paper prepared for the 1983 Annual Meeting of the American Political Science Association, Chicago, 1983.

6. An example is reformist leader, Elsie Elliot, O.B.E., who is the urban councillor representative of a sizable housing estate, and is a school principal. See her publication, *A, B, C's of Hong Kong* (or, "Avarice, Bureaucracy, and Corruption of Hong Kong").

7. Siu-kai Lau, *Society and Politics in Hong Kong* (Hong Kong: Chinese University Press, 1982).

8. Frances M. Geiger and Theodore Geiger, *The Development Progress of Hong Kong and Singapore* (New York: Macmillan, 1975); Mary Lee, "Work Suspended," *Far Eastern Economic Review* (August 21, 1981), 32–33.

9. David C. Chaney and David Podmore, *Young Adults in Hong Kong: Attitudes in a Modernizing Society* (Hong Kong: Centre of Asian Studies, University of Hong Kong, 1973); Joe England and John Rear, *Chinese Labor under British Rule: A Critical Study of Labor Relations and Law in Hong Kong* (Hong Kong: Oxford University Press, 1975); H. A. Turner et al., *The Last Colony, But Whose?* (Cambridge, England: Cambridge University Press, 1981).

10. Lau, Chapter 4; Chaney and Podmore, 46, 60; Sherry Rosen, *Mei Foo Sun Chuen: Middle Class Families in Transition* (Taipei: Orient Cultural Service, 1976).

11. Haggard and Cheng.

12. Lau, 174.

13. Christopher Howe, "Growth, Public Policy and Hong Kong's Economic Relationship with China," *China Quarterly* 95 (September 1983), 512–533, cited at page 521.

14. Tamera Hareven, *Family Time and Industrial Time* (Cambridge, England: Cambridge University Press, 1982); Lau; Larissa Adler Lomnitz, *Networks and Marginality: Life in a Mexican Shantytown* (New York: Academic Press, 1977); Keith Hopkins, ed., *Hong Kong: The Industrial Colony* (Hong Kong: Oxford University Press, 1971).

15. Turner et al., Chapter 6.

16. Richard E. Barrett and Martin King Whyte, "Dependency Theory and Taiwan: Analysis of a Deviant Case," *American Journal of Sociology*

87:5; 1064–1089. Cumings; Council for Economic Planning and Development, Republic of China, *Taiwan Statistical Data Book 1984* (Taipei: author, 1984); 23, 156.

17. Lydia Kung, *Factory Women in Taiwan* (Ann Arbor, MI: UMI Research Press, 1983).

18. Esther S. Lee Yao, *Chinese Women: Past & Present* (Mesquite, TX: Ide House, 1983).

19. Barrett and Whyte; Cumings; Walter Galenson, ed., *Economic Growth and Structural Change in Taiwan* (Ithaca, NY: Cornell University Press, 1979); Haggard and Cheng; Samuel P. S. Ho, *Economic Development of Taiwan 1960–1970* (New Haven, CT: Yale University Press, 1978).

20. Barrett and Whyte.

21. Kung.

22. There is some discrepancy in the labor force statistics. The *Yearbook of Labor Statistics* indicates that women's share in the labor force peaked in 1973, at 34.56 percent of the labor force; between 1973 and 1980, the trough was in 1976, at 31.91 percent of the labor force. The 1980 census report, however, claims that women's employment was only 29 percent of the labor force in 1975 and 27 percent in 1980 *(An Extract Report . . . ,* 113). The oil shock had much less of an impact on women's work in the former than in the latter statistics.

23. Myron Cohen, *House United, House Divided* (New York: Columbia University Press, 1976).

24. Yao, 209.

25. *An Extract Report . . . ,* Table 13; Council for Economic Planning and Development, Republic of China, 302.

26. Barrett and Whyte; Council for Economic Planning and Development, Republic of China, 54; Department of Agriculture and Forestry, Taiwan Provincial Government, *Report of Farm Record-Keeping Families in Taiwan, 1979* (Taipei: author, 1980); 20.

27. Geiger and Geiger.

28. V. G. Kulkarni, "Designer Genes," *Far Eastern Economic Review* (September 8, 1983); 23–24; Linda Lim, "A New Order with Some Old Prejudices," *Far Eastern Economic Review* (January 5, 1984), 37–38.

29. Linda Lim, "Multinational Export Factories and Women Workers in the Third World: A Review of Theory and Evidence," in Nagat M. El-Sanabary, compiler, *Women and Work in the Third World* (Berkeley: University of California, Center for the Study, Education, and Advancement of Women, 1983).

30. Geiger and Geiger.

31. Linda Lim, "Singapore's Success: The Myth of the Free Market Economy," *Asian Survey* 23:6 (June 1983), 752–764.

32. Janet W. Salaff and Aline Wong, "Country Study of Incentives and Disincentives in the Family Planning Program of Singapore" (New York: United Nations Fund for Population Activities, in preparation).

33. Kulkarni.

34. Siow Yue Chia, *Export Processing and Industrialization: The Case of Singapore* (Bangkok: International Labour Organization and Asian Regional Team for Employment Promotion, 1982).

35. The Hong Kong and Singapore studies employed purposive sampling. The ages of the Hong Kong women studied were 20 to 24 in 1973, and they were studied over a several-year time period. The Singapore women were married, with at least one child, and aged 20 to 30 when interviewed in the mid-1970s. They were also studied over time but, for ease of comparison with the other two studies, the present paper discusses only their mid-1970s work experience.

    Kung engaged in a two-pronged study of an ethnography of a market town and neighboring agrarian communities, and participant observation in an electronics factory west of Taipei (the capital city). Most of her respondents were unmarried. Arrigo similarly studied an American electronics firm in depth, through participant observation, survey, and case study methods. Although Kung and Arrigo did not explicitly select their sample of women workers within a particular age bracket, the labor force participation pattern of Taiwan women limits most workers to essentially the same ages of the Hong Kong and Singapore women studied, that is, their early twenties. For further discussion of sampling and other findings, see the following studies: Linda Gail Arrigo, "Taiwan Electronics Workers," in Mary Sheridan and Janet W. Salaff, eds., *Lives: Chinese Working Women* (Bloomington: Indiana University Press, 1984), 123–145; Kung; Lydia Kung, "Taiwan Garment Workers," in Sheridan and Salaff, 109–122; Janet W. Salaff, *Working Daughters of Hong Kong* (Cambridge, England: Cambridge University Press, 1981); Janet W. Salaff and Aline K. Wong, *State and Family in Singapore* (Ithaca, NY: Cornell University Press, in preparation).

36. Valerie Kincaide Oppenheimer, *The Female Labor Force in the United States: Demographic and Economic Factors Determining Its Growth and Changing Composition* (Berkeley: University of California, Institute of International Studies, Population Monograph Series, No. 5, 1970).

37. Arthur Wolf and Chieh-shan Huang, *Marriage and Adoption in China, 1845–1945* (Stanford, CA: Stanford University Press, 1980).

38. Margery Wolf, *Women and the Family in Rural Taiwan* (Stanford, CA: Stanford University Press, 1972).

39. William J. Goode, "A Theory of Role Strain," *American Sociologial Review* 25 (August 1960), 483–496.

40. William J. Goode, *The Family* (New York: Prentice-Hall, 1982).

41. Robert F. Winch, *The Modern Family* (New York: Holt, Reinhart and Winston, 1963).

42. *An Extract Report* . . . , 62.

43. Michele E. Barrett and Mary McIntosh, *The Anti-Social Family* (London: Verso, 1982).

44. "Interactors" are couples whose wives or husbands visited the same kin two or more times a week. Typically kin cared for their children during the week, which helped wives work. Some women or their husbands worked with kin. Many of the exchanges that occurred aimed to reduce

the homemaking burdens of these young mothers. Thus women could often draw upon this support system and go out to work.

45. In Singapore dollars, at the approximate rate of S$2.25 = U.S.$1.00.

46. Kung, *Factory Women.* . . .

47. Kung, *Factory Women* . . ., 200ff.

48. Cohen.

49. Marjorie Topley, "The Role of Savings and Wealth among Hong Kong Chinese," in I. C. Jarvie and Joseph Agassi, eds., *Hong Kong: A Society in Transition* (London: Routledge and Kegan Paul, 1969), 167–227.

RECOMMENDED READINGS

El-Sanabary, Nagat, compiler. *Women and Work in the Third World*. Berkeley: University of California, Center for the Study, Education and Advancement of Women, 1983.

Kung, Lydia. *Factory Women in Taiwan*. Ann Arbor, MI: UMI Research Press, 1983.

Lau, Siu-kai. *Society and Politics in Hong Kong*. Hong Kong: Chinese University Press, 1982.

Rosen, Sherry. *Mei Foo Sun Chuen: Middle Class Families in Transition*. Taipei: Orient Cultural Service, 1976.

Salaff, Janet W. *Working Daughters of Hong Kong: Female Filial Piety or Power in the Family?* Cambridge, England: Cambridge University Press, 1981.

——— , and Aline K. Wong. *State and Family in Singapore: Structuring an Industrial Society*. Ithaca, NY: Cornell University Press, in preparation.

15

Women in India: The Reality

Neela D'Souza
Ramani Natarajan

> In childhood a female must be subjected to her father, in
> youth to her husband, when her lord is dead to her sons; a
> woman must never be independent.
>
> — Manu's *Dharmasastra*

The future was bright and promising in 1947 when India emerged as a free nation from two centuries of British rule. Idealism permeated the atmosphere; the euphoria of the nationalist movement had blurred distinctions of caste and class—everyone was proud of the common denominator of being Indian.

Indian women had apparently vaulted with aplomb into the twentieth century and were highly visible in those years of breaking away from colonialism. Independent India had a woman governor of a state. Independent India sent a woman as head of the delegation to the United Nations; she became the first woman president of the General Assembly. Independent India had a woman minister of health. Indian women were progressive and emancipated and could tackle any kind of job—after the challenge of the nationalist movement nothing seemed difficult.

There was no need to agitate for equality and the right to vote; hadn't the women of India protested and marched and gone to jail along with their men to topple British rule? So it was only natural that the Constitution should guarantee them equality with men— something women in Western countries fought for long and bitterly.

The young women of independent India took up various professions and careers and were appointed to important public offices. Even though these were the educated, urban, middle class, it was only a matter of time before women all over the country, down to the remote villages, would benefit from the constitutional guarantees of equality.

As Madhuri Shah, well known for her work in women's education, writes, there was a general self-congratulatory air about the fact that women had been granted political rights and that quite a few of them were occupying positions of power.[1] Women deluded themselves into believing all was well, ignoring the ominous signs around them.

This complacency received a jolt in the 1970s when, at the prompting of the United Nations, the government of India set up a committee to survey the changing status of women as a result of the equality guaranteed by the Constitution and the reforms in law and policy. The committee was made up of nonofficials under the chairmanship of the minister for social welfare and included economists, social scientists, and lawyers with wide terms of reference to examine the administrative, demographic, educational, employment, health (including family planning), legal, political, and social status of women. Traveling across the country and holding discussions, the committee gathered valuable firsthand material; a number of studies were commissioned to provide material for investigation, and secondary data were also examined.

After months of surveys, investigations, and discussions with groups of women from different socioeconomic backgrounds in different parts of the country, the Committee on the Status of Women in India (CSWI) published its report, *Towards Equality: Report of the Committee on the Status of Women in India*.

Then came International Women's Year. Suddenly, the whole question of the status of women came under close scrutiny. Social scientists drew attention to the deterioration in the status of women that had accelerated in the years after independence; disturbing statistics indicated a steady decline in their value in society, leading the committee to declare: "Though women do not constitute a minority numerically, they are acquiring the features of one through inequality of class, status and political power."

On the subject of women in India it is difficult to generalize, for there are a number of variants. There are the obvious differences between rich and poor, urban and rural, educated and uneducated, upper, middle and lower class; there are also cultural, linguistic, regional, and other variables. The most important variant, with far-reaching consequences, is caste. The social norms and life-styles of upper-caste women are quite alien to those of the lower castes. Traditionally, upper-caste women are kept in seclusion (*purdah*) and do not work. Among the lower castes, economic necessity forces the women to work outside their homes, denying them the status symbols of the higher-caste women. Interestingly enough, a lower-caste family moving up the economic ladder is quick to acquire all the trappings of the higher castes, such as sexual segregation and confining women to decorative roles—a process referred to as Sanskritization.

In an autocratic, male-dominated society, sanctioned by scripture and tradition, a woman could not even inherit property; she was little more than a chattel and accepted her lot unquestioningly. Her role was defined in terms of wife and mother. Over the years an accumulation of myths relating to chastity, self-sacrifice, and wifely devotion gave these roles a deceptive gloss. So girls were married early,[2] subordinated themselves to their husbands and sons, and prayed for the reward of a timely death that would spare them the indignity and shame of widowhood.

It is strange that while society denigrated women, knowledge and wealth are personified by goddesses in the Hindu pantheon. There are various cults of the mother goddess as the source of energy, power, and fertility, as protection against evil and destructive forces. This is one of the many puzzling contradictions that complicate the subject of women in India.

Reformers of the nineteenth century, who had been exposed to Western intellectual liberalism, perceived women's problems in terms of these traditional attitudes and customs—child marriage, lack of property rights, purdah, the refusal to allow divorce or widow remarriage. They believed that if these customs were changed and if women were educated, they would make better wives and mothers. They did not think of women as individuals and so never contemplated equality of the sexes.

A closer look at these ideas shows how far removed the reformers were from the problems of women. The millions of illiterate poor owned little beyond the clothes they wore; denial of property rights and education affected only the wealthy. The real problems of the masses of women were poverty, insecurity, poor wages. The reform movements of the last century did accomplish a distinct improvement in the status of women—of the urban classes and only within the family. There was no place for women outside the family.

It was Gandhi who brought an entirely new dimension to the subject of women. While he admired and praised woman as wife and
mother and applauded her devotion to family responsibilities, he
insisted that she should be treated as an individual human being,
that she should not be singled out for legal disabilities because of
her sex. He deplored the state of women: "Today the sole occupation
of a woman amongst us is to bear children, to look after her husband
and otherwise drudge for the household. . . . not only is the woman
condemned to domestic slavery, but when she goes out as a labourer
to earn wages, though she works harder than man, she earns less."[3]

Gandhi's ideas were way ahead of the times—equal shares for
daughters and sons in parental property, joint ownership by husband and wife of the husband's earnings. He was uncompromising
in the matter of women's rights; women had a positive role to play
in the reconstruction of society, and recognition of their equality
was necessary to bring about social justice. At his urging, a variety
of measures were adopted for social reform and educating women.

"The women of India should have as much share in winning
Swaraj [freedom] as men and if the women of India arose, no one
could stop the country's march to freedom."[4] Under Gandhi's guidance, a concerted effort was made to involve large numbers of
women in the freedom movement. Not just the urban, educated,
middle-class women but also humble, unsophisticated women participated in civil disobedience, broke the salt laws, marched in
processions, picketed shops selling foreign liquor, faced police firing
and went to prison. As they took to political activity, they shook off
many of the restrictions society had placed on them.

Gandhi's charismatic personality and insistence on nonviolence
drew Indian women to the nationalist movement. But Nehru saw
another reason too for their large-scale participation: "The call of
freedom had always a double meaning for them and the enthusiasm
and energy with which they threw themselves into the struggle no
doubt had their springs in the vague and hardly conscious but
nevertheless intense desire to rid themselves of domestic slavery."[5]

The women in leadership roles were generally from educated,
liberal families and had little in common with the vast majority of
women in the country; they were not restricted by conventions or
traditions and took part equally with men in the decision-making
fora of the freedom movement. They were also involved with the
women's associations, such as the Women's India Association
(founded 1917) and the All India Women's Conference (founded
1927), which were interested in educational, legal, and social reform

and campaigned to get women the vote. Their main objective was the nationalist movement and not women's rights. Did they assume that the involvement of women in the freedom struggle would guarantee them their rights and equality of status in independent India?

Nehru's philosophy visualized a society where women would have a place equal to men. In an address to women students in Allahabad in 1934, he expressed quite revolutionary ideas: ". . . . the habit of looking at marriage as a profession almost and as the sole economic refuge for women will have to go before women can have any freedom. Freedom depends on economic conditions more than political and if woman is not economically free and self-earning, she will have to depend on her husband or someone else and dependents are never free."[6]

Against this background the Constitution of India was framed. It opens with the resolve to secure to all citizens justice, liberty, equality, and fraternity. Article 14 prevents the state from denying anyone equality before the law or equal protection of the law. Articles 15 and 16 reinforce the principle of equality: The former forbids discrimination against any citizen on grounds of religion, caste, sex, or place of birth; the latter gives all citizens equal opportunity for employment under the state. Further into the Constitution, Article 326 requires that adult suffrage will be the basis of elections—every citizen who is over 21 has the vote.

Deeply committed to the principle of equality for women, Nehru determined to give this proper legal authority when he became India's first prime minister. He was responsible for the reform of laws of marriage and succession for Hindu women. Against opposition from the traditional conservative elements in the Congress party, the Hindu Code Bill was passed, giving women rights of inheritance, divorce, and adoption. It was Nehru's new deal for women.

Independence had significantly changed the legal status of women by elevating them to the rights and privileges of citizens, including the right to vote. Women were offered the opportunity of rising to any position in the nation—even that of prime minister or president.

The importance of equality between men and women in nation building had been accepted in principle; it was not clear how this would be translated into reality, how the contradictions and difficulties in society that restricted women would be resolved. Perhaps it was the belief that in time, with education and progress, the

TABLE 15.1

Female Population in India, 1901–1981 (in millions)

YEAR	TOTAL POPULATION	MALE POPULATION	FEMALE POPULATION	FEMALES PER 1,000 MALES
1901	238	121	117	972
1911	252	128	124	964
1921	251	128	123	955
1931	279	143	136	950
1941	319	164	155	945
1951	361	186	175	946
1961	439	226	213	941
1971	548	284	264	930
1981	684	354	330	935

Source: Census of India, 1981.

benefits of equality would filter down and reach all women that convinced the leaders of the women's movement that all was well, and so they turned their attention to welfare work.

Twenty years later, the investigations of the CSWI uncovered a mass of shocking data; despite the legal and constitutional guarantees, the condition of women had deteriorated steadily.

In almost all countries of the world the sex ratio, the number of women per 1,000 men, in the population shows a marginally higher proportion of women. In India the opposite is true. There are fewer women for every 1,000 men. At the beginning of this century there were 972 women to 1,000 men, representing a 3.4 million gap between the sexes. The ratio declined steadily, dropping to 946 at mid-century and even more sharply in the next two decades to register a startling low of 930 in 1971 and a 20 million gap between men and women (see Table 15.1).

Various reasons have been suggested for the declining sex ratio, one being the underenumeration of women in the census. But surely mistakes of enumeration cannot account for a phenomenon that repeats itself time and again through seven censuses.

In almost all countries of the world women have a higher life expectancy than men. This was true for India too in the early years of this century; even though overall life expectancy was only 23 for the period 1901–1911, women could expect to live longer than men. Since 1931, expectation of life at birth has been lower for women than men. The deterioration in female life expectancy is evident from the fact that up to 1960, on reaching 45 years of age women

TABLE 15.2

Expectation of Life at Birth, 1921–1981

DECADE	YEARS	
	Male	**Female**
1921–31	26.9	26.6
1931–41	32.1	31.4
1941–51	32.4	31.7
1951–61	41.9	40.6
1961–71	47.1	45.6
1971–81	53.0	52.0

Source: *Towards Equality: Report of the Committee on the Status of Women in India*, Department of Social Welfare, Ministry of Education and Social Welfare, Government of India, 1975.

could hope to live longer than men; in the following decade women's life expectancy did not exceed that of men till they reached the age of 49 or 50 (see Table 15.2).

Put together, the declining sex ratio and the deteriorating life expectancy suggest that women are more vulnerable at certain times in their lives, particularly in the age group 1–5 and again between 15 and 34. More female children die between 1 and 5 than male; repeated and excessive child bearing has disastrous consequences, for more women than men die between 15 and 34 (see Table 15.3)

Behind the figures and charts, dismal in themselves, is the grim reality of neglect of female children, for the intense desire and preference for sons is linked to the often fatal neglect of daughters. If the practice of female infanticide belongs to history, the legacy of discrimination and the neglect of female children is validated in infant mortality rates, nutritional surveys, and hospital registers, which show that medical attention is sought much later for girls in case of illness—a delay with grave consequences. The male child is a potential source of economic support and so gets the major share of parental attention, better nutrition, and preferential treatment in all matters.

Reporting on social attitudes toward education, the CSWI found that they varied from acceptance to total indifference. In urban areas there is wider acceptance of education for girls; the middle classes regard education as a sign of modernization and accomplishment; among the lower-middle classes economic needs sanction education for girls, if their parents can make the sacrifices to

TABLE 15.3

Infant and Child Mortality

NO. OF INFANT DEATHS PER 1,000 LIVE BIRTHS

	Male	**Female**
Rural	130	142
Urban	69	71
Total	120	131

NO. OF CHILD DEATHS PER 1,000 POPULATION

Age group	**Rural**		**Urban**	
	Male	Female	Male	Female
0–4	52.1	60.4	26.4	27.8
5–9	4.0	5.5	2.2	2.5

Source: *Eve's Weekly*, March 24, 1984.

make this possible. For the vast numbers of poor families, the question of educating girls never arises.

> A large majority of girls have to undertake domestic chores, including looking after siblings, by the time they reach the age of eight years. A very large number are also engaged in earning for the family. We found girls from the age of five working with their parents in *beedi* [cigarette] factories and other industries in the unorganized sector for 12 hours a day and also as helpers of their mothers in domestic service. Some teenagers were supporting entire families of sick and unemployed parents and young siblings on their sole earnings. It should be noted that girls constitute a high proportion of the unpaid family workers throughout the country and that is a major reason for their exclusion from schools.[7]

In 1971, the female literacy rate stood at just 18.4 percent, about half the male rate. In the over-24 age group this rate sinks to 13.4 percent. The vast majority of the "literate" women have had only primary or middle school education. Surveys show that in the age group 6–11, two out of three girls are at school; between 11 and 14, one girl out of five is in school; and between 14–17 only one out of eight. University enrollment accounts for just 2.5 percent of the female population of the age group 18–23 years. (See Table 15.4.)

Literacy figures for India's rural women are even more disheartening. According to 1981 census figures, 214 million out of the total female population of 331 million live in rural areas; the rate of literacy among them is 18 percent as compared to 48 percent for urban women. So you have a sprinkling of highly visible educated

TABLE 15.4

Literacy, 1901–1981

YEAR	PERCENTAGE OF LITERATES TO TOTAL POPULATION	PERCENTAGE OF LITERATE MALES TO TOTAL MALE POPULATION	PERCENTAGE OF LITERATE FEMALES TO TOTAL FEMALE POPULATION	NUMBER OF LITERATE FEMALES TO 1,000 LITERATE MALES
1901	5.35	9.83	0.60	68
1911	5.92	10.56	1.05	94
1921	7.16	12.21	1.81	140
1931	9.50	15.59	2.93	132
1941	16.10	24.90	7.30	277
1951	16.67	24.95	7.93	299
1961	24.02	34.44	12.95	354
1971	29.45	39.45	18.69	435
1981	36.17	46.74	24.88	496

Source of Data: Census of India, 1981.

women, some of whom are the most progressive in the world, surrounded by masses of the most backward.

These are sobering thoughts for a country that had a woman prime minister for 16 years.

The lack of education emphasizes the lower status of women and firmly binds them there. Their work is confined to those areas where skills are not necessary, and it follows that wages will be low. That education is thought unnecessary for a girl only underscores the notion of male superiority; boys are regarded as more able and capable, and naturally they get the better-paid jobs.

Life for a girl is hard. Taking care of her younger siblings, helping her mother gather fuel, cook, clean, wash, and tend the animals. Learning early that her brothers are privileged and she is not, accepting as ordained that men come first in almost every aspect of life, so naturally they should eat first while she and her mother must be content to eat later whatever is left.

Even marriage emphasizes her secondary status. Dressed in her best clothes she is exhibited like any piece of merchandise to the prospective groom's family. She is scrutinized, and if approved the bargaining over her dowry begins. Dowry may have originated as a way to give a daughter a share of her father's assets, as she had no property rights. The sentimental view that dowry provides her with security overlooks the plain fact that dowry is seldom in the control of the girl, for it is immediately appropriated by the husband's family. When women got rights of inheritance with the Hindu Succession Act, the practice should have died out. It did not, even with the Dowry Prohibition Act of 1961. Originally practiced only among the upper classes, the spread of dowry to lower castes is a curious phenomenon. Among the poor and lower classes, the women work along with men because of economic necessity. As the men move upward to better-paid jobs, they insist on their women staying at home like those of the better-off upper castes. Women lose their productive role in the acquisition of dubious trappings of the upper castes, including dowry. The continuance and spread of dowry to all castes and even to other religions then suggests the real, if unpalatable explanation of this practice—it was a form of compensation for women's low economic value.[8]

A father had to get his daughter married, had to secure a "good" alliance for her, and the bait he held out was her dowry. It did not depend on his means or what he could afford. The groom's family stipulated their requirements, and for an educated, employed young man the price was high. There was no escape from dowry giving. It was a relentless system that spared no one. While the well off could meet steep and often preposterous dowry demands and even flaunt this as proof of wealth and social standing, the lower classes were reduced to misery and penury, particularly since quite often the demands for money and gifts by the son-in-law's family continued even after the marriage. The family suffered under the pressures of society and tradition and harsh economic reality—daughters drained their slender resources. Daughters were a liability.

India is primarily a rural society; the 1981 census showed that 76.3 percent of the population lived in villages. The agricultural sector remains the major field of employment, accounting for about 70 percent of the total workforce. Women's employment has been declining steadily since 1921, both in terms of the proportion of workers to female population and in the percentage of women in the total labor force.

The largest numbers of women workers are found in the unorganized sector of employment in the rural areas where they are agricultural workers, wives and daughters of small farmers, and in urban areas where they work as domestic servants, construction labor, and in unorganized small industries. With long hours of work, poor pay, and lack of security, these exploited women form 94 percent of the total female workforce. Because there are no labor organizations to help to knit them together and also because of the varied nature of their occupations, protective legislation is ineffectual in regulating their conditions. And even within the low wage scales common to the informal sector, women are paid less than men.

What are the sorts of jobs women find in the unorganized sector? What do they earn in these jobs?

Beedi (cigarette) making is an industry that has a much larger number of women workers than men—60 percent of beedi workers are women. This is because the industry has organized itself so that women can work at home and turn in the finished product—not out of concern for women or to enable them to take care of their families while earning a wage but because it is the simplest way of avoiding the rules and regulations of industry. With women working at home, the questions of conditions or hours of work do not arise. Equally so, minimum wages, leave conditions, payment of sickness or maternity benefits do not apply. Beedi making calls for no skills but is a tedious occupation with long hours of work. Payment is per 1,000 beedis rolled; this takes anything from 12 to 16 hours, and earns an incredible Rs 5 (U.S. \$1 = Rs 11). What the woman actually gets is often much less. The *Economic and Political Weekly* described a strike of the beedi workers of Bombay, who protested that the state government had not implemented the minimum wage and their wages had come down to Rs 2. According to the writer, the official attitude was that the beedi worker's wage was a supplement to her husband's, ignoring the basic principle that all labor must get a just wage and that there are some women who are heads of households and whose earnings support their families.[9]

The construction industry employs a large number of women as unskilled manual labor. Contractors hire labor from the poor and illiterate in remote villages and transport them to the building sites. Workers live on the sites in tents of sacking propped up on sticks; the women cook out in the open; sanitary facilities are nonexistent. The contractor guarantees himself an inexhaustible source of cheap labor by keeping his workers in a state of indebtedness; advances on wages are given at exorbitant interest rates. The illiterate worker puts his thumb impression on a scrap of paper that keeps him and his family even to successive generations in bondage to the contractor. The women are paid less than the men and suffer the additional indignity of sexual exploitation. Reporting on the construction industry, the CSWI stated:

> The women are mostly drawn from the rural poor and their earnings constitute the major share of the family's income. Nearly 80 percent of the sample were young women below 35

who began their working life as wage laborers and 98 percent were illiterate. Most of them were married in childhood. Infant mortality is high and in the absence of maternity relief or minimal health facilities, coupled with continuous malnutrition, the life expectancy of these workers remains low.[10]

Consider Jayamma, a middle-aged brick worker with a husband, daughter, and son at home. Her husband was a boatman but does not work now and spends his time tending their goats. He will not do any household chores—that is female work. Jayamma wakes at five, fetches water for the home, goes down the ravine for her toilet, has a wash, buys a cup of tea and is at work at seven. Her work is to carry dry bricks from where they are moulded to the kiln. She carries 20 bricks at a time, balanced on a plank of wood supported on a cloth coil on her head. It is a ten-minute walk from the moulding place to the kiln, and Jayamma virtually runs the distance; she stacks the bricks and unloads them herself, standing, as otherwise she might lose her balance or break her neck. She has done the same job for the last 30 years. Whatever the number of bricks she carries—this is between 500 and 700—her wages are never more than Rs 5 and she cannot hope for any improvement in her work or earnings. All the other jobs are done by men who earn higher wages, twice as much as Jayamma gets. The men are paid more for work that is less tedious, less physically exhausting.

After her long day's work, Jayamma still has to clean and cook the night meal; she feeds her husband and children well, and then she eats whatever is left.[11]

The women who make up the 6 percent of the female labor force that works in the organized sector—public sector undertakings and nonagricultural private sector establishments (employing ten or more persons)—are in a much better position. Here the various laws and regulations are enforced. The organized sector has been growing in the decade 1971–1981, and the percentage of women employed here has increased from 11 to 12.3. The increase has been mainly in the services and professions, while factories and mines have registered a sharp decline in the percentage of female employees. One explanation offered is that the protective labor laws that try to provide women with more benefits make female labor expensive and discourage employers from hiring women; another explanation is that the equal pay principle has affected women's employment.[12]

The real explanation may be the changes in the structure of industry, involving modernization and rationalization, which have resulted in the displacement of women:

Industries which have adopted a higher capital intensive technology resulting in displacement of labor have found it easier to displace women rather than men. They have justified this on the ground that women lack skills and are illiterate and unwilling to learn new processes. While a chance for on-the-job training is generally denied to women, there is evidence to show that where such training has been provided women have proved themselves capable of acquiring new skills and a few have proved to have greater aptitude than men.[13]

The low rate of literacy among women keeps them in ignorance of their rights. Because of Article 15 of the Constitution, which permits protective discrimination in favor of women and children, the state has been able to confer special benefits on women through labor and social welfare legislation. But these laws are disrgarded with impunity. The Equal Remuneration Act of 1976, which has as its object "the payment of equal remuneration to men and women workers and ... the prevention of discrimination on the grounds of sex against women in the matter of employment," is circumvented by simple expedients like confining women to lower-paid jobs.

Surprisingly, the government itself violates the constitutional guarantees with blatantly sexist regulations. The rules of the Indian Foreign Service decreed that a woman member of the service must get written permission from the government to marry; after her marriage she might be asked to resign if the government felt that her family and domestic commitments prevented her from discharging her duties efficiently. The rules prevailed until 1979 when Ms. C. B. Muthamma, a senior foreign service officer, challenged them as "hostile discrimination" against women. When the writ came up for hearing, the government hastily withdrew the offending rules. The Supreme Court urged government to examine all service regulations, "to remove the stain of sex discrimination without waiting for *ad hoc* inspiration from writ petitions or gender charity."[14]

How political are women in India? How interested are they in politics and the political process? While the total female electorate in the country has been increasing, the number of women returned to Parliament and the state legislatures has been decreasing, especially since 1962. The sixth general elections (1977) saw 70 women and 2,369 men contesting 542 seats; the total female electorate was 154 million, of whom 84 million actually voted. Nineteen women were successful in this election. The next parliamentary election in 1980 was a slight improvement. Out of a total number of 4,633 candidates contesting 529 seats, 142 were women, and 28 of them were elected—still a long way off from effective representation of half the population of the country.[15]

The politicians concede that the female electorate now has a mind of its own and so court the women's vote. At the same time they make little effort to include more women among the party candidates, nor do the parties think it necessary to take a stand on women's issues. Against this discouraging record, how does one explain the phenomenon of Indira Gandhi, who was prime minister of the country for over 16 years?

Mrs. Gandhi was born her father's daughter, which gave her a tremendous advantage. Prime Minister Nehru groomed his only child for a political future, and she entered politics at a high level. Though the politicians around him were resentful and secretly scornful of a woman, even if she were Nehru's daughter, the political bosses supported her, confident that they would be able to manipulate her. "She was named Prime Minister in 1966 because the bosses of her Congress party needed a marionette for the 1967 elections. As Jawaharlal Nehru's daughter she would pull crowds and votes; they would pull strings."[16]

Mrs. Gandhi proved them entirely wrong. With formidable political skill and capability she outmanoeuvred the old guard and swiftly pushed them aside and demonstrated her staying power by winning at three elections. If politics was a man's game, Mrs. Gandhi was infinitely superior at playing it. Now she set the rules, and they prevailed. A tough, strong-willed woman, she dominated Indian politics for over 16 eventful years, during which time India entered the nuclear and space age and established its dominance in the subcontinent.

She was an authoritarian ruler who brooked no opposition or rival seat of power and increasingly concentrated power in her own hands. The game of politics absorbed her completely, and there were innumerable problems that clamored for her attention—recession in the economy, the influx of refugees from Bangla Desh, two severe droughts, inflation, growing sectionalism, steering a course clear of the Big Powers, renewing ties with China, among others. Perhaps because of this, or because of expediency or simply because they were low on her list of priorities, Mrs. Gandhi did not concern herself overly with women's issues.

Yet in encounters with the media and at international conferences, she directed attention to and took advantage of the fact that she was a woman:

> In this political world of the masses, being a woman helped
> her even though she may have suffered from it in terms of

acceptance by the established elites. She could identify as a member of an oppressed section, and at the same time she could appeal to the deep emotional response of a mother-figure and the vast and ambivalent Hindu tradition of the mother-goddess who is both the benevolent Durga and the ferocious destroyer Kali.[17]

The declaration of 1975 as International Women's Year and the publication of the CSWI report sharpened the focus on women and their problems. The trend was noticeable from the early 1970s when women from different rural and urban areas began to organize and voice their concern over various issues—scarcity of essential commodities, adulterated foodstuffs, rising prices, etc. That was the time when the fiery Mrinal Gore, the Socialist leader, brought women out into the streets of Bombay, banging rolling pins on plates to protest against rising food prices. Sexual exploitation and crimes against women, like rape, came to be openly discussed. Women's organizations sprang up all over the country to fight for women and improve their status.

Horrifying reports of bride burning, "dowry deaths," appeared in the newspapers. Dowry deaths are not new in India. In fact, the government of the state of Gujarat had set up a commission in 1962 to inquire into the high incidence of suicide among brides in that state. But one heard more about them and realized how widespread the practice was only after 1975. Brides whose parents could not provide the exorbitant sums demanded by the husband's family were being burnt to death or driven to suicide. In all these cases, despite the desperate efforts of the girl's families to initiate an investigation, the police invariably closed the case with the observation, "accidental death while cooking." Women organized protest demonstrations to draw attention to dowry deaths, picketed the homes where they occurred, and demanded thorough investigation by the police.

In the recent case of Sudha Goel, who died in December 1980 of burn injuries in an advanced state of pregnancy, the prosecution case was that Sudha was burnt to death by her mother-in-law, husband, and huband's brother for not bringing sufficient dowry. The trial court convicted all three and sentenced them to death, but the Delhi High Court acquitted them. Several women's groups reacted strongly against the acquittal, and the case is now pending before the Supreme Court.

As a result of the efforts of women's organizations, amendments in the law have been proposed to facilitate investigation and punishment for dowry deaths, of which there are two every 24 hours in Delhi.[18]

The Mathura case brought rape out of the closet and into the open. Mathura was a young girl of 16 who alleged that she had been raped by police constables while in their custody in a police station in March 1972. The Supreme Court set aside the conviction for rape passed on the policemen by the Bombay High Court. While conceding that the policemen had had sexual intercourse with the girl, the Supreme Court held that there was no evidence to indicate that it was without her consent. The verdict infuriated the country, and the public discussion and criticism helped to mobilize action groups against rape; in turn, they encouraged rape victims to complain to the police and launch prosecutions.

An important aftermath of the Mathura case is the amendment to the criminal code making the rape laws more stringent.

Women won another battle in 1983 when the Supreme Court upheld the right of a young unmarried woman to live independently of her family if that gave her happiness.[19] The verdict was a blow to the popularly held belief fostered by Manu's *Dharmasastra*: "In childhood a female must be subjected to her father, in youth to her husband, when her lord is dead to her sons; a woman must never be independent."[20]

While the CSWI report makes depressing reading, the increase in the number of women's organizations and movements, the demonstrations and marches and protests on a variety of problems are all encouraging signs. A new consciousness is growing; it is seen in street plays and heard in songs about women's liberation and freedom from sexual exploitation, such as the one written by Madhav Chavan for the Women's Liberation Struggle Conference in 1975:

> To the women of this country, mothers and sisters
> We must go and say,
> Unite together, take up the battle
> We will smash this prison.

This awareness is not confined to the large cities like Bombay or Delhi or Calcutta, or to urban and educated women. It was as evident in the march to the police station in the village of Talasari in Maharashtra, when tribal women raised their voices against alcoholism and corruption, and demanded the right to work, as it was in the anger of women students of Delhi when they streamed out of their classrooms to protest against "eve-teasing" (sexual harassment).

The Self Employed Women's Association of Ahmedabad (SEWA) is an outstanding example of the ability of poor working women to organize themselves. In 1973 some women street vendors and laborers asked the Textile Labour Association (TLA) of Ahmedabad for help against exploitation by money lenders and harassment by the civic authorities. Gandhi had helped to found the TLA in this large city; it set up a women's wing in 1954 to look after the welfare problems of women mill workers and the families of male mill hands. Indian labor laws insist on an employer and an identifiable employer-employee relationship; the self-employed women challenged this, arguing that a trade union could be formed for freedom from exploitation and for workers' development, and won their point. So SEWA's registration was a minor triumph; it was founded by Ela Bhatt with the patronage of the TLA.

SEWA members set up their own cooperative bank—a big step forward for women who had no source of borrowing (other than money lenders), who had no personal security, who could not sign their names, and who had never approached a bank before. Over the years SEWA has grown and expanded under the able leadership of Ela Bhatt, who was awarded the Magsaysay prize for her work. Its membership, mostly illiterate women, is about 12,000. SEWA now organizes self-employment schemes, runs literacy classes, and offers several basic services such as bargaining and representation, legal aid and grievance resolution, supply of raw materials, marketing and management help. Members attend classes in family care and health, which lead to a natural interest and concern for family planning.

The growth of SEWA raised several interesting issues. TLA was not altogether supportive, as it felt threatened by the women's advance toward self-dependence—this from an organization Gandhian in origin and orientation! When Ela Bhatt took a stand in support of the oppressed lower castes, TLA resented her outspokenness and expelled her for indiscipline. So now SEWA functions independently.

In quite another part of the country another interesting development was taking place. This was the CHIPKO ("to hug")[21] movement to preserve the ecology of the hill districts of the state of Uttar Pradesh. For years this region suffered indiscriminate deforestation as government auctioned off vast tracts of forests to timber merchants, disrupting the lives of the people who live here. The men migrated to the cities to earn a living, leaving the women behind to look after the cattle and cultivate small family landholdings. The deforestation upset the weather pattern and deprived the people of grazing land, fodder for cattle, and wood for fuel. In a spontaneous and dramatic move to save their forests, the women wrapped their arms around trees, refusing to let them be felled. CHIPKO has grown into a regular ecological movement, effectively drawing attention to the grave problems of erosion and deforestation, which really affect women most. The same strategy has been adopted by organizations in other parts of the country also—the APIKO (also "to hug") movement in Karnataka, for instance.

In recent years the Indian government has displayed an increasing sensitivity to women's issues and has taken steps to find solutions to problems affecting women. One of these is the recognition of women's studies as a separate body of knowledge that views life and situations from a woman's point of view. Colleges have been encouraged to open departments of women's studies, and a university of women's studies has been set up in south India. A growing number of private agencies and associations are working to expand the body of information on this subject.

After the historic CSWI report in 1975, the Indian Council of Social Science Research (ICSSR) sponsored several in-depth studies of the factors contributing to the changes in status and condition of Indian women. These showed that government-sponsored developmental and welfare measures have affected the lives of only a small number of urban, middle-class women. The status of women will not improve unless adequate opportunities are provided for them to play socially and ecnomically productive roles. The ICSSR has identified employment, health, and education as priority areas for governmental intervention and has recommended several plans of action in these areas.

For the first time in the history of planning in India, a separate chapter on "Women and Development" was included in the Sixth Five Year Plan 1980–1985; this points out that the "excessive mortality in female children resulting in persistent decline in sex ratio, low rate of literacy and low economic status stress the need for greater attention to economic emancipation of women. . . ." Recognizing the plight of poor urban and rural women, the plan aims at their economic betterment through greater opportunities for salaried, self- and wage employment.

Indian women, irrespective of their political beliefs, are proud that their country is one of the very first in the world to have had a woman at the helm of affairs. But while the presence of a woman prime minister was a pointer to the abilities of Indian women and the possibilities ahead, it is not indicative of the condition of women in the country. India is not Indira. The absence of women on the political scene and in the decision-making process, despite the powerful presence of Mrs. Gandhi and her domination of politics for almost 17 years, is a matter of great concern to Indian women.

This is an area that women's organizations must tackle, and the emergence of grass roots movements—such as CHIPKO in the hill areas of Uttar Pradesh; women's water and forest protection committees as part of a people's ecological movement for the protection of the natural environment; organizations of women agricultural laborers, mine workers, tribal laborers; unionization of workers and women's cooperatives—is encouraging. As existing political mechanisms are generally male-defined, with little interest so far in women's issues, women's organizations at all levels of the political machinery will strengthen their voice and effectiveness.

In the face of all odds, girls are getting an education, even if it is rudimentary and involves only a few years of schooling. This, in turn, will lead to a later age at marriage, which will help a girl find a sense of her worth and capability as a person, and increase her aspirations.

Political parties are realizing the importance of female votes and are making efforts to woo them through welfare and legal schemes to improve women's lot. The ruling regional party on Andhra Pradesh, Telugu Desam, has structured itself so that every party office down to the village level has at least one woman on its executive.

The days when women's organizations concentrated their attention on social and welfare issues with little interest in increased involvement in the political processes are over. Inevitably they are drawn into political consciousness and activity. In this changing society, women's groups are examining the questions of power and its sources and the problems involved in social change. This is bringing the educated, middle-class activist into the homes of the working class and the poor in the effort to organize them, opening new channels of communication and understanding and sisterhood that will help build a larger women's movement. There is the very real dilemma of struggling for specific women's issues or making common cause with broader national issues and finding liberation on the way to "the socialist pattern of society" that is India's professed goal.

Women will have to reach the centers of decision making and reach these in strength if they are to have the power and ability to shape their own lives. If women's organizations—and there are a growing number of them all over the country—were to be more active in the political field and more interested in getting women into their rightful place in legislatures, they could reach this objective. For without the participation of women as equal partners, the egalitarian society promised to Indian women in the Constitution will remain illusory.

NOTES

1. Madhuri Shah, Chairman, University Grants Commission, in her foreword to "Symbols of Power," ed. by Vina Mazumdar, Vol. I in *Women in a Changing Society* (Bombay: SNDT Women's University).

2. According to ancient Hindu legal texts, the ideal age for a Hindu wife was one-third her husband's age.

3. "Young India," quoted in *Towards Equality: Report of the Committee on the Status of Women in India*, Department of Social Welfare, Ministry of Education and Social Welfare, Government of India, 1975.

4. "Young India," December 15, 1921.

5. Dorothy Norman, *Nehru: The First Sixty Years*, Vol. I (Bombay: 1965).

6. *Selected Works of Jawaharlal Nehru*, Vol. VI.

7. *Towards Equality.*

8. Dowry has now spread to all castes and to Christians and Muslims too. Islamic tradition calls for a man to pay a bride price, "mehr," to his wife. This is often just a token sum, far outweighed by dowry.

9. Amrita Abraham, "Beedi workers of Bombay," *Economic and Political Weekly*, Bombay, November 1, 1980.

10. *Towards Equality.*

11. Leela Gulati, "Female Labour in the Unorganized Sector," *Economic and Political Weekly*, April 21, 1979.

12. The CSWI found that the equal pay principle had not been seriously applied anyway and most industries continued to maintain wage differentials by direct and indirect methods. One successful method was to restrict women to certain jobs and prescribe lower wage rates for them.

13. *Towards Equality.*

14. *C. B. Muthamma v. Union of India and Others* (1979).

15. Figures from Election Commission, India.

16. Rajmohan Gandhi, "Creating India," *Washington Post*, November 1, 1984.

17. Gail Omvedt, *We Will Smash This Prison* (London: Zed Press, 1980).

18. From *Indian Express*, New Delhi, November 27, 1983.

19. The young woman, Asha, sought the help of "Saheli," a Delhi-based women's organization; her widowed mother and brothers were trying to force her into an unwelcome marriage.

20. Ancient Hindu legal text attributed to Manu, the lawgiver, 1200 B.C.

21. CHIPKO—Hugging trees and the movement to save forests—began in March 1973.

RECOMMENDED READINGS

Committee on the Status of Women in India. *Towards Equality: Report of the Committee on the Status of Women in India*, Department of Social Welfare, Ministry of Education and Social Welfare, Government of India, 1975.
Any study of women in India should start with this. The Indian Council of Social Science Research has published a synopsis of the report, *Status of Women in India*.

The Economic and Political Weekly, Bombay
Frequently carries articles, research reports, surveys and discussions on all aspects of the subject of women.

Everett, Jana M. *Women and Social Change in India*. New York: St. Martin's Press, 1979.
This discusses the emergence of the Indian women's movement in the historical context, examines early ideology, influence of Gandhi and other leaders, the campaign for Hindu law reform and political representation.

Jain, Devaki. *Women's Quest for Power*. Delhi: Vikas Publishing House, 1980.
Five interesting case studies of women's organizations in small towns, uneducated women organizing themselves, etc.

Mitra, Asok. *Implications of Declining Sex Ratio in India's Population*. Bombay: Allied Publishers, 1979.

Mukhopadhyay, Maitrayee. *Silver Shackles. Women and Development in India*. Oxford: OFXAM, 1984.
A good small study of the deteriorating status of women in India.

Omvedt, Gail. *We Will Smash This Prison*. London: Zed Press, 1980. A vivid description, in a personal account, of smaller radical women's organizations and movements, mainly in the state of Maharashtra.

Souza, Alfred de. *Women in Contemporary India*. New Delhi: Manohar Press, 1975.
A collection of articles by sociologists on traditional images and changing roles of women.

Part Three

Communist Countries

THE THREE COMMUNIST countries that conclude this volume are the Union of Soviet Socialist Republics, Yugoslavia, and the People's Republic of China. Joel Moses' chapter, "The Soviet Union in the Women's Decade, 1976–1985," finds the period a turning point because women's issues have received the most visibility since the 1920s. On the other hand, he notes the ideologically disturbing effects of the recent candor in discussing sex discrimination that continues to exist. In spite of impressive levels of women's political status and influence in national party congresses and in the state (Soviet) legislatures, real political power remains a man's domain. Although women comprise 51 percent of the labor force, they generally occupy the lower-skilled positions and tend to be the least mobile workers in both industry and the service sector. Moses comments that, in the past decade, Soviet women have been able to shape the direction of policy discussions on matters such as health, occupational safety, juvenile delinquency, and incentives to encourage population growth, family stability, and labor productivity. He suggests that the Soviet policies of the 1980s will include reforms to reduce the health risks of women and to improve the conditions for women to carry out their more traditional roles as mothers. He projects that women will be retrained into high growth areas that are in short supply of skilled workers, and notes the emergence of part-time work for women.

In Yugoslavia, Beverly Springer argues, economic development, combined with an official ideology that promotes sexual equality, has been moving women from centuries of rural, paternalistic living patterns into the labor force in urban areas. In "Yugoslav Women,"

she briefly traces the complex cultural history of this relatively new
nation, then discusses the present status of women. She analyzes
three events that have been important in the past decade. The 1974
Constitution decreed a new stage in worker self-management
through interlocking delegate systems at work and in social organization and communes. These have increased women's participation, but they play only a small role at the national level in both the
government and the Communist party. The world oil crisis of 1974
had a more significant impact than the constitutional changes because it slowed economic development and nearly stopped women's
urbanization. The third event was the International Women's Year.
The United Nations is a politically important forum for Yugoslavia,
and it played a visible role when the UN took up the women's issue.
This prompted Yugoslavian leadership into a self-study that has
resulted in several important domestic policy changes. Nevertheless, she concludes that these three events have brought about only
minor changes. Women made some political and economic gains,
and they experienced a small economic setback. She speculates that
women will continue to work, but their first obligation will be to
their families.

For Chinese women the reforms in the marriage law and the
traditional family institutions continue their salience because of
their connection to current family planning and population control.
Kay Johnson's chapter, "Women's Rights, Family Reform, and
Population Control in the People's Republic of China," notes that
since the 1940s the dominant party view is that mobilization of
women into the nondomestic labor force and abolition of private
property will lead to gender equality. Since 1953 the state has
focused on economic construction and on rural cooperatives. The
latter, however, need family stability as their basis, and this has
moved the Chinese leadership away from significant involvement in
family reform and women's rights policy. Collectivization has
increased women's participation in agriculture, but the male-
dominated cadres tend to discriminate against women in remuneration and have left rural women with most of the domestic
responsibilities. Johnson identifies substantial gaps between national goals and local rural practices. Peasants continue to prefer sons
rather than daughters, and they resist pressures to limit the number
of children until they have, preferably, two sons, because these
remain crucial to the support of the parents in their old age. Population limitation, however, is an urgent national priority and presents
a dilemma to the leadership. She concludes that the unfinished

rural family reforms of the original cultural revolution may cause policies that could again threaten an unknown number of Chinese female lives.

16

The Soviet Union in the Women's Decade, 1975–1985

Joel C. Moses
Iowa State University

G iven the closed and secretive nature of decision making in the Soviet Union, Western observers can never more than essentially speculate about the direction of change in Soviet policies or the underlying motivations and views of the collective Soviet leadership. Yet there seem fairly solid grounds to assume that, for the collective Soviet leadership, the international decade of women since 1975 may be remembered as both a political turning point and an ideologically disturbing time.

As a turning point, women's issues generally have emerged as priority concerns widely discussed in various facets of Soviet national decision making since 1975. Soviet women as a distinct interest group have been accorded greater political visibility than at any time since probably the mid-1920s, when semi-independent feminist organizations like the women's departments and feminist party officials like Alexandra Kollontai in the Central Committee focused national attention on women's problems before their elimination by Stalin in 1928 – 1933. As an ideologically disturbing time for the Soviet collective leadership, the period since 1975 has witnessed an unusual level of candor in policy debate for this otherwise authoritarian state. Wide-ranging discussion and published reports within the Soviet Union have questioned some of the most dogmatic

tenets and sources of political legitimacy for the Communist regime—particularly those asserting the superiority of communism
in eradicating since 1917 most causes of sexual discrimination still
identified as plaguing many women in Western capitalist nations.

To the likely consternation of the collective Soviet leadership, it
was not supposed to have turned out that way. The Soviet leadership has always been concerned with projecting internationally
only the most positive image of Soviet accomplishments in its
ideological rivalry with capitalism. Consistent with this reluctance
to admit national failings before a world audience, Boris
Ponomarëv, candidate member of the national Politburo and head
of the Central Committee's International Department for orches-
trating international campaigns to foreign audiences, had sounded
a predictably optimistic tone during a 1974 award ceremony, honor-
ing the Committee of Soviet Women and setting down the general
line to be defended by Soviet representatives participating in various 1975 international conferences on women's issues.[1] Ponomarëv
welcomed the forthcoming 1975 commemoration of International
Women's Year by the United Nations as a unique opportunity to
publicize worldwide the Soviet model of having resolved so successfully its "woman question" since the 1917 Bolshevik Revolution.
Thus, the decade commenced with Soviet delegations conspicuous
at internationally sponsored women's conferences in 1975, castigat-
ing the inhumane and sexist societies inherent to the nature of
capitalism and contrasting their own allegedly unblemished record
as a Communist society in having achieved complete equality between the sexes.[2]

Whatever success Soviet delegations achieved in persuading their
foreign audiences in 1975 about the accomplishments of the Soviet
model of sexual equality, political reality within the Soviet Union
since 1975 reveals quite a different perspective. Over the past decade, an almost unprecedented outpouring of frank discussion and
debate over various sources and consequences of sexual discrimination still afflicting many Soviet women has dominated Soviet mass
publications, specialized academic studies and reports, an array of
special women's forums established to investigate and correct discriminatory practices, and even the speeches of party-state leaders
before national audiences.

The awareness and discussion of problem areas had first emerged
tentatively in the mid-1960s. A few Soviet sociologists, demographers, and economists at the time had begun to draw attention in
their studies to conflicts between the working and family burdens
confronting many Soviet women, and the studies at least hinted

that Soviet women had yet failed to achieve complete factual equality of opportunity with men in the workplace and home. Then, seemingly legitimated by the events surrounding 1975 and the enhanced priority assigned women's equality as a measure of how far the USSR had progressed toward an egalitarian Communist society, many Soviet publications and conferences on women's issues appeared within the Soviet Union throughout 1975. It was very clear that several Soviet academics and political activists took advantage of 1975 to raise the volume and range of their criticisms against several aspects of Soviet reality to match the promise of sexual equality.

Since 1975, the wave of discussion and debate over women's status and related women's issues has not subsided within the USSR. As the Soviet leadership has struggled to define the causes and solutions for several critical economic-social problems, Soviet women in their varied roles as workers, wives, and mothers have increasingly been linked to these problems by Soviet academics and party-state officials.

Equally disturbing for the Soviet collective leadership must be the extent of this relatively candid discussion of problems affecting Soviet women and the manner in which issues have been defined and solutions offered. For, in this Marxist-Leninist society, any objective roots of sexual discrimination presumedly have been eliminated several decades ago with the abolition of private property and the full-time employment of more than 90 percent of all Soviet women throughout their adult lives. Marx, Engels, and Lenin—the ideological founders of the Soviet state—had identified the source of sexual discrimination as exploitative economic systems like capitalism, based on private property and the enslavement of women as unemployed and unpaid housewives of their equally exploited working-class husbands at home. Sexual inequality as a set of practices and values would only persist under capitalism, because the exploitation of women benefited the ruling capitalist class. Therefore, working full-time in the public sector of a society that had nationalized all means of production under the control of the working-class Communist party, Soviet women should have attained a factual state of liberation and equality unavailable to women in Western capitalism. Yet the past decade has witnessed public disclosures in the USSR about institutional and attitudinal factors limiting the opportunities of many Soviet women closely similar to those perpetuating inequality in Western capitalist nations.

In this still rigidly authoritarian state, views contrary to official policies or critical of political elites also cannot be expressed without utmost restraint. Yet the past decade has seen published criticisms within the USSR of governmental policies and practices as sexually discriminatory. Thinly veiled allegations have appeared in Soviet publications suggesting that sexist biases of the still predominantly male leadership and their traditional Russian view of the biologically distinct roles required of women in Soviet society have contributed to the problems of second-class citizenship still affecting many Soviet women.

The discussion and debate since 1975 has marked a qualitative change in Soviet politics. Always careful first to emphasize the positive changes in Soviet women's status since 1917, they have demonstrated a much greater official willingness to admit openly many problem areas in failing still to provide women complete and real equality to men in Soviet society.

Political Equality

A clear example of this change since 1975 has been the unfolding debate and reforms within the USSR over the issue of female political equality

Until 1975, Western observers of Soviet politics might have assumed that the problem of political equality for women had been successfully resolved in the Soviet Union. Until 1975 and to some extent even now, Soviet leaders have predictably cited several standard lines of argument to prove the major positive advances Soviet women have made since 1917 toward complete political equality. As Soviet leaders would contend, their commitment to female political equality has been an ongoing priority of state policy since the Bolshevik Revolution. Among the very first decrees of the Soviet leadership under Lenin in 1917–1918 were acts abolishing all forms of discrimination against women inherited from the prior tsarist system and the granting to women of complete juridicial and political equality in all areas of family and property rights, educational and employment opportunities, and access to elected-administrative offices. This formal commitment to equality was reaffirmed with explicit articles guaranteeing women complete equality in the 1922, 1936, and 1977 Soviet constitutions. As Article 35 of the current 1977 Constitution explicitly states: "Women and men have equal rights in the USSR."

At least on the surface, Soviet women have achieved an impressive level of political status and influence compared to women in many Western capitalist nations. Soviet leaders typically cite the average 25 percent of delegates to all national party congresses who are women and the 30 to 50 percent of deputies at various levels of state legislatures (Soviets) who have always been women since World War II. Women have also traditionally held at least one-third of elected positions on various administrative levels and governing organs of trade unions in the Soviet Union, and Soviet women individually can be found in influential leadership positions that would still be considered to be male-typed roles in the West. The Soviet leadership would also be expected to point out specific public organizations for women like the Committee of Soviet Women, which provide high visibility for women's concerns and a nationally identifiable corps of female political spokespersons. The long-time chair of this committee, herself an example of the nontraditional roles in which individual Soviet women can be found is Valentina Nikolaeva-Tereshkova, the first woman in space as a Soviet cosmonaut and a member of the national party's Central Committee since 1971.

On the other hand, these standard recitations of Soviet accomplishments for women in the political realm have been increasingly qualified since 1975 by admissions of major continuing shortcomings and failures. Thus, despite 68 years of constitutional guarantees of political equality, and despite the large percentage of women elected delegates to party congresses and deputies to state legislatures, published critiques in the Soviet Union over the past decade have alleged that much fewer than the normal or desired number of women hold really influential leadership roles. This allegation that Soviet women are significantly underrepresented in leadership roles has been documented since 1975 for a wide range of positions in Soviet society, including political-administrative elites in the government and party bureaucracies, directors of factories and collective-state farms, leaders of public organizations like trade unions, or heads of scientific and medical institutes. As one Soviet female academic summarized the pattern: "Even under socialism, the situation still prevails in which the higher the position held, the fewer the number of women represented in it. . . ."[3]

These published disclosures in the USSR during the past decade not only have contended that women lack true political equality, but in several instances they have explicitly cited or alluded to reasons for female underrepresentation in Soviet leadership roles not unlike those frequently analyzed in the West as obstacles in the political advancement of women in capitalist nations.[4] In the Soviet Union, one frequently cited factor, not unlike that limiting female political advancement in the West, has been the reluctance or inability of many Soviet women to set aside time to become active early in local politics. As in the West, early involvement in local politics is a major prerequisite and first stepping-stone to any future political leadership roles. In the Soviet Union, the only outlet for effective early political participation is membership in the Communist party, which currently includes 18 million Soviet citizens. The problem is that Soviet women have always made up a very low percentage of all Communist party members nationally, well below their proportion of the national population. Even by the mid-1980s, and following a concerted decade-long drive to increase the percentage of women in the party, female membership nationally stood at only 27 percent. Highly underrepresented in the party, Soviet women almost foreclose any opportunities for many of them to be recruited into higher leadership roles in the party and government bureaucracies, the factories or farms, and the scientific and medical institutes. Leadership roles in all of these institutions require as an absolute minimum of eligibility lengthy prior membership in the party.

As analysts in the Soviet Union who have criticized the low proportion of women in leadership roles since 1975 contend, the source of the problem probably has even more fundamental institutional and attitudinal causes. Even were Soviet women to increase significantly their percentage in the party, these diverse causes would continue to restrict the political advancement for many Soviet women to eventual influential leadership positions. As revealed and discussed by analysts in the USSR since 1975, they include stereotypes of the "natural" subordinate role of women in society perpetuated in Soviet school texts; the indifference or reluctance of political functionaries to push for greater female participation in jobs of real authority; the reluctance of many Soviet husbands to share domestic responsibilities and their failure to encourage their wives in leadership endeavors; the general unwillingness of male employees and lower party-state officials (and even women themselves) to take orders from female superiors; and widespread female psychological inhibitions.[5]

Given the very high value placed on children and the maternal role in Soviet culture, psychological inhibitions include guilt feelings among many Soviet mothers, internally pressured not to desert their primary maternal role responsibilities for the additional time away from their children required of any leadership role. Also, sexual equality in Soviet history has often meant women by default have almost been forced to deny their own femininity and adopt competitive and aggressive masculine personalities in performing male jobs in order to be accepted as true equals. In something of a counter-reaction and attempt by women to assert their own identity and values, it has been reported that particularly the current younger generation of Soviet women have adopted almost an idealized cult of Russian femininity. Their aspirations to become "liberated" in almost a nineteenth-century Victorian sense and to display tender and nurturing traits seem to them incompatible with assignments to Soviet leadership roles, stereotyped as demanding aggressive "masculine" personality types. Finally, Soviet analysts have attributed the low proportion of women in leadership roles to outright traditional male prejudices about women—namely, their presumed emotional instability and inability to cope with the additional responsibilities of leadership as well as men. Traditionally minded male factory directors may automatically discount the potential of women for promotion to key industrial managerial positions by assuming that married women cannot be expected to defer their primary homemaking and child-rearing responsibilities for the unpredictable and additional workload required of these positions.

Other unstated factors by analysts in the Soviet Union may also have a bearing. Some Western political scientists have concluded that the very kinds of early functional roles into which many Soviet female political activists become typecast, like ideology and social welfare, are so marginal in political status and visibility in the Soviet context almost to guarantee the low probability of many women ever being promoted to full-time higher offices of real influence in the USSR.[6] Given the prevailing patriarchal nature of Soviet culture and the importance attached to informal personal connections with a mentor or patron to advance politically, there also are unsubstantiated claims by Soviet emigres that many Soviet women deliberately shun leadership roles in the party and government. The women fear the stigma that, under prevailing Soviet norms, women who have achieved high political offices are widely assumed to have earned the support of their male mentor or patron only by engaging in sexual relations with him.

As a result of these diverse causes, real political power in positions of authority in the Soviet Union still remains a man's domain. At the present time, men make up all 109 members of the national Council of Ministers, the entire Politburo and Central Committee

Secretaries, and 97.5 percent of the 320 Central Committee members elected at the most recent national Party Congress in 1981.
Indeed, since 1917, only one woman, Yekaterina Furtseva, has been
elected to the national Politburo (and only for the brief period of
1957–1961); and women have never constituted more than 3 to 4
percent of Central Committee members elected at party congresses.
Even in secondary administrative positions of power, as heads of
Central Committee departments or deputy ministers, women historically have never represented more than a token few at any one
time.

To quote two Soviet female academics in 1973 and 1983 over a
ten-year span in which the situation may not have improved all that
much:

> Although the very highest posts in all areas of activity are
> accessible to women in socialism, at the same time we cannot
> ignore the factual situation by which in contemporary society
> men primarily direct state and public affairs and have greater
> possibilities of displaying their mental, organizational, and
> creative capabilities.[8]

> ... discussing the causes of some unresolved problems related
> to the status of women in socialist society, one should not forget
> such a factor as the backward consciousness of a segment of the
> population, expressed at times in an out-moded and disdainful
> view of the role and appointing of a woman ... not only in some
> families, but often in research establishments, industrial enter-
> prises, educational institutions, etc. And the situation is not so
> much in and by itself individual factors as it is that they have
> gradually formed a determined public opinion transferred into
> the practice of daily life....[9]

Despite the pessimism of these two Soviet female academics,
central male party officials since the mid-1970s have evidenced a
renewed sensitivity to the question of female representation in
leadership roles. While openly critical of Western feminist ideas
that real sexual equality necessitates a certain relative proportion
of women in leadership roles, Soviet leaders, nonetheless, appear to
have adopted their own formal affirmative-action policy for
women. Much more prominent during the past decade in speeches
by leaders at party congresses and in published reviews of party
membership and functionaries are now standard sections, detailing
the percentages of women in various positions and the measures
required to raise female representation even more. Prior to 1975,
gender as a category was more often omitted in listing the background characteristics of functionaries. Appeals to increase the
proportion of women assigned to various leadership roles have

become almost standard refrains by party-state officials in identifying still unresolved problems in the composition of leadership throughout the USSR. Thus, while critical of the fact that, even by the mid-1980s, women only make up 27 percent of all party members, party officials have lauded the increase from only 23 percent at the beginning of the 1970s and the trend over recent years for one of every three newly admitted party members to be a woman.

The need to expand female political participation through forms other than just the party has also received increased prominence in the Soviet Union in the past decade. With published reports citing the low level of political participation by women in trade unions and other organizations at work, previously dormant "women's councils" and "women's commissions" have apparently been reactivated in recent years. Women's councils, organized and run solely by female political activists in workplaces and housing areas, have been especially publicized in the Soviet Baltic republics—an area more directly influenced by Western cultural values and with a historical legacy of a more politically assertive and educated female labor force—and in the Central Asian republics—an area where women may confront even greater discrimination because of the patriarchal Muslim culture. Women's councils in these republics may now have emerged as a political outlet for more women. They have apparently been reactivated both to mobilize politically working women and homemakers and to articulate distinct female interests as an organizational counterweight to the still male-dominant local party and trade union committees. Even in small industrial centers of Central Asia, regions that employ many women workers may have as many as several thousand activists involved in their local women's councils. On Soviet collective farms, the deputy chairman is now more typically a woman who also heads the farm's women's council, invested with broadly defined responsibilities of defending women's interests on the farms.

Women's commissions, first established at the national and local levels of trade unions in 1962, have been charged with reporting on serious health and safety hazards for working women. Through the typical collusion of local male industrial officials, trade union leaders, and labor safety inspectors, these hazards have been allowed to continue because correcting them would cost the factories additional money and would complicate production by making special provision for the women. In some alleged instances, the women's commissions have been aggressive enough to force factories violating safety and health provisions, under threat of exposure and fines, to correct the problems. In April of 1983, the trade union women's commissions were renamed the "commissions for problems of women's labor and everyday life and the protection of motherhood and childhood."

The renaming of the women's commissions was not an isolated event. It occurred at the same time that the first national law on labor collectives in Soviet history was drafted and passed by the national legislature in 1983, amidst other signs that the Soviet leadership was cautiously attempting to provide some greater input for rank-and-file workers in administering Soviet industrial enterprises. For Soviet women, the renaming in 1983–1984 coincided with other signs on the national policy level that women's issues like day-care facilities, retaining and promoting women to higher-skilled and paying jobs in industry, and female medical facilities in industrial enterprises were to receive greater priority in future negotiations over collective contracts between trade union locals and enterprise management in the USSR. As a training ground for future women politicians, the trade union commissions also may have assumed increased importance. A reported 22 thousand female trade unionists were said to be active just in the women's commissions of Moscow,[10] and mass-publication studies on the women's commissions for local female trade union activists were distributed in large circulation runs of 50 and 100 thousand in 1984 throughout the Soviet Union.[11] In addition to the seemingly revitalized women's trade union commissions, since 1976 special legislative committees on women's issues have been formed in the national and republic legislatures of the Soviet state, with a broad mandate to promote women's interests, investigate wrongdoing, and prod compliance from ministries and trade unions. On the other hand, it is at least significant to consider that these various women's political organizations represent the first visible willingness of the Soviet leadership to provide women with even semiautonomous organizations, since special women's departments in the Communist party were abolished by the early 1930s. On the other hand, too much should not automatically be read into these recent policy changes and political fora to enhance female political participation in the Soviet Union. As overseers of an authoritarian state in which the Communist party remains the only legitimate representative of any group interests in Soviet society, the Soviet leadership will never tolerate any truly independent political interests not controlled at least indirectly by the party bureaucracy. With party members or officials heading all these various women's councils, commissions, and committees, there is little reason to expect that they would evolve into something of an independent feminist movement. Past organizations, like the Committee of Soviet Women, have long been notorious as extensions of the party's propaganda offensive in promoting a favorable image of women's accomplishments in the USSR to foreign audiences and channeling women's interests in directions acceptable to the male party elite.[12] One distraught Moscow woman interviewed by two female Swedish journalists in 1978 probably expressed the reaction of many Soviet women to these newly formed or reactivated women's political fora since 1975:

> And anyway, think of all our organizations! All they really boil down to is paying dues and obligatory attendance. We no longer think that anything can be accomplished by meetings and conferences. We've become immune to that.... [13]

On the other hand, there are signs that a group of younger and more outspoken female activists and officials may be emerging as an informal lobby for women's interests within the party and within the leadership of trade unions and other organizations more directly involved with women workers on a normal basis. They at least would have been provided the official encouragement from the party-state leadership and formal outlets to promote those interests to a much greater degree over the past decade. In this regard, there is indirect evidence that a potential common affinity or group awareness as women already has emerged among some female professional politicians in the Soviet Union. In their autobiographical accounts these women commonly mention their close friendships and informal interaction with other female activists and politicians in other parts of the country or in other countries (including the West).[14] Also intriguing are the comments of Tamara Glavak, a borough party secretary in her early forties from the Ukrainian capital of Kiev, and a party delegate to the 1981 Party Congress interviewed in *The New York Times*. In the interview, she disclosed that she was part of an informal feminine network active in Kiev to make sure that the current level of participation by women in local public life was not diminished. As she was quoted by the *Times* reporter:

> Some men try to lower it [the percentage of women assigned to positions in the party and state organizations in Kiev]. They say 'We're all for finding a woman for this position, but there aren't any.' What we have to do is prove to them that there are.[15]

Economic-Social Equality

Another common issue that has generated increased public discussion and debate within the Soviet Union during the past decade revolves around various facets of economic inequality still affecting many Soviet women. Despite women making up 51 percent of the entire Soviet labor force, and despite formal constitutional guarantees of equality in the workplace, published studies by Soviet economists (particularly by younger Soviet female economists) have increasingly disclosed during the past decade that Soviet women remain occupationally segregated and underemployed in the lowest-paying, less-skilled, and least vocationally mobile jobs in the Soviet economy. Despite the failure to report national average wages and salaries for male and female workers in the USSR, published studies of individual Soviet industries or regions since 1975 consistently find patterns in which women earn probably at best two-thirds the annual salaries of all men in the Soviet labor force.[16]

If these problems of economic inequality confronting many Soviet women do not differ substantially from those experienced by many women today in Western capitalist nations, their origin and perpetuation contrast with the otherwise very positive historical role of women in Soviet economic development.

In Western capitalist nations, the number of women working in the labor force has only significantly expanded during the past two decades, and at least part of the continuing problems of low job status and lower salaries for many Western women could be explained by their late entry into their nations' labor forces. In contrast, Soviet women have actually constituted a substantial percentage of all Soviet workers for the last five decades. During the Stalin era (1928–1953), a massive influx of women into the labor force, although heralded retrospectively as evidence of the state's long-term commitment to sexual equality, became a virtue as much out of economic and political necessity. The economy would never have been industrialized in the 1930s without the more than 8 of every 10 new industrial workers at the time who were women. Thoughout the Stalin era, the economy would never have successfully recovered from the devastation of World War II or expanded post-1945 without the millions of Soviet women—working full-time to compensate for the male population losses resulting from the Stalinist collectivization of agriculture, the purges and great terror of the 1930s, the labor camps of the 1930s and 1940s, and the more than 20 million men who perished during the war. Women have surged to over half of the entire labor force since the late 1960s; and over 60 percent of all new labor entries during a typical and most recent five-year period (1976–1980) were young women.

Few party-state leaders or economists in the USSR question the strategic dependence of the Soviet economy on its women workers nor the influence that women potentially derive from their majority status in the Soviet labor force. Surveys conducted among Soviet women consistently find wide support for female employment by a vast majority. The surveyed women have cited both the material necessity of their second salary to maintain even minimum living standards in average two-spouse Soviet families and the psychological satisfaction of their careers outside the home as motivations to continue working full-time their entire adult lives.

If few in the Soviet Union would deny the positive benefits for women's status of so many working full-time their entire adult lives, the problem increasingly raised by economists in the USSR since 1975 is that the real potentials and contributions to economic expansion of so many Soviet women have still not been realized to the fullest. The disparities in job status and salaries confronting many Soviet women derive from complex factors. These factors since 1975 have been both more openly and frequently criticized in studies by various Soviet research institutes and even by party-state leaders, unable to overlook the effect that female underemployment and their comparatively low labor productivity have had on declining economic growth rates nationally during the past decade. From these various Soviet published sources over the past decade, a fairly clear explanation of why women have failed to achieve economic and social equality with men in the USSR has emerged.[17]

One common explanation cited in these sources for the fact that Soviet women earn less than men in industry is that base salaries are set nationally according to attained occupational skills, the technical proficiency required to perform different jobs, and the specific industrial branch. The higher the occupational skills and technical proficiency and the more important the industrial branch in economic planning, the higher the hourly wage rate for the job on a comprehensive six-scale grade classification. Predominantly employed in unskilled or semiskilled manual jobs in the lowest-paying and least prestigious industrial branches in national economic planning (like textiles and food processing), many women are classified in the lower 1 and 2 skill grades and earn less than men, whose work typically in higher-paying industrial branches (like coal mining and metallurgy) has been classified in the higher 3–6 skill grades. Over the past two decades, even when women have broken out of traditionally low-paying female branches into higher-status and previously male-dominant branches like machine building (which now employs the largest absolute number of all women in Soviet industry), they still predominate in the least mechanized, unskilled, and lowest-paid and graded jobs in these branches. They seem as much preferred by plant managers in radio, electronics, and automobile assembly plants for their greater willingness than men to tolerate the intensely monotonous pace of work in these machine-building subdivisions. In addition, although only 40 percent of all women are employed in non–assembly-line auxiliary jobs in Soviet industry, most female auxiliary workers are hired for the most physically demanding and lowest-paying jobs (like packagers and warehouse loaders), while men in auxiliary work are employed more in the technically demanding and high-paying positions of machine repairers and assembly-line machinists.

The disparities in salaries and grade classifications persist despite the fact that women nationally equal or surpass men by total completed years of general secondary and higher education. Indeed, women overall tend to be the least mobile workers in industry. They constitute only one-third of those enrolled nationally in vocational-technical schools, where formal training over one to three years has more frequently been required to qualify for upgraded job classifications, and where evening sessions remain inaccessible to many women responsible almost solely for child rearing and housework. Even this one-third have been concentrated in a limited number of female vocational-technical schools because of prejudices against training women for allegedly male (and also typically high-paying) vocations in male-stereotyped industrial branches. Not unexpectedly, women often require more than twice as long as male workers to advance into higher skill grades. The total percentage of women in unskilled labor is 2.4 times higher than that of men and the percentage of women in skilled labor 1.8 times lower than that of men. And women even in surveyed factories where they far surpass their male cohorts in formal secondary-higher education remain almost perpetually underemployed in low-graded jobs as semimanual laborers.

The situation is not that much better for women employed in other sectors of the economy. Women make up approximately 55 percent of all collective farm workers, but hold fewer than 1 percent of skilled positions (like tractor drivers or combine operators) and, in some Soviet republics, constitute 90 to 98 percent of all manual laborers (like field workers or livestock growers). As in Western economies, women also comprise the overwhelming majority of all female-typed positions in the service sector, from secretaries (95 percent) and cashiers (94 percent) to hospital orderlies-nurses (99 percent) and retail shop attendants (79 percent). Even more so than in the West, these same service jobs in the Soviet Union are the very least skilled, lowest-paying, most personally and physically demanding, and very lowest in occupational prestige. Current projected economic trends in the USSR forecast a significant increase in the number of service sector workers required for the Soviet economy, with the probability that even a larger absolute number of women will be channeled into this very low-status and low-paid sector. Even the much lauded percentage of women doctors and teachers in the Soviet Union (approximately 7 of every 10) must be understood in the Soviet context and the comparatively low salaries of these professions in the USSR, averaging two-thirds or less of the average monthly take-home wage of a male welder in average monthly take-home wage of a male welder in industry.

As a Soviet female economist recently bemoaned in reviewing a study of labor force participation in the USSR:

> ... in which law or resolution, for example, has it been written that only women are to be employed for the position of maid, nurse, dish-washer, etc., while men are to be principally employed as the plant director, head of a department, or a brigade leader. Nowhere has this been said, but, nonetheless, it would seem that for the position of the first group (low skill level) they have always been designated to be of a female nature and practically exclusively women have been counted in these positions, while in the positions of the second group (high skill level), men predominate.... [18]

The problems Soviet women confront are not limited just to occupational segregation and low salaries. Despite the formal commitment to creating an egalitarian society and impressive state subsidies for preschool facilities, housing, and child support, the Soviet mass media in the past decade have been replete with articles on the hardships of Soviet women—working full-time at a job but then forced to bear the additional daily four- to five-hour double burden of shopping, housework, and child rearing almost completely unaided by their traditionally minded husbands. The reality in the Soviet Union is that housework and child rearing remain women's work and that the state's commitment to social equality has not altered women's status in many Soviet households.

Even Soviet public policy, critical of husbands' failures to share these responsibilities equally with their wives, and committed during the past decade to raise the quality of consumer services for the

Soviet public, unwittingly reinforces traditional stereotypes. As a former female deputy chairman of the Lituanian Council of Ministers pointed out in a forum on women's problems published in the republic newspaper, only plant meetings convened for their women workers ever discuss "female" subjects such as raising children, thus perpetuating conventional notions that child rearing should not be of any concern to male workers and emphasizing the second-class status of women workers. Furthermore, when government ministers and party officials herald improvements in consumer services for the Soviet public, they emphasize how these improved services will relieve the burdens of working housewives, as if consumer services should be solely women's concerns, and as if working husbands should not be responsible for dropping off laundry or preparing dinner.[19]

Difficulties for Soviet working women are compounded by the acute shortage and poor quality of preschool facilities (nurseries and kindergartens) available for young children. On one hand, it is true that a major effort has been initiated since 1975 to increase the number and improve the quality of these facilities, and the reported proportion of Soviet children between one and seven years old for whom preschool facilities are available has increased from 33 percent in the mid-1970s to 40 percent by the mid-1980s. On the other hand, this is a national average. Reports in the Soviet Union have also disclosed that available spaces for preschool children in some union republics and entire rural areas may still be less than one-tenth of those actually required. Throughout the past decade, overcrowding, unqualified supervisors, substandard and unheated buildings, inadequate nourishment, and unsanitary conditions have only been some of the standard criticisms leveled against preschool facilities in the Soviet national media like *Izvestiia*.

In addition, since the passage of a 1974 Soviet law providing child support payments for families falling below a certain monthly per-capita income categorized as poor in the USSR, a few specialized studies by Soviet sociologists, examining the implementation of the law, have offered partial glimpses into the extent of real poverty in the country. As in the West, they suggest an increasing association of poverty in the Soviet Union with single-parent, female-headed households with several underaged children, a failure for the support payments to reach many needy mothers, and an emerging feminization of poverty among working poor in the USSR not unlike the pattern emerging during the past decade in the United States.[20] Finally, despite the alleged social equality of Soviet women, published revelations in the USSR in the past decade have openly criticized the callous abuse of women by male superiors in factories and research institutes. Unpublished underground manuscripts distributed by Soviet female dissidents (before they were exiled from the country and stripped of their Soviet citizenship) cited even more widespread patterns of sexual mistreatment normally experienced by women in Soviet institutions ranging from medical clinics to prisons.[21]

Women's Issues

Western observers who have followed the preceding discussion of problem areas in Soviet publications in the past decade would be hard pressed to conclude that the status of women in the Soviet Union differs significantly in kind from that of women in many Western capitalist nations. As is still true in the West, these Soviet publications have revealed that Soviet women suffer from political discrimination and underrepresentation in leadership roles, insensitivity to women's problems by a dominant male elite, occupational segregation and lower wages, sexism at home and inadequate preschool facilities, the feminization of poverty, and sexual abuse and mistreatment as institutional norms.

At the same time, Western observers cannot but be impressed by the increasingly open admission of problem areas within the Soviet Union and the evident ability of Soviet women as a group at least to shape the direction of public policy discussions and decisions in the USSR during the past decade. Indeed, if the influence of a group is indirectly measured by the degree to which it can force political leaders to anticipate its demands and responses in making decisions, then Soviet women have achieved an unquestionably greater indirect influence this past decade. So wide-ranging are the policy issues to which Soviet women as a group have been linked that the issues almost span the domestic policy agenda and most critical domestic problems addressed by the Soviet leadership since 1975. In many instances, openly expressed conflict within these policy issues has revolved around those proposing solutions based on a more traditional view of woman as wife and mother against those proposing solutions based on a modern view of woman as both mother-wife and worker. The policy issues and manner in which women have been linked to make them almost defined "women's issues" in the Soviet political context include only some of the following.

Health

There has been increasing concern over irrefutable signs of deteriorating health in the Soviet population and dire warnings of its economic and societal consequences if unchecked. The factors contributing to the overall health crisis are complex and include environmental pollution, alcoholic addiction, poorly trained medical personnel, and administratively incompetent ministries responsible for health care. Yet one facet of this emerging concern over health during the past decade in the Soviet Union has been directed against rising infant mortality rates since the early 1970s and the many related health problems of women. In the Soviet specialized journals, the source of the problem has been attributed to the generally poor working conditions under which many women must labor, their prevalence in unskilled and physically arduous manual labor exposing them to all forms of health and safety risks, and the failure of many industrial and farm officials to enforce prescribed health and safety measures. As documented by analysts in the Soviet Union, health and safety laws designed to protect women have been systematically violated in certain industrial branches, unenforced in others because of the indifference of trade union and party officials (and the related political quiescence of women workers), underfunded by industrial managers reluctant to spend their own enterprise funds on improving working conditions for either their male or female employees, and generally sacrificed to the greater expediency of meeting monthly production quotas by the collusion of managers, trade union officials, and local party heads. Industrial managers have been more willing to pay the minimal fines if caught breaking the law or pay women wage supplements to work under unsafe conditions than to disrupt the production process and provide special dispensations for them.[22]

Occupational health and safety in this context has clearly emerged as a defined women's issue the past decade in the Soviet Union, and numerous actions since 1975 testify to the increased priority it has received. There are frequent reports about increased funding for medical research institutes investigating occupational health issues, and greater stress has been placed on the requirement that all industrial enterprises meet and fund annual targets in their social plans designed particularly to improve the working conditions of their women workers. To reduce the number of women potentially exposed to health and safety risks, a 1978 labor law amendment expanded the list of occupations prohibited to women because they were deemed unusually difficult or hazardous to female health, and since 1980 ministries have been instructed to meet annual quotas in reducing the number of their workers employed in manual and physically difficult jobs. With the large number of women employed in these kinds of jobs, the latter section has been widely and alternatively interpreted as a women's health reform.

In contrast to Western initiatives in the same area of female health and safety at work, however, very little concern (except by some female Soviet academics) has been expressed in the USSR over the fairness of these measures. Women are being prohibited from an even larger number of occupations that at the same time remain among the most highly paid and male-dominated in the Soviet economy. Granted, the same 1978 labor law amendment and post-1980 policy to reduce manual workers contained provisions specifying severance pay for the displaced workers and the intent to retrain and reassign the displaced workers to higher-skilled and paying jobs in related industries. Yet, when female employment in manual jobs is reduced, many of the displaced women workers, lacking any formal training to begin with and unqualified for anything but the most menial kinds of jobs, may have little option other than accepting work in the lower-paying service sector. Perhaps the real underlying implication of these recent policy reforms for women was tersely stated in a recent study distributed to female trade union activists in 1984, which concluded that the numerous recent mea sures "undoubtedly will reduce somewhat the participation of women in social production [i.e., the labor force]."[23] A tentative but probably valid conclusion would be that Soviet policy since 1975 appears set to improve the health and working conditions of women workers even at the expense of likely further occupational segregation and wage disparity between the sexes.

Population

The Soviet Union also confronts a critical population problem, resulting from the sharp decline of birthrates and imminent labor shortages projected for the rest of this century among its most highly educated and skilled Baltic and Slavic ethnic nationalities. For many Soviet demographers and party officials, this population decline has become defined as both a problem and a women's issue. The highly educated and career-oriented women among these ethnic groups are almost blamed for evolving life-styles in which having only one child has become the norm. Therefore, to correct the problem and induce these women to perform their socially necessary reproductive function of having two or three children on average, various pro-natalist measures have been instituted in the past decade: partially paid maternity leaves to one year; lump-sum allowances to mothers at the birth of their first through third children; and special privileges in housing, vacation centers, and retail consumer outlets for pregnant women and families with infants.

If in a minority, other Soviet academics have openly refuted both the underlying assumption that a critical population problem exists and the merit or efficacy of pro-natalist measures in raising birthrates. From their stated perspective, the desired or necessary population of the Soviet Union cannot be reduced to a quantitative measure but must consider the quality of those children raised in family units of different size and the effective contribution of those children later as adult workers to Soviet economic growth. If nothing else, smaller families permit parents to allocate more effort and financial resources to the education of their individual children, and the children as adult workers are more likely to be qualified to fill the new vocations created in a technologically expanding economy. The Soviet Union is not threatened with an absolute population problem, but a shortage of needed skilled and educated workers. Not only would the pro-natalist measures fail to induce highly trained women in these ethnic groups to have more children, but they would have the counterproductive effect of pulling them out of the labor force for extended periods during pregnancy and maternity leaves and depriving the Soviet economy already lacking in skilled workers of their vital number.

Family and Crime

Much alarm has been expressed in the Soviet Union during the past decade over the alleged destabilization of family life. One-third of all Soviet marriages now end in divorce, and Soviet divorce rates in Western European cities like Moscow and Leningrad now approximate those in countries with the highest world rates. Up to one-half of Soviet marriages in these cities end in divorce (and often within the very first few years of the marriage). The divorce rates threaten not only to worsen further birthrate declines, but to undermine the very traditional family unit, because it has tended to socialize children into pro-state supportive values and beliefs. Although some Soviet academics perceive the rising divorce rate as a positive expression and natural outgrowth of social emancipation for Soviet women, others have condemned the rate as a social problem. The problem is attributed partly to the sexual and emotional individualism of many younger Soviet women, who no longer seem as willing as their mothers and grandmothers to tolerate an unhappy marriage for the sake of their children and society.

In addition, rampant juvenile delinquency, with its clear manifestations in gang-organized crimes in large Soviet cities, has become a critical issue the past decade, blamed by some Soviet academics on the decline of parental oversight. The latter has been traced to mothers—more preoccupied by their careers outside the home, overindulging their single child with Western material goods and distorted life values, and more often raising their children in single-parent family units (the alleged pathology of children raised in fatherless families). Others reject the simplistic notion that juvenile delinquency can be equated solely with the decline of parental oversight, and they perceive its cause in the same complex of factors that has contributed to juvenile delinquency in Western societies. A few Soviet criminologists and sociologists in particular have argued that Soviet juvenile delinquency, as in the West, stems from the same breakdown in a sense of community and social order characteristic of neighborhoods in a rapidly changing urban environment.

Labor Productivity

Increases in labor productivity over the past decade in the Soviet economy have either leveled off or actually stagnated. The problem of labor productivity represents only one of several interrelated dilemmas plaguing the highly inefficient Soviet economy, but Soviet leaders have made a resolution of this problem their major economic priority for the rest of this century. With labor shortages projected for the next two decades, the smaller number of new workers added to the Soviet labor force must significantly increase what they produce hourly to prevent serious stagnation if not an absolute decline in Soviet economic growth.

To accomplish this increase in labor productivity, the Soviet leadership since 1975 have emphasized two policy lines. First, a segment of the current labor force who are not used efficiently are to be transferred after retraining to other jobs in the more high-growth areas of the economy or eased completely out of the labor force. Second, greater capital investments are to be made in automated technology to compensate for a smaller number of workers and produce more per hour from those who are employed.

The reason has been clearly stated by the leadership. While they have always boasted that unemployment does not exist in their socialist system, it does not mean that the approximately 130 million adult workers actually hold jobs economically necessary. To prevent unemployment, too many workers in the Soviet labor force are retained in make-work and low-productive jobs; and neither the way in which the economy is centrally administered nor the incentives provided local industrial managers encourage an efficient use of the national labor force nor the possible elimination of superfluous jobs and workers. Simply put, employing 130 million workers does not mean that 130 million real job positions exist in the Soviet economy. The current problem of labor productivity has thus emerged in policy discussions since 1975 as a women's issue for no other reason than that women personify this basic dilemma: As over half the entire labor force, women constitute the largest mass of underemployed and superfluous workers kept on in low-productive and make-work manual jobs.

The irony is that low labor productivity does not stem from any inherent faults of women workers themselves. Actually, published Soviet studies have consistently shown that Soviet women are much more diligent and hardworking than men and are much less likely to commit labor violations or be absent at work. The problem stems from the complex of previously cited factors that have occupationally segregated women, underutilized their real talents by channelling them into low-skilled and unproductive jobs, and consigned them to industrial branches with the fewest capital investments to automate production and make their workers more productive.

The alternatives underlying most Soviet policy discussion and reforms enacted since 1975 entail either retraining a large number of women in skilled vocations and redistributing them to high-growth areas of the economy, or easing a large number of the unskilled and unproductive women out of the labor force without appearing to backtrack from the state's commitment to full employment for all adult workers. The implication for the future role and status of Soviet women is obviously quite different, depending on which alternative prevails. The first would enhance female employment and status by providing women with a wider range of job opportunities in skilled positions with higher wages; the latter would negate even those advances Soviet women have made by their full employment since the 1930s, by relegating them back to the home and a more traditional role for women as solely wife and mother in Soviet society.

Soviet policy initiatives by the mid-1980s have been rationalized as fulfilling both alternatives, with some clear and openly expressed disagreements among Soviet academics as to their implications for the status and role of Soviet women. Thus, the previously cited 1978 amendment prohibiting women's employment in more industrial vocations and the post-1980 policy to reduce the number of manual workers have been rationalized as both female health reforms and economic reforms. As health reforms, their intent is to reduce the number of women in child-bearing years exposed to health and safety risks possibly harmful to their reproductive organs. In this sense, by reducing the number of women employed in arduous and hazardous manual work, the emphasis is to improve conditions for women to carry out their more traditional role of mother. At the same time, the reforms have been defended as a progressive economic change in the status of women. Workers displaced under the 1978 amendment and post-1980 policy are supposed to be retrained and reassigned to high-growth economic areas in short supply of skilled workers. In this sense, by increasing the number of women in skilled positions, the role and status of women in the labor force are to be enhanced.

Another emerging policy reform with divergent implications and rationales for women is part-time work.[24] Part-time work has been increasingly advocated as a reform since the 1970s, with two quite different justifications offered by its supporters. By reducing the number of hours women work, some advocates have contended that the economy would benefit in the long run by having women use their additional free time for retraining and then eventual reassignment to full-time highly skilled positions. Other advocates have defended the same reform as a pro-natalist policy in line with a more traditional role requirement for women. With the additional time at home and the option to work only part-time, more women would allegedly decide to have more children, under the expectation that they could remain home and care for their additional children during the first few years after their birth while still remaining somewhat active in the labor force by filling in part-time. Ironically, by indirection, the ideal labor status for women raised under this rationale is the prevalence of temporary jobs. In Western capitalist nations, temporary jobs have meant that many women remain occupationally limited by opportunities as part-time clerical and sales help. Soviet critics of part-time work for women in their own society have drawn the analogy to the West, by challenging the reform's advocates, who see merit in more Soviet women remaining active part-time as salesclerks, cashiers, dishwashers, and nannies.

The Future: The 1990s and Beyond

Predicting anything about the Soviet Union, let alone the role of women, is almost an impossible and foolhardy exercise. All that we can do is tentatively project the trends of the past decade and state with some probability that women will continue to achieve an indirect influence in Soviet politics by forcing the male collective leadership to consider them as a distinct group in formulating policies. In retrospect, the past decade has seen a much more visible importance attributed to women in Soviet policy making than at any time since the 1920s. It does not represent any sudden feminist consciousness on the part of the male leadership, but a pragmatic recognition that the major problems they face cannot be resolved unless policies anticipate the needs and likely responses of women. It is a recognition of the vital role that women occupy now and will continue to occupy for the rest of this century in the Soviet economy and society. In the past, policies have been made without much input from women, relatively absent from the party and leadership roles; and perhaps one reason the leadership have been so concerned since 1975 in expanding female participation in the party and in leadership roles has been an awareness that policies formulated without the involvement of this strategic group have been unrealistic and ineffective. This awareness is unlikely to diminish no matter who the Soviet leaders are during the next decade.

If women and women's issues continue to gain prominence during the next decade, it will also be without any pressure by an independent women's movement in the Soviet Union. That the Soviet Union is an authoritarian Communist state forbidding any independent political movement is a fundamental and likely unchanging reality the next decade. It definitely limits the degree of change in their condition that women will be able to initiate. Yet, as we have contended, there are indirect signs of an emerging stratum of younger female politicians within the party bureaucracy. These women and their male supporters are aware that the clock cannot be turned back in formulating policies. Their number and positions of authority may be sufficient to counter any policy decisions intended to ease women out of the labor force, arbitrarily limit divorces and raise birthrates, and otherwise reverse the status of Soviet women back into a more traditional role.

Finally, all of the above assumes a rational course of events predicated on the past decade. Given an authoritarian state in which the male collective leadership can arbitrarily initiate changes, rationality and the past can often be highly imperfect guides to the future in Soviet politics.

NOTES

1. "Vysokoe priznanie" (High Recognition), *Izvestiia*, February 16, 1974.

2. Extensive coverage and reports of the 1975 international conferences on women's issues appeared throughout the year in the Soviet press. See the reports and analyses of activities at the United Nations' Mexico City conference in *Pravda*, June 19, 21, 25–26, 29–July 1, and July 3, 1975; on the East Berlin conference organized by the Communist bloc, *Pravda*, October 19, 21–24, 28, 1975.

3. A. K. Iurtsinia, "Razvitie lichnosti zhenshchiny pri sotsializme" (The Development of Woman's Personality under Socialism), unpublished dissertation precis (Riga: Latvian State University, 1973), 19. An abbreviated and somewhat toned-down version of Iurtsinia's dissertation was published under her name as a research report of the USSR Ministry of Higher and Middle Specialized Education: "Sotsialisticheskii obraz zhizni i razvitie lichnosti zhenshchin" (The Socialist Way of Life and the Development of Women's Personality), *Nauchnyi kommunizm* 5 (September–October 1978), 52–59.

4. Over the past decade, several Western scholars who specialize in contemporary Soviet politics have published studies on the problems of female political participation and elite recruitment in the Soviet Union. These studies have been based in part on recent Soviet published sources and interviews with Soviet officials and emigres; and distillation of their major findings and conclusions has provided the source of my own generalizations on the post-1975 policy debate over female political equality within the Soviet Union. These Western studies include: Joel C. Moses, "Women in Political Roles," and Jerry F. Hough, "Women and Women's Issues in Soviet Policy Debates," in Dorothy Atkinson et al., eds., *Women in Russia* (Stanford, CA: Stanford University Press, 1977), 333–353 and 355–373: Gail Warshofsky Lapidus, *Women in Soviet Society: Equality, Development, and Social Change* (Berkeley: University of California Press, 1978), 198–231; Barbara Wolfe Jancar, *Women under Communism* (Baltimore, MD: Johns Hopkins University Press, 1978); and Joel C. Moses, *The Politics of Female Labor in the Soviet Union* (Ithaca, NY: Center for International Studies, Cornell University, 1978), 14–17.

5. Typically, more frank discussions of problems surrounding female elite recruitment have not appeared in the national Soviet newspapers with mass circulations like *Izvestiia* and *Pravda*, but in limited-edition regional periodicals and specialized academic journals published by government-academic research institutes in the Soviet Union. Several examples of specific sources from Soviet publications since 1975 can be found in the text and footnotes of Lapidus and Moses (1978).

6. Moses (1977).

7. Jancar, 201–203.

8. Iurtsinia (1973), 20–21.

9. Ye. P. Blinova, "Zhenshchina v razvitom sotsialisticheskom ob-shchestve" (The Woman in Developed Socialist Society), *Rabochii klass i sovremennyi mir*, 5 (September– October 1983), 173.

10. E. Ye. Novikova et al., *Sovetskiye zhenshchiny i profsoiuzy (Soviet Women and Trade Unions)* (Moscow: Profizdat, 1984), 165.

11. Novikova et al.; Z. A. Volkova et al., *Komissiia profkoma po voprosam truda i byta zhenshchin, okhrany materinstva i detstva (The Commissions of the Trade Union for Problems of Women's Labor and Everyday Life and the Protection of Motherhood and Childhood)* (Moscow: Profizdat, 1984).

12. In addition to general sources, this impression of the propaganda function by traditional women's organizations in the Soviet Union and their leadership by officials with little awareness of women's issues in their own country was reinforced by an extensive interview which I had in June of 1975 with Shirley Hendsch. At the time Hendsch served as director of international women's programs at the U.S. Department of State and had extensive personal experience and knowledge of her female counterparts from the Soviet Union through international contacts.

13. Carola Hansson and Karin Lidén. *Moscow Women* (New York: Pantheon Books, 1983), 152.

14. *100 interv'iu s sovetskimi zhenshchinami (A Hundred Interviews with Soviet Women)* (Moscow: Molodaia gvardiia, 1975), 30, 70, 116, 118–119, 121, 123, 132, 155, 169. A. P. Biriukova, a Central Committee member, secretary in the national trade-union council, and national chair of the same revitalized women's trade-union commissions, may reflect part of this emerging feminine network within the party establishment. See the interview with her and the assessment by Ned Temko, "Near the Top, But Still not Decisionmakers," *Christian Science Monitor*, October 9, 1981, 1 ff.

15. Anthony Austin, "Kiev Women Rises in Party Job, But Not to the Top," *New York Times*, March 6, 1981, 2.

16. Several of these regional or industry studies published in the USSR the past decade have been summarized by Western scholars on the Soviet Union: Moses (1978), 3–38; Michael Swafford, "Sex Differences in Soviet Earnings," *Amerian Sociological Review* 43:5 (October 1978); 657–673; Lapidus, 161–197, and "The Female Industrial Labor Force: Dilemmas, Reassessments," in Arcadius Kahan and Blair A. Ruble, eds., *Industrial Labor in the U.S.S.R.* (New York: Pergamon Press, 1979), 232–279. Examples can be found among several of the specialized studies from the Soviet Union over the past decade translated in Gail Warshofsky Lapidus, ed., *Women, Work, and Family in the Soviet Union*, Vladimir Talmy, trans. (Armonk, NY: M. E. Sharpe, 1982).

17. See, in particular, Moses (1978), 3–38; several of the translated selections from published studies in the Soviet Union in Lapidus, ed. (1982); Joel C. Moses, *The Politics of Women and Work in the Soviet Union and the*

United States, Institute of International Studies Research Series (Berkeley: University of California, 1983), 10–53.

18. Blinova, 173.

19. L. Iu. Dirżinskaite, "Dela and zaboty sovremennits" (The Pursuits and Concerns of Contemporary Women), *Sovetskaia Litva*, December 29, 1975.

20. V. Ia. Belen'kii, "Pomoshch' predpriiatiia maloobespechennym sem'iam" (Assistance of an Industrial Enterprise to Underprovided Families), *Ekonomika i organizatsiia promyshlennogo proizvodstva* 2 (February 1981), 114–121. It was noted in the study (p. 119) that 48 percent of the surveyed female-headed families eligible for assistance had not received any from their factory, at times for one and a half years.

21. On the feminist movement among Soviet dissidents, see the interviews with the exiled leaders: Robin Morgan, "The First Feminist Exiles from the U.S.S.R.," *Ms.* 9:5 (November 1980), 49 ff. Selected translations from the underground manuscripts can be found in the monthly journal of Freedom House in New York City: *Freedom Appeals*, May–June 1980, 3–12.

22. Analysis by Soviet academics of the reasons that labor-protection legislation for women workers has not been enforced in the Soviet Union include some of the following: T. Ye. Chumakova, *Trud i byt zhenshchin (sotsial'no-pravovye aspekty)* (Women's Labor and Everyday Life—Social-Legal Aspects) (Minsk: Nauka i Tekhnika, 1978), 40–52, 58–62, 73–78; E. Ye. Novikova and B. P. Kutyrev, "Kolichestvo i kachestvo truda—obsuzhdenie 'kruglogo stola,'" (The Quantity and Quality of Labor—A Round-Table Discussion), *Ekonomika i organizatsiia promyshlennogo proizvodstva* 3 (May–June 1978), 22–23, 27–28.

23. Novikova et al., 184.

24. On the complex factors and alternative rationales surrounding part-time labor reforms in the Soviet Union contrasted with those surrounding similar reforms in the United States, see Moses (1983), 10–170.

RECOMMENDED READINGS

Atkinson, Dorothy et al., eds. *Women in Russia*. Stanford, CA: Stanford University Press, 1977.
Analysis of Russian women from the range of historical, economic, sociological, legal, ideological, and political perspectives by 18 prominent Western scholars in the field of Russian and Soviet studies. Chapters assess the historical heritage, women's sex roles and social change, and the status of women in Soviet society and politics.

Hansson, Carola, and Karin Lidén. *Moscow Women*. Gerry Bothmer et al., trans. New York: Pantheon Books, 1983.
Transcriptions of 13 taped interviews with a representative cross-section of women in the Soviet capital by two Swedish feminists and journalists. With an introduction by Gail Lapidus, interviews offer a unique glimpse into the attitudes and perspectives of modern Russian women as expressed in their own words.

Jancar, Barbara Wolfe. *Women under Communism*. Baltimore, MD: Johns Hopkins University Press, 1978.
Sophisticated analysis of women's status and problem areas in contemporary Communist states based on secondary and primary sources, including extensive interviews with East European and Soviet women and emigres. Role and status of Soviet women in comparative perspective of women in similar states. Concludes that lack of political equality and inability to organize women's interests independently in Communist states preclude basic improvement in the lot of these women.

Lapidus, Gail Warshofsky. *Women in Soviet Society: Equality, Development, and Social Change*. Berkeley: University of California Press, 1978.
The best and most comprehensive single study of the topic by a Western scholar. Role and status of Soviet women as a consequence of Marxist-Leninist ideology, Soviet modernization, and Stalinist developmental priorities. Extensive analysis of current policy conflicts surrounding women in the Soviet Union.

————, ed. *Women, Work, and Family in the Soviet Union*. Vladimir Talmy, trans. Armonk, NY: M. E. Sharpe, 1982.
Excerpts from recent Soviet specialized periodicals and books on problem areas confronting Soviet women in the workplace and at home. Provides fair representation of divergent policy positions over issues by Soviet economists, demographers, jurists.

Moses, Joel C. *The Politics of Women and Work in the Soviet Union and the United States*. Institute of International Studies Research Series. Berkeley: University of California, 1983.

Comparative policy analysis of women's issues in both nations, particularly factors accounting for alternative work schedules like part-time work and work-sharing reforms. Political, economic, and cultural context of policy making. Finds parallels and major differences in reasons accounting for both nations expanding alternative work schedules for women at the present time.

17

Yugoslav Women

Beverly Springer
*American Graduate School
of International Management*

T he women in Yugoslavia today have experienced in their lifetime a remarkable transition for which they had no model. They were born in rural households. Their mothers were uneducated and led lives of drudgery, always subservient to the males in the household. The daughters left these rural households, gained an education, and went to work in urban areas. They have changed the pattern of female behavior that had existed for centuries. How has it happened? What does it mean? Most importantly, will women continue to experience an improvement in their status? These are the questions that this chapter addresses.

In the United States, we associate the recent improvement in the status of women with pressures created by the women's movement. We assume that progress will continue if women remain united in the demand for equality. Other factors, however, propel the improvement of the status of women in other parts of the world. A women's movement may not even exist in some societies where such change is taking place. Furthermore, many societies do not encourage pressure group behavior as Western, pluralist societies do.

In Yugoslavia, economic development appears to be the major factor propelling women out of rural households and into urban jobs. Economic development alone, however, would not account for the ease and speed of the change in Yugoslavia. We have only to consider the situation in some Middle Eastern countries where economic development has not led to comparable modernization of sex roles. The official ideology of the postwar regime in Yugoslavia has also facilitated the change. Traditional female roles have lost their legitimacy. The government has created a legal structure that recognizes the equality of men and women and an economic system that assumes all adults are employed. A women's movement does exist in Yugoslavia, but it does not—indeed, it cannot—operate as a powerful, determining agent for change, as does its Western counterpart. Rather, it acts to assist women in the transition.

The transition in Yugoslavian society has taken place so fast that it is very fragile. Attitudes, values, life-styles still retain a strong element of traditional paternalism. The government endorses equality, but government officials frequently are men whose attitudes toward women were formed in another era. Now even the economic development that was so instrumental in bringing about the change is in crisis. Indeed, it is questionable whether women will be able to maintain their position against the contrary pull of tradition now that economic development has lost its momentum. The world economic crisis hit Yugoslavia just when the government appeared ready to move from passive endorsement of the equality of women to affirmative action to establish that equality.

The study that follows is divided into three parts. The first provides the background—the history and culture that determined the traditional role of women in Yugoslavia and the history and ideology that led the new Communist government to change that role. The second provides information concerning the present status of women. The legal, political, and economic aspects of that status will be discussed. The third examines the evidence concerning the difficult question, Will the status of Yugoslav women continue to improve?

Some caveats need to be addressed to readers not familiar with Yugoslavia concerning the material that follows. Yugoslavia is a relatively new country formed after World War I from remnants of the Austro-Hungarian Empire and the Ottoman Empire. The Communist regime that took over after World War II created a federal system based on the historic divisions in the country. The six republics—Slovenia, Serbia, Macedonia, Bosnia-Herzegovina, Croatia, and Montenegro—and two autonomous provinces—Kosovo and Voyvodina—continue to bear the marks of their different heritages and are at quite different levels of economic development. Slovenia and Kosovo represent the two extremes. The people in Slovenia differ little from their Austrian neighbors. Their living standard is comparable. Their culture reflects Germanic and Roman Catholic influences. The people in Kosovo, in contrast, are more easily compared with their Albanian neighbors. Their life-style is derived from Turkish and Islamic influences. Their economy is among the least developed in Europe. Therefore, a balanced assessment of the current status of women in Yugoslavia is difficult. The countervailing forces of the patriarchal heritage and present official sexual egalitarianism produce uneven patterns of develop-ment. And because the situation is in flux, a statement true for Slovenia may be false for Kosovo; an assertion valid for 1970 may be invalid for 1984; a judgment based on scholarly information may be contradicted by visual observation. But some conclusions can be—indeed, need to be—drawn, even with those caveats in mind. Yugo-slavia is an important example of a nation making a conscious effort to transform rapidly a paternalistic society into an egalitarian one.

History and Ideology

History casts Yugoslav women into a more subservient role than that of women in many other parts of Europe. This was especially true in those parts that had a pastoral economy. The units in the pastoral economy were based on male blood ties. According to recent research, wives, as "outsiders," were viewed with suspicion and subjected to harsh treatment to force their compliance to the needs of the unit.[1]

In all parts of Yugoslavia, with the exception of Slovenia, the basic social unit was the *zadruga*, a patriarchal community whose mem-bers owned and worked land in common. The members were re-lated by blood or by marriage, and authority usually was vested in the eldest male member. Women were always subservient to men, and women performed much of the hardest work. Turkish domina-tion produced certain variations in this basic pattern. In Madedonia and in Bosnia-Herzegovina (although nominally under Austrian control) before World War I, it was customary for women to stand while men ate, to remove men's shoes, to kiss men's hands (espe-cially that of the leader of the zadruga).[2] Passive domestic roles remained the norm for women in these republics and in Kosovo, until very recent times. Most women never had the opportunity to even perceive any other possibility. They lived in rural isolation made complete by their almost universal illiteracy. But in Serbia, which gained its independence from Turkey in the nineteenth cen-tury, family life then entered an unstable period during which the subjugation of women lessened somewhat. The government opened a secondary school for girls, but husbands retained the right to beat their wives.[3] In Montenegro, the centuries of struggle against the Ottoman Empire produced a *machismo* culture in which strength and warfare were glorified. The lot of a woman was unfortunate from birth (a male birth was a cause for celebration, but a female birth was ignored) throughout her years as a hard-working wife under the complete control of her husband.

In Croatia, the dividing line between the Ottoman and the Austro-Hungarian empires, the influence of the latter predominated. Women were free from the extreme forms of suppression noted above, but they still were constrained by the norms of the patriarchal family characteristic of rural society in the Austro-Hungarian Empire. About the time of World War I, the strength of the traditional pattern began to wane. A few Croatian women participated in the peasant movement that was active in Croatia in the interwar period.[4]

Women in Slovenia probably had the best conditions in the period preceding the formation of Yugoslavia. Their role was defined by strict Roman Catholic values. However, contact with Western Europe and improving economic conditions allowed Slovenian women to experience the benefits of modernization earlier than women elsewhere in Yugoslavia.

After World War I, these diverse areas were united in the new state of Yugoslavia, which did little to improve the status of women. Women remained disenfranchised; local control of marriage practices (until 1935) meant that polygamy was still allowed in some areas. Divorce was difficult, and legal protections for women were minimal.

Economic modernization gradually undermined the basis of patriarchal society as the zadruga ceased to be a viable economic unit. In some ways this made the position of women worse. They lost their traditional role in the zadruga, which, despite the difficulties, had provided some security. Most were not prepared for any other role, and men were not prepared to accept women in new relationships. Instances of brutality toward women apparently increased.[5] But modernization also provided important opportunities. Education became available to women. Political activities extended into the grass roots of society. The peasant and socialist movements actively recruited women. Yugoslav women were gradually developing the skills, the confidence, and the awareness necessary for life outside the single role available for most Yugoslav women prior to the twentieth century. When World War II came to the Balkans, sweeping away the regime and bringing disruption and destruction, occupation by German and Italian troops, and the establishment of the resistance movement.

Socialist ideology began to spread to the area of Yugoslavia in the nineteenth century. It brought ideas that challenged traditional attitudes toward women. Yugoslav socialism was greatly influenced by Russian socialism during its formative period in the late nineteenth century. The drive for female equality in Europe was closely related to emerging European socialism. Important feminists, such as Clara Zetkin, Anner Kuliscioff, and Emmeline Pankhurst, were also active socialists.[6] One of the most famous books advocating equality for women was written by well-known socialist August Bebel in 1879. In *Women and Socialism*, he traced the exploitation and repression of women throughout history and dealt extensively with the position of women in the nineteenth century. He urged women to unite and strive for their freedom, "for there can be no liberation of mankind, without the social independence and equality of the sexes."[7]

Russia experienced, in the nineteenth century, a period of intellectual ferment in which women played an active role. Women participated as equals in the communes in which some young intellectuals lived. A group of Russian women traveled to Zurich where, in 1867, one of them was the first female to be graduated from a university on the continent of Europe. Their potential was glorified in Chernyshevski's novel *What Is To Be Done?*, the handbook of a generation of young idealists.

In 1866 Svetozar Markovic, a young Serb who was to become a major figure in the development of socialism in the Balkans, went to Russia on a government stipend to further his education. He entered the milieu of the Russian student intellectual, living in one of the communes, and was deeply influenced by Chernyshevski. Later, he studied in Zurich and joined the Russian group containing the women who broke the sexual barrier to university degrees. Other Serbs came to Zurich and accepted the ideas of their Russian comrades. After Markovic's return to Serbia, he introduced a resolution at an *Omladina* (an important youth group) congress that had as one of its seven parts the demand for "the right to work and the right to an education for both women and men."[8] He was also an important influence in the lives of two young women, Milica and Anka Ninkovic, who went to Switzerland at his urging and returned to be among the earliest participants in the Balkan socialist movement.[9]

Markovic died young, but he contributed significantly to the ideology of the present Yugoslav regime: He asserted that sexual equality is an essential aspect of socialism.

The modern form of Yugoslav socialism was influenced by later developments in Soviet socialism, which continued to incorporate sexual equality. Lenin, then as now a respected figure in Yugoslavia, advocated equality for women, and recognized the difficulty of its implementation in a traditional society. In 1919 he stated:

> You all know that even when women have full rights, they still remain factually downtrodden because all housework is the most unproductive, the most barbarous and the most arduous work a woman can do.[10]

During the interwar years, when united Yugoslavia had its first independent government, the Marxists were a small and persecuted group, but they maintained their close ties with the Soviet Union, where Stalin continued to give lip service to the ideal of sexual equality even though he did little to advance the status of women.

During World War II, Yugoslav socialism gained a power base in the guerrilla organization under Tito. Tito trained his partisans not only for resistance to the Germans but also for governance of the state of Yugoslavia after the war. His followers lived and fought together during the long years of the occupation; out of their experiences came the tales of heroism and glory that provide the unifying mythology of the present state. And women were counted among the founders of the current socialist regime. Supposedly, over 100,000 women were partisans, or members of the People's Army of Liberation, 25,000 of whom were killed and 40,000 wounded. And some two million women were alleged to have been participants in underground activities in the fascist-occupied territories.[11]

During the war, Tito promised women that the rights they had won during the struggle would not be snatched from them and that his followers "will stand behind the cause of women."[12] The first constitution of the new regime proclaimed, "Women shall have equal rights as men in spheres of state, economic and socio-political life. Women shall have equal pay for the same work as men.... "[13] Laws were passed in 1947 and 1949 to give women equal rights in the family. The new regime, in its first four years, swept away the legal structure of the old, paternalist system.

The regime did not direct a great deal of attention to women's issues in that period, however. Its very existence was threatened by the break with the Soviet Union. It had to define a course that differed from the Soviet model but one that was still Communist.

Three features characterized the new Yugoslav model of communism. Workers' self-management became the hallmark of its Communist ideology. Nonalignment determined its foreign policy. The regime sought to build a decentralized but modern economy in contrast to the centrally planned Soviet system.

The rapid improvement that took place in the status of women in the decades that followed was largely a consequence of the third feature of Yugoslav communism. The government embarked on an ambitious program of education. Female illiteracy, which had been as high as 90 percent in some areas, fell to 4 percent among females under the age of 19 by 1971.[14] Higher education was also expanded and opened to qualified women on an equal basis with men. Women composed more than one-third of university graduates in the years from 1946 to 1976. Equally dramatic developments took place in the society and the economy. The Yugoslav people, who historically lived and died within sight of the place where they were born, suddenly engaged in a massive immigration to urban areas.

By 1971, 40 percent of the population were living in a different place from the one in which they were born. The props of their traditional life-style were stripped away. They had to make a living in a structured work situation and seek a social life outside the cocoon of the extended family. Rapid economic developments pulled people who had known only the cycle of subsistence agriculture into the routine of paid employment. Total employment grew by 4.5 percent a year between 1953 and 1977. The employment of women increased 6 percent annually in the same period, so that the number of women working increased nine times. The liberation of women given by law in the 1940s took on reality in the 1950s and 1960s in the general rush toward economic development.

There were those who realized, however, that women were paying too high a price for this liberation and that the liberation itself was flawed. Women had assumed the new responsibilities of paid employment but lacked the infrastructure of an egalitarian society. They were modern at work but traditional at home. They lacked child care facilities, labor-saving devices, and husbands who shared domestic tasks. Moreover, liberation had given them an education and a paycheck but had not opened the doors to the best jobs or to positions that carried authority. The economic and political elite remained a private club for men only. Yugoslavia did not even practice the tokenism that placed a few women in visible political roles in the Soviet Union.

Interviews with women in Yugoslavia in 1974 brought some interesting insights. Working-class women expressed excessive

fatigue and frustration with their life. They were angry at the burdens of daily life, in which they had to cope with child care problems
and household tasks along with a paid job. They did not direct their
anger at the "system" or generalize it to an issue of sexual equality.
Most generally they directed it at their husbands for failing to share
the responsibilities of the home. On the other hand, women in
professional work more frequently expressed a desire for social
policies to alleviate some of the burdens. For example, young
women in Slovenia spoke with admiration about the long maternity
leave in Hungary compared with the one in Slovenia. (Both of which
are long by our standards.) Women in this class more frequently
remarked that their husbands shared, at least partially, household
tasks. Despite the frustrations, women in all groups believed that
their lives had improved and seemed to expect that they would
continue to improve. Many, however, defined improvement in the
sense of better material conditions rather than in the sense of better
status or greater authority.

The Status of Women in Yugoslavia, 1974–1984

In many respects, the decade starting in 1974 marked a new era for
Yugoslavia and for Yugoslav women. The rush for survival was over.
The regime was accepted at home and abroad. Modernization was
underway. Three separate events took place to inaugurate the decade. In Yugoslavia, a new constitution was adopted. In the world,
an economic crisis began when the price of oil escalated. In the
United Nations, the Women's Decade was proclaimed. Each of these
events was to have an important impact on the lives of Yugoslav
women.

The 1974 Constitution decreed a new stage in the evolution of
workers' self-management. Self-management means much more
than the right of workers to elect a council to oversee their work
place. Under the Constitution, the economic and political systems
are interlocked by an elaborate system of delegations arising from
workplaces as well as from social organizations and communes. The
delegations participate in the work of the commune assemblies, the
assemblies of the republics and provinces, and the national legislature. Delegations participate in the operation of social services such
as day care centers and hospitals. The delegate system mobilizes a
significant proportion of the population. Tens of thousands of delegations exist with hundreds of thousands of people participating in
them.

Women are supposed to participate in the delegations in the same proportion as their participation in the population from which the delegation is derived. In 1974 women composed 10 to 20 percent of the delegates to communal, republic, and federal assemblies. In 1982 the percentage differed very little. Women made up about 18 percent of the delegates to communal assemblies. Their proportion in the assemblies of the republics ranged approximately from 27 percent in Serbia to 12 percent in Macedonia. Fourteen percent of the delegates to the federal assembly were women.[15] Obviously women remain underrepresented compared to the total population, of which they are 50.9 percent. However, the extent of the underrepresentation is difficult to ascertain. The participation of women in the workplaces, communes, and sociopolitical associations from which the delegations are derived varies widely. Furthermore, the averages hide the large differences in participation rates among the republics. For example, women compose about 35 percent of the employed people in Yugoslavia, so women should make up about one-third of the delegates to the chamber of associated labor in the republics. In fact, they compose 30 percent of the Serbian chamber but only 15 percent of the Montenegrin.

The assessment of the figures needs to take into account several other factors as well. Women are underrepresented, in part, because many of them do not have jobs and many delegations are selected at places of work. They are also underrepresented in comparison with Eastern European countries, but their participation has more meaning since assemblies in Yugoslavia have more power than those in Eastern Europe. Finally, their rate of participation compares well with the rates found in Western Europe.

In general, women play a very small role among the national political elite, and little concern is expressed to change the situation. A recent book on leadership in post-Tito Yugoslavia contains no mention of the topic.[16] An appendix in the book that lists 31 persons who form the political elite contains the name of only one woman. A review of the five most recent years of the *Information Bulletin of the Communist League of Yugoslavia and the Socialist Alliance of Working People of Yugoslavia* revealed no mention of women despite extensive discussion of subjects that need improvement in Yugoslavia. Women have never been more than 3 of the 29 members of the Federal Executive Council (the highest political body).

The one woman who has penetrated the male club that is Yugoslavia's political elite is Milka Planinc. She was 58 years old in 1984. She is the first woman to head the Federal Executive Council (a position somewhat analogous to a prime minister in a cabinet government). She is a Croatian who joined the partisans in 1942 and became a party member in 1944. She was active in the Croatian Communist party but gained national prominence following a purge of Croatian party leaders who opposed Tito's policy to divert money from wealthy republics to poor ones. At that time she replaced Savka Dubcevic-Kucar, a woman who was deemed a threat because of her widespread support among Croatians. Indeed, she was called, "The one woman in a European communist party to have a popular following. . . . "[17] In contrast, Milka Planinc owed her success, in part, to her unquestioned loyalty to Titoism.

Yugoslav women do have one association that can and does work to promote their interests. The Conference on the Social Activity of Women is part of the Socialist Alliance, the mass organization in Yugoslavia, and it has branches throughout the country and is represented at the national level by a presidium of 28 women. Its members stress that the organization is not a women's liberation movement or a pressure group. Its visibility does not appear to be very high, but its effectiveness in assisting the achievement of sexual equality should not be discounted. Its active members appear to be limited to a small number of dedicated women who volunteer their time (a few members are paid).

The work of the Conference is widespread: It cooperates closely with organizations working on day-care centers and on spreading birth control information; it organized discussions on abortion and on women in the new constitutional system; it monitors the impact for women of various laws; and it may bring a suit against an enterprise that discriminates against women. It is a lower-key organization than are women's liberation groups in the United States. The main aim of the conference has been the establishment of preconditions for advancement, in contrast to the demands for immediate equality made by groups in the United States. In this manner, the conference may have been wiser and more productive, operating as it does in a society where attitudes are still largely traditionalist and where the regime would not tolerate either feminism or pluralism in the Western sense. Its effectiveness would be hard to measure, but its techniques deserve recognition and further study by those who are interested in advancing the cause of women in paternalistic societies. The conference is careful not to point to the government as the source of women's problems but rather at society. "Women have the laws but face social resistance."[18] It does work, however, to get government policies changed when they are detrimental to women. For example, it has been active to obtain changes in policies on rape.

The participation of women in the Communist party (LYC) parallels that of their participation in politics in general. Women make up about 22 percent of the members of the LYC, but their proportion declines at higher levels in the party organization. The most recent party congress elected 165 members to the Central Committee. Fifteen are women.[19] The powerful executive bureau has seldom had a woman on it. However, women have achieved positions of power in the party organization in the republics. Both the Croatian and Serbian parties have had women in top positions.

In general, the participation of women in Yugoslav politics appears to have reached a plateau. Their participation rate is obviously much greater than it was prior to World War II, and it is quite respectable compared to that found in other countries today. However, it does not achieve the equality promised in socialist ideology. The regime has taken no affirmative actions to move women into positions of authority. It did make some show of interest around 1974 but then lapsed back into a state of benign neglect.

The world economic crisis that began in 1974 probably has wrought more important changes for Yugoslav women than did the political events associated with the new constitution in that year. When the crisis started, Yugoslavia had just come through a remarkable period of economic development that was closing the gap between it and some of the countries in Western Europe. Per-capita income was almost 30 percent above the world average. Industrial output had increased on average 9.5 percent per year.[20] The proportion of the population involved in agriculture compared to the total population decreased from two-thirds to one-fourth—one of the most rapid decreases in the world. The proportion of the population living in urban areas doubled in less than 30 years.[21] These developments are all the more dramatic when contrasted with the facts that Yugoslav per-capita income was 30 percent below the world average before the war, that wartime destruction was higher than in most of Europe (including the proportion of the population killed), and that postwar reconstruction plans were seriously disrupted by the break with the Soviet Union.

In 1974, the total number of employed women was 43 percent higher than it had been ten years before. Women made up 34 percent of the workforce compared to 29.3 percent in 1964.[22] Now that women were a permanent part of the workforce, the next tasks were to broaden the range of work opportunities for women and to increase the number of women in positions of responsibility in the workplace. In order to determine the fate of these goals in the worsening economic situation, we shall survey where women are working according to the latest findings, then note the impact of unemployment on women compared to its impact on men, and finally consider the success of women in penetrating the Yugoslav economic elite. (Please note that the data that follow are not always based on the 1974–1984 decade due to lags in reporting data.)

Throughout the postwar period working women in Yugoslavia have been clustered in certain sectors. Agriculture, textiles, education, and service sector jobs are women's work. Despite the fact that this situation was deplored in the 1970s, work segregation had actually increased by 1980. Pedro Ramet found that, "in almost all sectors in which women constituted more than half of the work force in 1970, their numerical advantage actually increased between 1970 and 1980."[23] For example, women made up 52.8 percent of the employees in schools in 1970 and 56.6 percent in 1980. They composed 66.3 percent and 71 percent, respectively, of the workforce in textiles and social services in 1970 and 78.4 percent and 79.4 percent, respectively, in 1980.[24]

The role of women in agriculture deserves special attention not only because it concerns many women in Yugoslavia but also because it has relevance for the study of women in many parts of the world. It is common to speak of the feminization of agricultural work in Yugoslavia. Women account for over half of the persons working in agriculture. Most agricultural land is privately owned in Yugoslavia despite the fact that the country is Communist. (The constitution allows private farms of ten hectares or less.) In the period of rapid economic growth, men left their small farms, and women added the men's chores to their own. These women— frequently illiterate and always overworked—could not make productive farms out of their units, which were too small by modern standards. The government intervened. It set up cooperatives so that farmers could share modern equipment and dispose of their products more efficiently. The government also encouraged supplemental rural occupations—rural tourism and the marketing of local handicrafts. Thus, the life of rural women underwent significant changes even if the changes were not as obvious as those found in the cities. Rural women learned to make agreements with the cooperatives, to attend courses on rural tourism, and to participate in delegations managing the cooperatives or other local activities.[25]

Now that economic growth has slowed, another important change is taking place for women in rural areas. Full-time employment of women in agriculture is decreasing while part-time is increasing. The rate of change in the various republics correlates with the level of maturity of the economy. Ruza First-Dilic determined that the feminization of agriculture is a temporary phenomenon occurring in the early phase of industrialization.[26] At the present stage, the inexorable demand of the cities for workers has ended, and the modernization of farms has increased, so that men are no longer drawn out of agriculture at the rate that they were. At the same time, rural women are now more educated and aware, so they are more prepared to make choices rather than to become farmers by default. So, while agriculture remains "women's work," a redefinition is taking place in the nature and status of that work that portends more equality in the future.

Not only did women fail to break out of their work ghettos between 1974 and 1984, they lost a small portion of their participation rate in the total workforce. Yugoslav women never did go into the workforce to the same extent that they did in Eastern European countries. For example, 47.3 percent of Yugoslav women between the ages of 15 and 54 were in the workforce in 1970 compared to 76.5 percent in the Soviet Union and 77.7 percent in Poland.[27] When the number of women working is compared to the total female population, we find that the percentage for working women was 30.7 in 1971, 30.4 in 1980, and projected to be 29.4 in 1985 and 28.9 in 1990.[28]

Most authorities assume that the low participation rate for women in paid employment results from the persistence of traditional attitudes plus the chronic shortage of jobs in some parts of the country. The different employment rates between married and unmarried women indicate that traditional values may discourage married women from working. Between the ages of 30 and 34, 79.2 percent of unmarried women work compared to only 47.1 percent of married women. More divorced women work than any other category of women (widowed, never married, etc.) in all age groups from 20 to 54.[29] Participation rates also differ greatly among the republics, and the rates generally correlate with the level of development of the area. For example, in 1982 women made up 44.9 percent of the workforce in progressive, prosperous Slovenia but only 21 percent in Kosovo, where poverty and traditionalism prevail.[30]

Unemployment rates also show that women lost ground in the recent decade. Unemployment rates for women increased from 13 percent in 1974 to 17.5 percent in 1981. By comparison, the rates for men were 6.9 percent and 8.4 percent.[31] According to a study on employment trends in Yugoslavia, unemployment not only affected women more than men, but also the rate of female unemployment fluctuates more than the rate for men.[32] This probably indicates that work is regarded as less important for women than for men. Women are the first to be let go when a slowdown occurs, and so were very vulnerable in the economic crisis of the past decade.

Since a significant number of women have been in the workforce for several decades, it is reasonable to assume that women are now achieving positions of responsibility. The two most important positions in a Yugoslav workplace are those of director and member of workers' self-management councils. These councils have a great deal of power under Yugoslav law. The employees in all except very small private workplaces elect a council from among the workforce that has the responsibility to hire the director and to be the "powerful, driving force for the advancement of the entire social community."[33] Women have steadily increased their participation on these councils. In 1979, they composed 29 percent of the total members.[34] However, women do not appear to have made comparable gains as presidents of workers' self-management councils. This is an important position and one that attracts highly qualified employees. The figures are difficult to obtain, but indications are that the percentage of women who are presidents has "stagnated around the five percent level."[35]

Directors are professional managers who are "hired" by the workers' self-management council to run an enterprise. The position of director is lucrative and respected. It is one of the most sought-after careers in Yugoslavia today. A recent study of directors only mentioned women to note that wives of directors appear to be more active politically than other women.[36] No hint was given that any director might be female. In another study, it was noted that not one woman existed among 115 directors of enterprises and only 8 women were among the 318 directors of elementary schools in Kosovo.[37] Data is lacking to make any conclusive statements about changing rates of participation of women as directors. However, it does appear that women are not making the advances in leadership roles one would expect following several decades of employment. The most hopeful sign is that women have increased their participation on workers' self-management councils, so they are in a position to influence future decisions on presidents of the councils and directors.

To conclude this section on the economic crisis, it does appear that the momentum that had carried women forward until 1974 slowed, stopped, and possibly even reversed course after 1974. The decreasing participation rate coupled with increasing work segregation would seem to indicate the lingering impact of traditional values. Women were better educated by the 1980s, more experienced, and certainly had at least as much need to work as in the previous decades, but they did not make advances comparable with these facts. When an economy is not growing, women can only advance at the expense of those already holding the limited number of preferred positions. Economic recessions test the commitment of a society to the advancement of women. In the Yugoslav case, the forces of tradition are still strong enough to check the forward movement of women in the workplace.

The third event that helped to shape the decade under consideration was the proclamation by the United Nations of the year 1975 as the International Women's Year and of the years 1976–1985 as the Women's Decade. Skeptics regarded these proclamations as media events without real substance. For that reason, it is interesting to examine the impact of them on Yugoslavia. We find that they did much to promote public awareness of the concerns of women. Following the break with the Soviet Union, Yugoslavia sought international security through its policy of nonalignment. It has been a leader among Third World nations seeking a course between the two camps in the Cold War. The United Nations provides an important forum for Yugoslavia and other nonaligned nations. When the United Nations took up the women's issue, Yugoslavia immediately joined the effort and played a highly visible role in a number of activities associated with the effort. It sponsored international seminars on women's issues, and its women's association cooperated with women's associations in a hundred other countries. Yugoslavia served on the Preparatory Committee for the World Conference of the UN Women's Decade in Mexico City, and it was instrumental in calling the Bagdad conference on women in development in 1979, which was sponsored by the nonaligned nations.[38]

These international activities had important domestic consequences. Yugoslavia undertook a major self-study on the condition of women in order to make a report to the United Nations. Meetings and discussions were held throughout the country, engaging large numbers of people. Numerous reports were compiled on topics ranging from the practical needs of rural women to the subjective image of women in society. The government enacted two important policies in connection with the UN initiative. The Associated Labor Act reaffirms that sex discrimination at work is unconstitutional, and it also provides protections to working women in special situations.[39] For example, the health of expectant mothers must be safeguarded at work, and self-supporting mothers as well as mothers of small children should have priority when establishing a vacation schedule. In addition, the law extends job security to pregnant women and mothers of small children working in the private sector. (All employees have job security when working in the public sector, but employees in the small private sector are not protected.)

The second legislative act is the "Resolution on the Main Lines of Social Action to Promote the Socioeconomic Status and Role of Women in the Socialist Self-Managing Society." The resolution is self-congratulatory on the achievements of the country in regard to women but also notes that much remains to be done. A key passage reads, "The process of achieving equal living and working conditions for men and women is very complex and only feasible if there is an accelerated overall socioeconomic development with the corresponding structural changes in society."[40] The report concludes that further improvement in the status of women depends on accelerated economic growth and the provision of an infrastructure that will allow women to participate more fully in economic and political life.

This resolution brought women's issues into the spotlight of national politics. The government admitted that Yugoslavia was still distant from the international standards the government had endorsed. The government, therefore, pledged that every organization in the country would act to promote conditions that would facilitate the equal participation of women. This resolution stands as the most sweeping affirmation by the government of the need for more positive efforts to assist women to take their place as equals in the society.

In the case of Yugoslavia at least, it can be concluded that the work of the United Nations has had an important and beneficial impact on domestic policy. The UN work provided the legitimacy for women's issues to be raised. It caused the government to give priority to women's issues as it had not previously done. The work of the UN probably had more of an impact in societies such as Yugoslavia where traditionalism is still strong and where women are not organized than it did in Western societies with which we are more familiar.

As noted in the introduction, the personal lives of women in Yugoslovia today are vastly different from and better than they were even 30 years ago. Improvements have come rapidly and on several different fronts. However, a large proportion of women live a schizophrenic existence in which they combine modern public rules with paternalistic private ones. The infrastructure that facilitates household tasks in the West is still largely absent in Yugoslavia.

Shopping, cooking, cleaning, and child care are more time-consuming for Yugoslav women, and the tasks are less frequently shared with a male than they are in the West. In 1969, 69.5 percent of wives surveyed prepared all meals and did all the other household tasks. In 1973, only 30 percent of the homes had a vacuum cleaner, and only 35 percent had a washing machine.[41] There is almost unanimous agreement among persons studying the status of Yugoslav women—both foreigners and Yugoslavs themselves—that the lack of infrastructure combined with traditional attitudes constitute the major obstacle for women in Yugoslavia today.

The improvements in the daily life of women come in large part from economic development and increased per-capita income. However, improvements have also resulted from legislation that gives women rights comparable to those found in Western societies. Most family legislation is enacted by the republics, but trends are common throughout the country. Wives now have equal rights with husbands in marriage. Husbands and wives share the property acquired after a marriage, and each retains the right to property obtained before the marriage. Husbands and wives are equally responsible for their children. In case of a divorce, a guilty party no longer has to be designated, and children are awarded not to the "innocent party" but to the one deemed most capable of caring for them. A woman is entitled to assistance from the state for family planning. She also may obtain an abortion. (However, the government has tried to discourage abortions. In the past, Yugoslav women, as women in many underdeveloped areas, used abortions as their principal means of birth control. The government has sought to educate women that abortions are obsolete, primitive, and dangerous.) If a woman decides to have a child she is entitled to maternity leave from her job at full pay. The length of leave varies among the republics, but it is always more than three months and may be as much as nine months. (In Slovenia, the father may take part of the leave.)[42]

In Yugoslavia, the urban, nuclear family is becoming the norm. The average household has 3.8 persons.[43] This represents a radical change for Yugoslavia, where the extended family was the basic social and economic unit until 30 years ago. However, the new nuclear family differs from the one familiar in the West in several respects. Yugoslavs remain emotionally tied to members of the larger family even when they live separately from them. Women still frequently turn to other family members for companionship rather than to their husbands. Individuals still spend a large portion of their leisure time at home or visiting other family members.

Indeed, one authority observes, ". . . the evidence from Yugoslavia indicates the urbanization and modernization do not necessarily result in the demise of the family."[44]

In many respects, the development of the urban nuclear family has not been as traumatic for Yugoslav women as for women in many developing countries. It is true that a woman usually assumes the "double burden." However, she has gained new authority and a new sense of status within the home even when she does not take outside employment.[45] Her life also is not as lonely as that of many urban women because of continuing family ties. Moreover, the burden of urban life in Yugoslavia is not as great as it is in countries where urbanizaton means one overgrown megalopolis such as Mexico City or Seoul. Urbanization in Yugoslavia has retained a human scale. Each republic has its urban core that serves as a pole of attraction for migrants from the surrounding rural areas. A Yugoslav woman may lack the infrastructure that eases life in urban areas in the West, but she does not have to cope with the problems of congestion that add so immeasurably to life in urban areas in many developing countries.

In conclusion, women in Yugoslavia did not experience any dramatic changes in the decade 1974–1984. They made some political and educational gains. They experienced a small economic setback. The heroic years were over. The slow work of changing attitudes and of giving substance to the promises of the regime probably went on inside families and inside the women themselves, but on the surface the lives of women in Yugoslavia did not look very different in 1984 from 1974.

Prognosis for the Future

The study of women in Yugoslavia finds that the women today have the possibility of a richer and more varied life-style than their mothers could even contemplate. They have not, however, penetrated the seats of economic or political power, and they have not gained access to the most desirable jobs. The question remains, Is it only a matter of time before these remaining inequities disappear? The answer depends on the assessment of the evidence. We know from our own history that we cannot assume that progress, once set in motion, continues automatically. Women in the United States fought and won battles for equality earlier in this century. They then went dutifully back into the kitchen following World War II, only to emerge again two decades later to fight many of the same battles fought by their grandmothers.

Evidence to support an optimistic forecast is found in a variety of places. Improved education means that the next generation will have the qualifications for better positions. The traditional life-style that prevented women from even perceiving alternative possibilities is disappearing. The mass migrations that have affected 40 percent of the population, doubled the urban population in 30 years, and sent a million Yugoslavs to work in Western Europe have been some of the most dramatic in the contemporary world. Also, authorities generally agree that they have been less traumatic than such upheavals usually are. As a result, the experience has been relatively positive for Yusoslav women. They look forward to further modernization in the lives of their children and have similar hopes for their sons and daughters. Most migrant women desire both their sons and daughters to enter a profession that will require a university education.[46]

Laws and official government policy also support a prognosis of continuing progress for women. Progress in legislation for women in Yugoslavia is equal to that found almost anywhere in the world today. It is unlikely that there will be any erosion in this area. The ideology of the regime as well as its posture in international affairs will prevent a reactionary development such as we see in Iran today.

Some of the evidence found in the more subjective area of attitudes is less clear cut. A survey conducted in eight countries found that 67 percent of Yugoslav women answered "yes" to the question, "Do you wish that in the future there will be more women in leading positions?" A smaller but still significant percent (42) believe that women will be in these positions in the future. The troublesome aspect of this survey is the fact that the *aspirations* of Yugoslav women exceeded their *expectations* by a larger margin than that of women in the other countries. Furthermore, only 26 percent of Yugoslav men *wished* for women to be in these positions, but 40 percent *expected* women to be in them.[47] Conclusions based on a single poll can only be speculative, but these findings would seem to indicate that Yugoslav women still regard themselves as passive participants in the system.

The evidence that supports a more pessimistic prognosis for Yugoslav women is found primarily in the persistence of traditionalism and in the economic crisis. Yugoslav women simply do not have the time for added responsibilities outside their homes. Moreover, they are less likely to question the legitimacy of their family obligations than are more individualistic American women.

Traditional values are more resilient to changed environments than most authorities expected them to be. The traditional values of home and family serve an important function in "humanizing" urban life for women. In themselves, they are not an obstacle, but the underside of these values is the old idea that females are not worthy. That idea still persists and will continue to obstruct a fair assessment of the abilities of women.

Even though the worst of the economic recession may be over, no one expects that Yugoslavia will experience in the foreseeable future anything like the growth rates it had after World War II. This fact threatens not only future progress but even existing gains. Given the traditional attitudes and practices, it takes exceptional conditions and/or a high-priority commitment on the part of authorities to improve the situation of women. Exceptional conditions prevailed in the period of greatest improvements in the status of women. As we have seen, economic development was a major cause of changing life-styles for women. When economic growth slowed in the past decade, so did the development in the status of women. The linkage between economic growth and the conditions of women noted in this study should be considered in regard to women in other countries. Persons interested in the cause of women should consider the probable consequences for women of continuing international economic stagnation.

In the 1990s and beyond, Yugoslav women will probably experience a gradual amelioration in their personal lives. They will continue to be employed but to consider their first obligation to be to their family. An occasional woman will assume a position of authority, but in general the elite structures of the society will remain a men's club. The slow economy will tend to freeze employment practices. However, the government is unlikely to allow the conditions for women to worsen. Ideology, law, and the international posture of Yugoslavia remain as bulwarks to an erosion in the status of women. Equality is not in the forecast for Yugoslav women, but they have achieved much in terms of their own expectations and in comparison with women in many other countries.

In conclusion, American readers may feel a sense of frustration with the image of Yugoslav women as passive participants. These readers must realize, however, that Yugoslavia is a society only 100 years removed from one in which women were chattel. Females had no control over their destiny and no opportunity to see alternative possibilities. Life was drudgery for women to be accepted with the fatalism so characteristic of peasant societies. In contrast, today Yugoslav women have vast opportunities, and they have acquired a sense of their potential. In private conversation, Yugoslav women have ambitions and express frustration with the many obstacles that hinder the fulfillment of their ambitions. But they are not feminists in the American sense. They do not live in a society where the *individualism* and *pluralism* that are so intrinsic in American feminism are accepted values. The present regime, while espousing equality, would not tolerate organized attacks by women on it for failure to act affirmatively in the cause of equality. The women's association may and, indeed, does move to improve conditions for women, but as we have seen, it does so cautiously and without placing blame on the regime. The parameters in which Yugoslav women live differ from those that shape existence for American women. Apparent similarities in education, employment, and even frustration do not translate into common opportunities for women to act collectively in the cause of equality.

Sincere thanks to Sue Gumz and Nancy Greenberg for their excellent research assistance. The research for this article was funded by a grant from the President's Council of the American Graduate School of International Management.

NOTES

1. Bette S. Endich, "Sex and Power in the Balkans," in Michelle Zimbalist Rosaldo and Louise Lamphere, eds., *Women, Culture and Society* (Stanford, CA: Stanford University Press, 1974), 247, 252.

2. Vera St. Erlich, *Family in Transition* (Princeton, NJ: Princeton University Press, 1966), 228–234.

3. Ibid., 238–239.

4. Dinko Tomasic, *Personality and Culture in Eastern European Politics* (New York: George W. Stewart, 1948), 64.

5. St. Erlich, 285.

6. See, for example, Sheila Rowbotham, *Women, Resistance and the Revolution* (New York: Vintage Books, 1974); Richard Stites, *The Women's Liberation Movement in Russia* (Princeton, NJ: Princeton University Press, 1978); Jane Slaughter and Robert Kerns, eds., *European Women on the Left* (Westport, CT: Greenwood Press, 1981).

7. August Bebel, *Woman and Socialism* (New York: Socialist Literature Co., 1910), 7.

8. Woodford D. McClellan, *Svetozar Markovic* (Princeton, NJ: Princeton University Press, 1964), 130.

9. Ibid., 254.

10. Lenin as quoted in Alice Shuster, "Women's Role in the Soviet Union:

Ideology and Reality," *Russian Review* 30 (July 1971), 266–267.

11. "Impressions of Yugoslavia," *Women of the Whole World* 5 (1964), 13.

12. Vida Tomsic, *Woman in the Development of Socialist Self-Managing Yusoslavia* (Belgrade: Jugoslovenska stvarnost, 1980), 27.

13. Yugoslavia, *Constitution* (1946), Art. 26.

14. Tomsic, 113.

15. *Statistical Pocket-Book of Yugoslavia 1983* (Belgrade: Federal Statistical Office, 1983), 18–19.

16. Slobodan Stankovic, *The End of the Tito Era* (Stanford, CA: Hoover Institution Press, 1981).

17. Barbara Wolfe Jancar, *Women under Communism* (Baltimore, MD: Johns Hopkins University Press, 1978), 111.

18. Address by Hajra Marjanovic quoted in "Woman's Equality—A Class Struggle," *Yugoslav Information Bulletin of the League of Communists of Yugoslavia and the Socialist Alliance of Working People of Yugoslavia* 3 (1976), 14.

19. Richard F. Starr, ed., *Yearbook on International Communist Affairs* (Stanford, CA: Hoover Institution Press, 1983), 370.

20. Richard F. Nyrop, ed., *Yugoslavia: A Country Study*, Area Handbook Series, 2nd ed. (Washington, DC: U.S. Government Printing Office, 1982), 126.

21. "Movement of the Total Population," *Yugoslav Survey* 23 (February 1982), 93–94.

22. "Women's Employment," *Yugoslav Survey* 17 (May 1976), 57.

23. Pedro Ramet, "Women, Work and Self-Management in Yugoslavia," *East European Quarterly* 17 (January 1984), 463.

24. Ramet, 374.

25. Maria Rupena-Osolnik, "The Role of Farm Women in Rural Pluriactivity: Experience from Yugoslavia," *Sociologica Ruralis* 23:1 (1983), 89–94.

26. Ruza First-Dilic, "The Productive Roles of Farm Women in Yugoslavia," *Sociologia Ruralis* 28:2–3 (1978), 136.

27. Sharon L. Wolchik, "Ideology and Equality: The Status of Women in Eastern and Western Europe," *Comparative Political Studies* 13 (January 1981), 454.

28. Zvonimir Baletic and Ivo Baucic, *Population, Labour Force and Employment in Yugoslavia 1950–1990* (Vienna: Weiner Institut fur Internationale Wirtschaftsvergleiche, 1979), 55.

29. "Changes in the Economic Activity of the Population," *Yugoslav Survey* 28 (August 1977), 22.

30. *Statistical Pocket-Book*, 44.

31. International Labour Organization, *Yearbook of Labor Statistics* (Geneva: 1982).

32. Baletic and Baucic, 38.

33. Tomsic, 34.

34. *Statistical Pocket-Book,* 23.

35. Ramet, 465.

36. Richard P. Farkas, *Yugoslav Economic Development and Political Change* (New York: Praeger, 1975), 23–24.

37. Ramet, 465.

38. Tomsic, 148–155.

39. Tomsic, 158.

40. The document is reprinted in Tomsic, 181.

41. Jancar, 41, 50.

42. Tomsic, 99–100.

43. Tomsic, 132.

44. Andrei Simic, "Aging in the United States and Yugoslavia: Contrasting Models of Intergenerational Relationships," *Anthropological Quarterly* 50 (April 1977), 59.

45. Bette S. Denich, "Urbanization and Women's Roles in Yugoslavia," *Anthropological Quarterly* 40 (January 1976), 17.

46. Denich, "Sex and Power in the Balkans," 261.

47. Jancar, 187.

RECOMMENDED READINGS

Flanz, Gisbert H. *Comparative Women's Rights and Political Partici-pation in Europe*. Dobbs Ferry, NY: Transitional Publishers, 1983.
This book, which covers all of Europe, contains valuable current information on women and also provides the reader with the opportunity to compare trends in individual countries. The section on Yugoslavia is excellent.

Jancar, Barbara Wolfe. *Women under Communism*. Baltimore, MD: Johns Hopkins Press, 1978.
This book is somewhat dated, but it provides comparative data concerning women in Communist countries in Eastern Europe as well as China. It covers a broader range of topics than do many studies on women, ranging from demography to the female self-concept. The book is very readable and raises points that should stimulate further consideration.

Nyrop, Richard F., ed. *Yugoslavia: A Country Study*. Area Handbook Series, 2nd ed. Washington, DC: U.S. Government Printing Office, 1982.
The book provides a handy reference source for basic information on Yugoslavia. Since the Yugoslav system is so unique and the republics so diverse, readers of this chapter on Yugoslav women may wish to consult the country study for background on the society and the economy.

St. Erlich, Vera. *Family in Transition*. Princeton, NJ: Princeton University Press, 1966.
Although this book has been supplemented by later studies, it still remains a good starting point for readers seeking a vivid picture of the lives of women in a traditional paternalistic society.

Tomsic, Vida. *Woman in the Development of Socialist Self-Managing Yugoslavia*. Belgrade: Jugoslovenska Stvarnost, 1980.
This book is the single, best source on the subject of Yugoslav women. It is a quasi-official study, so readers should assume that findings are presented in the most favorable light. However, it contains extensive current data, interesting discussions, and reprints of important documents.

18

Women's Rights, Family Reform, and Population Control in the People's Republic of China

Kay Johnson
Hampshire College

The dominant policies and theories concerning women's emancipation developed by the Chinese Communist party (CCP) during the revolution and early postrevolutionary period have continued to shape the party's approach to women ever since. This essay examines these policies and theories, focusing on the reform of traditional marriage practices and the traditional family institution in rural areas, for family and kinship practices have shaped women's place in traditional and contemporary Chinese society more than any other single set of factors. Indeed, family reform issues have been closely associated with the liberation of Chinese women ever since the radical intellectual ferment of the New Culture– May Fourth era of the 1910s and 1920s. Today these issues have renewed importance because they impinge directly and indirectly on the urgent family planning and population control efforts the government has pursued with increasing vigor and insistence since the mid-1970s.

The CCP has long claimed that women, and the cause of their emancipation from traditional forms of oppression, have constituted important allies in building a peasant revolution and then in constructing socialism. Yet examination of policies toward women and the family reveals that party efforts to promote key women's rights and family reform issues have been characterized in most periods by varying degrees of political avoidance, organizational neglect, and indirect accommodation to the traditional aspirations of the male peasants, who became the party's most crucial constituency once it was forced to shift the focus of its revolutionary strategies from urban to rural areas in the late 1920s and 1930s. The fact is that issues surrounding the reform of rural women's traditional subordinate family and social status have rarely been the subjects of serious or sustained politically directed efforts toward change, despite the continually reiterated ideological commitment to gender equality. For the most part, issues involving gender equality have been promoted only when they directly impinged on other priorities considered more immediate and more important by the predominantly male party leadership.

To some extent this pattern must be understood as a reflection of the political outcome of a revolutionary coalition of radical iconoclastic intellectuals and peasants, marginal peasants, and disenfranchised ex-peasants. On the culturally fundamental issues of women and the family, these two main revolutionary forces have held sharply conflicting values and expectations, shaped and politically mobilized by their different experience and understanding of the impact of nineteenth- and early twentieth-century disruptions of the traditional family institution. Intellectual youth of the May Fourth era, many of whom later became CCP leaders, came to see the Confucian family as an institution that oppressed and stifled the energies of youth and women.[1] For this group, mainly the sons and daughters of a declining gentry and rising commercial class, egalitarian reform of the traditional patriarchal family and the promotion of equal rights for women in family and society were integral to the "anti-feudal" cultural revolution they felt was necessary to save China and restore her strength in a modern era of imperialist depredations. When the party first turned its attention to organizing the countryside, these family reform and women's rights issues seemed to appeal powerfully to at least a minority of rural women and youth, who, as the most subordinate groups within the traditional family, sought refuge from particularly severe forms of family oppression.[2] Yet, once in the countryside, the party became increasingly wedded to a poor male peasant constituency whose aspirations and sense of manhood were shaped by and tied to traditional patriarchal, patrilineal, familial-religious institutions and ideals. While the most crucial source of recruits for the Red Army probably came from those already pushed from the land and deprived of the ability to live by traditional family ideals, these men were nonetheless likely to aspire to regain the wherewithal to return to the land and rebuild their manhood on its honored traditional, familial basis. Indeed, the deprivations of this group were perhaps all the more likely to be expressed in the stridently misogynous, macho ethos that has traditionally characterized the rituals and popular heroic legends of social banditry in China.[3] Landless and familyless, such men were forced to turn to the "brotherhood of the green-woods" both as a means of survival and as a salve of masculine self-respect when the inability to pay a bride price and produce male progeny for their ancestors made them less than whole men.[4] Not surprisingly, issues of family reform and women's rights caused considerable conflict within the revolutionary coalition. As the party tried to build a rural male army, it increasingly shied away from attempts to propagandize and implement women's rights, especially those that directly challenged traditional masculine rights over women in the family.[5]

This is not to assert that, during the revolution or after, the party did not attempt to change women's traditional roles and some of the traditional restrictions placed on women in the countryside. When central party priorities have been involved, the party has moved to enlist women's involvement in revolution and socialist construction in ways that have required changes impinging on the family and traditional female roles, especially economic roles. Through waging a protracted revolutionary guerrilla war, the party came to recognize the important contribution that mobilized rural women could make. Women's labor and support were crucial in recruiting husbands and sons into the army, in replacing men in the agricultural economy, and in performing essential (if "secondary") services for local guerrilla forces and the army (ranging from intelligence gathering to making shoes). The mobilization of women's labor was also key to the success of the labor-intensive "production war" strategy in the early 1940s that saved the Communist-led anti-Japanese base areas during the Yenan era from economic collapse and strangulation by the enemy.[6] Years later, with China again encircled and blockaded by foreign enemies, without reliable international allies, the draft mobilization of women's labor into agriculture was a key to the precipitous collectivization drives of the late 1950s and a self-reliant, Maoist development strategy that in some ways recalled the once-successful model of the Yenan days. In Yenan, as in later mobilizations, economic strategies often required that the party confront certain aspects of traditional taboos and family restrictions on women's time and labor in order to make full use of the resources of women and the family.

One of the first comprehensive statements of the dominant party approach to women was issued in a directive on the party's work among women in the anti-Japanese base areas in the early 1940s. Instead of raising sensitive issues concerning women's family rights and status, this major wartime document focused overwhelmingly on women's expanded contribution to productive labor. While emphasizing the need to expand women's wartime contribution, the document noted somewhat defensively that the new policies would also strike at the very essence of women's inferior status, their lack of productivity and economic independence.[7]

The document rested squarely on the orthodox materialist Marxist view as elaborated by Friedrich Engels, which stressed that women's inferior status is directly and primarily a function of their exclusion from productive economic roles.[8] The implication, made clear in contemporary party policy and theory, was that the general emancipation of women, including family reform, was primarily, perhaps wholly, dependent on enlarging women's economic role outside the family and changing their relationship to production. In short, oppressive family relationships, and the culturally defined patriarchal attitudes and family structures that support and justify these relationships, should be treated as dependent variables in the process of social change. Women's economic role can be treated as the primary independent variable, the key that unlocks the inner recesses of the "women's problem." Carried to the extreme, this produces a unidirectional, unicausal economic theory of gender inequality in which change in the economic realm will automatically induce thoroughgoing changes in the social superstructure, including the full range of social relations and ideas.

The dominant view within the party since at least the 1940s has been that once women are fully integrated into remunerative social production, interrelated changes in all other areas of family, society, and culture will naturally follow: Women's traditional dependence on men will be broken; women will play a larger role in community and family life; and new norms of equality and female worth will reflect the new relationship of women to production. Collectivization and the abolition of private property, which eliminates the family as a basic economic unit and provides the organizational basis for the large-scale participation of women in production outside the home, will eliminate the remaining bases of patriarchal power and ideology and usher in a society characterized by complete gender equality.

Although this presentation necessarily oversimplifies the theory, the key underlying factors in this dominant view are economic: the abolition of private property and, above all, the mobilization of women into nondomestic production. Economic change is assumed to be both necessary and sufficient to induce sweeping changes in all other areas of women's lives and relationships.

During the period of war and revolution, the Engelsian theoretical approach to gender inequality provided a rationale for a conservative and passive approach toward women's political, social, and family roles. In focusing on the expanded productive role of women, it temporarily postponed division and conflict within the revolutionary coalition between iconoclastic family reform ideals of a generation of educated urban youth and the traditional family aspirations of a male poor peasant base. Likewise, during most of the post-1949 period, as well, the official view of women has continued to stress heavily, often exclusively, the economic determinants of women's status, with the major concern placed on mobilizing women into social production.

The dominant view that changing women's relationship to production will ineluctably change their family, social, and political status has not, however, been the only perspective advanced since 1949. In the early 1950s, in an atmosphere temporarily more conducive to the promotion of "bourgeois democratic" rights, considerable attention was directed toward the democratic reform of patriarchal family attitudes and customs, even at some risk of creating conflict with male supporters. The proponents of these efforts criticized the overly sanguine views that had dominated "women's work" in the 1940s. These reformers stressed that patriarchal structures, customs, and ideology were deeply rooted in popular attitudes and had a tenacity independent of the "feudal" economic and political system that presumably gave rise to and supported them. Such patriarchal structures, beliefs, and customs would not automatically collapse in response to the new political and economic relations being established in the villages.

The relationship between cultural-social change and economic change was complex and multifaceted. The two areas were not perfectly correlated, nor was causation and influence unidirectional from the economic to the social and cultural. Culturally transmitted attitudes concerning women and family could persist despite economic changes and reforms that seem to make them objectively "outmoded." Moreover, traditional attitudes and customs could slow the realization of economic reforms. Thus, they pointed out that "feudal" ideology and the "feudal"-patriarchal family system constituted obstacles to other kinds of changes for women, including women's economic participation. In order to fully release women's productive energies, to enable them to broaden their social activities and raise their public status, it was necessary to overcome traditional attitudes and customs that treated women as family property and second-class human beings. These family reformers in the early 1950s insisted that patriarchal ideology and family practices, which for centuries defined women's lowly family and social status, had to be directly confronted as an independent variable that crucially affected the broad range of economic and political changes.

Whether male supremacist ideology and patriarchal family and marriage practices should be treated primarily as dependent or independent variables in the processes of social and economic change reflected different policy choices and levels of priorities for "women's issues." To argue for a more politically activist approach to women's rights and marriage reform—an approach that had definite "costs" in terms of organizational time, political energy, and social conflict—reformers had to do more than pinpoint the serious nature of women's traditional oppression. They implicitly had to argue for a different view of the dynamics of change and of causal relationships. In the spring of 1950, when the National Marriage Law was promulgated, it was increasingly argued in editorials and speeches that reforming "feudal" attitudes and oppressive family practices were the necessary prerequisites to enable women to make greater economic contributions.[9] "Feudal" patriarchal ideology, both inside and outside the party, had to be exposed and attacked so as to alter people's consciousness about relationships that were accepted as "natural." Deeply rooted notions and practices of male superiority and authority over women would not, as Mao Zedong sanguinely predicted in his 1927 "Report on the Peasant Movement in Hunan,"[10] "naturally" disappear with the seizure of political power and the destruction of the "feudal" landlord political and economic system. Such problems could not, therefore, be ignored, nor could it be conveniently assumed, as it was in the 1940s, that patriarchal ideology and practices would "take care of themselves" in the course of fulfilling other revolutionary goals.

In an historical sense, this position might be seen as a reassertion of the more radical anti-patriarchal, anti-Confucian impulses of the May Fourth tradition. Perhaps significantly, this reemergence coincided with the reincorporation of urban areas into the revolutionary fold, including areas such as Shanghai and Beijing that had once been the major centers of radical May Fourth activity and the site of early women's rights activities among intellectuals. Family reformers of the early 1950s, some of whom had themselves been youthful participants in the May Fourth movement of 1919, not only shared the anti-Confucian spirit that sought a joining of interests of radical youth and young women against patriarchal authority, they also shared the conviction that *cultural revolution* could serve as a primary means to change and rejuvenate Chinese society.[11] Implicit in their approach to reforming the family and furthering women's rights was the faith in the importance and power of ideas in shaping society.

Thus family reformers in the early 1950s sought to directly challenge the patriarchal rural family system, much as urban intellectual youth had done during the 1910s and 1920s. To be sure, the rural family already showed signs of disintegration. Poverty, natural disaster, and, above all, war had disrupted traditional family life, forcing many to seek security in religious sects, secret societies, social banditry, and revolutionary "brotherhoods."[12] Nevertheless, after years of war and famine, the moral order and security of the ideal traditional family surely retained its appeal for many. The task of marriage reformers was to introduce a new vision of a reformed egalitarian family system at a time when millions who had effectively lost all meaningful family relationships, and millions more who had desperately managed to maintain some semblance of the traditional normative relationships, were attempting to reknit their families. To initiate and guide the destruction of the old and creation of the new family, marriage reformers believed the ideological seeds of a more just, egalitarian system had to be sown. Above all, political forces had to organize to encourage women to use their new legal rights and to protect them when they did.

While the reformers sought to eliminate oppressive features of family life, the family *per se* was not attacked. Chinese marriage reformers were not looking toward a future in which the family would cease to be an important basic social unit of society, as had some radical feminists of the Russian revolution.[13] They believed that in the long run the reforms would and should strengthen long-cherished ideals of "family harmony." Indeed, they held, this harmony would be possible only after the establishment of the more egalitarian principles of the new democratic family system.

Furthermore, marriage reformers never seriously questioned the larger kinship structures within which the family was embedded. Structurally, the target of family reform was quite narrow—the internal gender and, to some extent, age hierarchy of individual family units. Indeed, one could argue that the reformers' greatest practical and theoretical weakness was a failure to understand the relationship between larger kinship structures and patterns and the specific features of female subordination they sought to change. Reformers failed to analyze how kinship and marriage patterns shaped the fabric of local society and women's position within communities and individual families. In focusing on patriarchal ideology and attitudes (and specific practices these engendered, including blind marriages, the sale of daughters through bride prices, and mistreatment of daughters-in-law), the reformers failed to strike at important links between ideology and patrilineal kinship structure.

Throughout the 1930s and 1940s, party leaders, fearful that marriage reform might prove divisive and weaken the military struggle for survival, had repeatedly retreated on marriage reform issues in the face of resistance. In 1950, with the establishment of the People's Republic, the time seemed at hand for full-scale implementation of the reforms.[14] Between 1950 and 1953, the party launched a series of educational campaigns to popularize and implement the National Marriage Law promulgated in May 1950. Yet, despite the greater visibility of women's rights and family reform issues in the early 1950s, efforts to promote the reforms were at best sporadic. During these years the campaigns were repeatedly stalled. Lack of responsiveness to the reforms was strongest at the bottom of the hierarchy, dominated by predominantly male rural cadres, many of whom ignored, slighted, or actively subverted the marriage law.

But reformers also met indifference or resistance from highly placed authorities who sought to downgrade family reform in favor of other campaigns and tasks. For example, central and regional land reform directives pointedly omitted marriage reform as a legitimate concern in organizing rural women in the early 1950s.[15] Investigative reports by the woman minister of justice, Shi Liang, and by a few regional officials actively supporting marriage reform, showed that many county, provincial, and regional authorities did not accord the reforms priority status as called for by central marriage reform directives.[16]

Not all cadres were ignorant of the law or recalcitrant in applying it, but getting the political apparatus to popularize family reform and to protect those who asserted their new rights was only the first hurdle. The reforms met various forms of resistance, sometimes violent, within the villages. Male resistance to reforms that challenged the normative basis of their traditional family power and privileges was predictable and well documented in articles published during this period. Somewhat less well documented, but clearly evident, was the fact that many women, especially older women, also often resisted the introduction of the new marriage and family practices. Reformers of many kinds have been confronted with the disconcerting phenomena of the assumed beneficiaries of their reforms, the victims of a system of subordination and discrimination the reformers seek to change, actually forming part of the resistance to those reforms. Family reform in China clearly witnessed this familiar pattern.

Yet the apparent conservative attachment of many women to traditional norms and practices should not be interpreted as merely a defense of a male-dominated patriarchal system that women had been socialized to accept all of their lives. Women's traditional view of the family was not likely to be synonymous with the dominant, male-centered, patrilineal Confucian ideal; peasant women were far more likely to place what Margery Wolf has identified as their own mother-dominated "uterine family," based on mother-son bonds, at the center of their vision of the traditional family.[17] Nonetheless, women's ideal of the uterine family, built of necessity on sons rather than daughters, who were lost to their mothers at marriage, was shaped by the traditional ideals and norms of the patriarchal Confucian family within whose structures it existed. The strength of these informal uterine families provided women with their primary means for overcoming loneliness and the powerlessness that the formal patrilineal, patriarchal family structures and norms sought to impose upon them. For many women living in the aftermath of decades of war and disruption, the marriage reformers' attack on old ideals and the reformers' desire to rebuild family life on a new reformed basis must have appeared as a threat, coming precisely at a time when many women hoped to be able to reconsolidate their uterine families.

Thus there were a number of hard-headed, self-protecting reasons for older women to resist some of the new family practices. Women who had had no voice in their own marriages, who had already struggled to overcome the traditional lowly status of new stranger-bride and daughter-in-law, expected in their older years to have a strong voice in their children's marriages, especially in the matter of acquiring a daughter-in-law. An obedient, hard-working daughter-in-law who accepted her traditional role could greatly ease the burden on her mother-in-law, while a rebellious, independent, or "modern-minded" young woman (such as the kind who would dare to take a hand in her own marriage) would be far more likely to violate such expectations. Most importantly, an arranged blind marriage and the traditional daughter-in-law's lowly status helped protect the crucial mother-son bond from the potential threat of a strong husband-wife bond or a strong-willed daughter-in-law striving to establish her own independent uterine family. In this way, the traditional family system pitted women against each other and created generational cleavages that cut across a gender-defined underclass. The Marriage Law threatened not only patriarchal power but, inadvertently, older women's uterine families as well.[18]

It is doubtful that many marriage reformers fully understood the nature of older women's "conservatism" on family reform issues—that it was not simply a reflection of "remnant feudal ideology," but that it grew of necessity out of the larger structures of male kinship and community that marriage reformers failed to address. Nor were reformers likely to appreciate the extent to which women's resistance to marriage reform was less a defense of the traditional patriarchal family than, ironically, a defense of the subtle ways women had traditionally used to resist the powerless position such male-defined families placed them in. But marriage reformers were not unmindful of the fears and concerns for security of older women, and men. Over the months they sought to reassure such people by moderating the tone of the marriage reform campaigns and giving greater prominence to the legal obligation of all children to support and respect elderly parents.

But despite resistance in the first years, marriage reformers persisted in trying to prod the party apparatus into more serious implementation efforts, while at the same time emphasizing more moderate methods. A spate of horrific local accounts appeared in the press, drawing on reports of investigation teams dispatched by Shi Liang. These not only detailed widespread cadre failure to support women struggling for their rights, but revealed cadre complicity in oppressing and punishing those who defied traditional family norms. The results were sometimes fatal.[19] In 1953, the Ministry of Justice reported that 70,000 to 80,000 women a year were "murdered or forced into suicide" due to family conflicts and oppression.[20] Support in their family struggles was a life-and-death matter for tens of thousands of women.

Finally, the top leadership increased its organizational and political commitment briefly in late 1952 and early 1953, and the political system did in fact respond. In preparation for the campaign, work teams, cadre training classes and thousands of "key-point" experiments in selected villages and counties were set up.[21] Furthermore, newly formed marriage law committees, partially coinciding with but structurally independent of regular party channels, were organized from the regional to the county level to direct the campaign.[22] Around this time, the courts also underwent a general rectification to retrain, discipline, or replace judicial personnel to make local courts more responsive to party policy. As a result of these activities, women and young people in the countryside became more aware of their new rights, and larger numbers began to use these rights.[23] In at least some local areas pro-reform forces emerged and appear to have gained in strength.[24] Yet even before the campaign began, and before the issues had been effectively joined in most areas, there were signs of vacillation at the highest levels. Would not the campaign create divisive social conflict among peasant activists? Central directives increasingly cautioned marriage reformers against confronting traditionalist elements in the villages.[25] "Struggle meetings" and investigations were prohibited, and local cadres were assured that, except in extreme cases involving loss of life, no disciplinary action would be taken against them as a result of their actions in the campaign.

Top marriage reformers on the National Committee for the Thorough Implementation of the Marriage Law, which was set up to coordinate the campaign, supported the moderate tone but called for greater organizational energies in the campaign.[26] Given widespread resistance, the National Committee held that a moderate-but-extensive campaign was the most realistic way to initiate change in the countryside. The main goals were to educate the population about the reform principles and to move toward creating a local political and legal apparatus that would uphold the law for women and young people who sought to use it. At the same time, the National Committee saw the 1953 campaign as the first of a series of national campaigns. Following the campaign, they called for a long-term process of regularized educational and political work that would be periodically punctuated by national political mobilization on the scale of the 1953 campaign.[27]

Yet after 1953 not even the moderate proposals of the National Committee commanded the necessary leadership support. Marriage reform never again commanded sufficiently high priority among the party leadership to warrant a national campaign. It was argued that material conditions were not ripe for making further progress in marriage reform and that the goals would gradually be attained in the process of economic development and socialist construction. It was again stressed that the key to women's emancipation was the expansion of their economic role.[28] Indeed, as socialist construction and large-scale collectivization rapidly eclipsed the "new democratic" phase of reconstruction, the women's rights issues associated with marriage reform were often cast as "bourgeois" and outdated for the New China.[29] Some would have it that the reform issues had been surpassed once China began to build socialism, even though in reality these fundamental reforms had never been achieved at all. On these issues leftist Maoist proclivities against individual rights often dovetailed with the most conservative "feudal" sentiment against family reform.

Perhaps most importantly, as the state focused on economic construction and cooperative transformation in the countryside, it became increasingly concerned with maintaining family stability and reinforcing the patrilineally shaped traditional bases of community solidarity upon which new cooperative structures could be built. Thus, far from pursuing marriage reform vigorously, it encouraged increasingly restrictive interpretation of the Marriage Law's divorce clause to reduce the peak divorce levels reached in 1953.[30] Women found it increasingly difficult to exercise their divorce rights, and it became increasingly easy for husbands and in-laws to protect bride price investments, which even today remain widespread in many parts of rural China.[31].

In effect, the pre-1953 pattern of implementation reemerged, and conservative forces reasserted themselves in an atmosphere that effectively decentralized and depoliticized family reform and related women's rights issues. The responsibility for overseeing reform and the protection of women's and young people's new family rights fell to unsupervised local male cadres whose political and social orientation in their native villages were heavily shaped by patrilineal kinship ties and networks of male-defined family groups that have traditionally formed the basis of community in rural China. Collectivization, which the party in the mid- and late 1950s claimed to be the key to fully realizing family reform and women's emancipation, actually reinforced these networks. Policies then froze them in place by prohibiting significant population movement among rural collective units (except, of course, for the movement of women through patrilocal marriage) or from rural units to urban areas. Moreover, from the late 1950s on, "anti-bureaucratic," "mass line" legal reforms and guidelines on family dispute mediation further reduced the role of county courts and the legal bureaucracy in controlling and overseeing the implementation of reforms and the protection of the rights of women and youth.[32]

Over the years, the leadership's decision to back off from significant involvement in implementing family reform and women's rights policy and to decentralize enforcement has slowed the realization of reform goals in the villages. While the marriage reformer's approach certainly provided no panacea for bringing about these changes, the abandonment of their politically directed approach undercut ideological, political, and legal sources of support that were essential if subordinate women and youth were to effectively translate the presumed greater economic independence from patriarchal control brought about by collectivization and the gradual expansion of women's economic roles into greater self-determination and influence in marriage and the family.

Since the early 1950s, with few exceptions, issues of gender equality have been raised only when the leadership has felt they bore a direct relation to the success of campaigns and central efforts aimed at other priorities, such as increasing agricultural production and, more recently, controlling population growth.

The major focus of policy toward rural women in most periods has been on the mobilization of their labor. The collectivization drives of the late 1950s were predicated on the notion that there was a reservoir of "underutilized" labor in the countryside that the collectives could productively tap. A major source of this underutilized labor was women. While collectivization, and the state centralization of markets for raw materials, further undermined many cottage handicraft industries that traditionally employed women in some parts of the countryside, women's participation in field labor and collective agricultural sidelines was increased under the collectives. By the late 1970s, relatively high and stable rates of female participation in agriculture had been attained.[33] Efforts to increase these rates over the years were occasionally accompanied by efforts to overcome the nearly universal tendency of the collectives, dominated by male cadres, to discriminate against women in remuneration. While significant improvements were made in many places, many collectives persisted in policies that systematically discriminated against women, such as setting a ceiling of seven work points per day for women while allowing men to earn up to ten work points. In order to facilitate women's higher participation rates, local units were also encouraged to establish day-care services. Such services were set up in increasing numbers of villages in the late 1960s and 1970s, but they remained inadequate to relieve the burdens of more than a minority of working rural mothers. For example, one study of rural Guangdong, where women's participation rates have been among the highest, only slightly less than men's, found that only 19 percent of the production brigades had any kind of year-round day care.[34] Left with most domestic responsibilities, rural Chinese women have been trapped with the classic double-burden of two jobs. The redistribution of domestic work that has occurred has mostly involved a shift from younger to older women within the family. Though women have benefitted from expanded economic roles in many respects, they have had to bear a significantly unequal burden for their "liberation through labor." Shulamith Firestone's observation that as a result of the Russian revolution "women's roles have been enlarged rather than re-defined" applies as well to China, and to most other socialist and capitalist nations where women work in significant numbers out-side the domestic sphere.[35]

It is too early to know how the economic reforms of the early 1980s and the current "responsibility system," which decentralizes the management of rural labor to the family, will affect these patterns. Some have argued that the new policies will worsen the position of women. At this point, however, the picture is at worst mixed, and it seems unlikely that policies will result in any radical alterations in either direction. In some areas there are indications that women's agricultural labor has decreased under the new system, while women have taken advantage of new opportunities to take up more highly remunerated (and traditionally preferred) handicraft pro-duction for local, national, and even international markets. In other areas, such as those close to major urban centers, women seem to be left playing an increasingly dominant role in low-status field labor as men are drawn off to more lucrative nonagrarian work opportu-nities. With fewer funds available for collective services, it also seems likely that day-care services will diminish, though this will not represent a change for the majority of rural women. Certainly, the double day and double-burden are likely to continue for most women as families struggle to take advantage of new income-earning opportunities to improve their still too meager standard of living.

In the 1980s, the family, and women's relationship to it, has remained one of the most traditional features of a predominantly rural Chinese society. The outcome of nearly a century of upheaval and revolution, born partly of widespread family crises among intellectuals and peasants, has done more to restore the traditional role and structure of the rural family than to fundamentally reform it. Greater progress toward family reform and gender equality probably could have occurred with the benefit of consistent state support for politically directed change over the years. Yet it is also true that the marriage reformers of the early 1950s overstated the role that ideological agitation could play in changing attitudes and practices over time. Neither the dominant Engelsian approach adopted by the party nor the activist approach advocated by mar-riage reformers directly addressed a number of social patterns related to traditional patrilineal family and kinship structure that have crucially affected women's status and made them "outsiders" to the family and kinship system, and to the communities and local power structures shaped by these structures. The impact of kinship practices and customs of patrilocality and village exogamy on women's subordinate family and community status, the ways in which women were systematically made outsiders to both while men remained rooted natives and life-long members of their parents' family with permanent obligations of loyalty and support, remained unrecognized by party policy.

This is not to suggest that traditional and restorationist aspirations among the peasant base have remained constant and that no change has occurred in family and marriage practices over the years. As several studies have shown, changes have occurred, some of them in the direction of the goals of the marriage reformers.[36] Yet these studies also reveal the substantial gap between national goals and local rural practice. With respect to "buying and selling" marriages, bride price practices, and the realization of women's property, child custody, and divorce rights, the evidence is that little if any change has occurred in many rural areas.

In the mid-1970s, problems posed by traditional, exclusively patrilineal patterns finally gained official recognition for the first time. In the context of the 1974 anti-Confucian campaign (the only campaign since the early 1950s to address the impact of traditional male supremacist attitudes on family and society) matrilocal marriage was proposed as a progressive alternative to exclusive patrilocal patterns.[37] For the first time, it was suggested that the insistence that women always marry into their husbands' family and community, rather than vice versa, was a manifestation of "feudal" male supremacist attitudes.

Significantly, the issue surfaced not primarily out of concern for gender inequality, but in connection with urgent state efforts to promote rural family planning. As family planning cadres and top policy-makers became more concerned with reducing fertility rates, they had to confront the reasons peasants continued to prefer sons over daughters and therefore resisted pressures to limit the number of children until they had at least one, and preferably two, sons. The fact is that, regardless of how much progress is made in expanding women's remunerative economic roles and making women equal breadwinners with men (a goal far from realization), as a result of patrilineal family structures and patrilocal marriage practice, daughters are "lost" at marriage to their husband's family. Even though village exogamous taboos seem to have weakened over the years, they continue to operate in many areas, so daughters usually marry into another village.[38] Embedded in the meaning of marriage for women is the transfer of their labor, filial obligations, and fertility to another patrilineal family group. Bride price practices both symbolize and reinforce this transfer of "rights in women" at marriage, while restricting women's own rights to the fruits of their labor, the determination of their personal obligations, and control over their fertility.

Given these traditional practices and structures and given the central importance of traditional corporate forms of family security in dealing with elderly and disabled family members, sons remain crucial to the support of parents in their old age.[39] It was in this context that matrilocal marriage was first raised. Parents who had no sons might then be able to substitute daughters to fulfill their old age security needs, and younger couples might be more easily convinced that it was not essential to continue to bear children until they produced a son.

Since the mid-1970s, population limitation has become an increasingly urgent state priority.[40] It is now clear that lack of progress for three decades in formerly "low-priority" areas such as women's emancipation had direct and adverse affects on such current priorities as population control and increased living standards for rural people. In a sense, problems that were readily slighted when seen as merely related to women's issues, gender equality and family reform have come back to haunt the leadership.

Some side effects of family planning are likely to contribute to gender equality by weakening traditional patrilineal family orientations. On the other hand, as the state moves vigorously against behavior rooted in traditional family structures and attitudes, women are sure to be caught in the crossfire. Since the late 1970s, women have been pressured to drastically reduce their fertility, in many cases through late abortion,[41] while remaining trapped in unreformed family structures in which their status, personal influence and security, indeed their very membership in their husbands' family and village, depend on traditional child-bearing functions, on the successful development of their own uterine families, and on their personal relationships with sons. In extreme cases, the consequences of current policies for females may prove dangerous and life-threatening. Family pressure on women—presumed to determine the biological sex of their offspring—to produce a son on the first try can readily spill over into abuse when the stakes are so high.[42] Moreover, the clash between unreformed family structures and attitudes, on the one hand, and forcefully implemented government demands for one—or at most two—children per family, on the other, led in the late 1970s and early 1980s to a revival of female infanticide in some areas, repeating the fate of unknown numbers of unwanted females during cycles of poverty and disruption in the "old society."[43]

The government, of course, has firmly condemned the practice of infanticide. By 1983, the government was calling for greater vigilance by local authorities and was publicly prosecuting those found guilty of the crime.[44] But the collision of forces that have recreated conditions hazardous to the lives of infant girls are not likely to change radically in the near future. There is some evidence of efforts to pull back from the more coercive excesses in implementing the policy that have occurred in recent years, and there may even be government acceptance for some rural areas of a de facto two-child family policy. At the same time, however, the possible pro-natalist tendencies inherent in the new family "responsibility system" (which, among other things, make the economic rewards and penalties attached to "excess" births less significant to many peasants) may lead the government to turn toward even greater coercion to achieve its goals in the future.

In the long run, family planning approaches that seek to overcome attitudes toward fertility rooted in traditional structures exclusively by means of economic incentives, harsh punishments, and political coercion rather than investing in efforts to reform these structures are not only inhumane but may produce a powerful backlash. Current population and family policies are politically and morally costly (far more costly than serious marriage reform efforts ever were); a successful program ultimately requires basic changes in structures and attitudes.

While greater gender equality and more egalitarian family structures and practices would not necessarily and automatically produce the extremely low fertility rates the government now seeks, many family reform goals would contribute to this result. For example, vigorous promotion of free-choice marriage practices, unimpeded by traditional taboos and parental control, would help keep women in or near their natal community, making possible stronger parent-daughter ties as well as creating a better community base for women to develop public roles and influence not dependent on their children or their position in their husbands' family. Free-choice, youth-dominated marriages are also likely to contribute to stronger conjugal bonds, which relieve the traditional loneliness felt by young women at marriage. Margery Wolf has argued that this loneliness and insecurity in a strange man's family is a major factor leading young brides to desire children, particularly sons, as soon as possible after marriage. Similarly, the reduction of bride price practices, which would become easier with the loosening of exclusive patrilocal residence, relaxation of restrictions on divorce, and the enforcement of women's full property and child custody rights, would help reduce traditional family claims to control women's fertility, allow women more easily to reduce fertility in response to their expanded economic and community roles, and strengthen ties and obligations between daughters and parents after marriage. Indeed, any loosening of patrilineal patterns is likely to lead to closer relations between daughters and parents and to a greater value being placed on women in their natal communities and families, reducing the necessity for sons.

The impetus for promoting women's rights and family reform within the revolutionary coalition that the May Fourth heritage once provided has repeatedly been overwhelmed by other political forces and priorities. A "coalition within the coalition" of radical intellectuals and rural women and youth never emerged with sufficient cohesion and power to sustain rural family reform as an ideological force that could shape new values and behavior as people adapted to structural change. Family reform remains an uncompleted task of the original cultural revolution. Marriage reformers in the early 1950s echoed a number of impassioned May Fourth writers in arguing that family reform was a life-and-death matter for tens of thousands of Chinese women. Today unreformed rural family structures and attitudes, coupled with a government crash program for population control, may threaten again an unknown number of Chinese female lives.

For a detailed analysis of party policy toward women and an elaboration of the ideas presented in this essay see Kay Ann Johnson, *Women, the Family and Peasant Revolution in China* (Chicago: University of Chicago Press, 1983).

NOTES

1. For a much-celebrated May Fourth era article on the liberation of women and youth from Confucianism and the Confucian family, see Ch'en Tu-hsiu, "The Confucian Way and Modern Living," translated in Theodore De Bary et al., eds., *Sources of Chinese Tradition*, Vol. 2 (New York: Columbia University Press, 1964), 153. A detailed discussion of the attitudes toward women of three famous May Fourth figures is provided in Christine Chan, *May Fourth Discussions of the Woman Question: Hu Shih, Ch'en Tu-hsiu and Lu Hsun* (unpublished master's

thesis, History Department, University of Wisconsin–Madison, 1980).

2. See for example, Anna Louise Stong, *China's Millions* (New York: Coward-McCann, 1928), 113–114.

3. The ethos and many of the rituals of the brotherhood are portrayed in the popular epic novel, *Water Margin*. In many parts of rural China, the characters and legends of *Water Margin* and similar tales recounted by storytellers were an integral part of a living popular culture. On the misogyny of these tales, see Yi-tse Feuerwerker, "Women as Writers in the 1920's and 1930's," in Margery Wolf and Roxane Witke, eds., *Women in Chinese Society* (Stanford, CA: Stanford University Press, 1975), 145–148; C. T. Hsia, *The Classic Chinese Novel: A Critical Introduction* (New York: Columbia University Press, 1972), 105–106.

4. Edward Friedman, *Backward toward Revolution* (Berkeley: University of California Press, 1974), Part III and Conclusion. This analysis has also been suggested by Phil Billingsley. See his Ph.D. thesis, "Banditry in China 1911–1928, with particular reference to Henan province" (Center for Research on China, University of Leeds, U.K.). For an interesting cross-cultural perspective that presents a complementary analysis of the role of fraternal societies in Europe, see Mary Ann Clawson, "Early Modern Fraternalism and the Patriarchal Family," *Feminist Studies* 6:2 (Summer 1980).

5. P'eng Teh-huai, "Report Concerning Work in the North China Base Areas," in *Kung-fei huo-kuo shih-liao lei pien* (Collection of Historical Materials on the Communist Bandits [*sic*]) (Taipei: Chung-hua min-kuo kuo-chi kuan-hsi yen-chiu suo, 1961), Vol. III, 346–406. For a woman cadre's view of the conflict caused by women's family rights, see the interview with Ts'ai Ting-li in Helen Foster Snow, *The Chinese Communists: Sketches and Autobiographies of the Old Guard* (Westport, CT: Greenwood Press, 1970), 119–202. Also see Strong, 125.

6. Mark Selden, *The Yenan Way in Revolutionary China* (Cambridge, MA: Harvard University Press, 1971), 208–212, 258–260.

7. "Decision of the CCP CC Concerning the Policy on Current Women's Work in the Anti-Japanese Base Areas, February 26, 1943," in *Zhongguo funu yundong di zhongyao wenxian* (Important Documents on the Chinese Women's Movement) (Beijing: Renmin chubanshe, 1953), 1–3.

8. *The Origin of the Family, Private Property and the State* (New York: International Publishers, 1942).

9. On the promulgation of the marriage law, see *Renmin Ribao* (People's Daily, hereafter *RMRB*), May 1, 1950, 1.

10. Mao Tse-tung, *Selected Works of Mao Tse-tung* (Peking: Foreign Languages Press, 1965), Vol. I, 23–59.

11. Maurice Meisner, *Mao's China* (New York: Free Press, 1976), Chapter 2.

12. Friedman, Part III.

13. H. Kent Geiger, *The Family in Soviet Russia* (Cambridge, MA: Harvard University Press, 1968); N. Timasheff, "The Attempt To Abolish the Family in Russia," in N. W. Bell and E. F. Vogel, eds., *The Family* (Cambridge, MA: Harvard University Press, 1960).

14. Deng Yingchao's "Report on the Marriage Law of the People's Republic

of China," *RMRB*, May 24, 1950, is a major statement initiating the reform movement. Reprinted in *Hunyin fa jiqi yuguan wenjian* (The Marriage Law and Related Document) (Shanghai: 1950).

15. See, for example, "Directive Concerning the Strengthening of Women's Work during Preparations for Land Reform," issued by the Central Committee of the East China Region, in *Xin zhongguo funu* (New Women of China, hereafter *XZGFN*), 14 (September 1950).

16. Shi Liang, "Report of the Central Inspection Group on the Situation Concerning the Implementation of the Marriage Law," *RMRB*, July 4, 1952.

17. Margery Wolf, *Women and the Family in Rural Taiwan* (Stanford, CA: Stanford University Press, 1972).

18. See William Hinton, *Fanshen* (New York: Vintage Books, 1966), 353–354, for an account of the reaction of one older peasant woman, soon to become a mother-in-law, to the notion of according higher status to daughers-in-law in the family and to the idea of free-choice marriage.

19. See, for example, New China News Agency (hereafter NCNA), "Women Still Persecuted and Murdered as Marriage Law Fails to Be Thoroughly Implemented," in *Survey of China Mainland Press* (hereafter *SCMP*) 499, 22–24.

20. *RMRB*, May 30, 1953, 3; *RMRB*, February 25, 1953, 2.

21. "Cadres Trained throughout the Country for Marriage Law Publicity Campaign," *RMRB*, March 19, 1953. For a report on one of the key-point experimental areas see Liang Hong, "Experience in the Implementation of the Marriage Law in Zhenggong County, Yunnan," *XZGFN* 1 (January 1953).

22. "Government Administrative Council Directive on the Thorough Implementation of the Marriage Law," *RMRB*, February 1, 1953.

23. As a result of the campaign, the number of divorces granted by the courts reached a peak in 1953 of 1.1 million. These figures again fell rather sharply from 1954 through 1956, the last year for which there are reported divorce figures. These statistics were published in *RMRB*, April 13, 1957.

24. See, for example, Liang Hong's report on Zhenggong County, Yunnan, cited in note 21. Also see NCNA, "Achievements throughout the Country in Movement To Publicize Marriage Law," May 6, 1953, *Current Background* (hereafter CB), 243; Liu Jingfan, "General Summary Report on the Movement for the Thorough Implementation of the Marriage Law," *RMRB*, November 19, 1953.

25. See "Supplementary Directive of the Central Committee, CCP, on The Movement for the Thorough Implementation of the Marriage Law," NCNA, February 19, 1953, *CB* 236. Compare this with the less cautious GAC directive issued less than three weeks earlier on February 1, cited in note 22 above. This GAC directive was itself apparently a diluted version of an earlier Central Committee–GAC directive that was never published.

26. NCNA, "National Committee on Campaign for Thorough Implementation of the Marriage Law Holds Second Session," March 18, 1953,

SCMP 535.

27. Liu Jingfan, "General Summary Report on the Movement To Thoroughly Implement the Marriage Law."

28. An editorial at the conclusion of the 1953 campaign signalled this new tone. "The Thorough Implementation of the Marriage Law Is an Important Regular Task," *RMRB*, May 6, 1953.

29. See for example, Tzu Chi, "In the Handling of Divorce Cases, We Must Struggle against Bourgeois Ideology," *Extracts from China Mainland Press* 65, 5–11 (December 15, 1956); Wan Mu-ch'un, "How To Look at the Women Question," *Hong Qi* (Red Flag) 20 (October 16, 1964).

30. See note 23 above.

31. William Parish and Martin Whyte, *Village and Family in Contemporary China* (Chicago: University of Chicago Press, 1978), 180–192. Also see "Resolutely Oppose Marriage by Purchase," *RMRB*, July 25, 1978; "Arranged Buying and Selling Marriages in Guangdong," *Wenhuibao* (Hong Kong), August 8, 1978.

32. On the way in which divorces and mediation are handled largely by local cadres outside of the courts, see Parish and Whyte, 193–197. For a general discussion of the "anti-bureaucratic," "mass line" legal reforms see Victor Li, *Law without Lawyers: A Comparative View of Law in China and the United States* (Boulder, CO: Westview Press, 1978).

33. Marina Thorborg, "Chinese Employment Policy in 1949–78, with Special Emphasis on Women in Rural Production," in U.S. Congress, Joint Economic Committee, *Chinese Economy Post-Mao* (Washington, DC: U.S. Government Printing Office, 1978).

34. Parish and Whyte, 81.

35. Shulamith Firestone, *The Dialectics of Sex: The Case for Feminist Revolution* (London: Cape, 1971), 248.

36. The most detailed comprehensive study on contemporary rural family practices is Parish and Whyte, *Village and Family*. Also see Janet Salaff, "The Emerging Conjugal Relationship in the People's Republic of China," *Journal of Marriage and the Family*, November 1973, 705–717.

37. See, for example, "Destroy Old Habits, Establish New Customs: An Investigation of the Promotion of Matrilocal Marriage in Dingxian," *RMRB*, March 14, 1975.

38. Parish and Whyte, 169–192.

39. For an excellent analysis of aging strategies, see Deborah Davis-Friedmann, "Strategies for Aging: Interdependence between Generations in the Transition to Socialism," *Contemporary China* 1:6 (March 1977). Also see her more recent book, *Long Lives: Chinese Elderly and the Communist Revolution* (Cambridge, MA: Harvard University Press, 1983).

40. See, for example, Hua Guofeng's address to the Fifth National People's Congress in *Beijing Review* 38 (September 22, 1980). For an analysis of the current family planning policies, see Leo Orleans, *China's Population Policies and Population Data: Review and Update*, prepared for the Committee on Foreign Affairs, U.S. House of Representatives (Washington, DC: U.S. Government Printing Office, 1981).

41. See, for example, Steven Mosher, *Broken Earth* (New York: Free Press, 1983), Chapter 9.

42. For hints of the emotional pressures and physical abuse some women experience for their "failure" to produce a son within the one or two births now permitted by the government, see Tung Tung, "One Baby for You, One Baby for Me," *American Spectator*, January 1981; "Wife Beater Sent to Chinese Prison," *Korea Herald*, September 18, 1980.

43. By the spring of 1983, the official Chinese press openly admitted the problem and urged that those responsible for killing infant girls be severely punished. See, for example, *Women of China*, March 1983. Lucien Bianco reports instances of female infanticide in Shanxi in cases where the first two children were girls, "Birth Control in China: Local Data and their Reliability," *China Quarterly* 85 (March 1981), 131. The crime is a very difficult one to detect, since it may be accomplished by inconspicuous neglect. Also see Orleans, 31; Jay Mathews, "Odyssey of Love," *Washington Post*, August 17, 1980; Jonathan Mirsky, "The Infanticide Tragedy in China," *The Nation*, July 2, 1983.

44. *Women of China*, March 1983.

RECOMMENDED READINGS

Croll, Elizabeth. *Chinese Women since Mao*. Armonk, NY: M. E. Sharpe, 1983.
Examines the most recent policy changes associated with the economic reforms and modernization drive launched in the late 1970s and early 1980s. The book suffers from having been written as these policies are unfolding and while their effects on women remain very unclear. Nonetheless, it provides an excellent review of the relevant official literature, and it raises a number of common concerns about the implications of the new policies for women that can be weighed against the evidence as it becomes available.

Johnson, Kay Ann. *Women, The Family and Peasant Revolution in China*. Chicago: University of Chicago Press, 1983.
Provides a critical historical overview of policies and changes affecting rural women under Communist party leadership since the early years of the revolution. The primary focus is on reform of marriage and family because, it is argued, traditional marriage family and kinship practices have been, and continue to be, the most central factors shaping women's place in Chinese society. The book also makes an effort to relate the Chinese case to larger theoretical issues relevant to comparative family studies and feminist studies.

Parish, William, and Martin Whyte. *Village and Family in Contemporary China*. Chicago: University of Chicago Press, 1978.
The best sociological account we have of women's position in rural families and the communities in post-1949 China. It is based primarily on extensive interviews conducted in Hong Kong with recent immigres from rural Guangdong Province.

_____ . *Urban Life in China*. Chicago: University of Chicago Press, 1984.
The urban counterpart of the same study, also based on interviews in Hong Kong. Both are excellent sources of information on women's family, work, and political roles and on contemporary marriage and family practices.

Pruitt, Ida. *Daughter of Han: The Autobiography of a Chinese Working Woman*. Stanford, CA: Stanford University Press, 1967.
Tells the firsthand story of a poor but resourceful woman struggling to cope with the problems posed by poverty and family disintegration that plagued tens of millions of peasants in late

nineteenth- and early twentieth-century China. It is an outstanding oral history, one of the few available on nineteenth-century
women.

Wolf, Margery. *Women and The Family in Rural Taiwan.* Stanford,
CA: Stanford University Press, 1972.
A classic study of the Chinese family as seen from the perspective
of females in various stages of their life cycles. Rather than por-
traying women as mere victims of a male-dominated family system, Wolf delineates the regularized ways through which women
resist, subvert, and avoid, as well as accommodate, the powerless
position that formal family structures and norms assign to them
at birth. Though her study is based on field work in rural Taiwan,
the basic family structures she observes are roughly typical of the
"traditional" Chinese peasant family.

CONTRIBUTORS

ELLEN BONEPARTH is a former professor of political science at San Jose State University and editor of *Women, Power and Policy* (Pergamon Press, 1982). In 1981, she founded the International Women's Studies Institute, which offers summer travel/study programs in Greece, Israel, and Kenya. She is currently serving as a political officer in the Foreign Service of the U.S. Department of State.

BARBARA J. CALLAWAY, after earning her B.A. degree at Trinity University in San Antonio, Texas, earned her M.A. and Ph.D. degrees in political science at Boston University. Her early research was on processes of change and development in African societies and her field research was conducted in Nigeria and Ghana. In recent years she has focused on women and social change and has conducted a large research project in Kano, Nigeria. She is associate professor of political science at Rutgers University in New Brunswick, New Jersey, where she is chair of the Comparative Politics field and director of a new Ph.D. program in Women and Politics. Her articles have appeared in the *Journal of Politics, Journal of Contemporary African Studies, African Studies Review,* and *Women and Politics.* She is completing a book-length monograph on women in Kano.

NEELA D'SOUZA is a free-lance writer who has taught history and worked several years in advertising in India. She has written three books for children and has worked as a volunteer with welfare agencies in India.

FADWA EL GUINDI received her doctorate in anthropology in 1972 from the University of Texas at Austin, where she could best combine her two areas of research interest: Middle East and Middle America. She is author of *Religion in Culture, The Myth of Ritual: A Native's Ethnography of Zapotec Life-Crisis Rituals*, and over 30 articles on ritual, belief, and gender among Nubians, the Zapotec, and in the Arab Islamic East. She was a recipient of a Fulbright Senior Research Scholarship in Islamic Civilization, 1981–1982, taught at UCLA since 1972, was engaged in full-time research on Egypt's contemporary Islamic movement since 1979, and is currently visiting professor at the University of Southern California in Los Angeles.

LYNNE B. IGLITZIN is executive director of the American Foreign Service Association in Washington, D.C. Previously she served as Executive Director of the National Council for the Social Studies, also headquartered in Washington, D.C. She served as a lecturer in the Department of Political Science at the University of Washington, Seattle, from 1968 to 1982, where she also held the title of associate director of undergraduate studies. She is the author of *Violent Conflict in American Society* and numerous articles on women's issues, including women and welfare, and sex-role stereotyping.

JANE S. JAQUETTE is a professor and chair of the Department of Political Science at Occidental College. She edited *Women in Politics* (1974) and co-edited *Women in Developing Countries: A Policy Focus* (1983). She has published articles on women in development, female political participation, and Latin American politics. She is currently studying international feminism and working on a book on women and power.

KAY JOHNSON is associate professor of politics and Asian studies at Hampshire College and is the author of *Women, the Family and Peasant Revolution in China* (Chicago: University of Chicago Press, 198). She is currently working with three other colleagues on a village study based upon field work they have carried out in a North China rural community since 1978.

JOELLE RUTHERFORD JUILLARD obtained her Ph.D. in political science from UCLA and lived in France from 1968 to 1974, where she administered the Institute for Comparative Politics at the University of Nice, acting subsequently as a corresponding research attaché with the institute. Formerly the Director of the Program for the Study of Women and Men in Society at the University of Southern California, she has published articles in the field of feminist theory and has a biographical study in preparation.

MARJORIE LANSING is a professor of political science at Eastern Michigan University. Her publications include: senior author, Baxter and Lansing, *Women and Politics: The Invisible Majority* (1980, rev. ed., 1982); chapters in *Women in Politics* (ed. by Jane S. Jaquette, 1974); *A Portrait of Marginality: The Political Behavior of American Women* (ed. by Marianne Githens and Jewel L. Prestage); and *The Contemporary American Woman* (ed. by Marie Richmond-Abbott). Her research interests include the effects of religion on the politics of women and contemporary biography.

PETER H. MERKL is a professor of political science at the University of California, Santa Barbara. He has written and edited numerous books and articles on comparative politics and West German politics, the most recent being *New Local Centers in Centralized States, Religion and Politics in the Modern World* (with Ninian Smart), and *West German Foreign Policy: Dilemmas and Directions*. His current interests include the new social movements in Europe and small-town politics in Bavaria.

JOEL C. MOSES is professor of political science at Iowa State University. He is the author of *Regional Party Leadership and Policy-Making in the USSR, The Politics of Women and Work in the Soviet Union and the United States*, and several published articles and monographs on the Communist party, women, and labor policy in the Soviet Union.

RAMANI NATARAJAN practices law in Madras, India, handling tax matters, law, and divorce. She has taught law at evening classes and

spoken widely on the position of women in India. She is the sister of
Neela D'Souza.

INGUNN NORDERVAL teaches political science at Møre and Romsdal
College in Molde, Norway. She obtained her Ph.D. at the University
of Washington in Seattle, and taught in the United States and
Canada for many years before returning to Norway. She has pub-
lished several articles on Scandinavian politics in American and
Canadian journals, and a book on women in Norwegian politics
(Kvinner i norsk politikk). An active politician herself, she represents
the Labor party in the Møre and Romsdal Provincial Assembly.

MARY CORNELIA PORTER was co-editor with G. Alan Tarr of *State
Supreme Courts: Policymakers in the Federal System*. She has pub-
lished articles in: *The Supreme Court Review, Baylor Law Review,
Hastings Constitutional Law Quarterly, Ohio State Law Journal,
Women and Politics, Publius, PS*, and Jane Jacquette, ed., *Women in
Politics*. Current research focuses on state supreme courts and the
judicial function from the perspective of the Alabama, New Jersey,
and Ohio judiciaries.

ADALJIZA SOSA RIDDELL, Ph.D., currently is teaching at the University of California, Davis, in the Chicano Studies Program and the
Political Science Department. She is also director of the Chicano
Studies Program and is involved in several professional, campus,
and community organizations. Her current major project is developing a research support group for Chicanas, Mexicanas, and
Latinas in teaching, research, and community activities. The group
is called Mujeres Activas en Letras y Cambio Social (MALCS). Dr.
Sosa Riddell is a native Californian, of Mexican descent, and received her B.A. and M.A. degrees from the University of California,
Berkeley, and her Ph.D. from UC Riverside. Her research interests
include women in Mexico, Chicanas in the U.S., Chicano communities in California, Chicano political thought, and Chicano
studies.

RUTH ROSS is an associate professor in the Graduate Center for
Public Policy and Administration, California State University at

Long Beach. She is a specialist in community development, financial resource management, and intergovernmental fiscal relations. Her publications include "Federal Decentralization and Its Diverse Effects on CDBG," in *Publius* (1983), and *The Impact of Federal Grants in the City of Los Angeles* (United States Department of Labor, 1980). In addition, she has been a research associate for the Brookings Institution and for the Princeton Urban and Regional Research Center at Princeton University.

JANET W. SALAFF is professor of sociology at the University of Toronto. She is interested in family roles of Chinese women and has completed a monograph containing the lives of ten Hong Kong women, *Working Daughters of Hong Kong*, published by Cambridge University Press in 1981. She is currently researching family structures of married Chinese women in Singapore and recently completed a monograph, *State and Family in Singapore*, with Aline Wong.

ELIZ SANASARIAN was born and raised in Iran. She is a visiting assistant professor in the Department of Political Science at the University of Southern California. She is the author of the book *The Women's Rights Movement in Iran: Mutiny, Appeasement, and Repression from 1900 to Khomeini*. Professor Sanasarian's research interests lie in comparative women in politics and Middle East politics, and she has published and lectured extensively on these topics. She is currently working on a comparative study of feminist goals in Egypt and Iran during the 1920s and 1930s.

ENID SCHILDKROUT, after earning her B.A. degree at Sarah Lawrence College, earned her M.A. and Ph.D. degrees in anthropology at Newnham College, Cambridge University. Her doctoral research was on migration and ethnicity in urban Ghana. She has subsequently been working on the economic roles of women and children in northern Nigeria. She is curator of anthropology at the American Museum of Natural History in New York City. She has published numerous articles on her research in Ghana and Nigeria, and a book, *People of the Zongo, Transformations of Ethnic Identity in Ghana* (Cambridge University Press, 1978). She is currently writing a book on child workers in Africa, editing a volume of papers on the

Asante of Ghána, and working on the analysis and publication of her Kano data. In addition she has had curatorial responsibility for a number of major African exhibitions at the American Museum of Natural History.

STEFFEN W. SCHMIDT is associate professor of political science at Iowa State University. He received his Ph.D. from Columbia University. His recent publications include the book *El Salvador: America's Next Vietnam?* and a forthcoming co-authored book, *American Government and Politics Today.* He has published numerous articles on women in politics and the role of women in development, with primary emphasis on Latin America and Colombia and is chair of the Women in Development (WID) Committee at Iowa State. He has also done research and published in the area of patron-broker-client relations, including the co-edited volume *Friends, Followers and Factions,* published by the University of California Press, Berkeley. Dr. Schmidt is active in Hispanic affairs and serves as co-chair of the Iowa Governor's Spanish Speaking Peoples Commission.

BEVERLY SPRINGER is professor of international studies of the American Graduate School of International Management in Glendale, Arizona. She is a member of the board of the Southwest Labor Studies Association and the board of the Arizona Chapter of the Society for International Development. She received an American Association of University Women grant for research in Yugoslavia and Italy. Her current interest is labor policies in Europe. She received a grant from the National Endowment for the Humanities for research on labor participation in the European Community.

KAZUKO SUGISAKI, M.A. in English, Whittier College, Ph.D. in Anglo-American Literature, Occidental College, taught English at Obirin College, Tokyo for 15 years. She is now teaching at Meijo University, Nagoya, Japan. She has translated for publication Oscar Wilde, Kate Chopin, Anais Nin, Ursula K. Le Guin, and others into Japanese, and Okamoto Kanoko (woman novelist and poet) into English. Her published literary essays and criticisms on Anais Nin, Kate Chopin, Margaret Anderson, Charles Dickens, etc. are published both in Japanese and English in books and journals and include *Anais: An International Journal,* a book yet untitled (Sharon Spencer, ed., in press), and one of the back-to-back series for Capra Press, Santa Barbara (in press).

COREY VENNING is associate professor of political science and associate director of the Honors Program at Loyola University of Chicago. She is a former U.S. Foreign Service officer, and has lived in India, Greece, Italy, and the United States. Her research and publications include work on the theory of empire and on aspects of women's life and roles.

INDEX